ARCHAEOLOGICAL LANDSCAPES OF
LATE ANTIQUE AND EARLY MEDIEVAL TUSCIA

MediTo | ARCHAEOLOGICAL AND HISTORICAL LANDSCAPES
OF MEDITERRANEAN CENTRAL ITALY

VOLUME 3

GENERAL EDITORS

Alessandro Sebastiani – *University at Buffalo – SUNY*
Carolina Megale – *Università degli Studi di Firenze*
Riccardo Rao – *Università degli Studi di Bergamo*

EDITORIAL BOARD

Giorgio Baratti – *Università Cattolica del Sacro Cuore, Milan*
Emeri Farinetti – *Università Roma Tre*
Todd Fenton – *Michigan State University*
Michelle Hobart – *The Cooper Union University, New York*
Richard Hodges – *American University of Rome*
Daniele Manacorda – *Università Roma Tre*
Marco Paperini – *Centro Studi Città e Territorio, Follonica*
Anna Maria Stagno – *Università di Genova*
Emanuele Vaccaro – *Università di Trento*
Edoardo Vanni – *Università per Stranieri di Siena*

Submissions should be sent to:
Alessandro Sebastiani – as424@buffalo.edu
Carolina Megale – carolina@archeodig.net
Riccardo Rao – riccardo.rao@unibg.it

Archaeological Landscapes of Late Antique and Early Medieval Tuscia

Research and Field Papers

Edited by

RICCARDO RAO and ALESSANDRO SEBASTIANI

BREPOLS

To Stephen L. Dyson
A pioneer of late antique and early medieval Tuscia

British Library Cataloguing in Publication Data
A catalogue record for this book is available from the British Library.

© 2023, Brepols Publishers n.v., Turnhout, Belgium.

All rights reserved. No part of this publication may be reproduced, stored
in a retrieval system, or transmitted, in any form or by
any means, electronic, mechanical, photocopying, recording,
or otherwise without the prior permission of the publisher.

D/2023/0095/118
ISBN: 978-2-503-60499-2
e-ISBN: 978-2-503-60500-5

DOI: 10.1484/M.MEDITO-EB.5.132620

Printed in the EU on acid-free paper.

Table of Contents

List of Illustrations   7

Alessandro Sebastiani and Riccardo Rao
Introduction   11

Antonio Alberti
1. The City of *Pisae* from Late Antiquity to the Early Medieval Period   21

Stefano Campana
2. Infrastructure, Water Management, Settlement, Agriculture, and Funerary Landscapes
    near *Rusellae* in the *longue durée*   39

Federico Cantini and Gianluca Martinez
3. 'The River and the Villa'   55
    The Arno and the Vetti Villa between the Late Roman and the High-Middle Ages:
    A Complex Relationship

Maria Grazia Celuzza, Elena O. Watson, Alexis C. Goots, Mari I. Isa, Jared S. Beatrice,
Emily R. Streetman, and Todd W. Fenton
4. Late Antique and Early Medieval *Rusellae*   65
    Archaeology and Anthropology of the Cemetery of the Episcopal Church

Elena Chirico and Alessandro Sebastiani
5. The Coastal *ager Rusellanus* between the Fourth and Sixth Centuries AD   88

Luisa Dallai and Lorenzo Marasco
6. The nEU-Med Project: Archaeology of a Coastal District in Tuscany during the Early Middle Ages   107

Andrea U. De Giorgi, Michelle Hobart, Melissa Ludke, and Russell T. Scott
7. Cosa during Late Antiquity   126

Richard Hodges
8. Cityness: A Chimera in Early Medieval Tuscany   141

Simonetta Menchelli, Stefano Genovesi, and Rocco Marcheschi
9. Late Roman Luna in the Light of the Porta Marina Excavations   148

Fabio Saggioro
10. When the Countryside Changes   163
    Landscape between Places of Power and the Environment in Central and Northern Italy

Francesca Romana Stasolla
11. Landscapes between the Sea and the Hills: An Early Medieval City in Roman Tuscia   172

Paolo Tomei
12. The Landscapes of Power in Mediterranean Tuscany (*c.* 750–850)   185

Index   198

List of Illustrations

1. The City of *Pisae* from Late Antiquity to the Early Medieval Period

Figure 1.1.	The Pisan coast between Late Antiquity and the early Middle Ages, with its ports (P) and moorings.	23
Figure 1.2.	*Pisae*, Piazza Duomo.	24
Figure 1.3.	Plan of the city of *Pisae*.	25
Figure 1.4.	Map and photoplan of the wall found along the via Maffi.	26
Figure 1.5.	Plan of *Pisae*.	29
Figure 1.6.	A: marble barrier found in Piazza Duomo during the excavations of Sanpaolesi in 1949–1950, sixth century (after Alberti and others 2011a, 199); B: Marble slab from Piazza Duomo. Opposite fan decoration, the first half of the ninth century (after Belcari 2011, 542); C: Piazza Duomo, Excavations 2004 (Area 8000). Fragmentary slab. Mesh decoration of free circles, the first half of the ninth century.	30
Figure 1.7.	Area of origin of the amphorae between Late Antiquity and the early Middle Ages.	31
Figure 1.8.	*Pisae*, the early medieval necropolis.	32
Figure 1.9.	*Pisae*, the early medieval necropolis.	33

2. Infrastructure, Water Management, Settlement, Agriculture, and Funerary Landscapes near *Rusellae* in the *longue durée*

Figure 2.1.	The Ombrone and Orcia valleys in southern Tuscany.	40
Figure 2.2.	The territory between *Rusellae* and Grosseto.	41
Figure 2.3.	The lowland north-west of Grosseto.	43
Figure 2.4.	The valley immediately west and south-west of the city of *Rusellae*.	45
Figure 2.5.	The area west of the city of *Rusellae*.	46
Figure 2.6.	Plan of detected roads, settlements, and funerary areas south-west of the city of *Rusellae*, showing in black a diachronic view of all the elements interpreted as parts of the road system in this area.	47
Figure 2.7.	Excavations south-west of the city of *Rusellae*.	48
Figure 2.8.	The Lombard cemetery south-west of the city of *Rusellae*.	49
Figure 2.9.	The landscape between *Rusellae* and Grosseto.	50
Figure 2.10.	3D digital record of the section of an exploratory trench at Brancalete, north-east of the city of Grosseto and south-east of the Roman villa at Aiali.	51
Figure 2.11.	The landscape between *Rusellae* and Grosseto: hypothetical reconstruction of the main road system.	53

3. 'The River and the Villa'

Figure 3.1.	Location of the Vetti dell'Oratorio in Italy.	55
Figure 3.2.	The structures of the villa.	56
Figure 3.3.	The territory between Capraia e Limite and Montelupo Fiorentino with the sites mentioned in the text.	57
Figure 3.4.	Bar cores and canal cores.	59
Figure 3.5.	Stratigraphy reconstructed from SO_24 (left) and SO_6 (right).	59
Figure 3.6.	Drawing known as 'Isbozzo del taglio di Limite' (1550).	60
Figure 3.7.	Meander cutoff chute.	61
Figure 3.8.	GIS The Medici Villa dell'Ambrogiana.	62

4. Late Antique and Early Medieval *Rusellae*

Figure 4.1.   *Rusellae*, the area of the church inside the Roman bath building, after the excavations in 1942.   66
Figure 4.2.   *Rusellae*, the church and the cemetery after the excavations 1987–1991.   67
Figure 4.3.   *Rusellae*, excavations 1987–1991: the church and the cemetery.   67
Figure 4.4.   Museo Archeologico e d'Arte della Maremma, inscribed pluteus and small pillars from *Rusellae* (eighth century).   68
Figure 4.5.   Location of the church of *Rusellae* and the churches in the nearest surroundings.   69
Figure 4.6.   Frequencies of lesions in the *Rusellae* sample compared to Smith-Guzmán's (2015) endemic and non-endemic samples.   75
Figure 4.7.   Individual 5523, *in situ* (left) and anterior view of proximal left femur displaying femoral cribra (right).   77
Figure 4.8.   Linear discriminant analysis (LDA) for ancestry at the *Rusellae* cemetery.   79
Figure 4.9.   Individual 82–1103, *in situ* (left) and anterior view of the skull (right).   80
Figure 4.10.   Individual 82–1284, *in situ* (left), anterior view of the skull (right), and associated grave goods (bottom).   80
Figure 4.11.   Museo Archeologico e d'Arte della Maremma, Individual 82–1284, associated grave goods.   81

5. The Coastal *ager Rusellanus* between the Fourth and Sixth Centuries AD

Figure 5.1.   GIS view of the investigated area between the third and the fourth centuries AD.   88
Figure 5.2.   GIS view of the coastal land between Cosa and *Rusellae* showing the Imperial estates between the first and the second centuries AD.   88
Figure 5.3.   Plan of the *positio* of *Umbro flumen*.   91
Figure 5.4.   Plan of the manufacturing district at Spolverino.   91
Figure 5.5.   Plan of the sanctuary area dedicated to *Diana Umbronensis*.   92
Figure 5.6.   Plan of the *mansio* of Hasta.   92
Figure 5.7.   Plan of Podere Passerini/*Aquae Rusellanae*.   95
Figure 5.8.   Plan of villa/harbour at Serrata Martini-Paduline.   96
Figure 5.9.   Drawing of the gilded glass from Serrata Martini/Paduline.   97
Figure 5.10.   GIS view of the investigated area in the fifth century AD.   99
Figure 5.11.   GIS view of the investigated area in the sixth century AD.   99
Figure 5.12.   Golden earring *a cestello* from Grosseto.   101
Figure 5.13.   Lead stamp with the representation of the *menorah* from Sterpeto-San Martino.   101

6. The nEU-Med Project: Archaeology of a Coastal District in Tuscany during the Early Middle Ages

Figure 6.1.   (A) Overview of the two coastal districts investigated by the nEU-Med Project research. (B) Distribution of the main archaeological survey areas (squares), location of the geognostic cores (stars), and multidisciplinary surveys (grids). (C) Panoramic view of the coastal plain between Piombino and Follonica.   108
Figure 6.2.   Archaeological excavation at Carlappiano (Piombino, Livorno).   110
Figure 6.3.   Archaeological excavation at Carlappiano (Piombino, Livorno).   112
Figure 6.4.   The lower Cornia valley and the ERC multidisciplinary research.   113
Figure 6.5.   The lower Val di Pecora and the site of Vetricella.   117
Figure 6.6.   (A–B) Period plans of the first and second occupation at Vetricella (Periods 1 and 2). (C) Examples of a possible forge and kiln from Period 1. (D) Test trenches carried out in the enclosing ditches.   118
Figure 6.7.   (A–B) Period plans of the fourth phase of occupation at Vetricella, divided into two sub-phases (Period 4.1 and Period 4.2). (C) Detail of the first mortar mixer, located to the south of the tower. (D) Aerial view of the stone and mortar cobbling set directly over the innermost ditch.   121

7. Cosa during Late Antiquity

Figure 7.1. Cosa, the site. — 126
Figure 7.2. Cosa, the territory and Succosa. — 129
Figure 7.3. Cosa: The medieval wall on the Arx. — 130
Figure 7.4. Cosa: The forum in the fourth/fifth century. — 131
Figure 7.5. Cosa, the bath and its sectors of excavations. — 132
Figure 7.6. Cosa, the bath: slabs of mosaic floors lifted and left *in situ*. — 133
Figure 7.7. Cosa, the bath: *labrum* prepared for demolition. — 133
Figure 7.8. Cosa, the 1948–2019 coin finds. Graph of coin distribution at Cosa by century. — 134
Figure 7.9. Coin of Gordion III. AD 241–244. — 135
Figure 7.10. Coin of Philip I. AD 244–249. — 135

9. Late Roman Luna in the Light of the Porta Marina Excavations

Figure 9.1. Porta Marina excavations. The rediscovered buildings. — 148
Figure 9.2. Porta Marina excavations. The late antique phases. — 150
Figure 9.3. Aerial view of the area of *domus* B, including the water well and the squared structure resting against the foundations of the Temple. — 153
Figure 9.4. Room B1. The water well viewed from east. — 154
Figure 9.5. Area of *domus* B. The northern foundations of the Temple and the squared structure viewed from the west. — 155
Figure 9.6. Area of *domus* A. Aerial view of the *atrium* of the *domus* after the building interventions of the mid-fifth century AD. — 157
Figure 9.7. Area of *domus* A. The southern perimeter wall of the Byzantine house (on the left) and aerial photo of Rooms D1 and D2. — 158
Figure 9.8. Pottery finds and glass vessels from the late sixth–seventh centuries AD. — 159

10. When the Countryside Changes

Figure 10.1. Mapping of anthropogenic and paleoenvironmental traces detected by aerial photography and LiDAR in the low Veronese plain. — 165
Figure 10.2. Reconstructive hypothesis of the paleoenvironmental topography in the lower Brescia plain. — 165
Figure 10.3. Image of the early medieval phases of the alpine town of Piuro during the excavation phases 2021. — 168
Figure 10.4. Early medieval building under excavation in Piuro, during the 2019 research campaign. — 168

11. Landscapes between the Sea and the Hills: An Early Medieval City in Roman Tuscia

Figure 11.1. Cencelle: aerial view of settlement. — 172
Figure 11.2. Cencelle: inscription of Pope Leo IV. — 172
Figure 11.3. Cencelle: aerial view with the early medieval phase highlighted. — 175
Figure 11.4. Cencelle: on the right, the Romanesque church; on the left, the political pole of the town. — 175
Figure 11.5. Cencelle, sector III, aerial view of the residential buildings. — 177
Figure 11.6. Cencelle, artefacts for women's work. — 180
Figure 11.7. Cencelle, majolica vessels produced locally. — 180
Figure 11.8. Cencelle, game pieces. — 181

Introduction

This volume collects essays presented during the second day of studies organized in Paganico as part of the MediTo – Mediterranean Tuscany initiative in the summer of 2019, together with others that were not included in the original programme. After the publication of the first seminar (Sebastiani and Megale 2021), attention shifted to the late antique and early medieval periods of the ancient region of Etruria, which in those periods became known as Tuscia. In continuity with the previous volume, the analysis focuses again on the coastal area of modern Tuscany between the fifth and eleventh centuries AD, a key moment for the definition of new political, administrative, economic, and social structures of medieval Europe.

The fall of the Western Roman Empire represented only a first fundamental piece of these profound transformations; the exegesis of written sources, as well as the scrutiny of new archaeological data, shows a varied reality in which certain regional peculiarities lead to the progressive, albeit slow, formation of medieval landscapes. The increasingly marked closure of Mediterranean markets and the reduction in the volume of international trade led to the creation of purely regional or local trading places, in line with those *Mediterranean Ecologies* already encountered twenty years ago in the *Corrupting Sea* (Horden and Purcell 2000). Great commercial traffic gave way to coastal cabotage routes, while new forms of communities and settlements took over the Roman villas, the classical cities, and the scattered agglomerations of the countryside.

By taking account of new research conducted in recent years in Tuscia, this volume seeks to frame new problems that add to those of classical historical and archaeological literature for late antique and early medieval Tuscany, providing further ideas for reflection and directions for future analyses.

The Rural and Coastal Landscape

Rural landscapes have been the focus of intense research for the classical period in recent decades. Evidence of this is the recent publication of the Roman Peasant Project, where a substantial synthesis is presented on the settlement and social strategies behind the territorial organization following the Roman conquest of part of Etruria (Bowes 2021). The first volume in the MediTo series was particularly interested in these aspects and in the rural context, presenting the research in progress and showing a classical landscape very different from what had been previously postulated (Sebastiani and Megale 2021). If previously the focus was mainly on the analysis of central settlements such as villas, now the research shows a variety of settlements, minor in their monumentality but equally important for a better definition of the classical society at the basis of the territorial expansion of Rome, in the construction of that distinctive settlement network necessary for the agricultural exploitation and utilization of natural resources fundamental to the Roman economy as a whole.

This approach to so-called *minor sites* has always been necessary in the search for early medieval landscapes. The dissolution of the socio-political and above all economic system of the Western Roman Empire led to the birth of a myriad of settlements built on the ruins of the large estates that had characterized the classical countryside from the fourth century AD on. The increasingly cumbersome presence of the Church resulted in the establishment of parishes and parish churches, which became new poles of aggregation of the rural settlement fabric, although in this case the archaeological research of Tuscia still lags behind in

Alessandro Sebastiani (as424@buffalo.edu) University at Buffalo (SUNY)

Riccardo Rao (riccardo.rao@unibg.it) Università di Bergamo

Archaeological Landscapes of Late Antique and Early Medieval Tuscia: Research and Field Papers, ed. by Riccardo Rao and Alessandro Sebastiani, MEDITO 3 (Turnhout 2023), pp. 11–19

demonstrating the impact of the Christianization of the countryside.[1]

The sumptuous, finely decorated buildings of villas as well as the productive or service settlements along the coast gave way to new forms of community, now gathered in villages and in houses scattered across the landscape or perched on the ruins of ancient classical cities, as in the case of *Rusellae* and Cosa. From the mid-sixth century, rural and coastal landscapes underwent profound transformations, and Tuscia has always been the favoured research laboratory for investigating these changes.[2] This tradition continues with some of the contributions presented in this volume, where the advancement of studies allows us to better outline the transformations of Late Antiquity and the early Middle Ages for the coastal landscapes of the territory of the *ager Rusellanus* (Chirico and Sebastiani, *infra*), of the immediate suburb of the city of *Rusellae* (Campana *infra*), of the territorial district of the city of Florence (Cantini and Martinez *infra*), and of the coastal area of the ancient city of Populonia (Dallai and Marasco, *infra*).

The investigative path starts from the coast of the *ager Rusellanus* and the transformations that can be recorded by analysing in tandem the excavations carried out by the University of Sheffield in the landscape of the Maremma Regional Park and the previous research of the administrative areas of the Etruscan-Roman city. After seven years of intense research, it became possible to reconstruct the emergence and progressive dissolution of Roman landscapes, identifying in the mid-sixth century the moment of a full break between the classical world and the developing world of the early Middle Ages. The data of the Alberese area (Chirico 2019c, 2020; Sebastiani 2016, 2017) have now been added to those relating to the site of Castiglione della Pescaia and the immediate vicinity of the city of *Rusellae*, where

the analysis presented here is able to summarize for the first time data that have always been heterogeneous, or linked to single case studies (Chirico 2019a, 2019b).

Stefano Campana's contribution broadens the scope and the diachrony of the same territory, illustrating a wide range of settlements belonging to the early medieval period and discovered through the EmptyScapes project. The data collected in his contribution to this volume bring together and amplify the conclusions already partially published (Campana 2017, 2018; Vaccaro and others 2009), providing a much more detailed picture of the complex settlement dynamics that were formed between the seventh and the eleventh centuries.

Moving north along the coast, the contribution of Luisa Dallai and Lorenzo Marasco emphasizes the results obtained from the *nEU-Med Project*, with particular reference to the Vetricella site and the wider area of the Pecora river valley, where the settlement of Carlappiano lies.[3] The multidisciplinary approach proposed here allows for the innovative reconstruction of the natural environment in which a series of sites aimed at increasing administrative control of the landscape and the natural resources it made available were installed over the course of the early medieval centuries. It would be precisely this widespread arrangement of the territory that would favour the rise of the centres of royal power, located both on the now-recognized high ground sites but also in the flatter areas of the Pecora valley.

The relationship between settlements and the natural environment is at the centre of the contribution of Federico Cantini and Gianluca Martinez. The case study of the *Villa dei Vetti* takes us back to the late antique period, when starting from the mid-fourth century, we witness the construction of a sumptuous residential structure, the owner of which could be recognized in the *Vettio Agorio Pretestato* mentioned in a marble inscription. The archaeological research of the various rooms of the villa is accompanied by an accurate poli-environmental reconstruction, which will show how the proximity to the Arno river was a fundamental deterrent for the topographical choice of the settlement.

Finally, Fabio Saggioro provides a general overview of the early medieval settlement networks in Tuscia and details a comparison with the area of central and northern Italy. His analysis is based on recent archaeological investigations, as well as the tight relationship between sites and the surrounding natural environment. The establishment of centres of power is, in fact, now

---

1 There is, however, a growing interest in this, as is outlined in Campana and others 2008; Christie 1991; Valenti 2016.

2 The transformations of the late antique and early medieval countryside have been the subject of heated debates and interventions since at least the 1970s, when medieval archaeology as a discipline was taking its first steps. Fundamental for the understanding of the subsequent fortified high-ground settlements (the *castelli*), the early medieval campaign has been the subject of wide discussion in research over almost fifty years and culminated in excellent syntheses, including, amongst others: Bianchi and Hodges 2018; Brogiolo 1996b; Castrorao Barba 2020; Cavalieri and Sfameni 2022; Francovich and Hodges 2006; McCormick 2001; Valenti 2004; Wickham 2005; Cavalieri and Sacchi 2020. The impetus to undertake an ever more detailed analysis of early medieval rural landscapes was certainly stimulated by research in the French and British contexts, which saw from the beginning historians and archaeologists in opposition, on post-classical villages (Chapelot and Fossier 1980; Hamerow 2002, 2012; Zadora-Rio 1995) and on the research history of the foundation of castles (Toubert 1973, 2002).

---

3 On the *nEU-Med Project* in general and on the results of this important study, refer to the numerous publications published in recent years, in particular to Bianchi and Hodges 2018, 2020; Briano 2020; Dallai and others 2020.

approached via historical and archaeological debates regarding dependence on natural resources such as rivers, forests, and agricultural fields.

The Urban Landscape

The urban archaeology of late antique and early medieval Tuscia has certainly seen different research approaches in recent years, especially with respect to the pioneering research of the last century (Hodges *infra*). The 1980s and 1990s saw an exceptional ferment of studies on urban transformations, following in the wake of what was initially found in *Luna* (Ward-Perkins 1981) and then in the major cases of Brescia (Brogiolo 1993), Milan (Caporusso 1991), Pavia (Hudson 1981), Verona (La Rocca 1986) and Roma (Arena and others 2012; Manacorda 2001). The debate on urban archaeology and the birth of early medieval cities was fuelled by encounters/clashes between archaeologists and historians, culminating in the creation of contrasting models between those who saw an ideological and settlement continuity in the reused material remains of the classical city and those who, instead, used these to affirm and to emphasize a total discontinuity with the past.[4]

In this cultural environment, the two urban contexts in Tuscia that stood out were those of Cosa, the subject of systematic excavations by the American Academy of Rome (Brown 1980; Fentress 2003), and the ancient city of *Rusellae*, which right at the turn of the 1980s and 1990s, saw its last major urban excavations (Celuzza and Fentress 1994) before a systematic archaeological revival during recent times (Celuzza and others 2021; Zifferero and others Forthcoming). This was joined by the city of *Luna*, the object of systematic research by English and Italian teams (Durante 2001; Lusuardi Siena and Sannazaro 1990, 1995; Ward-Perkins 1981) and belonging to the Augustan *Regio VII*, although today it is included in the administrative territory of the Liguria region and for this reason is included in this volume. A first synthesis on urban research saw the light at the end of the last century (Gelichi 1999), while the excavation activities in other centres such as Populonia (Dadà 2007; Cavari 2009; Camporeale and Mascione 2010) or Vetulonia (Cygielman and Millemaci 2007) found few and unsystematic traces of early medieval occupation.

The advent of the new century saw, however, a revival of interest in post-classical Tuscan cities; examples are the works presented for Siena (Cantini 2005; Castiglia 2014) and Florence (Cantini 2007; D'Aquino and others 2015), as well as several pieces of evidence obtained from rescue excavations in Lucca (Ciampoltrini 2006), the subject of a preliminary synthesis in recent times (Castiglia 2016).

This volume updates the reader on at least five urban case studies: *Rusellae*, Cosa, *Pisae*, *Luna*, and Leopoli-Cencelle. In the first case, the city of *Rusellae* and its early medieval transformations are analysed through the lens of forensic archaeology. The study proposed by the team of Todd Fenton and Maria Grazia Celuzza emphasizes the analyses conducted on the skeletal remains of about 120 identified individuals, coming from excavations around the urban cathedral in the 1980s (Celuzza and Fentress 1994; Celuzza and others 2002). These have returned interesting data on the distribution of malaria, which has always been indicated as one of the main reasons for the abandonment of the classical city in favour of the nearby medieval centre of Grosseto. The topic is particularly valuable at this time, not only because we are still experiencing the COVID-19 pandemic emergency but for the interest that molecular and forensic archaeology have garnered in recent years for understanding the dramatic changes of Late Antiquity and the early Middle Ages.[5] The study places a new emphasis on the presence of malaria in the late antique and early medieval population of *Rusellae*, certainly changing the perspective of a disease that was considered to be one of the main causes of the abandonment of the city. It would be interesting in the near future to be able to repeat this type of analysis also for other coastal centres in the region, first of all that of Cosa, together with rural places such as the nearby villa of Settefinestre explored during the last century, whose skeletal remains seem to have similar characteristics. Furthermore, the craniometric analysis of the individuals buried in the urban cathedral at *Rusellae* revealed the presence of individuals of probable African and North-European origin within the sample. This is a fundamental first step for understanding the mobility of people within the borders of early medieval Tuscia and for starting a process of genetic identification within post-classical urban societies. The deposition of an African individual inside the Christian cemetery of *Rusellae* may also favour in the immediate future studies

---

4 There is a large bibliography referring to these debates, and this note tries to summarize the main interventions over time, with the excellent summaries recently released. See, at least, Augenti 2006, 2014; Brogiolo 1996a; Brogiolo and Gelichi 1998; Brogiolo and Ward-Perkins 1999; Christie and Loseby 1996; Gelichi 1999, 2010; La Rocca Hudson 1986; Ward-Perkins 1983, 1997, 2006; Wickham 2005.

5 In this regard, see Harper 2021, together with the contributions on the subject in Little 2006; McCormick 2008; Keller and others 2019.

of a religious and social nature and on the perception of identity in early medieval society, often enclosed within anthropological binomials in strict dichotomy.

Excavations conducted by Florida State University (De Giorgi, *infra*) at the remains of an Imperial bathhouse building are showing new data on late antique presence at the Roman city of Cosa. This new information adds to what is already known for the city, especially in its sixth-century settlement forms (Fentress 2003; Celuzza and Fentress 1994), and opens up new directions for research on the transformations of the urban fabric of Cosa before its conversion to a late medieval settlement.

In the chapter dedicated to the maritime city of *Pisae*, Antonio Alberti presents the evolution of the centre from the fourth century up to the dawn of the late Middle Ages. The analysis starts from both the critical reading of the written sources and the material evidence obtained from the numerous archaeological excavations that have taken place over time. The urban fabric seems to remain fairly unchanged at least throughout the fifth century, while with the sixth the first systematic changes due to Byzantine intervention in the city begin to be glimpsed. *Pisae* certainly encountered a reduction of its settled area, with the construction of a fortified redoubt linked both to the changed geological situation around the river and to the coast, as well as an objective decrease of the urban population. Special attention is paid to the proliferation of churches within the walls, as well as outside them in the Lombard period. The early medieval city was taking shape, with its new points of aggregation and reference, including the cathedral that houses the necropolis, which has returned important information.

The research on early medieval *Luna* starts from the report published in the first volume of the MediTo series (Menchelli and others 2021). The authors now provide a narrative around the life and frequentations of the insula located near Porta a Mare, along the defensive wall circuit. The Roman structures, mainly two *domus*, had different destinies. On the one hand, the so-called Domus B saw the construction of an Imperial temple in its immediate vicinity, which was already subject to dispossession and systematic destruction during the fourth century. The presence of a religious building leads the authors to believe that a purely domestic use of the complex is unlikely, and it was abandoned and destroyed during the fifth century AD; right after its destruction, the building changed its intended use, becoming a workshop dedicated to washing clothes, probably in leather. Its lifetime, however, was relatively short, if already during the second half of the sixth and until the eighth centuries, the area was affected by the construction of at least one residential building, based on a substantial rise of surfaces that obliterated the productive facility. The area of the so-called Domus

A experienced alternating occupation phases in the late antique and early medieval periods. Having lost its residential function already during Imperial times, it saw the construction of at least one well during the sixth century; this infrastructure remained in use until the next century, when it was sealed and obliterated with land and building material. Its construction took place at a time when the city of *Luna* saw the construction of similar structures in other urban portions, perhaps in support of the inhabited area recognized in the Forum and in the nearby theatre and, most likely, of buildings in perishable materials arranged in the immediate vicinity of the well itself.

The last urban complex examined in this volume is represented by the city of Leopoli-Cencelle. In truth, the geographical context of this site does not correspond to the territorial limits of Tuscia, placing itself instead in the landscapes controlled by the papacy. The decision to include this case study in the volume aims to underline the differences as well as the similarities in the settlement choices used during the early medieval period in neighbouring territories that were nevertheless subject to different political authorities. As mentioned in the *Liber Pontificalis*, the city of *Leopolis* (the city of Pope Leo IV) was built to help the inhabitants of *Centumcellae* in response to the constant Saracen attacks along the Tyrrhenian coast of Latium. We are therefore faced with a newly founded city, an element that already distinguishes it from the previous cases analysed, all united by a classic urban tradition that was then revisited and remodelled in the post-Roman period. Nonetheless, the medieval settlement was built on top of some pre-existing structures from the Etruscan and Roman periods. The hill, in fact, had been occupied by an Etruscan *oppidum*, abandoned during the period of Roman expansion and no longer rebuilt. The presence of a place of worship would be dated to the following period, the location and dating of which is still a matter of debate. The cultic memory of the place had to survive for a long time if, in the late antique phase, a church was built into the hill, perhaps becoming a point of reference for the Christianization of the countryside and local communities; however, we are not faced with any type of extensive occupation of the hills, at least not since the eighth century when the city was founded. The evolution of the urban layout, which can be followed through the analysis of the inscriptions, written sources, and archaeological data recovered during the excavations by La Sapienza University of Rome, allows us to understand the involutions and transformations of a centre of the papacy's political-territorial power. The excavations have managed to bring to light sections of daily life and the ecclesiastical and military architecture, as well as the domestic and artisanal structures of a community that managed to delay the abandonment of the centre until at least the fifteenth century, when the political changes in the eastern Mediterranean also entailed dramatic consequences in commercial traffic to which the fate of *Leopolis* was closely connected.

Between City and Countryside: Written Sources and Landscapes of Power

Overall, historical research on landscape in recent decades has assumed an increasingly intense exchange with archaeological literature (Rao 2015, 27–28). Within a historiographical panorama less dynamic than the archaeological one as regards the landscape, beyond singular, specific research, the most significant ideas came first of all from the re-evaluation of the role of the public during the early Middle Ages, with important reflections also on the transformation of landscapes, as the works on public goods, now interpreted as a fundamental moment of action by the public on the territories analysed in this volume (Bianchi, Lazzari, and La Rocca 2018; Bougard and Loré 2019). There is no doubt that the framework of knowledge appears decidedly changed today as compared to fifty years ago, when the founding works of landscape and settlement history began to be developed on which historiographic interpretation is still being built — think of Latium by Pierre Toubert (Toubert 1973) — and when the main actors of landscape transformations were identified in the aristocracies, which were, moreover, at the centre of debate in European political-institutional history. Today, the action of the aristocracies is recognized but framed within a dialectic with the public powers.

Starting from these research paths, in this volume Paolo Tomei proposes a close reading of early medieval written sources up to the ninth century, comparing them with archaeological data. The perspective of written sources makes it possible to better integrate the transformations of the countryside, connecting them with the power groups operating in the cities. In particular, Tomei develops here the concept of 'Landscape of Power', with the aim of recovering the material elements of anthropic action on the territory and the environment 'that fulfill political functions in a performative sense'; in other words, identifying which powers organize physical space. In particular, the wide Tuscan coastal strip, with large swampy and uncultivated stretches, appears in Late Antiquity and the early Middle Ages as an area of fiscal relevance. Indeed, thanks also to his work on onomastics, Tomei underlines the dominant aspects of continuity of the parental groups that operated in the area for centuries, at least until the middle of the seventh century, starting

with the great families of the senatorial aristocracy. In particular, the landscape of power is built around the action of the regional elite, which included the major political and ecclesiastical authorities in close connection with the kingdom. Although gravitating primarily around cities, the regional elite groups also operated intensively in the countryside, thanks to their network of residences (*salae*) and directly related managed branches (*sundria* or *cafaggia*). These favoured the construction of a local connectivity of Mediterranean projection, which opened up to the island system of Corsica and Sardinia.

Starting from the mid-eighth century with the end of the Lombard kingdom and the Carolingian conquest, the rise of new power groups, characterized by a greater involvement with the continent, also changed the management of the coastal strip: it lost the connection network with the islands. Finally, the *curtis* model was implanted, with also significant lexical substitutions (*dominicum* replaces *sundrium*).

Dynamic Landscapes of the Early Middle Ages

Overall, the collected essays contribute to restoring a decidedly more dynamic picture of early medieval landscapes than that which was still visible only a few decades ago in Italian historiography. Stripped of all monolithic and static dimensions, the early medieval centuries appear marked by strong moments of continuity with the ancient world but also by important phases of dynamic rethinking of environmental balances.

Certainly, the tenth century, at the end of the period considered, can no longer be seen as 'the century of iron'; rather, it must be considered as a decisive junction fully inserted in a new phase of growth. As is now clearly evident, especially from the works of *nEU-Med* presented here, embattling, deforestation, and large-scale reclamation, thanks also to the initiative of the public authorities, end up producing new landscapes. Onto this new environmental framework, further phases of modelling the landscapes of the late Middle Ages are grafted; these are perhaps better known thanks to research paths consolidated through written sources, but they are to be re-read again for the Tuscan Mediterranean in the light of a now-renovated, early medieval interpretative framework.

Acknowledgements

The editors would like to thank first of all the various contributors to this volume. As with the previous publication of the MediTo series, we found ourselves obtaining the definitive texts and curating the edition during the COVID-19 pandemic, which has slowed down the research due to closed libraries as well as to the accumulation of academic commitments following the establishment of online teaching.

Heartfelt thanks also go to Brad Ault, Stephen Dyson, Carolina Megale, Marco Paperini, Riccardo Santangeli Valenzani, and Giulia Vollono for their advice and the exchange of ideas on the issues of the volume, together with Elisabeth Woldeyohannes, who edited all the texts.

The municipal administration of Civitella Paganico, in the persons of the mayor Alessandra Biondi and the city councillor Luca Giannuzzi Savelli, has allowed for the holding of international conferences from which the idea of the editorial series was born; our recognition goes to these individuals for being able to attract interest and resources for the conferences' development and final realization.

Finally, we thank the anonymous reviewers for their suggestions to improve the volume, together with Rosie Bonté, publisher editor of the series on behalf of Brepols, for her constant professionalism and support.

Works Cited

Arena, Maria Stella, Paolo Delogu, Lidia Paroli, Marco Ricci, Lucia Saguì, and others (eds). 2012. *Roma. Dall'antichità al Medioevo. Archeologia e Storia nel Museo Nazionale Romano Crypta Balbi* (Milan: Electa)

Augenti, Andrea (ed.). 2006. *Le Città Italiane tra la Tarda Antichità e l'alto Medioevo: Atti del Convegno (Ravenna, 26–28 Febbraio 2004)*, Biblioteca di Archeologia Medievale, 20 (Florence: All'Insegna del Giglio)

—— . 2014. 'Archeologia della Città Medievale', *Archeologia Medievale*, Numero Speciale: 173–82

Bianchi, Giovanna, and Richard Hodges (eds). 2018. *Origins of a New Economic Union (7th-12th Centuries): Preliminary Results of the NEU-Med Project, October 2015-March 2017*, Biblioteca di Archeologia Medievale, 25 (Florence: All'Insegna del Giglio)

Bianchi, Giovanna, and Richard Hodges (eds). 2020. *The NEU-Med Project: Vetricella, an Early Medieval Royal Property on Tuscany's Mediterranean*, Biblioteca di Archeologia Medievale, 28 (Florence: All'Insegna del Giglio)

Bianchi, Giovanna, Tiziana Lazzari, and Maria Cristina La Rocca (eds). 2018. *Spazio pubblico e spazio privato. Tra storia e archeologia (secoli VI-XI)* (Turnhout: Brepols)

Bougard, François, and Vito Loré (eds). 2019. *Biens publics, biens du roi. Les bases économiques des pouvoirs royaux dans le haut Moyen Âge* (Turnhout: Brepols)

Bowes, Kimberly Diane (ed.). 2021. *The Roman Peasant Project 2009–2014: Excavating the Roman Rural Poor*, University Museum Monograph, 154 (Philadelphia: University of Pennsylvania, Museum of Archaeology and Anthropology)

Briano, Arianna. 2020. *La Ceramica a Vetrina Sparsa nella Toscana Altomedievale: Produzione, cronologia e distribuzione*, Biblioteca di Archeologia Medievale, 31 (Florence: All'Insegna del Giglio)

Brogiolo, Gian Pietro. 1993. *Brescia Altomedievale*, Documenti di Archeologia, 2 (Mantua: Società Archeologica Padana)

—— (ed.). 1996a. *Early Medieval Towns in the Western Mediterranean. Ravello, 22–24 September 1994*, Documenti di Archeologia, 10 (Mantua: Società Archeologica Padana)

—— (ed.). 1996b. *La Fine delle Ville Romane. Trasformazioni nelle campagne tra Tarda Antichità e Alto Medioevo: 1° Convegno Archeologico del Garda, Gardone Riviera (Brescia), 14 Ottobre 1995*, Documenti di Archeologia, 11 (Mantova: Società Archeologica Padana)

Brogiolo, Gian Pietro, and Sauro Gelichi. 1998. *La Città nell'alto Medioevo Italiano. Archeologia e Storia* (Rome: Carocci Editore)

Brogiolo, Gian Pietro, and Bryan Ward-Perkins (eds). 1999. *The Idea and Ideal of the Town between Late Antiquity and the Early Middle Ages*, The Transformation of the Roman World, 4 (Leiden: Brill)

Brown, Frank E. 1980. *Cosa. The Making of a Roman Town* (Ann Arbor: The University of Michigan Press)

Campana, Stefano. 2017. 'Emptyscapes: Filling an "Empty" Mediterranean Landscape at Rusellae, Italy', *Antiquity*, 91.359: 1223–40

—— . 2018. *Mapping the Archaeological Continuum*, SpringerBriefs in Archaeology (Cham: Springer International Publishing)

Campana, Stefano, Cristina Felici, Riccardo Francovich, and Fabio Gabbrielli (eds). 2008. *Chiese e Insediamenti nei secoli di formazione dei paesaggi medievali della Toscana (V–X secolo). Atti del Seminario, San Giovanni d'Asso-Montisi, 10–11 Novembre 2006*, Quaderni del Dipartimento di Archeologia e Storia delle Arti, Sezione Archeologia, Università di Siena, 64 (Florence: All'Insegna del Giglio)

Camporeale, Stefano, and Cynthia Mascione. 2010. 'Dalle cave ai cantieri: estrazione e impiego della calcarenite a Populonia fra periodo etrusco e romanizzazione', in *Arqueologia de La Costruccion II. Los Procesos Constructivos en el mundo Romano: Italia y Provincias Orientales, Workshop I Cantieri edili dell'Italia e delle Province Romane: Italia e Province Orientali, Siena (Italia) 13–15 Novembre 2008*, ed. by Stefano Camporeale, Hélène Dessales, and Antonio Pizzo, Anejos de Archivio Español de Arqueologia, LVII (Merida: Artes Gráficas Rejas), pp. 153–72

Cantini, Federico. 2005. *Archeologia urbana a Siena: L'area dell'Ospedale di Santa Maria della Scala prima dell'Ospedale Altomedioevo*, Biblioteca del Dipartimento di Archeologia e Storia delle Arti, Sezione Archeologica, Università di Siena, 11 (Florence: All'Insegna del Giglio)

—— (ed.). 2007. *Firenze prima degli Uffizi: Lo scavo di via de' Castellani. Contributi per un'archeologia urbana fra tardo antico ed Età Moderna* (Florence: All'Insegna del Giglio)

Caporusso, Donatella (ed.). 1991. *Scavi MM3. Ricerche di archeologia urbana a Milano Durante la costruzione della Linea 3 della Metropolitana 1982–1990* (Milan: Edizioni ET)

Castiglia, Gabriele. 2014. *Il Duomo di Siena: Excavations and Pottery below Siena Cathedral* (Oxford: Archaeopress)

——. 2016. 'Lucca e Siena a confronto. Trasformazioni urbane nella Tuscia Annonaria dall'età classica alla fine dell'altomedioevo', *Mélanges de l'École française de Rome – Moyen Âge*, 128.1 <https://doi.org/10.4000/mefrm.3008>

Castrorao Barba, Angelo. 2020. *La fine delle ville romane in Italia tra tarda antichità e alto medioevo: III–VIII secolo*, Munera, 49 (Bari: Edipuglia)

Cavalieri, Marco, and Furio Sacchi (eds). 2020. *La Villa dopo la Villa. Trasformazione di un sistema insediativo ed economico in Italia Centro-Settentrionale tra Tarda Antichità e Medioevo*, Fervet Opus, 7 (Louvain-la-Neuve: Presses universitaires de Louvain)

Cavalieri, Marco, and Carla Sfameni (eds). 2022. *La Villa dopo La Villa – 2. Trasformazione di un sistema insediativo ed economico nell'Italia centrale tra Tarda Antichità e Medioevo*, Fervet Opus, 9 (Louvain-La-Neuve: Presses universitaires de Louvain)

Cavari, Fernanda. 2009. 'Rivestimenti pavimentali e manufatti in marmo dagli edifici dell'acropoli di Populonia', in *Materiali da costruzione e produzione del ferro: studi sull'economia populoniese fra periodo etrusco e romanizzazione*, ed. by Franco Cambi, Fernanda Cavari, and Cynthia Mascione (Bari: Edipuglia), pp. 97–104

Celuzza, Maria Grazia, S. Cencetti, and Elsa Pacciani. 2002. 'Scavi nel cimitero della più antica cattedrale di Roselle', in *Antropologia del Medioevo: Biologia e Cultura*, ed. by Elsa Pacciani, Rosa Boano, and Margherita Micheletti (Arezzo: L.P. Grafiche), pp. 77–87

Celuzza, Maria Grazia, Matteo Milletti, and Andrea Zifferero. 2021. 'Rusellae and its Territory. From the Etruscan to the Roman City', in *Archaeological Landscapes of Roman Etruria*, ed. by Alessandro Sebastiani and Carolina Megale, MediTo – Archaeological and Historical Landscapes of Mediterranean Central Italy, 1 (Turnhout: Brepols), pp. 79–92

Celuzza, Mariagrazia, and Elizabeth Fentress. 1994. 'La Toscana Centro-Meridionale: i casi di Cosa-Ansedonia e Roselle', in *La storia dell'altomedioevo italiano (VI–X Secolo) alla luce dell'archeologia. Atti del Convegno (Certosa Di Pontignano – Siena 1992)*, ed. by Riccardo Francovich and Ghislaine Noyé, Biblioteca Di Archeologia Medievale, 11 (Florence: All'Insegna del Giglio), pp. 601–14

Chapelot, Jean, and Robert Fossier. 1980. *Le village et la maison au Moyen Âge*, Bibliothèque d'archéologie (Paris: Hachette Littérature)

Chirico, Elena. 2019a. 'Aquae Rusellanae: Il complesso termale di carattere pubblico a Bagni di Roselle (GR, Italia)', *Orizzonti*, XX

——. 2019b. 'Il brigantaggio in Maremma in età tardoantica', in *Antico e non Antico. Scritti multidisciplinari offerti a Giuseppe Pucci*, ed. by Valentino Nizzo and Antonio Pizzo (Milan: Mimesis Edizioni), pp. 125–36

——. 2019c. 'Prima Golena (Alberese, GR): Umbro Flumen una *mansio-positio* a servizio della viabilità', *Bollettino Di Archeologia Online*, X.1–2: 85–96

——. 2020. 'La *mansio* di Hasta ad Alberese (GR, Toscana, Italia)', *Journal of Fasti Online*, 458: 1–15

Christie, Neil (ed.). 1991. *Three South Etrurian Churches: Santa Cornelia, Santa Rufina and San Liberato*, Archaeological Monographs of the British School at Rome, 4 (London: British School at Rome)

Christie, Neil, and Simon T. Loseby (eds). 1996. *Towns in Transition: Urban Evolution in Late Antiquity and the Early Middle Ages* (Aldershot: Scolar Press)

Ciampoltrini, Giulio. 2006. 'Lucca tardoantica e altomedievale (IV–VII secolo). Archeologia di una struttura urbana "allo stato fluido"', *Geschichte Und Region*, 15: 61–78

Cygielman, Mario, and M. Millemaci. 2007. 'Vetulonia, via Garibaldi (Castiglione della Pescaia, GR) Scavi 2003–2006', in *Materiali per Populonia, 6*, ed. by Lucia Botarelli, Marta Coccoluto, and Cristina Mileti (Pisa: Edizioni ETS), pp. 343–88

Dadà, Massimo. 2007. 'Ceramica medievale e moderna dall'acropoli di Populonia (Saggio XX)', in *Materiali per Populonia, 6*, ed. by Lucia Botarelli, Marta Coccoluto, and Cristina Mileti (Pisa: Edizioni ETS), pp. 169–87

Dallai, Luisa, Giovanna Bianchi, and Francesca Romana Stasolla (eds). 2020. *I paesaggi dell'allume: archeologia della produzione ed economia di Rete*, Biblioteca di Archeologia Medievale, 29 (Florence: All'Insegna del Giglio)

D'Aquino, Valeria, Guido Guarducci, Silvia Nencetti, and Stefano Valentini (eds). 2015. *Archeologia a Firenze: Città e Territorio. Atti del Workshop. Firenze, 12–13 Aprile 2013* (Oxford: Archaeopress)

Durante, Anna Maria. 2001. *Città antica di Luna. Lavori in corso* (La Spezia: Luna Editore)

Fentress, Elizabeth (ed.). 2003. *Cosa V: An Intertmittent Town, Excavations 1991–1997*, Supplements to the Memoirs of the American Academy in Rome (Ann Arbor: University of Michigan Press)

Francovich, Riccardo, and Richard Hodges. 2006. *Villa to Village: The Transformation of the Roman Countryside in Italy, ca. 400–1000*, Duckworth Debates in Archaeology (London: Duckworth)

Gelichi, Sauro (ed.). 1999. *Archeologia urbana in Toscana: la città altomedievale*, Documenti di Archeologia, 17 (Mantova: Società Archeologica Padana)

——. 2010. 'La città in Italia tra VI e VIII secolo: riflessioni dopo un trentennio di dibattito archeologico', in *Espacios urbanos en el Occidente Mediterraneo (S. VI–VIII)*, ed. by Alfonso García, Ricardo Izquierdo, Lauro Olmo, and Diego Peris (Toledo: Anebri Artes Gráficas), pp. 65–85

Hamerow, Helena. 2002. *Early Medieval Settlements: The Archaeology of Rural Communities in North-West Europe, 400–900* (Oxford: Oxford University Press)

——. 2012. *Rural Settlements and Society in Anglo-Saxon England* (Oxford: Oxford University Press)

Harper, Kyle. 2021. *Plagues Upon the Earth: Disease and the Course of Human History*, The Princeton Economic History of the Western World, 46 (Princeton: Princeton University Press)

Horden, Peregrine, and Nicholas Purcell. 2000. *The Corrupting Sea: A Study of Mediterranean History* (Oxford: Blackwell)

Hudson, Peter. 1981. *Archeologia urbana e programmazione della ricerca: l'esempio di Pavia*, Biblioteca di Archeologia Medievale, 1 (Florence: All'Insegna del Giglio)

Keller, Marcel, Maria A. Spyrou, Christiana L. Scheib, Gunnar U. Neumann, Andreas Kröpelin, and others. 2019. 'Ancient *Yersinia Pestis* Genomes from across Western Europe Reveal Early Diversification during the First Pandemic (541–750)', *Proceedings of the National Academy of Sciences*, 116.25: 12363–72

La Rocca, Cristina. 1986. 'Dark Ages a Verona. Edilizia privata, aree Aperte e strutture pubbliche in una città dell'Italia settentrionale', *Archeologia Medievale*, XIII: 31–78

La Rocca Hudson, Cristina. 1986. 'Città altomedievali, storia e archeologia', *Studi Storici*, 27.3: 725–35

Little, Lester K. (ed.). 2006. *Plague and the End of Antiquity: The Pandemic of 541–750* (Cambridge: Cambridge University Press)

Lusuardi Siena, Silvia, and Marco Sannazaro. 1990. 'Luni. Area della Cattedrale', *Archaeologia in Liguria*, III.2: 222–28

——. 1995. 'Gli scavi nell'area della Cattedrale lunense: dall'uso privato dello spazio all'edilizia religiosa pubblica', in *Splendida Civitas Nostra. Studi Archeologici in onore di Antonio Frova*, ed. by Giuliana Cavalieri Manasse and Elisabetta Roffia, Studi e Ricerche sulla Gallia Cisalpina, 8 (Rome: Quasar), pp. 191–216

Manacorda, Daniele. 2001. *Crypta Balbi. Archeologia e storia di un paesaggio urbano* (Milan: Electa)

McCormick, Michael. 2001. *Origins of the European Economy: Communications and Commerce, A.D. 300–900* (Cambridge: Cambridge University Press)

——. 2008. 'Molecular Middle Ages: Early Medieval Economic History in the Twenty-First Century', in *The Long Morning of Medieval Europe. New Directions in Early Medieval Studies*, ed. by Jennifer Davis and Michael McCormick (London: Routledge), pp. 83–97

Menchelli, Simonetta, Paolo Sangriso, Alberto Cafaro, Stefano Genovesi, Silvia Marini, and others. 2021. 'Luna: The Area of Porta Marina between the Republican and the Imperial Periods', in *Archaeological Landscapes of Roman Etruria*, ed. by Alessandro Sebastiani and Carolina Megale, MediTo – Archaeological and Historical Landscapes of Mediterranean Central Italy, 1 (Turnhout: Brepols), pp. 163–74

Rao, Riccardo. 2015. *I paesaggi dell'Italia medievale* (Rome: Carocci)

Sebastiani, Alessandro. 2016. 'New Data for a Preliminary Understanding of the Roman Settlement Network in South Coastal Tuscany. The Case of Alberese (Grosseto, IT)', *Res Antiquae*, 13: 243–72

——. 2017. 'From Villa to Village. Late Roman to Early Medieval Settlement Networks in the Ager Rusellanus.', in *Encounters, Excavations and Argosies. Essays for Richard Hodges*, ed. by John Moreland, John Mitchell, and Bea Leal (Oxford: Archaeopress), pp. 281–90

Sebastiani, Alessandro, and Carolina Megale (eds). 2021. *Archaeological Landscapes of Roman Etruria. Research and Field Papers*, MediTo – Archaeological and Historical Landscapes of Mediterranean Central Italy, 1 (Turnhout: Brepols)

Toubert, Pierre. 1973. *Les structures du Latium médiéval: le Latium méridional et la Sabine du 9e siècle à la fin du 12e siècle*, Bibliothèque des Écoles françaises d'Athènes et de Rome, 221 (Rome: École française de Rome)

——. 2002. *Dalla terra ai castelli: paesaggio, agricoltura e poteri nell'Italia medievale*, Biblioteca Einaudi, 13 (Turin: Einaudi)

Vaccaro, Emanuele, Mariaelena Ghisleni, and Stefano Campana. 2009. 'The Site of Aiali from the Late Republican Period to the Middle Ages in the Light of Surface Potter Analysis', in *Seeing the Unseen. Geophysical and Landscape Archaeology*, ed. by Stefano Campana and Salvatore Piro (London: CRC Press), pp. 303–24

Valenti, Marco. 2004. *L'insediamento altomedievale nelle campagne toscane. Paesaggi, popolamento e villaggi tra VI e X Secolo*, Biblioteca del Dipartimento di Archeologia e Storia delle Arti – Sezione Archeologica, 10 (Florence: All'Insegna del Giglio)

——. 2016. 'Fortified Settlements of the 8th to 10th Centuries. Italy and the Case of Tuscany', in *Fortified Settlements in Early Medieval Europe. Defended Communities of the 8th-10th Centuries*, ed. by Neil Christie and Hajnalka Herold (Oxford: Oxbow Books), pp. 289–301

Ward-Perkins, Bryan. 1981. 'Two Byzantine Houses at Luni', *Papers of the British School at Rome*, 49: 91–98

——. 1983. 'La città altomedievale', *Archeologia Medievale*, X: 111–24

——. 1997. 'Continuists, Catastrophists and the Towns of Post-Roman Northern Italy', *Papers of the British School at Rome*, 65: 157–76

——. 2006. *The Fall of Rome and the End of Civilization* (Oxford: Oxford University Press)

Wickham, Chris. 2005. *Framing the Early Middle Ages. Europe and the Mediterranean, 400–800* (Oxford: Oxford University Press)

Zadora-Rio, Elisabeth. 1995. 'Le village des historiens et le village des archéologues', in *Campagnes médiévales: L'homme et son space. Études offertes à Robert Fossier*, ed. by Élisabeth Mornet (Paris: Publications de la Sorbonne), pp. 145–53

Zifferero, Andrea, Stefano Camporeale, Luca Passalacqua, Elisabetta Ponta, Benedetta Baleani, and others. Forthcoming. 'Roselle: indagini archeologiche sulla collina Nord (2018–2019)', *Bollettino di Archeologia Online*, XI

ANTONIO ALBERTI

1. The City of *Pisae* from Late Antiquity to the Early Medieval Period

Introduction

Urban archaeology at *Pisae* has seen an extraordinary development in the last fifteen years. Several enhancement projects within the urbanscape have allowed us to investigate multiple sites in the city, both in the historical centre framed by the medieval fortification walls and in its immediate surroundings.

With its large section dedicated to the history of the ancient city, the opening of the *Museo delle Navi antiche di Pisa* witnesses the dramatic changes that archaeological data have imprinted onto the historical sequence of the urban centre (<www.navidipisa.it>).

The chronological focus proposed here, which spans from the sixth to the tenth century AD, suffers from a lack of written sources, as these start to be more present only from the late eighth century; moreover, few contemporary, early medieval structures are well attested, and archaeological stratigraphy for the period is not too visible either. Nonetheless, more information comes from the material culture: albeit less in quantity in comparison with previous and later periods, pottery is quantitatively represented and clearly shows a constant economic decline, although the city is still inserted in extra-regional trade routes.

The Roman period has so far given back a few useful indications, both architectural and archaeological, for the reconstruction of the urban layout: if the epigraphic and narrative sources describe a city of Imperial age rich in temples, structures for entertainment, public baths, and shops, the available archaeological data is essentially reduced to portions of houses mainly located in the northern sector of the city;[1] on the other hand, there is a rich evidence of locally produced and imported contemporary ceramics, collected in the phases of use of the *domus* and also in late contexts as residual material.[2]

For the following periods, between the reign of Theodoric into the Lombard age, accompanying a few material traces there is the sporadic survival of written sources, which define the role of *Pisae* on the sea and in the territory. It seems clear that there was a continuity of organization in the layout of the city, in the functionality of its ports, in the maintaining of an adequate hydrogeological structure, and in the content of trade, at least until the fifth century AD.[3]

The few reports about *Pisae* in the sphere of the Byzantine dominion are characterized by the affirmation of the abilities that the city seems to have acquired in the difficult art of navigation since antiquity. It would be this sort of *genetic predisposition* that would find affirmation in the central centuries of the Middle Ages (Tangheroni and others 2004, 119).

Among the traditional sources used to contextualize *Pisae* in the Byzantine period, the best known is the letter of Saint Gregory the Great I to the Byzantine exarch Smaragdo from June AD 603. The correspondence

---

see Paribeni and others 2011, 71–78; Segenni 2011"event-place":"Ghezzano","page":"71–165","publisher":"Felici Editore","publisher-place":"Ghezzano","title":"Un quartiere residenziale di Pisa romana (Periodo II. For parallels, see also Rizzitelli and Fabiani 2020, 39–48.

2 For the production of Terra Sigillata at *Pisae*, see Sangriso 2018; Menchelli, Baronti, and Sangriso 2020, 57–64.

3 In this regard it should be emphasized that, during the reign of Theodoric, attention was assigned to the navigability of the *Auser*. The maintenance of this communication route had the objective of making it easy for Mediterranean goods to reach both Lucca and Pisa.

---

1 The difficulty of reaching the stratigraphic levels of the Roman period is due to the intense medieval building activity and, also, to the hydrogeological and subsidence characteristics of the area. For a summary of Roman Pisa,

---

Antonio Alberti (antonalberti65@gmail.com) Independent Scholar

Archaeological Landscapes of Late Antique and Early Medieval Tuscia: Research and Field Papers, ed. by Riccardo Rao and Alessandro Sebastiani,
MEDITO 3 (Turnhout 2023), pp. 21–37
BREPOLS ❧ PUBLISHERS   DOI 10.1484/M.MEDITO-EB.5.133991

shows the city with a remarkable maritime vitality and an autonomous political initiative towards both the Byzantines and the Lombards. A recent assessment underlines the real autonomy of *Pisae* towards Byzantium, where its dependence was only nominal (Tangheroni 2004). In the letter, in addition to ecclesiastical matters of Istria related to the Tricapitolinian schism, Saint Gregory writes about an epistolary exchange that he had with the Lombard chief Cilliane regarding a truce agreed to with the exarch. The failure of the embassy of a pontiff's envoy could have resulted in the departure of the *dromones* of the Pisans; therefore, in 603 *Pisae* was able to have a fleet, which was to have a decisive role in the attempts of the Empire to defend the coast. The risk of making this source the proof of the uninterrupted seafaring activity of *Pisae* between the Roman period and the Middle Ages has been underlined, although on the other hand, the archaeological evidence makes it probable, even with a considerable decrease in traffic, at least throughout the seventh century. This is when a 'break' with the political and economic reality inherited from the Empire in the coastal centers of Etruria happens, a crisis accelerated by the Lombard advance in the *Maritima italiorum* (Baldassarri 2013).

The sources are not explicit about the manner and time of the fall of *Pisae* under the Lombard rule. The letter of AD 603 provides the *terminus post quem* and testifies to the real autonomy of the city from Byzantium, while the *terminus ante quem* is identified as AD 643, the year of the expedition of Rotari (king of the Lombards from 636 to 652) to *Maritima*. The city was linked to the Dukedom of Lucca, as the seat of *iudiciaria*, where a royal *gastaldo* resided. Based on the toponymy, the seat of the *gastaldo* should be located near S. Pietro in Cortevecchia, in the modern Piazza dei Cavalieri. Besides the attestation of a series of religious buildings, the few documents dating back to the Lombard period do not allow us to say much about the urban organization of the city, which in these centuries was probably constituted by settlements belonging to the city churches. As for the territory, the sources of the eighth century describe a strong presence of public goods, royal and marquisate, in Valdiserchio, north of *Pisae*, with a strong bond with nearby Lucca, seat of the duchy.[4]

From the last thirty years of the eighth century, other sources record *Pisae* and its active role as a port of the upper Tyrrhenian Sea (Tangheroni and others 2004, 121–25). In AD 774 Adalgis, King Desiderius' son, embarked for Constantinople from the *portu Pisano*; the ambassadors of Caliph Harum al-Rashid entered from *portum Pisas* in 801; and King Hugh of Italy arrived with a ship into *Pisae, Tusciae provinciae caput*, in 926. In addition, the interests of some representatives of the Lombard aristocracy of *Pisae* and Lucca with possessions of land and property in Corsica lead us to deduce the existence of a periodically regular navigation between the island and the Tuscan coast, probably related to *Pisae*.[5]

The Pisan port seems to have had a leading role against the raids of Muslims in the Upper Tyrrhenian Sea: from the beginning of the ninth century, Muslim maritime attacks on the cities and the main islands of the western Mediterranean became increasingly frequent. In this context, in AD 828 King Lothair I charged Boniface II, Count of Lucca, with leading an expedition on the sea against the Ifrigiye Arabs. The count was able to undertake a navigation first to Sardinia and then to Tunisia, and the port where the fleet was fitted out could only have been the port of *Pisae*. The Tuscan Count thus assumed the title of Marquis from AD 846, with the function of vassal of the crown, and was responsible for the protection of the kingdom's borders. In this evolution of the political power of Lucca, the primary role of the Marquis of Tuscia in the economy of the city of *Pisae*, holder of a consolidated ability to go to sea, is more conceivable (Tangheroni and others 2004, 123). The affirmation of King Hugh of Italy, who in AD 926 called *Pisae Tusciae provinciae caput*, underlines the political and economic development that characterized the city from the tenth century onwards.

---

4 The oldest document dates back to AD 720 and concerns a piece of land in Arena, granted by the king to Pertualdo, *vir devotus*, who on his return from a pilgrimage to Rome, donated it to the church of S. Michele, which he founded near the walls of Lucca (Ceccarelli Lemut 1994, 228). In other Lombard documents appear the localities of Limite (739), Vecchiano (762), and the church of S. Giuliano sul Monte Pisano (772), belonging to the diocese of Lucca (Ceccarelli Lemut 1994, 228). The most consistent testimonies of the Carolingian period often concern

ecclesiastical patrimonies of Lucca with wide interests in the area of the Pisan Valdiserchio: the monastery of S. Pietro di Bellerifonsi of Lucca had a *curtis* in Arena; the bishopric of Lucca had a *curtis* in Filettole and one in Vecchiano (Ceccarelli Lemut 1994, 228–39).

5 The interests mentioned concern two documents of AD 754: in the first one, before leaving for the war, the bishop of Lucca Vualprando has all his substance and leaves to his brothers, among other things, all that he owns in Corsica; in the second document, Vualfredo of the former Ratcauso of *Pisae* founds the monastery of Monteverdi and gives it his possessions, among which was the monastery of San Pietro 'in Acci' in Corsica (Tangheroni and others 2004, 122–23).

Pisae in Late Antiquity

To understand the role of *Pisae* on the sea, it is necessary to define the structure of the Pisan coast and its documented landing sites between Late Antiquity and the early Middle Ages.

The definition of the coastline between the Roman period and the Middle Ages is complex. However, it has been outlined by a series of geomorphological and archaeological studies that have reconstructed its ancient shape and evolution over the centuries. It is necessary to remember that the coastline was a few kilometres further back than the present one, following a curvilinear course that leaned towards the sea in the city's southern area, forming the Pisan gulf (*Sinus Pisanus*). In Late Antiquity, the presence of real ports can only be hypothesized in the localities of San Piero a Grado and *Portus Pisanus*/S. Stefano ai Lupi, located near the northern and southern branches of the Arno delta, while in the other numerous sites, one has to assume the existence of harbours, even if only temporary. From these berths, goods were directed toward *Pisae* via the other branches of the Arno to the South and via the channels and tributaries of the Serchio basin to the north. Near the mouth of the Serchio river, known in its urban trait as *Auser*, there were several landing areas: Isola di Migliarino, situated north of *Pisae* on the right side of the Serchio river (today located about 4 km from the coastline) and used between the middle and late Republican periods and the fifth/sixth centuries AD; and also immediately south of the Isola di Migliarino with the nearby Poggio al Marmo (the toponym of which is attested at the mouth of the Serchio river) and Porto alle Conche (Fig. 1.1).

Finally, although the toponym Livorno is attested in medieval sources only from the ninth century onwards, some scholars identify it as a landing area for Byzantine ships called *liburne*, which had been established since the end of the sixth century (Gattiglia 2013, 68).[6] The two main ports (S. Piero a Grado and *Portus Pisanus*) are mentioned by Rutilius Namatianus in the fifth century AD (*De reditu suo*, I, 527–40) and in the *Itinerarium maritimum* in the beginning of the sixth century (Baldassarri and Gattiglia 2009, 181), but only the first is attested on both archaeological and geological bases (Baldassarri 2011). A separate case is the area investigated in recent years at the railway station of S. Rossore, where numerous Roman shipwrecks have been found. The archaeological data do not indicate the presence of port infrastructures of the Roman and/

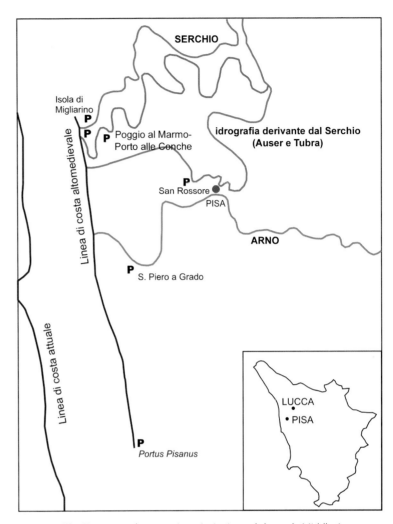

Figure 1.1. The Pisan coast between Late Antiquity and the early Middle Ages, with its ports (P) and moorings (re-elaboration by the author after Gattiglia 2013, 70, fig. 2.30, reproduced with permission).

or late antique periods and show a continuity in the navigation of this stretch of the *Auser* until the sixth century AD (Bruni 2003, 65–66; Camilli 2004, 2019). The absence of port facilities has suggested the possible presence of a docking area near the current cathedral square (Gattiglia 2013, 69).

This system of 'widespread' landings on the Pisan coast declined in the passage between Late Antiquity and the early Middle Ages. Archaeological research has shown a substantial abandonment of these locations after the sixth–seventh centuries, often following the silting of the landings, in a situation similar to that highlighted for the sixth century in other coastal sites of Tuscany (Baldassarri 2011; Baldassarri and Gattiglia 2009, 181). Written sources record a break between the beginning of the seventh century and the middle of the eighth century, and, equally, archaeological investigations have not identified phases of use of the Pisan port facilities between the end of the seventh/

---

6 For a summary of the written sources and of the results of archaeological investigations at the *Portus Pisanus*, see Ducci and others 2011.

Figure 1.2. *Pisae*, Piazza Duomo. A: Excavations 2004 (Area 8000). Re-occupation of a portion of *domus* between the end of the fifth and the first half of the sixth centuries AD. Post holes and other interventions cutting the floor of the *domus* (after Alberti and others 2011b, 167). B: Excavations 1998. Late antique context with post holes, prior to the deposition of the inhumation with Lombard trousseau (after Alberti and others 2011b, 173, reproduced with permission).

beginning of the eighth and the entire ninth centuries (Baldassarri and Gattiglia 2009, 181). The survival of maritime routes and the activity of the ports of the upper Tyrrhenian Sea and *Pisae* between the seventh and eighth centuries seem to be confirmed by ceramic findings, which attest to the rare presence of globular amphorae dated within this chronology. In this regard, it has been hypothesized that since Late Antiquity *Pisae* inherited at least the ports of *Portus Pisanus* and S. Piero a Grado, the only ones that are attested even in the Middle Ages (Baldassarri 2011; Baldassarri and Gattiglia 2009, 181). Thanks to the particular wealth of these places, suitable for landing near the mouths of rivers, and the possibility of supplying wood for the construction of boats, the city would therefore have kept the possibility of going to sea even during the early Middle Ages.

The Roman urban organization was preserved, without obvious transformations, at least until the fifth century AD, while the suburban area north of the city indicates signs of profound changes already from the fourth. Literary sources confirm that the city remained intact until the beginning of the fifth century. The forum of the city, although no archaeological traces indicate its location, is still in operation at the beginning of the

fifth century when Rutilius Namatianus, travelling from Rome to Gaul, stopped in *Pisae* and went to the forum to pay homage to the statue of his father Lacanius, *consularis* of Tuscia and Umbria (Celuzza 2010, 2015).

Although limited in quantity, archaeological data show that the *domus* discovered in Piazza Duomo continued to be inhabited until the fifth century, with renovations and changes that never altered the original layout. It was only between the end of the fifth and the first half of the sixth centuries that the buildings were reoccupied after a phase of abandonment. From the end of the fifth century, the layout of the *domus* began to break down: some areas seem to have been abandoned and to have collapsed, while in other portions buildings were certainly reused for residential purposes, emphasizing a completely different approach than in the past. A series of post holes that cut the *cocciopesto*, at this point obliterated by the abandonment, would testify to the use of perishable materials for the construction of a new, small building (Fig. 1.2).

Belonging to the same phase are also some spoliation pits reused as waste dumps. In these fillings, many ceramics have been collected that testify to a frequentation around the mid-sixth century (Eastern amphorae: late Roman 4; African amphorae: Keay

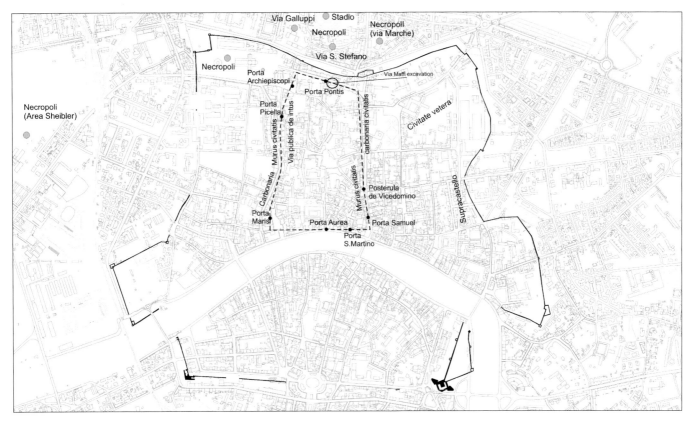

Figure 1.3. Plan of the city of *Pisae* with medieval toponymy indicating the presence of the late antique wall circuit (dotted line) and location of the necropolis (plan by the author).

62 G; African Red Slip Ware D Hayes 80B/99, 89B, 98; Alberti and others 2011b, 168–73; Costantini 2011, 416–20). Some similar but more structured contexts have been documented in the excavation carried out behind the apse of the Cathedral in 1998: here, in the phase preceding the burials with Lombard period grave goods, the traces of a structure, built in perishable material and defined by a line of single and double holes, probably parallel to a masonry base with reused material, have been found (Alberti and others 2015).

The materials collected in the stratigraphies of Piazza Duomo, especially amphorae, indicate *Pisae*'s active participation in Mediterranean trade until the end of the fifth century (Alberti and Costantini 2015; Alberti and others forthcoming). In the panorama of the third–fifth centuries AD, the presence of the so-called amphorae of Empoli stands out, which constitute the most attested transport container and which alone almost equal the total African imports (Cantini and others 2014). This is a testimony to the consistent production of wine in Valdarno and Etruria and of its diffusion in local markets. During the fifth century, imports from the eastern Mediterranean also began to appear, with sporadic examples of late Roman amphorae 1A and 4. The quality and quantity of imports attested in archaeological contexts, therefore, show a specific organization for this period, testifying to how in Late Antiquity *Pisae* was still well inserted in the economic and commercial circuits of the Empire, thanks to its strategic position and the functionality of its ports (Alberti and Costantini 2015; Costantini 2011, 405–07).

The drastic change of destination suffered by the artisan districts that in the Roman period occupied the northern area of the city, beyond the ancient route of the *Auser* (now via Galluppi and via Santo Stefano), indicates a decisive break with the past; here, in fact, in the fourth century, some burials were installed and testify to the disposal of the production workshops of the *terra sigillata* produced within the city (Anichini and Bertelli 2009; Costantini 2014, 346). The same happens a little further north, in the suburban villas discovered near the Stadium: they too are abandoned, and some tombs are installed into their rubble (Anichini and Bertelli 2009; Costantini 2014, 346; Genovesi and Bueno 2020, 65–74) (Fig. 1.3).

These episodes testify to the approach of the burial areas towards the inhabited area and show, for this period, the loss of importance of the northern suburb, once the fulcrum of the city's artisanal activities. This phase of slow deconstruction of the city's suburbs

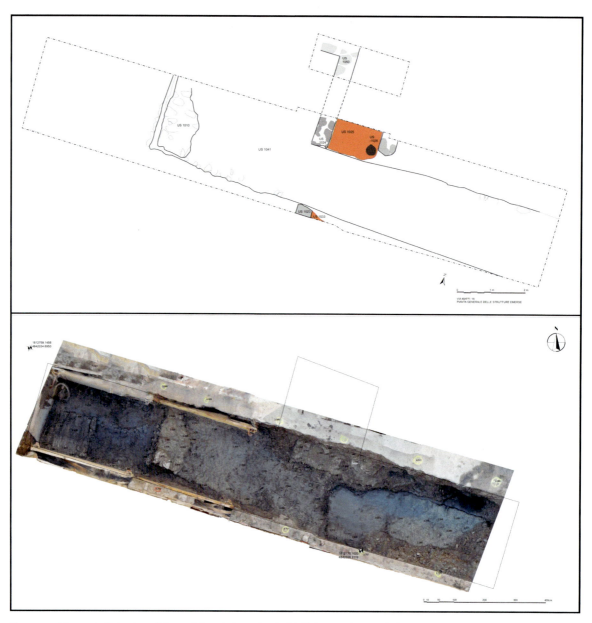

Figure 1.4. Map and photoplan of the wall found along the via Maffi (excavation 2016; direction of excavation Soprintendenza Archeologia Belle Arti e Paesaggio for the provinces of *Pisae* and Livorno: Claudia Rizzitelli; Archaeologists: Antonio Alberti, Monica Baldassarri, Fabio Stratta, reproduced with permission).

would end with the construction of a wall circuit that enclosed the town centre (Cantini 2012, 175). The existence of the late antique city wall has long been hypothesized on the basis of citations of place names, relating to the presence of stretches of city walls that are quite clear in the medieval documentation of the tenth–twelfth centuries, that is, before the construction of the municipal walls.[7] The interaction between written and literary sources and the archaeological data would place the construction of this important masonry work, hypothetically, between the fifth and the sixth centuries AD. Recent archaeological investigations conducted in via Cardinale Maffi, along the road that connects Piazza del Duomo to the Roman baths, have brought to light

---

7 For a complete discussion of the research on the late antique and early medieval city walls, see Garzella 1990, 26–58; for the urban history of *Pisae* in the Middle Ages, see Redi 1991.

a portion probably related to that fortification. It is a wall more than 2 m thick, with a slightly north–west/south–east course, discovered for more than 12 m (corresponding to the length of the excavation test) and continuing towards the east. The structure was found completely dismantled up to the foundation level and composed of only hewn stones bonded with abundant mortar. Its construction caused the cutting of portions of a Roman *domus* (Fig. 1.4).[8]

On the western edge of the trench, the wall is defined by a regular opening that might correspond to that *Porta Pontis* mentioned in medieval documents. The chronology of the wall is challenging to determine. The materials collected are just a few;[9] still, from the archaeological point of view, the construction of this wall is between the phases of abandonment and reoccupation of the *domus*, which for comparison with the excavations of Piazza Duomo, would date between the end of the fifth and first half of the sixth centuries and the subsequent plundering that would precede the construction of the municipal walls of the twelfth century, as confirmed by the ceramics of the layers that cover the phases of disassembly of the structure.

For *Pisae*, therefore, the sixth century has come back under scrutiny as a moment of particular political importance for the city, dictated by relations with Byzantium and the control of the coast; on the other hand, the role of the city during the Gothic War and the first phase of the Lombard conquest, during which *Pisae* remained within the Byzantine orbit, is still uncertain. Would the role of the Byzantine stronghold on the Tyrrhenian coast, therefore, have contributed to the fortification of the city by Byzantium? This is a stimulus for historians to further investigate the subject.[10]

Following the written sources, the presence of late antique walls is repeatedly the subject of spatial references in the determination of land and building properties. The same documents do not allow for the advancement of certain hypotheses about the chronology of this first circuit of walls, but dating it back to the early fifth century would seem justified by a literary source: the lack of mention by Rutilius Namatianus, generally careful to describe or mention the walls of the centres that he visited during his travel (Costantini 2014, 347). From the point of view of urban planning, it is important to focus attention on the exclusion of the episcopal area from the space enclosed by the walls. The archaeological data indicate a complete reorganization of the area of the current Duomo by the sixth century, when the Roman houses were obliterated, and a necropolis was organized on the new surfaces that coexisted with residential buildings characterized by the use of perishable materials.

Based on the reconstruction of the city-wall circuit, *Pisae* also falls within the cases of those cities of ancient foundation presenting the cathedral outside the walls (such as Florence, for example). The primary church was built in a suburban area, which acquired a new religious function starting from the sixth century with the organization of a necropolis immediately outside the city walls, most likely around the *domus ecclesiae*. The location between the coast and the city also acquires a symbolic value concerning the Christianization of *Pisae* (Ceccarelli Lemut 2005, 87–101).

It is likely that this phase corresponds to the construction of a primitive cathedral, no traces of which have been found even in the most recent investigations, while the presence of the octagonal baptistery, excavated in the 1930s inside the Monumental Cemetery and traditionally dated to the sixth century, has in fact turned out to be a late medieval building.[11]

It would therefore seem likely that the construction of the city walls took place before the area of Catallo, the Episcopal area of *Pisae*, took on the function of the city's religious centre, regaining its ancient function as a cult area abandoned since the late Etruscan period. The city walls, which testify to the narrowing of the perimeter of the previous inhabited area, would therefore be the result of the contraction of the city within the limits of the Arno to the south and the *Auser* to the north, caused both by slow depopulation and by a

---

8   The wall structure was unearthed during excavations for public works in February 2016 (archeologists Antonio Alberti, Monica Baldassarri, Fabio Stratta; scientific director Soprintendenza Archeologia Toscana: Claudia Rizzitelli).

9   The excavation made it possible to identify only a short section of the foundation cut on the south side of the wall. In this, a single piece of pottery was recovered: it is common pottery, produced during the fourth century in coastal Etruria and along the Arno valley and also documented in contexts dating back to the sixth century AD (Menchelli and others 2017, 305).

10   An interesting parallel is with the city of *Luna* (see also Menchelli and others in this volume). Lusuardi Siena recently stated that in the sixth century the city witnessed the refortification of a part of the city walls, in addition to the construction of the cathedral. In this regard, it is hypothesized that this intervention can be interpreted as the result of a coordinated operation of the Byzantine authority and the bishop, aimed at consolidating the coastal *castra* of the *Maritima* to ensure continuity of maritime communications and landing sites (Lusuardi Siena 2007, 117–52).

11   The recently proposed reassessment of the archaeological and architectural documentation relating to the remains of the octagonal building, which is based on the mensiocronological analysis applied to the bricks of the building, on the determination of the variety of the lithotypes of the stone drafts used in the base of the perimeter, and on the information derived from the written sources, could make the structure coincide with the funeral Church dedicated to the Holy Trinity, built before the Monumental Cemetery, in the 70s of the thirteenth century (Alberti and others 2011a, 195–204; Meo 2014).

dramatic environmental and settlement change that archaeological and geomorphological data clearly show for the sixth century.

The passage between Late Antiquity and the early Middle Ages, particularly the sixth century, witnessed a moment of a great transformation of the hydrogeological order, and the archaeological data of the urban and suburban areas show it. The stratigraphic sequence of the San Rossore shipyard documents the continuous difficulty of an area subject to periodic flooding in the place where the *Auser* crossed a canal. The context is quite evident in defining the last flood event that caused the sinking of the so-called ship 'D' and the end of the use of this river branch, probably within the sixth century AD (Camilli 2004, 71). The same phase of abrupt transformation is witnessed in the northern part of the city. In the necropolis of via Marche, an event of filling and deactivation of the canals caused the rapid obliteration of the late antique necropolis and the abandonment of the entire area, where only a few burials of the second half of the seventh century persist. Along the nearby via Galluppi, a similar phenomenon can be seen but dated to the end of the fourth century AD, where a vast area of necropolis is covered by a sandy clay layer. In the ex-Marzotto area (eastern part of the city), a structure of the first Imperial period was obliterated by flooding activities dated between Late Antiquity and the early Middle Ages (Costantini 2014, 347; Gattiglia 2013). The phenomenon is also found in the stratigraphy of Piazza Duomo. The excavations from 2003–2009 and the reassessment of old survey have defined a phase of obliteration of the rich Roman *domus* chronologically dating back to the mid-sixth century (Alberti 2011a, 68–69).

Due to the extension of the activity and the homogeneity of the carry-over, there was a levelling and covering operation of the pre-existing structures, which assisted in the definitive conversion of the residential area into a cultic area and most probably was a consequence of episodes of flooding of the nearby *Auser*. It is in this moment that the necropolis and probably the first nucleus of the episcopal area of the city began to be structured, even if the first bishop of *Pisae* is recorded as early as 313.[12]

According to the proposed reconstructions, the portion of the city enclosed by the late antique walls was much smaller than what should have been the extension of *Pisae* in Roman times. It would have included the strip that went from the *Auser* in the north to the Arno in the south. The western portion, towards the coast, probably already swamped, was excluded from the current via S. Maria, which is the road that has connected the Cathedral with the right bank of the Arno since the Middle Ages. The eastern boundary left out a portion of ancient settlement and monumental buildings of the Roman period, such as the baths and the amphitheatre. The city gates opened within the walled circuit, also mentioned on several occasions in medieval archival sources: the *Porta Aurea* opened on the southern side, at the only bridge connecting the city with the left bank of the Arno and with the streets coming from the south, in particular, the *via Aemilia Scauri* and on the same side also the Porta di S. Martino; on the northern side was the *Porta Pontis*, which connected with the bridge over the *Auser*, while other accesses to the city were on the east (*Posterula de Vicedomino* or S. Felice) and west sides (*Porta Archiepiscopi, Porta Picelle,* and *Porta Maris*).[13]

Even in this case, the exclusion of part of the settlement of the Roman period from the circuit of this wall seems to be testified by some medieval toponyms, including for example the *in civita vetera*, referring to an older area outside the eastern walls of the city where Roman structures were probably still visible, although they may have lost their original function. This part of the city was almost completely abandoned during the early Middle Ages because it began to be overtaken by swampland, which probably had already begun during the sixth century due to the hydrogeological phenomena mentioned above. Another medieval toponym, which probably referred to the remains of the Roman period, is to be recognized in the above-mentioned *castello*, located in the south-eastern sector of *Pisae*, which could refer to a *castellumaquae*, the arrival point of the aqueduct coming from the north, from the slopes of Monte Pisano (Garzella 1990, 26–58; Baldassarri and Gattiglia 2009, 64–65).

Studies conducted on the altimetry of the Pisan area and its variations over the centuries show that the wall circuit would have included only the most surveyed areas of the city and instead excluded, both to the east and west, large portions of land subject to periodic flooding; this hypothesis seems once again confirmed by the medieval toponymy of *Pisae*, which

---

12 The birth of the Pisan Church is certainly earlier than AD 313 since the bishop of *Pisae*, Gaudentius, appears among the twenty-one participants in the Roman synod organized to resolve the issue between Cecilianus and the schismatic Donatus, a piece of information that presupposes the presence in the city of a church already well rooted and structured. After Gaudentius, the sources remain silent about the representatives of the local church for almost two centuries, until the letter that

Pope Gelasius I (492–496) wrote to the Pisan bishop Johannes. For the origins of the Pisan Church, see (Ceccarelli Lemut 2005, 3–28).

13 For the complete data about the early medieval city, see Garzella 1990, 26–58.

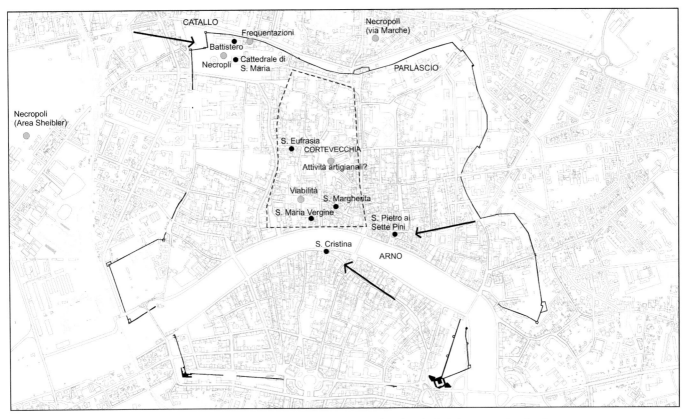

Figure 1.5. Plan of *Pisae* with the indications of churches as drawn from written and archaeological documentation for the Lombard period (plan by the author).

indicates to the west the area called 'Paludozzeri', from *palus Auseris*, and to the east a more generic area *in palude* (in swamp) (Garzella 1990, 52).

The Early Medieval Period

The greater availability of written sources and the limited material sources also tell us about the Lombard period of a city that was still organized mainly within the limits of the late antique urban space. The early medieval city is organized inside and outside the late antique walls, thus constituting the future urban layout of the medieval city. The political and administrative centre where the *gastaldo* resided was probably near the actual Piazza dei Cavalieri, where medieval toponymy documents the church of S. Sisto in Cortevecchia.

The Lombard period has left rare testimonies of the urban settlement, which can be deduced from the written documents concerning goods of city churches (Garzella 1990, 13–18). In addition to the bishop's church of S. Maria, which is attested for the first time in AD 748 in an area outside the walls, the documents of the Lombard period recall the presence of three other churches: S. Margherita, '*sita hic intra civitate nostra Pisana*', is remembered in a donation in AD 765; S. Pietro ai Sette Pini (*ad SeptemPinos*) is mentioned in a donation of goods of which it is the beneficiary in AD 763; and finally, S. Cristina, south of the Arno, is attested in the same year. Two other churches are documented in the last twenty years of the eighth century: S. Maria Vergine and S. Eufrasia (Fig. 1.5).[14] Two of these, S. Pietro and S. Cristina, are outside the city walls but located along the main access roads to the city.

The buildings do not show evident construction phases of the Lombard period because they underwent total rebuilding during the exceptional development of the Pisan Romanesque period between the eleventh and twelfth centuries. Only some reused architectural elements in the Cathedral building and others recovered during the archaeological investigations around it allow us to consider a building phase of the late Lombard and Carolingian ages, which affected the Episcopal

---

14 The baptistery of S. Giovanni is attested for the first time in AD 953 (Garzella 1990, 18–19); for its documentation during the excavations in Piazza Duomo, see Alberti and others 2011a, 207.

Figure 1.6. A: marble barrier found in Piazza Duomo during the excavations of Sanpaolesi in 1949–1950, sixth century (after Alberti and others 2011a, 199); B: Marble slab from Piazza Duomo. Opposite fan decoration, the first half of the ninth century (after Belcari 2011, 542); C: Piazza Duomo, Excavations 2004 (Area 8000). Fragmentary slab. Mesh decoration of free circles, the first half of the ninth century (after Belcari 2011, 529, reproduced with permission).

area between the eighth and ninth centuries.[15] In addition to the well-known elements reused in the external elevations of the cathedral, almost all pilasters variously decorated with interwoven ribbons, another five elements have been collected in the stratigraphies of Piazza Duomo: the oldest piece is a marble barrier of a window datable to the sixth century and found during the excavations of Sanpaolesi in 1949 (Fig. 1.6A);[16] another later architectural element, of which we do not know the history of the discovery, is a marble slab with a decorative motif with opposing fans (Fig. 1.6B). In phase with the construction of the pre-Buschettian cathedral that dates to the end of the tenth–early eleventh centuries (Alberti and others 2011c) are: a fragmentary marble slab with a quadrangular shape and a decorative motif of free circles, intersected by isolated ribbons with a diagonal pattern, probably a pluteus; two fragments that refer to another slab with a decorative motif of 'double-pointed knots'; and a small portion of a cornice with a three-banded braided decoration (Fig. 1.6C). For all these elements the comparisons refer principally to Rome and Latium, where liturgical furnishings with interlaced decoration were particularly popular between the eighth and early ninth centuries.[17]

For this same period, no documents mention any foundation of new churches. It is only from the 930s that the church of S. Giorgio (disappeared but located near the actual archbishop's palace) is recorded, inside the late antique walls. Its presence is accompanied by other documents that describe a rather scattered settlement (Garzella 1990, 21). Starting from the tenth century, the documents are clear about the reorganization of the suburban areas to the west and north-east of the city, as well as about the agents of this undertaking. Near the cathedral, an area known as 'Catallo' (name of Lombard origin) since AD 937, the baptistery of S. Giovanni has been documented since AD 953 (Garzella 1990, 19). The entire north-western suburban portion was originally predominantly public property, as is evidenced by some documents that mention *in loco et finubus Catallo* of *terra dominis regis*. Still in the western strip is to be reported the locality *Vinregi* (*Vinea Regi*). These are all lands of public property that were gradually acquired by the Church. The same happened in the area of *Civitate Vetere*, also affected by a process of acquisition of cultivable land from the second half of the tenth century, under the impulse of the churches and monasteries of the city (Garzella 1990, 25–26). It is, first of all, the bishop's church, but also the private ones, which recovered wide spaces for cultivation and later for the settlement, thus giving new development

---

15 For a complete study of early medieval architectural elements from Pisa and the surrounding area, see Belcari 2011.

16 For a new interpretation of the context of discovery, see Alberti and others 2011a, 199.

17 The nucleus of the furnishings seems homogeneous and referable to an updating of the liturgical apparatus of the presbytery throughout the first half of the ninth century, a period that coincides with the episcopate of Bishop Johannes, attested between AD 826 and 858. The prelate participated in the

year 826 in the Roman Synod, which introduced the principles of the Council of Aachen in AD 816; Johannes in particular is credited with the initiative of establishing the common life of the canons. The need to provide a seat for the community life of priests, which became an obligation after Aachen, may have been the occasion to organize the spaces of the sacred buildings connected to it (Belcari 2011, 550).

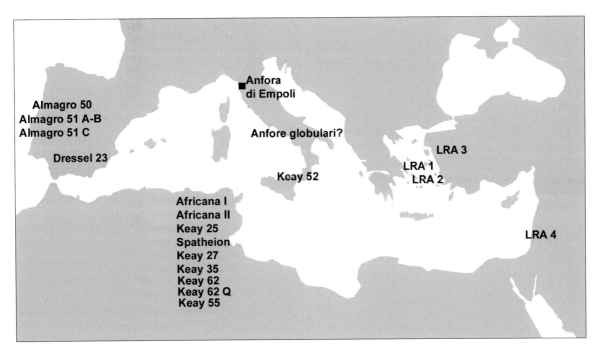

Figure 1.7. Area of origin of the amphorae between Late Antiquity and the early Middle Ages (after Alberti and Costantini 2015, 169, reproduced with permission).

to the urbanization of the city beyond those walls, that would surround and defend the town at least from the sixth century.

It was in this socio-economic context that a building fever began to develop again, with the employment not only of local workers but also of external groups of specialized builders. The search for a more precise social connotation also passed through new and better types of buildings, by the rising city *élite* that was developing thanks to land estates and Mediterranean trade. This stimulated the introduction in the city of a building technique characterized by squared stones, the start of the splendid Pisan Romanesque style. This adoption took place first thanks to external itinerant workers and then, after the acquisition of the building technique, through skilled labourers who were working in the area.[18]

Written evidence for housing typologies that in this period occupied the spaces of a largely ruralized city is very rare. The oldest document dates to AD 720 and concerns the sale of a house located *infra civitatem*. The house was built partly in wood (the elevations and the roof) and partly in stone (*solamentum*: foundations and lower part of the building) (Febbraro 2011, 560–61; Garzella 1990, 17–18). Some traces of similar dwellings have been documented in archaeological surveys conducted in the city in recent years, while the levels of occupation of the excavations in Piazza Dante refer to generic phases of early medieval frequentation; some doubts remain for the attribution to the late Lombard period of production activities documented in Piazza dei Cavalieri.[19] The best-preserved stratigraphy for the seventh and eighth centuries is that of Piazza Duomo. With the excavations of 2004, the periodization defines a chronology of the seventh–eighth centuries that can be referred to as phases of frequentation, accompanied by traces of the use of the area above the *domus*, now obliterated, with post holes, rubbish pits, dry-stone walls, levels of beaten earth, and traces of fireplaces (Alberti and others 2011b, 175–83): these are all elements that indicate the presence of buildings built in perishable materials. The contemporary ceramics find comparisons with household and transport artefacts dating back to the seventh century and, in some contexts, to the eighth century. It is, above all, amphorae that measure the extent of both local and international trade, and it is precisely through the attestation of these transport containers that the marked decline in arrivals compared to previous centuries can be observed, although imports from Africa still maintain a prominent role (Keay 62, 62Q, and 55). After this, containers from the Aegean and Asia Minor began to appear, which were poorly represented until the sixth century. Fragments of

---

18 For a complete study of the masonry techniques documented in Pisa between the sixth and eleventh centuries, see Febbraro 2011.

19 Bruni, Abela, and Berti 2000; Bruni 1993.

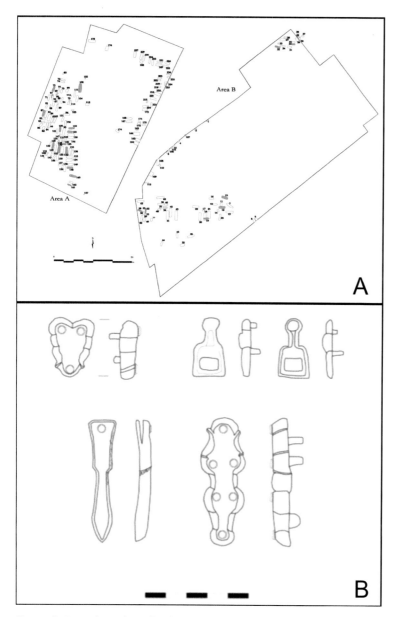

Figure 1.8. *Pisae*, the early medieval necropolis. A: Distribution of the burials of the necropolis along the via Marche. The campite tombs are those that have returned a trousseau (after Costantini 2007); B: Elements from tomb 11 of the Scheibler Area (after Fabiani and others 2019, 22, fig. 21, reproduced with permission).

concave-shaped bottoms, probably produced in the centres of the eastern Mediterranean, as well as maybe in some production centres of south and central Italy (Costantini 2011, 421–22). This amphora is present in Tuscany in a very sporadic way, with single finds found in Florence and Vada (on the Livorno coast) (Fig. 1.7).

Between the sixth and seventh centuries, there was a sharp drop in the volume of imports, but this did not correspond to a drastic reduction in the repertoire of amphorae, which were present with a good number of variants. The same economic liveliness of *Pisae* in this period is represented by imports of African Red Slip Ware C and D. The types of bowls, cups, plates, and vases collected in the stratigraphies of Piazza del Duomo document the continuity of trade relations with the African coast into the seventh century (Mileti and Rizzitelli 2011, 369–80). Starting from the sixth and throughout the seventh centuries, there were also important quantities of pottery painted in red or with dripping red or brown engobe (jugs, vases, bowls), probably locally produced (Alberti 2011b, 445–54). Graffito decorations, wave or zig-zag decorations, parallel lines with waved lines or simple parallel lines characterize some examples of flasks and jugs. This type of engraving can be accompanied by drippings of a red slip or appear on achromatic fragments, however similar in the fabric to those with traces of slip (Alberti 2011b, 452–53).

The deconstruction of the Roman city layout in the transition between Late Antiquity and the early Middle Ages is quite evident in the formation of the cemetery in the city's northern areas. The Roman artisan district was abandoned and underwent a dramatic change of destination. Starting from the fourth century, some burials were installed on the site of production workshops, and the same happened on the suburban villas discovered at the Stadium (Genovesi and Bueno 2020, 65–74). Proof of the change of use of the northern suburban strip over time is the extensive cemetery nucleus found in the area of the current via Marche (Fig. 1.8A), located on the ancient bank of the *Auser* river, used from the third to the fifth century and partially re-occupied during the seventh century. It is the largest cemetery area excavated in *Pisae*, composed of 194 burials: inhumation in an earthen pit represents 44 per cent of the assemblage, depositions in amphora make up 40 per cent, tile tombs stand for 13 per cent, while only 7 per cent are in wooden caskets. Among these, six burials have grave goods that archaeologists have attributed to the Germanic sphere, and these are generally dated to the seventh century (Costantini 2007; Fabiani and others 2019). Burials of Germanic culture have also been found in the burial ground of Area Scheibler, located north-west of the city, towards the ancient coast and the lagoon areas. In this case, two

late Roman 2, 3, and 4, and the Samos Cistern type, have been identified and testify to the demand in the Pisan markets for fine wines from the Near East and the growing influence of oriental production in the commercial traffic of the Mediterranean West. These exchanges in the northern Tyrrhenian Sea concern only a few critical centres besides *Pisae*, such as Luni, Florence, and Lucca (Alberti and Costantini 2015). More important is the presence of the globular amphorae, datable to the second half of the seventh century AD (although production continued into the following centuries) and represented by some fragments of burials have been excavated, partly upset by modern ploughing, which have very rich goods composed of belt elements, with a buckle, plaque, counter plaque and pendants, armilla, and necklace composed of perforated Roman coins (Fabiani and others 2019) (Fig. 1.8B).

The slow abandonment of the suburban necropolis could be related to the development of the cemetery built in Piazza del Duomo around the primitive cathedral. The suburban cemeteries of the Roman and late antique periods, at least those identified and excavated in the northern sector of the city, remained in full operation until the end of the fifth century; then the necropolis excavated around the Duomo began to take shape. It seems therefore that, from the beginning of the sixth century, there was a shift of the cemetery area to the north of the city. This choice could have been determined by the presence of a cult building, until then absent or not particularly important, which attracted the burials around it.

The necropolis of Piazza Duomo was an area of considerable extent. Indeed, the late antique burials were found in the eastern and north-western part of the square, to the north and south of the Romanesque Cathedral. The cemetery limit was probably identified near the western perimeter of the Monumental Cemetery: here a *temenos* of land was found where a significant number of carapaces had been deposited, which has been interpreted as the boundary of the necropolis (Alberti and others 2011a, 205–06; Bruni 1995, 172–73). The documented burials, which from the evidence of the excavations seem to be limited in number, are generally in earthpits, some with the pit cut delimited by stones of medium and small size, with filling and without covering; some have reused stone elements recovered from Roman structures. Others are characterized by a roofing with large, reused tiles; some instead are covered with simple slate slabs. The tombs of the 1998 excavation were inserted in the layers earlier than the tombs of the Lombard period, others (excavation 2004) were cut into the obliteration layer of the *domus*, and others (excavation 1992) were set into the collapse of the *domus*. From the middle of the seventh century, this area was also used by the Lombards who arrived in the city at that time and who occupied and shared with the native population the cemetery space, at this point probably organized around the Cathedral (Fig. 1.9A).

The tombs of the Lombard *élite* were installed during the seventh century. Excavations in 1949 made it possible to identify five tombs between the Cemetery and the north corner of the cathedral façade; of these, it seems that only two have returned abundant material (tombs A and B) (Pani Ermini and Stiaffini 1985; Von

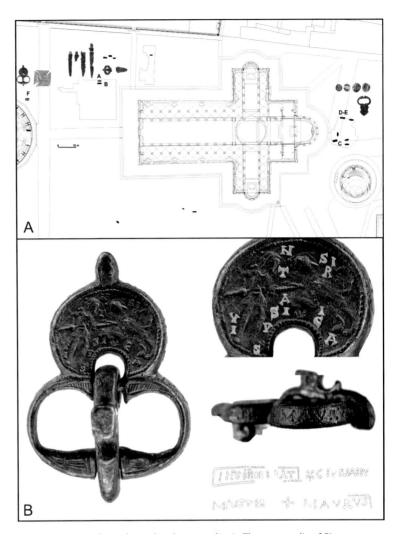

Figure 1.9. *Pisae*, the early medieval necropolis. A: The necropolis of Piazza Duomo. Late antique and Lombard tombs (A–F) (after Alberti and Baldassarri 2015); B: The necropolis of Piazza Duomo. The buckle of tomb F with engraved inscription (after Alberti and Baldassarri 2015, reproduced with permission).

Hessen 1975, 51–57).[20] The complex of materials is composed of various belt elements, including three Byzantine buckles, a bone comb, numerous *spatha* and *scramasax*, decorative elements, an *umbo* of a parade shield, gold plates and foil, and belts with ageminate pendants, all datable to the second half of the seventh century. The archaeological excavation of 1998 between the apse of the Cathedral and the leaning tower led to the identification of two more box tombs (C and E). The tombs had skeletal remains still in connection, while a third deposition (D) was found bumpy in the surface filling of E with some materials: glass beads, a Byzantine-type buckle, and a bronze belt tip. The burial

---

20 For a complete catalogue of the Lombard graves found in Piazza dei Miracoli, see Alberti and others 2011a, 209–25.

E goods are characterized by the presence of a coin set in a draft of the wall that forms the long north side of the case, at the height of the skull: this is half of a *follis* of the Mint of Rome (AD 674–685), which attests to a certain permeability of the different monetary areas during this period, as well as a particular use of *nummi* of this type. The accompanying materials of the three burials date this phase of frequentation to the second half of the seventh century.[21]

Of considerable interest is the monumental tomb, sealed in ancient times, of the late Lombard period, inserted into a masonry structure initially above ground. The tomb (F), a sarcophagus, consisted of a tufa box and was found with a lid, closed and therefore not stripped in ancient times. The type of cover, however, documents its use on at least two occasions: The original one is made of medium-sized tufa slabs, rectangular, regular in execution, and still *in situ* in at least one part of the tomb; the remaining space is closed by a monolithic, reused limestone cover of a displuviated shape with corner acroteria. The sarcophagus was placed inside a larger masonry structure that was to constitute a burial chamber, perhaps for a family.[22] The burial chamber contained the remains of at least three individuals (a, b, and c), of which probably b) is the original one. The grave goods consist of a golden cross of quadrangular shape and medium-small size. The gold foil is embossed with interlaced bands of the *Schlaufenstil* type, with a stylized frontal face of a subcircular shape at the centre of the cross (first half of the seventh century).[23] It is associated with the larger belt buckle with a shaped silver movable plate. Also, in this case, the decoration is relatively rich. It consists of plant elements and stylized palm leaves coming out of a double horn, underlined by comma-shaped engravings and circles. The third element comprises a small, silver buckle with a fixed plate of 'Byzantine type', which presents a representation surrounded by letters on the plate and an inscription running along the edge of the ring. The engraving depicts an army wielding a spear (right), against a fair in the act of

attacking (left).[24] The rest of the field of the plate is occupied with enhanced capital letters, with a type of epigraphy similar to that used on the obverse of several coin series at the time of *Heraclius* and his successors. Along the whole edge runs an inscription, divided into two parts: in the first one we read the inscription 'MA[g]ISTER MAVRVS', and the remaining letters make up the inscription 'INV[icto] D[omi]NO BIBAT * CIPRIANV' (Fig. 1.9B).[25]

The *magister Maurus* is probably the creator who made the piece, while the addressee would be the *Ciprianus*, to whom the augural formula is addressed. Although the other elements of the trousseau date back to the first half of the seventh century, the morphological data, the figurative typology, the presence of the goldsmith's 'signature', and the handwriting of the dedicatory inscription place the element between the end of the second and the third quarter of the seventh centuries. It could be a family tomb of Byzantine persons who still found an important role in the society of the new Lombard city and in the service of which there was an artifex of Roman origins, *Maurus*, who continued to work in *Pisae* for old and new clients. This would testify to the high degree of integration between Lombards and natives in the complex Pisan society that would start, from the late ninth and then fully in the tenth centuries, to build its political, economic, and commercial affirmation in the western Mediterranean.

Conclusions

Although affected by a general lack of written sources and material data, the late antique and early medieval history of *Pisae* confirms a distinctive trait of the city, constantly linked to the nearby presence of the sea. This remains evident in all the crucial passages of the city, especially in the establishment of relationships with subsequent conquerors.

The presence of one or more ports was fundamental in the established relationship with the Byzantines (the *dromones* of the Pisans), during the Lombard period (in AD 774 Adalgis, King Desiderius' son, embarked for Constantinople in *portu Pisano*), and until the subsequent *Regnum Italiae* (King Hugh of Italy arrived with a ship in *Pisae, Tusciae provinciae caput*, in 926). The mention

---

21 A similar example is reported in Cividale del Friuli for the so-called tomb of Gisulf, even if in that case it is contextualized inside a previous building (Brogiolo 2001).

22 For the description of the grave goods, see Alberti and others 2011a, 218–21, with an extensive bibliography and specifically Baldassarri in the same contribution, from which the description and interpretation of the 'Byzantine type' buckle with engraving is taken from; see also Alberti and Baldassarri 2015.

23 For the precise description and comparisons, see Alberti and Baldassarri 2015. This type of representation is widespread in Mediterranean mosaics between the fourth and the beginning of the seventh centuries, but it is also found on ivory plates and other artifacts, as well as on fabrics of the same chronology.

---

24 For the interpretation of the inscription, we refer to the work of Monica Baldassarri in Alberti and Baldassarri 2015.

25 The legend is engraved as in the Byzantine coinage of the Heraclian dynasty from about AD 620 and then of Lombard Tuscia from the end of the seventh century. The construction technique and the different style used with respect to the plaque suggest an intervention subsequent to the manufacture of the buckle.

of King Hugh who addressed *Pisae* as the capital city of Tuscany highlights the hegemonic position in politics and economy that the city had reached in its regional context during the tenth century; this position would be the base on which to affirm its maritime supremacy in the next two centuries, especially in the western Mediterranean.

The maintenance of the activities of its ports and docks in the large marshy area of the coastal strip until the definitive structuring of the *Porto Pisano*, the continuous presence of imported vessels (such as African productions, globular amphorae, etc.) until at least the seventh or eighth century, including goods transported with them, and the maritime connections attested by written sources with Corsica, Sardinia, and the islands of the archipelago return a picture of social vivacity that would be the main stimulus for the incredible development of economic and commercial policy that would distinguish *Pisae* in the central centuries of the Middle Ages.

Works Cited

Alberti, Antonio. 2011a. 'Gli scavi 2003–2009', in *Archeologia in Piazza dei Miracoli: Gli scavi 2003–2009*, ed. by Antonio Alberti and Emanuela Paribeni (Ghezzano: Felici Editore), pp. 61–70

——. 2011b. 'Ceramiche con rivestimenti e decorazioni a ingobbio', in *Archeologia in Piazza dei Miracoli: Gli scavi 2003–2009*, ed. by Antonio Alberti and Emanuela Paribeni (Ghezzano: Felici Editore), pp. 445–54

Alberti, Antonio, and Monica Baldassarri. 2015. 'Sepolture di epoca longobarda a Pisa: La tomba "di Cipriano"', in *VII Congresso Nazionale di Archeologia Medievale (Lecce, 9–12 Settembre 2015)*, ed. by Paul Arthur and Marco Leo Imperiale (Florence: All'Insegna del Giglio), pp. 3–8

Alberti, Antonio, Monica Baldassarri, and Antonio Fornaciari. 2011a. 'L'area episcopale e l'organizzazione della necropoli tra VI e VII secolo', in *Archeologia in Piazza dei Miracoli: Gli scavi 2003–2009*, ed. by Antonio Alberti and Emanuela Paribeni (Ghezzano: Felici Editore), pp. 195–242

Alberti, Antonio, Emanuele Bovi Campeggi, and Claudia Rizzitelli. 2011b. 'La trasformazione dell'area tra tardoantico e altomedioevo', in *Archeologia in Piazza dei Miracoli: Gli scavi 2003–2009*, ed. by Antonio Alberti and Emanuela Paribeni (Ghezzano: Felici Editore), pp. 167–94

Alberti, Antonio, Luca Parodi, and John Mitchell. 2011c. 'La Cattedrale prima di Buscheto', in *Archeologia in Piazza dei Miracoli: Gli scavi 2003–2009*, ed. by Antonio Alberti and Emanuela Paribeni (Ghezzano: Felici Editore), pp. 243–67

Alberti, Antonio, and Alessandro Costantini. 2015. 'Commerci a Pisa tra tardoantico e altomedioevo. Nuovi dati da Piazza dei Miracoli', in *Le forme della crisi. Produzioni ceramiche e commerci nell'Italia centrale tra Romani e Longobardi (III–VIII sec. d.C.). Atti del Convegno (Spoleto-Campello Sul Clitunno, 5–7 Ottobre 2012)*, ed. by Enrico Cirelli, Francesca Diosono, and Helen Patterson (Bologna: Ante Quem), pp. 159–69

Alberti, Antonio, Maria Letizia Gualandi, Federica Logiudice, Ornella Raffo, Claudia Rizzitelli, and others. 2015. 'Pisa, Piazza dei Miracoli: Materiali dagli scavi 1998', *Agoge*, VIII–IX 2011–2012: 57–106

Alberti, Antonio, Luca Parodi, and John Mitchell. 2011c. 'La Cattedrale prima di Buscheto', in *Archeologia in Piazza dei Miracoli: Gli scavi 2003–2009*, ed. by Antonio Alberti and Emanuela Paribeni (Ghezzano: Felici Editore), pp. 243–67

Alberti, Antonio, Alessandro Costantini, and Claudia Rizzitelli. (forthcoming). 'Pisa. Piazza Duomo. Nuovi dati sulle fasi tardo antiche e altomedievali', in *LRCW 6. Sixth International Conference on Late Roman Coarse Ware. Cooking Wares and Amphorae in the Mediterranean: Archaeology and Archaeometry. Land and Sea: Pottery Routes* (Oxford: Archaeopress)

Anichini, Francesca, and Elisa Bertelli. 2009. 'Pisa. Via Galluppi, via Piave: Indagine archeologica 2009', *Notiziario della Soprintendenza ai Beni Archeologici della Toscana*, 5: 336–38

Baldassarri, Monica. 2011. 'Strutture portuali e comunicazioni marittime nella Toscana medievale alla luce della fonte archeologica (VIII-Inizi XIII sec.)', in *I sistemi portuali della Toscana mediterranea. Infrastrutture, scambi, economie dall'antichità ad oggi*, ed. by Giuseppe Petralia (Pisa: Ospedaletto), pp. 81–116

——. 2013. 'Approdi, rotte e distribuzione della ceramica in area alto-tirrenica (VIII–XIII secolo): Riflessioni in margine ai recenti studi', in *Navi, relitti e porti: Il commercio marittimo della ceramica medievale e post-medievale, Atti del XLV Convegno Internazionale della ceramica (Savona, 25–26 Maggio 2012)* (Florence: All'Insegna del Giglio), pp. 17–34

Baldassarri, Monica, and Gabriele Gattiglia. 2009. 'Tra i fiumi e il mare. Lo sviluppo di Pisa nel suo contesto ambientale tra VII e XV secolo', in *Atti del V Congresso Nazionale di Archeologia Medievale. Palazzo della Dogana, Salone del Tribunale (Foggia); Palazzo dei Celestini, Auditorium (Manfredonia); 30 Settembre-3 Ottobre 2009*, ed. by Giuliano Volpe and Pasquale Favia (Florence: All'Insegna del Giglio), pp. 181–87

Belcari, Riccardo. 2011. 'Elementi di arredo liturgico altomedievali da Piazza dei Miracoli', in *Archeologia in Piazza dei Miracoli: Gli scavi 2003–2009*, ed. by Antonio Alberti and Emanuela Paribeni (Ghezzano: Felici Editore), pp. 527–50

Brogiolo, Gian Pietro. 2001. 'Urbanistica di Cividale longobarda', in *Paolo Diacono e il Friuli altomedievale (Secc. VI–X), Atti del XIV Congresso Internazionale di Studi sull'Alto Medioevo (Cividale del Friuli-Bottenicco di Moimacco, 24–29 Settembre 1999)* (Spoleto: Centro Italiano di Studi sull'Alto Medioevo), pp. 357–86

Bruni, Stefano. 1993. *Pisa. Piazza Dante. Uno spaccato della storia pisana* (Pontedera: Bandecchi e Vivaldi)

——. 1995. 'Prima dei Miracoli. Aspetti e problemi dell'insediamento antico nell'area della Piazza del Duomo', in *Storia ed arte nella Piazza del Duomo. Conferenze 1992–1993*, ed. by Mariagiulia Burresi and Vigo Cursi, Quaderni dell'Opera della Primaziale Pisana (Pontedera: Bandecchi & Vivaldi), pp. 163–95

——. 2003. *Il porto urbano di Pisa antica. La fase etrusca. Il contesto e il relitto ellenistico* (Cinisello Balsamo: Silvana)

Bruni. Stefano, Elisabetta Abela, and Graziella Berti. 2000. *Ricerche di archeologia medievale a Pisa. I. Piazza dei Cavalieri, la campagna di scavo 1993* (Florence: All'Insegna del Giglio)

Camilli, Andrea. 2004. 'Le strutture "portuali" dello scavo di Pisa-San Rossore', in *Anciennes routes maritimes mediterranéennes. Le strutture dei porti e degli approdi antichi, Atti del II Seminario ANSER (Roma-Ostia Antica, 16–17, aprile 2004)*, ed. by Anna Gallina Zevi and Rita Turchetti (Soveria Mannelli: Rubbettino), pp. 67–86

——. 2019. *Le navi antiche di Pisa. Guida al Museo* (Pisa)

Cantini, Federico. 2012. 'La Tuscia settentrionale tra IV e VII secolo. Nuovi dati archeologici sulla transizione', in *La trasformazione del mondo romano e le grandi migrazioni. Nuovi popoli dall'Europa settentrionale e centro-orientale alle coste del Mediterraneo. Atti del Convegno Internazionale di Studi. Cimitile-Santa Maria Capua Vetere, 16–17 Giugno 2011. Giornate sulla Tarda Antichità e il Medioevo*, ed. by Carlo Ebanista and Marcello Rotili (Cimitile: Tavolario), pp. 163–75

Cantini, Federico, G. Boschian, and M. Gabriele. 2014. 'Empoli, a Late Antique Pottery Production Centre in the Arno Valley (Florence, Tuscany, Italy)', in *LRCW 4 Late Roman Coarse Wares, Cooking Wares and Amphorae in the Mediterranean Archaeology and Archaeometry. The Mediterranean: A Market without Frontiers*, ed. by Natalia Poulou-Papadimitriou, Eleni Nodarou, and Vassilis Kilikoglou, BAR Series, 2616 (Oxford: British Archaeological Reports), pp. 203–12

Ceccarelli Lemut, Maria Luisa. 1994. 'Il Valdiserchio', in *La pianura di Pisa ed i rilievi Contermini. La natura e la storia*, ed. by Renzo Mazzanti, Memorie della Società Geografica Italiana, L (Rome: Società Geografica Italiana), pp. 228–39

——. 2005. *Medioevo pisano: Chiesa, famiglie, territorio*, Collana Percorsi, 13 (Pisa: Pacini Editore)

Celuzza, Maria Grazia. 2010. 'Il De Reditu di Rutilio Namaziano e l'archeologia tardoantica delle coste tirreniche', in *Il Mare degli antichi*, ed. by Carlo Casi (Pitigliano: Laurum), pp. 193–232

——. 2015. 'Ancora su Rutilio Namaziano e l'archeologia delle coste tirreniche', in *Diana Umbronensis a Scoglietto. Santuario, Territorio e Cultura Materiale (200 a.C. – 550 d.C.)*, ed. by Alessandro Sebastiani, Elena Chirico, Matteo Colombini, and Mario Cygielman, Archaeopress Roman Archaeology, 3 (Oxford: Archaeopress), pp. 367–74

Costantini, Alessandro. 2007. 'Primi dati sulla necropoli tardoantica rinvenuta nel suburbio settentrionale di Pisa (via Marche)', *Rassegna di Archeologia*, 23B: 149–68

——. 2011. 'Le anfore', in *Archeologia in Piazza dei Miracoli: Gli scavi 2003–2009*, ed. by Antonio Alberti and Emanuela Paribeni (Ghezzano: Felici Editore), pp. 393–430

——. 2014. 'Pisa. L'evoluzione della città e del suburbio tra antichità e altomedioevo', in *Ciudad y Territorio: Transformaciones Materiales e Ideológicas Entre La Época Clásica y El Altomedioevo*, ed. by Desiderio Vaquerizo Gil, José Antonio Garriguet Mata, and Alberto Leon Munoz, Monografia de Arqueologia Cordobesa, 20 (Cordoba: Universidad de Córdoba, Servicio de Publicaciones), pp. 339–53

Ducci, Silvia, Marinella Pasquinucci, and Stefano Genovesi. 2011. 'Portus Pisanus nella tarda età imperiale (III–VI secolo): Nuovi dati archeologici e fonti scritte a confronto', in *I sistemi portuali della Toscana mediterranea. Infrastrutture, scambi, economie dall'antichità ad oggi*, ed. by Giuseppe Petralia (Pisa: Ospedaletto), pp. 29–58

Fabiani, Fabio, Claudia Rizzitelli, Davide Caramella, Giulia Feriani, Rossana Izzeti, and others. 2019. 'Longobardi a Pisa: Le necropoli di via Marche e dell'Area Scheibler', *Journal of Fasti Online*, 436: 1–38

Febbraro, Mara. 2011. 'Prima della Cattedrale. Un contributo alla conoscenza dell'architettura altomedievale a Pisa', in *Archeologia in Piazza dei Miracoli: Gli scavi 2003–2009*, ed. by Antonio Alberti and Emanuela Paribeni (Ghezzano: Felici Editore), pp. 551–70

Garzella, Gabriella. 1990. *Pisa com'era. Topografia e insediamento. Dall'impianto tardoantico alla città murata del secolo XII*, Europa Mediterranea, 6 (Naples: Liguori)

Gattiglia, Gabriele. 2013. *MAPPA. Pisa Medievale: Archeologia, analisi spaziale e modelli predittivi* (Rome: Edizioni Nuova Cultura)

Genovesi, Stefano, and Michele Bueno. 2020, 'Il quartiere suburbano intorno all'Arena Garibaldi (fine II a.C.-IV secolo d.C.)', in *Le case di Pisa*, ed. by Federico Cantini, Fabio Fabiani, Maria Letizia Gualandi, and Claudia Rizzitelli (Florence: All'Insegna del Giglio), pp. 65–74

Lusuardi Siena, Silvia, 2007. 'L'antica Luni e la sua Cattedrale', in *Da Luni a Sarzana – 1204–2004. VIII centenario della traslazione della sede vescovile*, ed. by Antonio Manfredi and Paola Sverzellati (Città del Vaticano), pp. 117–52

Menchelli, Simonetta, Tatiana Baronti, and Paolo Sangriso. 2020. 'Gli scavi di via Galluppi', in *Le case di Pisa*, ed. by Federico Cantini, Fabio Fabiani, Maria Letizia Gualandi, and Claudia Rizzitelli (Florence: All'Insegna del Giglio), pp. 57–64

Menchelli, Simonetta, Alberto Cafaro, Claudio Capelli, Stefano Genovesi, and Paolo Sangriso. 2017. 'Vada Volaterrana (Vada, Livorno). Un contesto tardo-antico dalle piccole Terme. Anfore e vasi comuni e da fuoco', in *LRCW 5. Late Roman Coarse Wares, Cooking Wares and Amphorae in the Mediterranean: Archaeology and Archaeometry*, ed. by Delphine Dixneuf (Alexandria: Centre d'Études Alexandrines), pp. 287–312

Meo, Antonino. 2014. 'Alfea e la sua eredità. Un modello interpretativo sulle metamorfosi della città di Pisa tra antichità e Medioevo', in *Studi di storia degli insediamenti in onore di Gabriella Garzella*, ed. by Enrica Salvatori, Percorsi, 18 (Pisa: Pacini Editore), pp. 67–95

Mileti, Maria Cristina, and Claudia Rizzitelli. 2011. 'Terra Sigillata Africana', in *Archeologia in Piazza dei Miracoli: Gli scavi 2003–2009*, ed. by Antonio Alberti and Emanuela Paribeni (Ghezzano: Felici Editore), pp. 445–54

Pani Ermini, Letizia, and Daniela Stiaffini. 1985. *Il Battistero e la Zona Episcopale di Pisa nell'alto medioevo*, Biblioteca del Bollettino Storico Pisano (Pisa: Pacini Editore)

Paribeni, Emanuela, Luca Parodi, Stefano Genovesi, Federico Mani, and Daniela Stiaffini. 2011. 'Un quartiere residenziale di Pisa romana (periodo II)', in *Archeologia in Piazza dei Miracoli: Gli scavi 2003–2009*, ed. by Antonio Alberti and Emanuela Paribeni (Ghezzano: Felici Editore), pp. 71–165

Redi, Fabio. 1991. *Pisa com'era: Archeologia, urbanistica e strutture materiali (Secoli V–XIV)*, Europa Mediterranea, 7 (Naples: Liguori)

Rizzitelli, Claudia, and Fabio Fabiani. 2020. 'Area dell'Arcivescovado. La ricomposizione di contesti residenziali da vecchi e nuovi scavi', in *Le case di Pisa*, ed. by Federico Cantini, Fabio Fabiani, Maria Letizia Gualandi, and Claudia Rizzitelli (Florence: All'Insegna del Giglio), pp. 39–48

Sangriso, Paolo. 2018. 'La produzione di Terra Sigillata a Pisa: Economia e società', in *Una Città Operosa. Archeologia della produzione a Pisa tra età romana e Medioevo*, ed. by Federico Cantini and Claudia Rizzitelli (Florence: All'Insegna del Giglio), pp. 11–19

Segenni, Simonetta. 2011. *I Decreta Pisana: Autonomia cittadina e ideologia imperiale nella Colonia Opsequens Iulia Pisana*, Documenti e Studi, 47 (Bari: Edipuglia)

Tangheroni, Marco. 2004. 'Pisa. I Longobardi e la Sardegna', in *Il mare, la terra, il ferro. Ricerche su Pisa medievale (Secoli VII–XIII)*, ed. by Graziella Berti, Catia Renzi Rizzo, and Marco Tangheroni (Pisa: Pacini Editore), pp. 143–61

Tangheroni, Marco, Catia Renzi Rizzo, and Graziella Berti. 2004. 'Pisa e il Mediterraneo Occidentale nei secoli VII–XIII: L'apporto congiunto delle fonti scritte e di quelle archeologiche', in *Il mare, la terra, il ferro. Ricerche su Pisa medievale (Secoli VII–XIII)*, ed. by Graziella Berti, Catia Renzi Rizzo, and Marco Tangheroni (Pisa: Pacini Editore), pp. 109–42

Von Hessen, Otto. 1975. *Secondo contributo alla archeologia longobarda in Toscana. Reperti isolati e di provenienza incerta*, Studi, 41 (Florence: Leo S. Olschki)

STEFANO CAMPANA

2. Infrastructure, Water Management, Settlement, Agriculture, and Funerary Landscapes near *Rusellae* in the *longue durée*

Introduction

In recent years there has been a revolution in the archaeological methodologies used for the study of the ancient landscape. A wide variety of 'new' remote sensing methods are now increasingly widely deployed for archaeological exploration and mapping. In addition to the improvement in technical capabilities, we have also seen the beginnings of a conceptual change. Archaeology has traditionally been focused upon individual locations — 'sites' — which we have sought to identify and then to explore through excavation and the analysis of the finds from them. Although pragmatically understandable, the division of the world into a series of isolated sites is conceptually problematic since human beings do not just exist at particular points in the landscape but rather utilize the whole of their surroundings in a wide variety of different ways. Given that the same was true in the past, and that we increasingly have technologies to explore whole tracts of landscape, archaeology is moving towards changes in approach that seek to explore and to understand the reality of total past landscapes.

The Emptyscapes project is part of this new approach to the study of landscapes and represents the first experiment of this type in the Mediterranean area. The University of Siena has been active in southern Tuscany with landscape archaeology projects for more than forty years (Fig. 2.1). In the last twenty years, the *ager Rusellanus*, the countryside around the ancient city of *Rusellae* in southern Tuscany, has been subjected to intense research involving archaeological questions and methodological tensions that have developed in constant interaction with one another, stimulating the

attention of fellow researchers towards highly innovative archaeological themes and issues, in particular the transformation of settlement networks, agricultural landscapes, the rural infrastructure, the Christianization of the countryside, and the discovery of a new type of so-called 'mound-settlement', previously unknown in Tuscany (Campana and others 2008, 2009; Campana 2018; Vaccaro 2011).

In effect this sample area inspired the implementation and development of a new paradigm for the study of landscapes, capable of responding to temporal and spatial gaps as well as to the absence of some important aspects of information, in particular concerning transformations in the related ecosystems (fauna, flora, geomorphology, etc.).

This realization arose in around 2007 from an awareness that, after an intense and decades-long research activity in the area by archaeologists at the University of Siena, we had reached, at least to a reasonable extent, a level of substantial saturation in the discovery of 'new' sites. Among the areas of greatest interest, we identified at the beginning of this new phase of research an area of about 2500 hectares in south-western Tuscany that includes and connects the suburban and rural territories of the Etruscan and Roman city of *Rusellae* and the medieval town of Grosseto (Fig. 2.2). The questions that fostered this intensified programme had a double character, historiographical and methodological. As a result, the area has been subjected over the past thirteen years to a new research initiative based on systematic and continuous investigation and mapping (with as few gaps as possible) using 'traditional' methods such as

Stefano Campana (stefano.campana@unisi.it) Università di Siena

Archaeological Landscapes of Late Antique and Early Medieval Tuscia: Research and Field Papers, ed. by Riccardo Rao and Alessandro Sebastiani, MEDITO 3 (Turnhout 2023), pp. 39–54
BREPOLS ❧ PUBLISHERS
DOI 10.1484/M.MEDITO-EB.5.133992

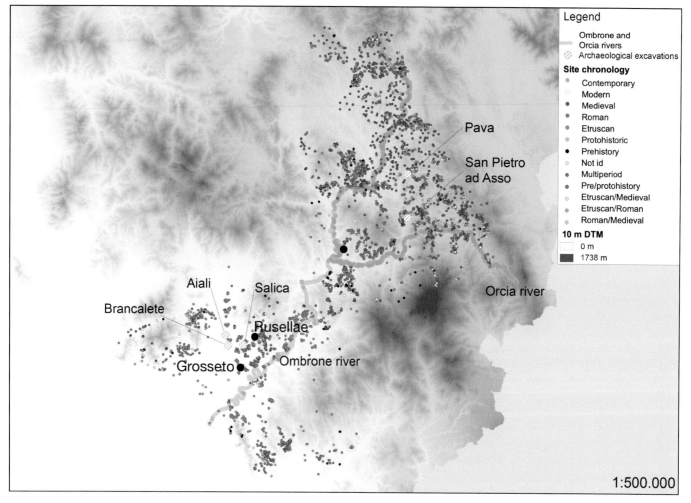

Figure 2.1. The Ombrone and Orcia valleys in southern Tuscany. Showing the geographical distribution of the archaeological evidence (sites, finds, and documentary references) identified so far. Together, the two river basins occupy an area of about 2500 km² and currently contain about 4800 archaeological 'sites' of one kind or another (image by author).

field-walking survey and surface collection *in symbiosis* with geophysical prospection (850 hectares to the end of 2020). The work has also taken in the exploration of wooded areas by high-resolution LiDAR scanning and drone survey, supplemented by radiocarbon dating, geo-archaeological sampling (reconnaissance, core sampling, and stratigraphic analyses), and bioarchaeological studies (macrorest, palynology, and palaeopathology).

The main archaeological questions can be traced, in essence, to the identification of transformations in the agrarian, settlement, and infrastructural patterns of the *Rusellae*-Grosseto landscape, the resources and influence of the natural environment (the geo- and bio-archaeological background), and transformations in the relationship between the suburban landscapes and the cities over time, including the dynamics of urbanization at *Rusellae* and the movement of the city's key functions to Grosseto in the early Middle Ages. The chronological scope of the investigations is broad, open to any archaeological evidence from prehistoric times to the present day; however, in practice we have focused in particular on the period from the beginning of the first millennium BC to the early and later parts of the Middle Ages.

The work carried out so far, in what over time has become known as the Emptyscapes project, has made it possible to recognize a significant amount of archaeological evidence that would have been entirely unidentifiable if restricted solely to the use of the 'traditional' research methods of field-walking survey, surface collection, artefact studies, and documentary research. Effectively, the overall results to date have multiplied the amount of previously known information by a factor of thirty or more; however, this is not just a matter of the simple *quantity* of evidence but also of improvements in the *quality* and *articulation* of the interpretations that can be achieved, providing new opportunities for understanding a variety of phenomena,

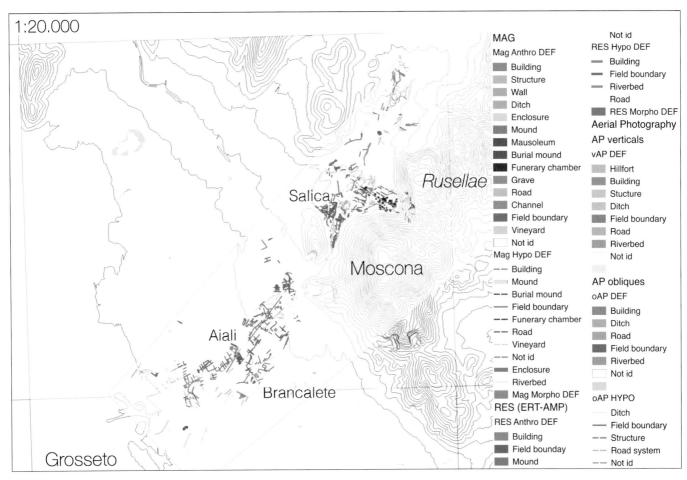

Figure 2.2. The territory between *Rusellae* and Grosseto: general visualization of the evidence identified through the integration of 850 hectares of extensive geophysical survey, several episodes of exploratory aerial survey by light aircraft, four years of aerial survey by drone, analysis of high-resolution LiDAR data (airborne and by drone), and the detailed examination of high-resolution satellite imagery (image by author).

contexts, and phases of development within entire socio-economic systems (Campana 2017, 2018; <http://www.emptyscapes.org>).

Within the tightly focused sample area between *Rusellae* and Grosseto, outlined in Figure 2.2, systematic investigation using the traditional sources of ancient topography had already identified a considerable amount of information. Overall, there were eighty known archaeological 'sites' of various kinds (Roman villas, farms, cemeteries, furnaces, etc.) within the sample area. Caution is of course required in making a comparative quantification of results produced by the 'traditional' methods as compared with the wider and more closely integrated range of activities and analytical methods used in the most recent work. That said, these integrated methods have so far produced 2746 new items of evidence, considerably expanding not only the quantity but also the varying *types* of evidence, in many cases recording features entirely undetected in the past — fences, settlements, burial mounds, tombs, agricultural field systems, buildings, ditches, pits, roads, canals, and so on (Fig. 2.2).

The long and continuing period of research based on non-invasive detection systems has been complemented since 2017 by three small-scale excavation campaigns at key locations, Salica, Brancalete, and Aiali (Fig. 2.2), aimed at achieving a better understanding of the evidence identified so far, both at those locations in particular but also within the wider area under investigation through the analysis of stratified geomorphological samples and organic remains, linked wherever possible to radiocarbon dating. Overall, we have carried out an open area excavation (600 m^2) and twenty targeted test excavations of varying sizes between 15–100 m long and 1.3 m wide for a total of 2000 m and a surface of 2600 m^2 with depths of up to 3 m below the topsoil.

The Current Archaeological Framework

During its lifetime *Rusellae* was an important Etruscan and subsequently Roman city, which survived until the Middle Ages before finally being abandoned, more or less, in the twelfth century AD. Starting from the Orientalizing period in around the mid-seventh century BC, there appear to have been city walls, a transformation in the topographic layout of the city, and a generalized phase of public and private building activity. The process was continued and reinforced during the Archaic period, with a general growth of the city and the progressive development in the surrounding landscape of a pattern of dispersed settlements that were probably related to agricultural production. There also grew up a network of roads and other communication routes, no doubt including the waterway of the Ombrone river to gain ready access to inland Etruria. In 294 BC the Etruscan city was conquered by the Romans and, from the end of third century to the middle of the first century BC, there ensued a long process of further building activity within the city walls. In the *Rusellae* area, as in the rest of Etruria, later centuries saw a major restructuring of the landscape, introducing Roman villa settlement and productive systems aimed at improving agricultural productivity. In the first century BC, *Rusellae* was designated as a Roman Colony and, from the first century AD, there began another phase of building activity, both within the city and in the surrounding landscape: forum, amphitheatre, temple, *domus*, further Roman villas in the countryside, and perhaps a pattern of centuriation (Nicosia and Poggesi 2011). During the fourth century AD, there is clear evidence of a further transformation including the conversion of public buildings into workshops and the abandonment and subsequent redevelopment of the public baths as a church. In the countryside, the pattern developed during the late Republican and early Imperial phases fell into crisis during the Antoninian age in the middle and later parts of the third century AD. From the fourth up to the mid-sixth century, a slight recovery is visible in the revival of a number of Roman villas, both close to *Rusellae* and in the more distant hinterland, at Aiali, Sterpeto, and Casette di Mota for instance (Citter 2007; Campana and Piro 2019; Vaccaro 2011; see also Chirico and Sebastiani in this volume); however, *Rusellae* maintained its role as an administrative centre with a complex urban topography. Documentary evidence shows that, from at least AD 499, the bishopric had its seat at *Rusellae*, remaining in that area until a move to Grosseto in 1138 (Celuzza 1998). This shift of the area's main functions does not, however, appear to have been a unitary and linear process, and it would be extremely interesting (in the longer term) to analyse whether any relevant evidence of the process has been left in the landscape between these two central places — changes in the settlement or agricultural patterns, for instance, or transformations in the area's communication systems. Whatever the details, the relationship between *Rusellae* and Grosseto must have played a significant role within the early Middle Ages, involving first the Lombard and later the Carolingian lordships, the Papacy, and a number of prominent aristocratic families, in particular the Aldobrandeschi. Evidence of urban activity in *Rusellae* is attested until the tenth to eleventh centuries AD, mainly in improvements to the fortifications. Up to that time Grosseto, roughly 8 km to the south-west, still served in a 'secondary' role, but recent archaeological excavations within the present-day city have demonstrated a progressive development of the settlement area from the ninth to the eleventh century, providing conditions for the transfer of the bishopric to Grosseto, as noted above, during the first part of the twelfth century (Citter 2007).

This historical framework of great vigour and unremitting transformation provides the context for a decade and more of non-destructive research by Siena University and the Emptyscapes project in the *Rusellae*-Grosseto area, complemented recently by three tightly focused campaigns of small-scale excavation involving revelatory geo-archaeological investigations and archaeometric analyses. As described and discussed below, the cumulative outcomes have prompted a completely new reading of the area under examination.

Unravelling the *Rusellae* Hinterland: Landscape Transformations across Historical Time

The articulation and transformation of the road system may represent an effective theme to link together some of the changes in the territory in historical times. In fact, this area is known for the crossing of the *via Aurelia* (*Vetus* and *Nova*) and the *Aemilia Scauri* (Fig. 2.11). The suggested routes of these two roads have been the subject of much debate among scholars for over a century, the conjectured route between the Ombrone and Populonia being particularly complex and controversial, including a stretch that runs through the *ager Rusellanus* and the key area of interest within the Emptyscapes project (Citter 2007).

We have so far identified 141 features interpreted as elements of the road network, of which 127 were detected by gradiometric survey and 14 by aerial photography. The distinguishing characteristics of these features are closely consistent with the well-known specialized literature, generally consisting of linear elements of variable width depending on the importance of the roadway. In aerial photographs the colour or tone of the

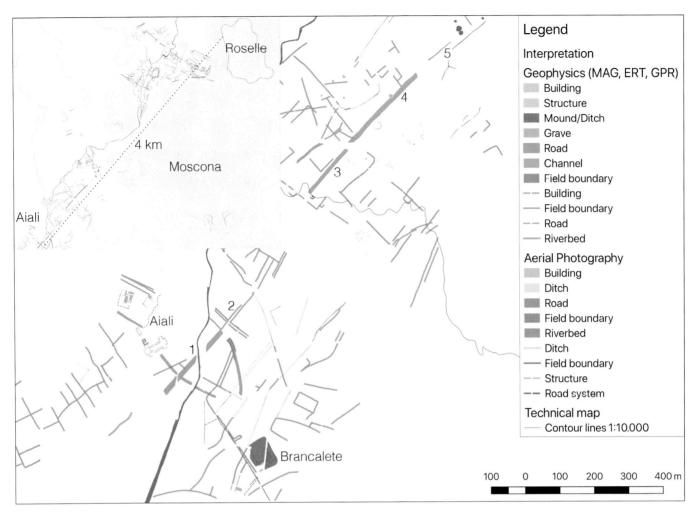

Figure 2.3. The lowland north-west of Grosseto. The map shows the dense network of evidence obtained for the most part through non-invasive survey, in particular the villa at Aiali and the lengths of assumed road to its north-east (numbered 1 to 5 in this Figure). The upper left box indicates the rest of the hypothetical route to *Rusellae*, firstly along the lowland and then exploiting the gentle north-western relief of Moscona to reach the city approximately 4 km north-east of Aiali (image by author).

features generally appears lighter than the surrounding context. The presence of smaller and darker linear anomalies running along one or both sides generally correspond to the presence of drainage ditches up to about 1 m width.

A first element of particular importance that enriches the emerging picture of communication routes and settlements at the regional level is the identification at Aiali, about 3 km north-east of Grosseto, of a large and complex Roman villa. The discovery was first made during exploratory aerial survey in late spring of 2001 and was followed first by field-walking survey, systematic artefact collection, and then integrated geophysical survey (Campana and Piro 2019). The settlement shows distinctive characteristics from various points of view. The size of the complex as a whole, about 4 hectares, makes it one of the largest villas known in this region, including structures along the Maremma coast. The formal characteristics of the individual building suggest an integrated complex of stone-and-brick structures, in one case consisting of a central body about 80 m long and 35 m wide, with projecting square elements at each corner, perhaps representing towers rising above the roof line of the main body of the building. The chronology extends from the late Republican period (200 BC) to the Middle Ages (AD 1000) with a gap between the early seventh and late ninth centuries evidenced by an absence of ceramic remains on the present-day surface. The Aiali villa must have played a central and imposing role in Roman rural settlement hierarchy of the *ager Rusellanus*, attaining its greatest development between the second and mid-third centuries and again in Late Antiquity (fifth and sixth centuries). After that we have a long hiatus in the archaeological sequence, from the beginning of the seventh century up to the late ninth century, after which we suppose that a new pattern of settlement emerged at the villa site, though its detailed character will not be recoverable without extensive excavation.

A little further south-east, to the east and north-east of the villa, the gradiometric survey identified several clearly defined stretches of roadway, aligned with one another from a few tens of metres south-east of the villa complex and continuing for a total distance of a little over 900 m in the general direction of *Rusellae*. The first section (numbered 1 in Fig. 2.3), which appeared to have a narrow crossroad pointing directly toward the imposing facade of the villa's main building, measured 112 m in length with a width varying from 13.5 m at the south to 11.5 m at the north. The next section, which also involved an east–west crossroad, measured about 7 m across, and this width remained more or less constant for three further lengths to the north (Fig. 2.3, nos 2–5). These features, not yet explored through excavation, would appear to constitute the connecting axis between the conjectured route of the *via Aemilia Scauri* (passing from west to east just north of Aiali) and the city of *Rusellae*. For the rest of the assumed route, we have as yet only circumstantial evidence, which will be discussed later in the chapter. It is highly plausible, however, that the connection between Aiali and *Rusellae* took an almost straight path along the lower slopes of Moscona and then onward in a northeasterly direction for the gradual climb into *Rusellae* (Figs 2.3 and 2.11).

At this point in the discussion, we can in our mind's eye now follow this route northward until we reach the low land of the valley floor immediately west and south-west of *Rusellae*. Here, non-destructive investigation has allowed us to identify a dense pattern of previously unsuspected features ranging widely in type and likely chronology, an amazing fossilized landscape which in terms of density and complexity finds few if any parallels in Italy other than the air-photo evidence collected in the 1940s and 1950s by John Bradford (and by many others since) on the Tavoliere Plain in Puglia (Bradford 1957).

Among the most evident features in this area, we have identified the western access road into and out of the city, along much of its length about 6 m wide but then progressively increasing to about 14 m as it approaches the city itself. This newly discovered route is flanked on both sides by thirty or more circular anomalies in the geophysical data, varying from 14 to 43 m in diameter and undoubtedly (despite the complete lack of surface evidence) representing the former mounds of Etruscan funerary monuments (Fig. 2.4, no. 1; Campana 2017). In addition to this evidently monumental road and its funerary landscape that finds wide comparisons in the Etruscan world (at

Cerveteri, Vulci, and Veio for instance), a second road system has emerged a little further to the south (no. 2 in the right-hand part of Fig. 2.4). The geophysical evidence in this case is rather different in character, the width of the roads being more modest, with the central track measuring only 3–4 m across, often with traces along one side (usually to the north) of a drainage ditch about 60 cm to 1 m across. The overall layout is also less strictly orthogonal, with curving or sinuous sections in places, along with obvious junctions and at least one well-defined crossroad. Also present in this area there is a network of geophysical traces clearly representing the drainage and boundary ditches of a wide-spreading field system (no. 2 in Fig. 2.4 and in closer detail in the left-hand part of Fig. 2.6).

The available evidence in this area is very complex, with a dense web of archaeological and geoarchaeological features consisting not only of the road network but also involving settlements, individual structures, field boundaries, and (on recent excavation evidence) an inhumation cemetery. In this regard we must always keep in mind that we are not entirely in the open countryside here but still quite close to the suburban area and to *Rusellae* itself; the city, with its ups and downs over the centuries, must surely have played a significant role in the landscape development of this area from the first half of the first millennium BC to the beginning of the second millennium AD when many of its functions were transferred to the growing medieval town of Grosseto.

The non-invasive study of this piece of landscape over more than a decade has allowed us to identify a very significant density of previously inaccessible evidence, while targeted excavations in more recent years have contributed substantially to a better understanding of the settlement dynamics and environmental changes, at least from the middle of the first millennium BC onwards, providing a striking example of the way in which, even at this scale of detail, it is possible to understand at least some of the transformations of the landscape through long-term commitment and the innovatory use of non-invasive methods, small-scale excavation, and targeted environmental analyses.

The targeted small-scale excavations of recent years in this part of the valley lowland have produced results that have proved critical in the environmental interpretation of the area close to the city of *Rusellae*. In particular, two machine-dug trenches over 2 m deep enabled the collection of crucial soil samples aimed at analysing the geomorphological history of the area.

The results made it possible to identify, in the area now crossed by the course of the Salica stream, the presence of a layer of blue clay, a distinctive sign of the presence of still water, either a pond or an area of permanent wetland or marsh that, on radiocarbon

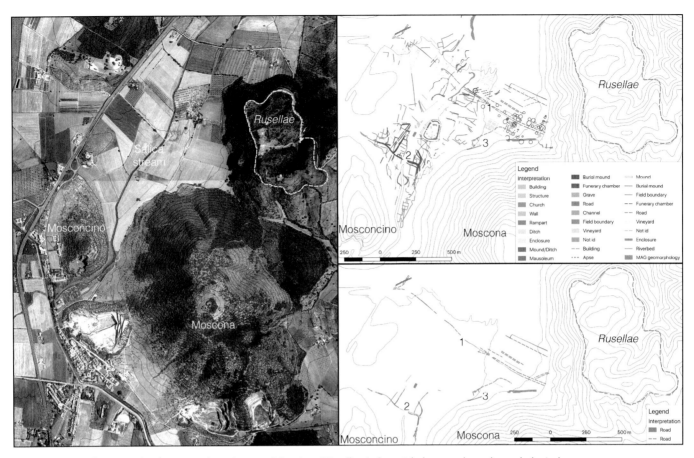

Figure 2.4. The valley immediately west and south-west of the city of *Rusellae*. Left, aerial photography and morphological characteristics of the area. Top right: cumulative map of the archaeological evidence. Lower right: map of all of the features interpreted as parts of the area's road network over the passage of time (image by author).

evidence, appears to have existed from at least the mid-sixth century BC (Fig. 2.5). This situation lasts until around the fifth century AD (again on radiocarbon evidence) when the samples indicate the formation of late antique and early medieval palaeosoils, with finds of ceramic material from these periods beginning to appear both in the stratified deposits and on the surface of the present-day fields. A crucial observation in this respect is that, in the whole area over which we estimate the lake or wetland to have extended, there were virtually no finds of ceramic material attributable to the chronological period between the sixth century BC and the fifth century AD. The absence of ceramic material belonging to this time-span — extremely common elsewhere and exceptionally durable as regards long-term survival — is an anomaly which we were unable to explain in any credible way until the geomorphological evidence about the long-term development of the local soils was obtained and analysed by our colleagues in the Soil Science Department of the University of Siena in the attempt to understand the environmental dynamics of the area under investigation.

The magnetic data interpreted as parts of road systems, field boundaries, settlements, and other features were selectively targeted by small-scale trenching and limited open-area excavation between 2017 and 2019. The overall picture that emerges at the current state of research allows us to assert that in this area, starting from the sixth century BC, we have a lake or area of permanent wetland that covers about 34 hectares of the valley floor 1.5 to 2 km to the west and south-west of *Rusellae* (Fig. 2.5, lower part). This may well have formed naturally under particularly favourable environmental and geomorphological conditions, though an alternative possibility of deliberate anthropic intervention is also considered later in this chapter. The limits to the east and west are defined by the rising slopes of the Moscona and Mosconcino foothills, but to the south the shorelines converge towards a passage so narrow that a modest embankment or sluice of some kind would have been able to block (or, if necessary, to adjust) the southerly outflow of the water (Figs 2.4, 2.5, 2.7, and 2.9). Between the fifth and sixth centuries AD, roughly half of the wetland area (Fig. 2.5) was apparently reclaimed, but it was not until the late ninth or early tenth century that

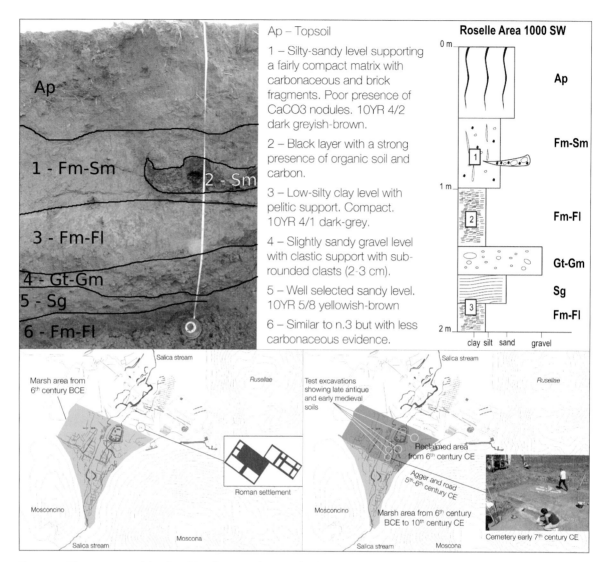

Figure 2.5. The area west of the city of *Rusellae*. Top: the crucial soil analyses from one of the excavation trenches. Lower left: the area in grey represents the pond or marsh limited on the north by a Roman settlement (inset) and on the east and west by rising land at the foot of the Moscona and Mosconcino hills. Lower right: the dark grey area represents the original extent of open water or wetland reclaimed for cultivation during the late Roman period or Late Antiquity, bounded on the south by the embankment and road along which the inhumation cemetery of the Lombard period was later formed (image by author).

the rest of the area dried out or was artificially drained through the creation of drainage channels and boundary ditches like those depicted within the magnetic data. Approximately contemporary with the final draining of the southerly part of the wetland area, the already-dry land to the north saw the development of a large oval mound-settlement (Figs 2.4, 2.5, and 2.6) occupying a little less than 2 hectares on a natural hillock that may once have formed an island in the former wetland. Sample excavation and ceramic evidence have shown that the settlement was surrounded by two substantial ditches and was already in existence by the tenth to twelfth centuries; for the moment, however, its interior remains largely unexplored.

South of this settlement the features of the road identified by aerial photography and magnetometry were investigated by small-scale excavation in 2017, showing them to have been placed in a highly dynamic and significant context at the northern end of the reduced wetland area. Mechanical and hand-dug excavations on the main east–west road line revealed a high density of stones corresponding with the line of the roadway itself, especially compared with the surrounding areas. The stones were homogeneous in character (limestone) and dimensions (medium and small), though they had clearly been disturbed and scattered to some extent by present-day (and perhaps earlier) ploughing. Below this level there were occasional stones still *in situ*, placed

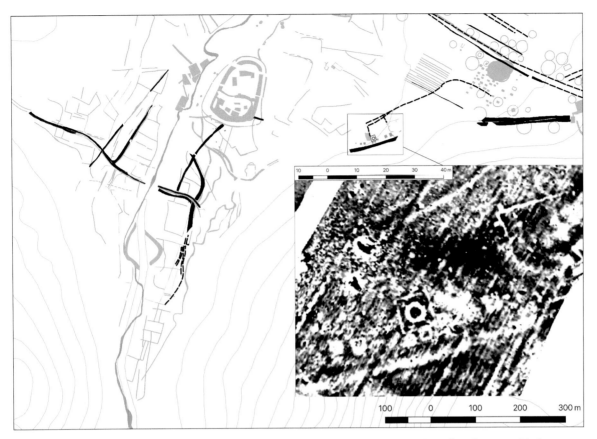

Figure 2.6. Plan of detected roads, settlements, and funerary areas south-west of the city of *Rusellae*, showing in black a diachronic view of all the elements interpreted as parts of the road system in this area. All of the other features, along with the present and past courses of the Salica stream, are shown in grey. The area marked as no. 3 in Fig. 2.4 and illustrated closer up at the upper and lower right in this Figure shows the magnetic traces of roads and a series of square anomalies assumed to represent graves or tombs, along with a larger square anomaly that has a smaller circular feature at its centre — a pattern which finds close parallels in size and shape with well documented mausolea elsewhere in Italy (image by author).

on a bed of gravel and fine pebbles, making it clear that we were dealing here with a typical *via glareata*, presumably finished at the top with a gravel surface now entirely dispersed by the subsequent ploughing. Deeper excavation showed that the substrate of the road consisted of extremely compact and coherent inert material, with rare intercalations of brick and generic Roman pottery fragments at the top of the layer. Further deepening and extension of the excavation revealed an impressive, stratified section down to a depth of about 2 m from the present surface, showing that the road had been set on an artificial embankment of trapezoid section measuring about 8.5 m across at the base and around 3 m at the top (Fig. 2.7, bottom right).

This imposing engineering feature, which appears in the aerial photography as well as on the magnetic map for an east-west length of about 500 m, must have been necessary to stabilize the crossing of the unstable and easily flooded land to the north and to hold back the remaining water to the south, guaranteeing viability of the road in all seasons and particularly after heavy rainfall

(Quilici Gigli 1992). The choice of a basal layer of inert material characterized by river pebbles of various sizes seems to be associated, as often reported by literary sources, with the local availability of this material, in this case easily found along the margins of the Salica stream (Matteazzi 2012). Particular interest attaches to the structural features of this rural (or perhaps sub-urban) engineering work: toward the south the embankment slopes steeply down from its peak, while on the north it descends more gradually, defining a structure that seems to have been created to contain a thrust from the south. In addition to guaranteeing the stability of the east–west road on its upper surface, the embankment therefore served the function of an *agger*, bounding the wetland to the south and protecting the reclaimed land to the north.

A further element in the story of this area's occupation and development takes the form of a Lombard inhumation cemetery of the early seventh century AD, barely represented in the magnetic data but found by chance during the exploratory excavation across the

Figure 2.7. Excavations south-west of the city of *Rusellae*. Top: plan and partial section of the 'embankment' roadway: from top to bottom, surviving stretch of the roadway with medium and small stones; views of the embankment from the south and from the north. Bottom: general view of the excavation across the road, highlighting the scattered stones of the road itself with the structure of the embankment to its left and right; the small detail on the left shows the composition of the embankment in its central part; the drawn detail on the right shows a simplified representation of the trapezoid cross section of the embankment, sloping gently on the 'dry' side to the north and more steeply on the 'wetland' side to the south (image by author).

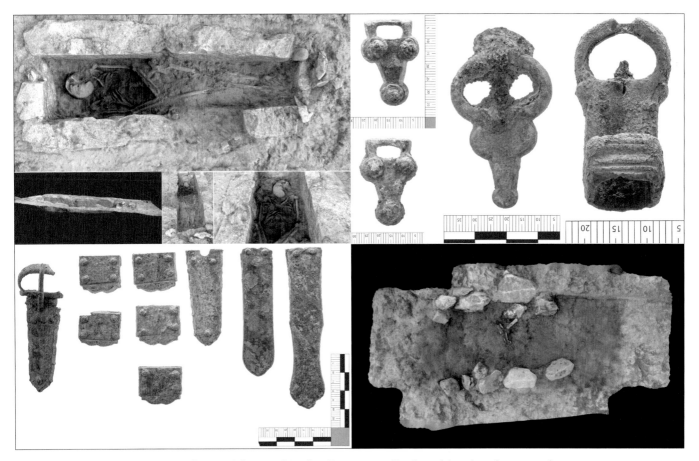

Figure 2.8. The Lombard cemetery south-west of the city of *Rusellae*. Top: stone coffin of an adult male and grave goods consisting of bronze belt elements (right). Bottom: child's grave simply bordered by stones but containing parts of a bronze belt (left) (image by author).

road and beyond (in a local widening of the trench to about 9 m north of the road and its supporting embankment). So far, the cemetery has produced about twenty-five burials (of adults, infants, and at least one juvenile), some of them in stone coffins and accompanied by readily datable but weapon-free grave goods (Fig. 2.8). On the basis of similar examples elsewhere, the cemetery can probably be attributed to an extended family group, composed of weaponless freemen who nevertheless flaunted a certain degree of wealth by way of their stone coffins and the quality of their accompanying grave goods. Several scholars have identified this kind of context as belonging to a middle-class family, living and owning land locally but occupying a social position somewhat below the highest (armed) aristocracies with their more generous access to goods of greater value and opulence.

In much the same area, two settlements have emerged, both referable to the early medieval period. The first is located immediately to the west of the cemetery and therefore quite close to the embankment road, while the second lies between the cemetery and the tenth-century and later mound-settlement in the former wetland to the north. The reasons for the intensity of anthropic activity in this area, and the obviously substantial economic investment made in construction of the embankment and its crowning road, are probably to be found in the importance to the region's 'central places', the nearby city of *Rusellae* and, from Late Antiquity to the Middle Ages, Moscona, Mosconcino, and the growing town (and later city) of Grosseto, up to the definitive shift of power and population in AD 1138.

In the wider compass of the early medieval period and the succeeding centuries, the settlement dynamics within this kind of investigation present the greatest problems of interpretation. We are inclined to believe that this stage of the process can only be solved by extending the strategy of non-invasive survey, environmental analysis, and small-scale excavation to include more extensive open-area excavation on larger samples of the lowland area just discussed but also by carrying out investigations on the flanking hills of Mosconcino and Moscona. At least in part this reflects

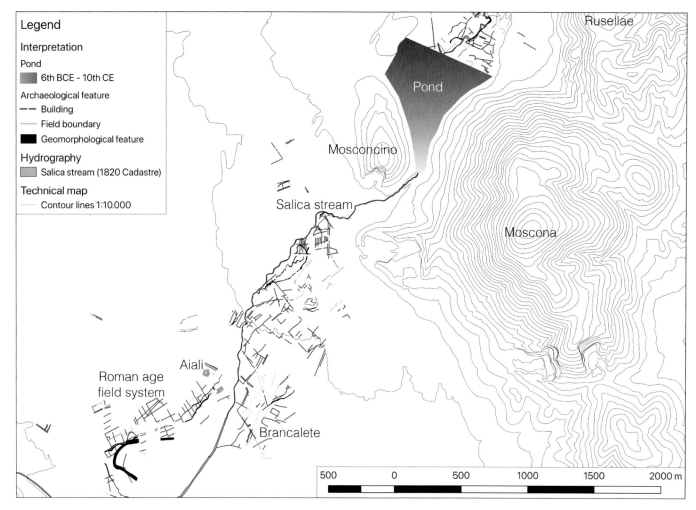

Figure 2.9. The landscape between *Rusellae* and Grosseto, showing the relationship between the lake or wetland area near *Rusellae*, the course of the Salica stream, and field systems and settlements of the Roman and later ages, in particular the monumental Roman villa at Aiali (image by author).

the fact that hilltops and highlands throughout Italy display obvious signs during the early Middle Ages and later centuries of large investments by both the secular and the ecclesiastical ruling classes, building in the case of Mosconcino a settlement on the top of the hill and a monumental church along its northern slopes, while on Moscona archaeological evidence and documentary sources attest to the development of a large hilltop settlement. Finally, a critical element for understanding the dynamics of this territory consists of the advancement of knowledge about transformations within the city and defences of *Rusellae*, especially from Late Antiquity onward (Fig. 2.9).

Other questions remain open; for example, it is not clear whether the lake or wetland was the result of a natural process generated by the displacement of the Salica stream (meander jump or similar) and/or perhaps by a landslip at the meeting of the Moscona and Mosconcino reliefs. Alternatively, the wet area might have owed its existence to the capacity and determination of the creators of *Rusellae* to conceive and to execute a transformation of the landscape during the Etruscan age, the lake or wetland then being kept unchanged during Roman times before being progressively reclaimed between Late Antiquity and the early part of the Middle Ages. In any case, whatever the circumstances that produced it, this waterscape survived for as much as twelve centuries throughout much of the Etruscan and Roman periods. If it had not been seen as a valued part of the landscape, it would have been very simple to reclaim it at an earlier date. Much more likely, as underlined by Horden and Purcell (2000), wetlands in the Mediterranean area were understood and valued as a precious natural resource — a readily managed ecosystem rich in amphibians, reptiles, fish, and both sedentary and migratory birds, a large food reserve located in this case only a few hundred metres from the city of *Rusellae*. Moreover, it also served as a large

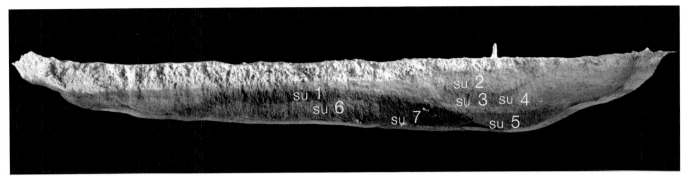

Figure 2.10. 3D digital record of the section of an exploratory trench at Brancalete, north-east of the city of Grosseto and south-east of the Roman villa at Aiali (image by author).

but shallow reservoir, a fundamental freshwater reserve for livestock and agricultural exploitation. In this last respect it is interesting to note that the irrigation of the plain further south could easily have taken place through the same Salica stream that in its ancient development traversed the length of the valley and passed close to the future villa site at Aiali, intercepting on its way a number of different field systems identified through the recent survey work and small-scale excavation as dating to the Roman period and Late Antiquity. It is notable in this respect that at least some of the field systems are characterized by a dense network of channels in direct stratigraphic relationship with the palaeo-riverbed of the Salica stream (Fig. 2.9).

At this point we can fruitfully turn our attention to the lowland south-east of the Aiali villa, where at Brancalete fieldwork and small-scale excavations confirmed the stratigraphical relationships and possible functions of the features detected in the magnetic data. Here, too, we also identified another mound-settlement, rectangular in this case (Fig. 2.3), along with possibly related but mostly 'negative' archaeological features that left no trace at the present-day ground surface — ditches and small channels, palaeosoils, and settlement evidence of one kind and another.

The settlement at Brancalete, in addition to its surrounding ditch, produced surface evidence of walls and deposits of ceramic material belonging exclusively to the early medieval horizon in the tenth–twelfth centuries AD. In all the areas investigated so far, we found medieval palaeosoils, consistent with the chronological range of the settlement, located at differing depths and clearly signifying various geomorphological transformations in this area. Paradoxically, however, we have not yet identified hereabouts any earlier palaeosoils belonging to the Roman, Etruscan, or any previous ages. This is a significant but rather puzzling point considering that, a few hundred metres away, there once stood the vast Roman villa at Aiali; nevertheless, collaboration with the geomorphologists of the University of Siena has allowed for analysis and interpretation of samples from one of the trench-sections to highlight a number of interesting stratigraphical relationships (Fig. 2.10).

The section shown in Figure 2.10 shows a series of layers. Beneath the present-day plough soil, the layer numbered su 1 is an example of an easily identifiable agricultural palaeosoil having an undulatory surface and producing pottery entirely consistent with the chronology of the nearby mound-settlement. The surface morphology is reminiscent of the outcome of the ridge-and-furrow ploughing system that is so widespread in the early Middle Ages in Central Europe and Great Britain, functioning (among other things) as a means of drainage on land exposed to high hydraulic risk. It is interesting to note that above su 1 another soil, su 4, is in turn cut by a channel (su 3), probably a subsequent agricultural partition covered by su 2 and in turn by the present-day plough soil. With the exception of su 1, the layers examined so far lack any significant finds or dating evidence.

Interim Assessment of the Results Achieved So Far

In the first place it is essential to clear the field of a recurring misunderstanding: the scenario that emerges from targeted small-scale excavations based on non-destructive survey data is not limited to confirming or denying what has already been observed by prospection. The integration of extensive and continuous prospection with targeted small-scale excavation is of course aimed at understanding the character of features identified in the survey data but even more importantly at exploring the physical relationships between the features and improving our understanding of their possible function and dating, not least by involving soil and environmental experts and implementing archaeometric analyses. This approach has allowed us, both in the area near *Rusellae* and further south at Aiali and Brancalete, to access completely new scenarios, far beyond our expectations.

Innovative elements and new questions are manifold. Putting the various pieces back together, in the Etruscan Age we have a city that is perhaps able to plan and to implement the creation of a lowland reservoir serving water supply and food sustenance functions. Even if the appearance of the lake resulted from natural phenomena, its subsequent maintenance would nevertheless bear implicit testimony to the value attributed to it by the local population as a productive part of the area's natural environmental resources. The presence of a large reservoir already in the Archaic period could perhaps be an indication of the use, even at that early period, of irrigation systems and advanced methods for cultivating the land downstream in the wide plain south of Moscona and Mosconcino. Although a hypothesis rather than proven fact, this seems a sustainable suggestion at least for the Etruscan and Roman periods, though there is clearly much to do in terms of identifying physical or other support for the conjecture. It is interesting to note in this respect that, for a long-time, archaeologists have denied the presence of these kinds of systems in Mediterranean contexts, on the argument that there is no material evidence for their existence. The apparent lack of evidence, however, is almost certainly attributable to the fugitive nature of the material remains in hydraulic landscapes — a problem, therefore, of visibility and research methodology rather than a real absence, as is clearly demonstrated by literary sources but also by recent interest in these aspects that has allowed for the identification of impressive irrigation and water-management systems elsewhere (Horden and Purcell 2000).

The embankment and road built across the former wetland are two elements of the same engineering intervention at the centre of a wider reorganization of the territory south-west of the developing city of *Rusellae*. Starting from Late Antiquity we have clear evidence showing a partial conversion of the area from lake or wetland to agricultural exploitation, probably following a premeditated act of reclamation or a change in the climate (or both; McCormick and others 2012; Büntgen and others 2016). A few metres to the north of the embankment, we find the Lombard cemetery along with evidence of settlements and production sites which were arguably placed there in strict relationship with the new road system, occupying an area that was wet until about the fifth or sixth century AD. To the south of the embankment, on the other hand, the survey work and excavation did not return any stratigraphy or other significant evidence of further transformation of the area until the early tenth century.

The features of the embankment and road are visible in a west–east direction for about 500 metres, connecting the Mosconcino relief to that of Moscona; they clearly represent, at least until about the tenth century, the northern limit of the surviving part of the lake or marsh. Their relationship with events or situations closer to the city of *Rusellae* is not entirely clear, however: perhaps they were built to replace the monumental road of the Etruscan age that may have fallen into disuse at times and for reasons that we as yet do not know.

Whatever the cause, the embankment and its crowning road guaranteed continued access from the west to the lowermost slopes of Moscona and from there in a northeasterly direction (either directly or by way of a junction with the roadway from Aiali) to *Rusellae* along two stretches of road clearly represented in the geophysical data (Fig. 2.11 and no. 3 in Fig. 2.4). A possibly relevant point here, as shown in greater detail in Figure 2.6, is that one of these stretches has clear magnetic evidence along its northern side of small square burials or tombs as well as a much larger structure measuring about 11 × 11 metres across with a circular structure about 7 metres in diameter at its centre, which could very well represent a mausoleum of the kind discussed by Johnson (2009). This route, perhaps initially alternative, could have become over time a substitute for the monumental road of the Etruscan age. The presence along its suburban route of monumental tombs and a possible mausoleum may well testify to the road's importance in providing additional or alternative access from the west by way of the embankment and the road that it supported.

What has been described in this chapter still suffers from many uncertainties and gaps, leaving much work still to be done, especially through non-invasive survey, targeted minimalist excavations, and equally importantly, the collection and analysis of geomorphological and bio-archaeological samples; however, we believe that the results achieved so far should make us reflect on what has been achieved so far and what our next moves might be. We have shown that in appropriate circumstances this type of landscape survey can be extremely effective, allowing for a substantial reduction in the physical and chronological gaps traditionally present in the archaeological record. The gains made so far undoubtedly move us significantly closer to achieving the exploration of the past as a true archaeological *continuum*. The research approach based on the integration of radiocarbon dating, geophysical prospection, and other methods of remote sensing can clearly have a fundamental impact on our understanding of landscape transformations by clarifying the physical characteristics and stratigraphical relationships of the features concerned (both structural and infrastructural components). The geo- and bio-archaeological sampling and analysis adds another invaluable instrument to our

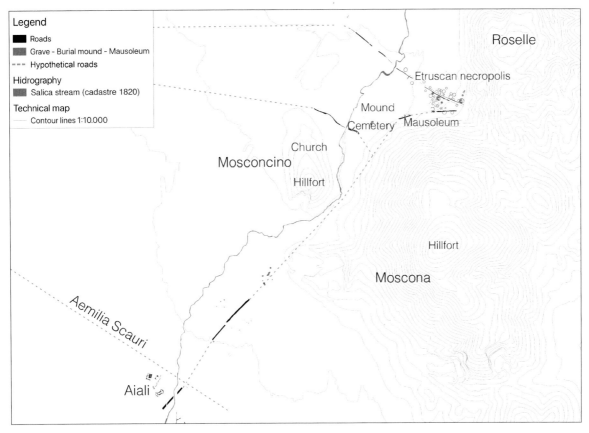

Figure 2.11. The landscape between *Rusellae* and Grosseto: hypothetical reconstruction of the main road system, showing the results of geophysical prospection in solid black (image by author).

toolkit, leaving little doubt that in positive circumstances the overall outcome of this kind of survey work and field investigation may allow the creation of what one might call a 'landscape matrix'.

Finally, and as a spur to further endeavours, we should recall that our landscapes are under constant threat from intensive agricultural exploitation, infrastructure development, residential and industrial expansion, pollution, erosion, climate change, clandestine excavation, and other destructive forces. It is therefore essential for us to develop and apply new paradigms, capable of responding effectively to the progressive disappearance of the traces of ancient activities by improving our ability to document even the most ephemeral elements in the search for a better understanding of the past while fostering a stronger public, specialist, and political awareness of the need to protect and preserve what still remains of our invaluable archaeological heritage.

Acknowledgements

The research for this chapter would not have been possible without the financial support of the Marie Curie action for the Emptyscapes project (FP7-PEOPLE2013-IEF n. 628338), the Culture 2007 ArchaeoLandscapes Europe project (Grant Agreement nr. 2010/1486/001–001), ARCUS, and two Italian research grants within the scheme of the Project for Research of Relevant National Interest (PRIN 2008 and PRIN 2015). The generosity and support of these institutions has been greatly appreciated.

The initiation and build-up to the Emptyscapes Project would not have happened without the initial urgings of Professor Riccardo Francovich around the turn of the millennium in what we now know as landscape archaeology. The project itself has benefitted from the advice and support of many friends and colleagues, to whom it is now a pleasure to express my sincere gratitude and appreciation. I am particularly grateful to Chris Musson, Professor Dominic Powlesland, and Professor Martin Millett for longstanding advice and encouragement. Dr Ken Saito, of all the project's workers in the field, deserves my very sincerest thanks for his perseverance and resilience in the decade-long task of collecting the vast amount of geophysical data that lies at the very heart of the project. Others who provided invaluable support included Professor Emanuele Vaccaro (University of Trento), Professor Charles French (University of Cambridge), Professor Pierluigi Pieruccini

(University of Turin), Davide Susini (University of Turin), Professor Gaetano di Pasquale (University Federico II), Dr Mauro Buonincontri (University of Siena), and Professor Annamaria Mercuri (University of Modena and Reggio Emilia).

The targeted excavations during the summers of 2017, 2018, and 2019 were generously supported by the local administration of Grosseto and the Province of Grosseto, enabling a small team of highly motivated archaeologists to achieve outstanding results in a very short time; for this my gratitude goes to Drs. Cristina Felici, Marianna Cirillo, Ken Saito, Prospero Cirigliano,

Virginia Sommella, Benedetta Baleani, Alessia Mandorlo, Alberto Massari, Olga Ciaramella, Luca Agresti, and to the skilful drivers of the mechanical excavator of the Province of Grosseto.

The University of Siena spin-off company ATS srl played a crucial role, generously sharing with us the use of its Foerster magnetometer system essential in the survey work.

Sincere thanks are also owed to the Superintendency of Siena, Grosseto e Arezzo, and in particular to Dr Andrea Pessina and Dr Matteo Milletti for the intellectual debate and problem-solving approach.

Works Cited

Bradford, John. 1957. *Ancient Landscapes: Studies in Field Archaeology* (London: G. Bell and Sons Ltd)

Büntgen, Ulf, Vladimir S. Myglan, Fredrik Charpentier Ljungqvist, Michael McCormick, Nicola Di Cosmo, and others. 2016. 'Cooling and Societal Change during the Late Antique Little Ice Age from 536 to around 660 AD', *Nature Geoscience*, 9.3: 231–36

Campana, Stefano. 2017. 'Emptyscapes: Filling an "Empty" Mediterranean Landscape at Rusellae, Italy', *Antiquity*, 91.359: 1223–40

——. 2018. *Mapping the Archaeological Continuum*, SpringerBriefs in Archaeology (Cham: Springer International Publishing)

Campana, Stefano, Michel Dabas, Lorenzo Marasco, Salvatore Piro, and Daniela Zamuner. 2009. 'Integration of Remote Sensing, Geophysical Surveys and Archaeological Excavation for the Study of a Medieval Mound (Tuscany, Italy)', *Archaeological Prospection*, 16.3: 167–76

Campana, Stefano, Cristina Felici, Riccardo Francovich, and Fabio Gabbrielli (eds). 2008. *Chiese e insediamenti nei secoli di formazione dei paesaggi medievali della Toscana (V–X Secolo). Atti del Seminario, San Giovanni d'Asso-Montisi, 10–11 Novembre 2006*, Quaderni del Dipartimento di Archeologia e Storia delle Arti, Sezione Archeologia, Università di Siena, 64 (Florence: All'Insegna del Giglio)

Campana, Stefano, and Salvatore Piro (eds). 2019. *Seeing the Unseen: Geophysics and Landscape Archaeology* (London: Routledge)

Celuzza, Maria Grazia. 1998. 'Rusellae: la tarda antichità e il Medioevo', in *Rusellae. Guida al Parco Archeologico*, ed. by Francesco Nicosia and Gabriella Poggesi (Siena: Nuova Immagine), pp. 43–48

Citter, Carlo. 2007. 'Il sistema viario tirrenico romano: strategia, cronologia, obiettivi', in *Archeologia urbana a Grosseto. I. La città nel geografico della bassa Valle dell'Ombrone*, ed. by Carlo Citter and Antonia Arnoldus-Huyzendveld (Florence: All'Insegna del Giglio), pp. 156–98

Horden, Peregrine, and Nicholas Purcell. 2000. *The Corrupting Sea: A Study of Mediterranean History* (Oxford: Blackwell)

Johnson, Mark Joseph. 2009. *The Roman Imperial Mausoleum in Late Antiquity* (Cambridge: Cambridge University Press)

Matteazzi, Michele. 2012. 'Ne Nutent Sola. Strade e tecniche costruttive in Cisalpina', *Agri Centuriati. An International Journal of Landscape Archaeology*, 9: 21–41

McCormick, Michael, Ulf Büntgen, Mark A. Cane, Edward R. Cook, Kyle Harper, and others. 2012. 'Climate Change during and after the Roman Empire: Reconstructing the Past from Scientific and Historical Evidence', *The Journal of Interdisciplinary History*, 43.2: 169–220

Nicosia, Francesco, and Gabriella Poggesi (eds). 2011. *Roselle. Guida al Parco Archeologico* (Siena: Nuova Immagine)

Quilici Gigli, Stefania. 1992. 'Opere di bonifica in relazione a tracciati', *Atlante Tematico Di Topografia Antica*, 1: 73–83

Vaccaro, Emanuele. 2011. *Sites and Pots: Settlement and Economy in Southern Tuscany (AD 300–900)*, BAR International Series, 2191 (Oxford: British Archaeological Reports)

Web Sites

<http://www.emptyscapes.org>

3. 'The River and the Villa'

The Arno and the Vetti Villa between the Late Roman and the High-Middle Ages: A Complex Relationship

Figure 3.1. Location of the Vetti dell'Oratorio in Italy (elaboration by Federico Cantini, reproduced with permission).

Introduction: The Villa

The site of 'Villa dell'Oratorio', located in the town of Capraia-Limite sull'Arno (Florence), is a great late Roman villa built in the mid-fourth century AD. A marble inscription found on the site would suggest that the villa was the property of *Vettio Agorio Pretestato*, a Roman Senator, or at least of his family (Fig. 3.1).

The structures of the building reflect a prestigious owner. In particular, the villa has a thermal bath and a hexagonal structure with five apsed rooms facing a central one, all enriched with polychrome mosaic floors. The archaeological evidence reveals that the villa was renewed during the fifth–first half of the sixth centuries and abandoned in the mid-sixth century because of a fire; after this event, the architectural

Federico Cantini (federico.cantini@unipi.it) Università di Pisa
Gianluca Martinez (gianlucamartinez@hotmail.it) Università di Pisa

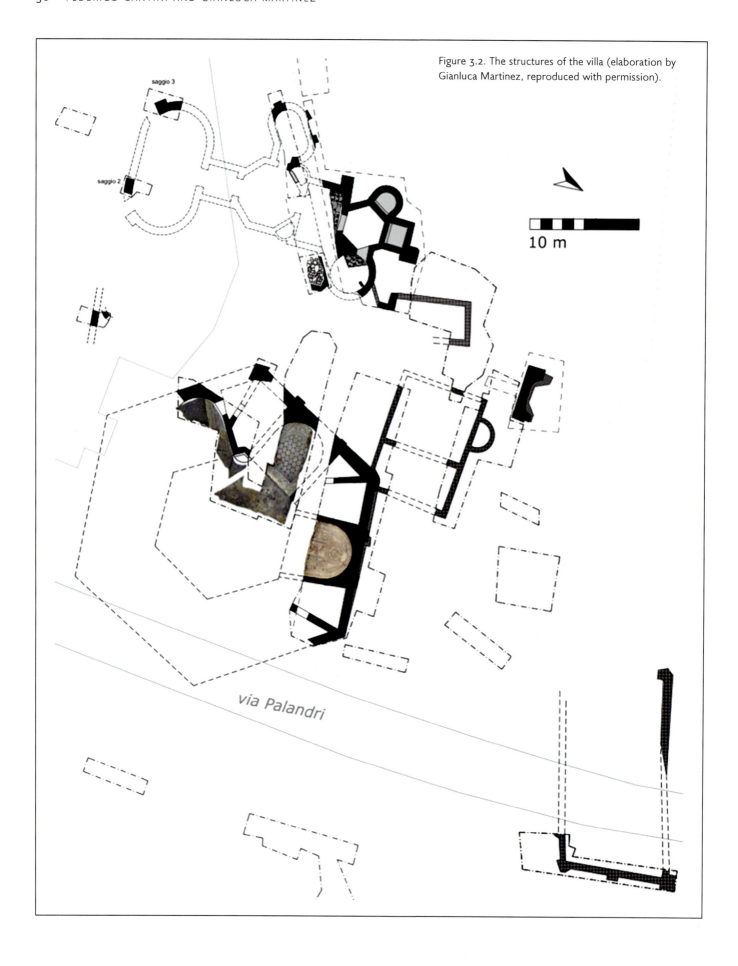

Figure 3.2. The structures of the villa (elaboration by Gianluca Martinez, reproduced with permission).

Figure 3.3. The territory between Capraia e Limite and Montelupo Fiorentino with the sites mentioned in the text (elaboration by Gianluca Martinez, reproduced with permission).

complex was despoiled (Cantini 2017; Cantini and others 2018) (Fig. 3.2).

The villa was built near the Arno river, at the foot of the Albano Mountain. Today we can observe a distance of 460 metres between the late Roman complex and the river. Still, we know that Arno has undergone several significant changes in its path from Ancient to the Modern times due to natural and anthropogenic events, such as large floods, course adjustments, and meanders cutting.

The main goal of this study is the reconstruction of the Arno riverbed between Capraia e Limite and Montelupo Fiorentino (Fi), to understand the relationship between the river and the villa.

[FC]

The River

This territory crossed by the river, between Capraia e Limite and Montelupo Fiorentino (Fi), and bounded to the north by the rocky complex of Albano Mountain and to the south by hilly reliefs, is now highly anthropized, with large industrial areas and communication routes, whereas in the past it had a predominantly agricultural economy (Fig. 3.3).

The area is part of the Arno floodplain, and it has been subjected to many works of water reorganization and river embankment from the Roman Age until the eighteenth/nineteenth century (Canuti and others 1994, 862–63). To reconstruct the Arno ancient canal between Roman and medieval times, we analysed with GIS tools the data from written sources, cartography, geomorphological analysis, and laser surveys. Using the open-source software Qgis, we have created a map organized in several layers:

- CTR 2k: raster containing regional technical map at a scale of 1:2,000;
- OTF: raster containing ortho-photo-maps of the years 1954, 1965, 1988, 1996, 2002, and 2016;
- Hydrography: vector (linear) layer with the georeferenced drawing of the primary and secondary hydrography;
- DTM 10 m: raster containing laser surveys performed with lidar scanning and processed through *second-impulse* techniques;
- Layer contour: vector layer (linear) obtained extracting z value from DTM 10 m layers;

- BDIG: vector layer (point) with the cores and the penetrometer tests made in the area. It was downloaded from Geoportale Regione Tosca as a layer WMS;
- Geomorphological database: raster of the primary geomorphological forms combined with the wms service database of the Geoportale Regione Toscana;

In addition to the geological and geographic data, we used the cartography preserved in the Florentine Historical Archive:

- 'Isbozzo del taglio di Limite': this is a schematic drawing of the 'Arno Vecchio' meander cut, dating back to 1550;[1]
- the plan of the Farm of Empoli estate, owned by the Medici (1746): this represents the bed of the old meander, filled and parceled (Guarducci and Rombai 1998, 47).

We also processed in GIS the archaeological map of Capraia and Limite, which has been georeferenced in a raster file.[2]

After collecting all the data, we analysed the geomorphological and geological information to identify the areas with a higher probability of having hosted the river. In this process, we checked the historical sources and the archaeological findings to exclude the presence of human settlements inside the reconstructed riverbed. In particular, the study began with observing aerial and satellite photographs to identify the settlement and hydrographic network transformations from 1954 to 2016. The land structure of agrarian parcels and the trace left by the ancient embankments show an Arno meander that today has been filled and transformed into cultivated fields. In the written sources, it is called 'Arno Vecchio': it is the product of a vast work of rectification carried out in the sixteenth century (Guarducci and Rombai 1998, 47–48).

We wanted to verify if, before this meander and moving to the hydrographic right of the river, the Arno could have flowed closer to the foot of the Albano Mountain and the late Roman villa, defining a second river bend that today is no longer visible in the aerial and satellite photographs. The absence of its traces in the contemporary landscape could be determined by the parcelling and agricultural alterations of the soil after the abandonment of this meander.

The study of land geomorphology and sediment lets us identify the sedimentary forms typical of the meander-form rivers. Working in a GIS environment, it was possible to consult the Geoportale Regione Toscana geomorphological database.[3] In addition, river morphology was also considered, referring to the cases of meander-form rivers and their depositional forms. This work allowed us to highlight what sediments could be taken as a reference for the construction of the paleo-path. The morphology of a riverbed is the result of the combined processes of erosion, transport, and deposition. These processes in the meander-form rivers determine the particular configuration of the canal and of the meanders themselves. According to the dynamics of the river sedimentation, a meander-form river tends to accumulate coarse sediments, such as gravels and sands, on the inner side of the lobes, while it facilitates bank erosion on the outer side. When the river changes course and abandons the old riverbed, the canal is gradually filled with finer materials (silts and clays) carried by the water that goes to settle on the bottom.[4] The sediments were verified through the database provided by the Geoportale as WMS service, which contains the results of all the cores made in the area. From a sedimentological point of view, this area is characterized by a complex succession of sands, gravels, slits, marnes, and clays, also in combination with each other.[5] Based on the stratigraphy of the different cores, we grouped the areas with the same sedimentological characteristics and identified those that have the typical geological sequence of an abandoned riverbed (with a section filled by loams and clays). In this way, we traced on the map a hypothetical ancient path of the Arno following the points with the suitable sedimentological characteristics and taking into account both the orography of the area to avoid 'obstacles' and the ancient meander of the 'Arno Vecchio'.

We have examined all the available cores present in the area (eight cores labelled SO 'Sondaggio geognostico'). These cores were executed in the context of the different planning activities on the territory carried out by Regione Toscana,[6] physically executed by 'Studio Geologico Aiello&Neroni'. The cores reach a depth of 15 m underground and present two main clusters of sediments: four referable to the paleo-path (SO-4; SO-5; SO-6 and SO-23), that present a stratigraphic

---

1 <www502.regione.toscana.it/searcherlite/cartografia_storica_regionale_scheda_dettaglio.jsp?imgid=16266>; last accessed 16 May 2019.

2 <www.comune.capraia-e-limite.fi.it/images/stories/StrumentiUrbanistici/Piano%20Strutturale/1_8.JPG>; last accessed 16 May 2019.

3 <www502.regione.toscana.it/geoscopio/geologia.html>; last accessed 16 May 2019.

4 Ricci Lucchi 1980, 63.

5 </www502.regione.toscana.it/geoscopio/geologia.html>; last accessed 16 May 2019.

6 Metadata: <www502.regione.toscana.it/geonetwork/srv/ita/csw?SERVICE=CSW&VERSION=2.0.2&REQUEST=GetRecordById&ID=r_toscan:ffbf3bab-0964-484c-b963-b174056c6e93>; last accessed 13 October 2022.

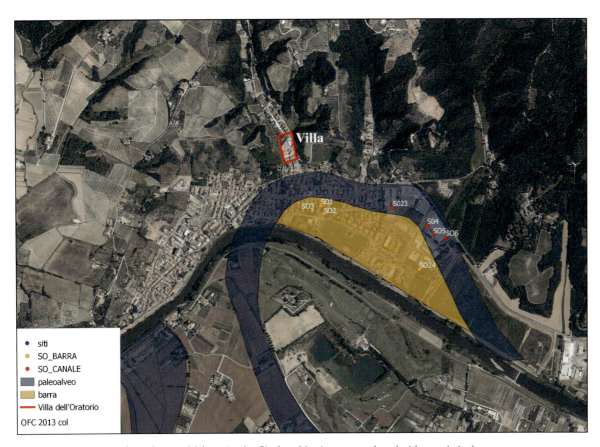

Figure 3.4. Bar cores and canal cores (elaboration by Gianluca Martinez, reproduced with permission).

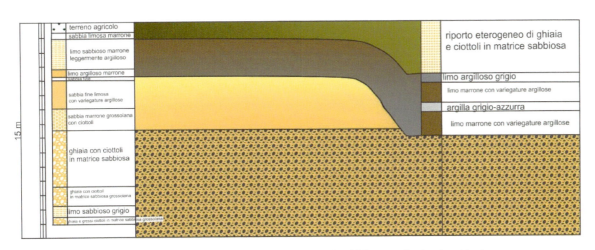

Figure 3.5. Stratigraphy reconstructed from SO_24 (left) and SO_6 (right) (elaboration by Gianluca Martinez, reproduced with permission).

profile mainly composed of clay loam and brown and blue clay, which are typical of residual canals; four linked to the meandering bar (SO-1; SO-2; SO-3 and SO-24), that present, instead, a stratigraphy of sands, gravels, and sandy silage. Using the cores SO-6 and SO-24, we drown an N-S section of the terrain that stresses out the differences in stratigraphy between the two main clusters of sediments and allow us to visualize the profile of the ancient canal (Fig. 3.4).

The comparison between the SO-6 and the SO-24 also shows differences in depth between two similar stratigraphic profiles, suggesting a jump due to the ancient canal, which is filled mainly by clays and loams (Fig. 3.5).

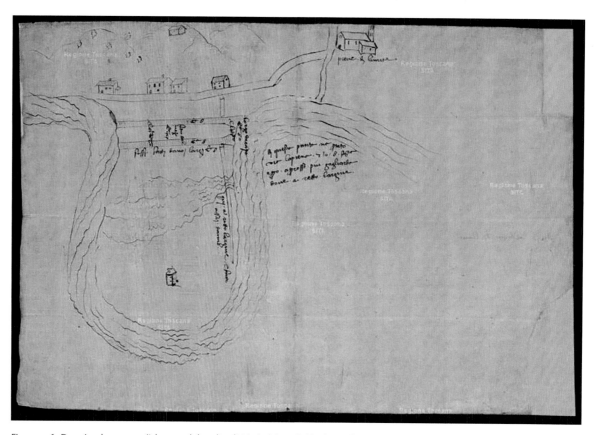

Figure 3.6. Drawing known as 'Isbozzo del taglio di Limite' (1550) (Archivio di stato di Firenze, Fondo miscellanea medicea, mappe e disegni, nº 93/ III, reproduced with permission).

After charting the hypothetical ancient river path, we verified it with historical sources and archaeological finds (Berti and Fenu 2008, 523–25). None of the findings dated before the Middle Ages are in the reconstructed path of the river. In particular, the 'Campi Bagni' archaeological site was interesting for our study. In the area, extended over a triangle of land between the provincial road (via Traversa) and the via di Pulignano, at the foot of the Montereggi hill, many Etruscan and Imperial (second–third-century) pottery fragments have been found as a result of an extensive agricultural activity. It is important to note that no other Etruscan-Roman finds were discovered outside this area, which is the only one not to be affected by the passage of the reconstructed river path. Furthermore, precisely at the 'Campi Bagni' site, close to the ancient canal, in January 2008 some wall remains, identified as a sixth–fifth-century BC river landing, were found (Alderighi and others 2009, 146).

The next step was to define how and when the hypothesized river path changed in to the present one. We know from written sources and historical cartography that the 'Arno Vecchio' meander was cut and filled during the sixteenth century, with a great work of rectification desired by Cosimo I de Medici (1553) for the construction of the Tinaia farm (Guarducci and Rombai 1998, 47). The first evidence in the historical cartography of this work dates to about 1550: it is the schematic drawing known as the 'Isbozzo del taglio di Limite' (Fig. 3.6). This map shows the excavation of the canal that would become the new Arno bed. In this drawing, the old meander presents the 'break' in the embankments at the beginning of the curve to divert the water from the original canal to the new one.

Yet in the same drawing, we also can see that, right before the meander of the 'Arno Vecchio', the river already presents the current shape: indeed, the S. Maria Assunta church, still existing (Fig. 3.3), is placed along a little road north of the river, while it should have been in the riverbed. Because the first mention of the church is dated to AD 1132 (Rauty 1974, 26), we can assume that the change in the path of the river must have taken place before the twelfth century.

We must consider that, after the Roman period, the first new settlement of the plain and foothills in the area dates to AD 957, when Limite is mentioned in a donation of the Count Guido to the Pistoia's cathedral. In this document, we read that in *loco Limite* were a *casa et res Massaricia* (Sestan and Savino 1973, 62). The archaeology also shows a human use of the plain

3. 'THE RIVER AND THE VILLA' 61

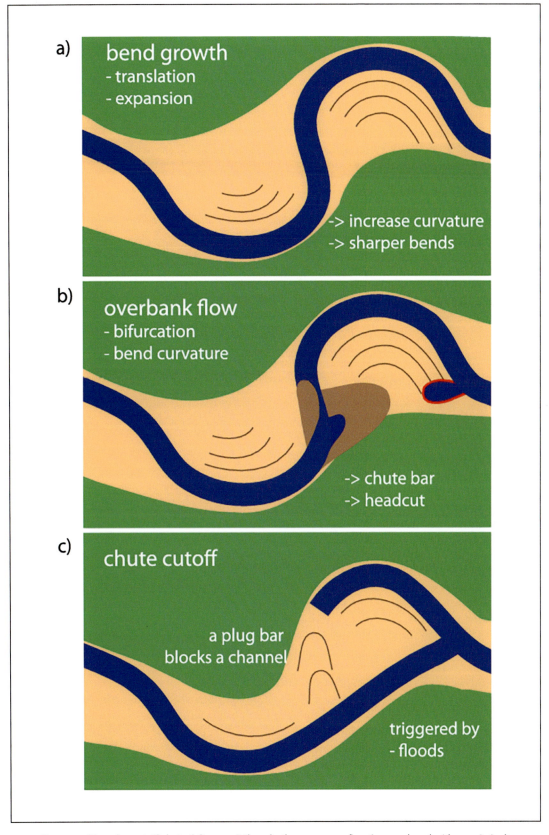

Figure 3.7. Meander cutoff chute (after van Dijk and others 2012, 15, fig. 16, reproduced with permission).

Figure 3.8. GIS The Medici Villa dell'Ambrogiana (1744, reproduced with permission).

area from the sixth century BC to the fourth century AD (Campi Bagni) and until the middle of the sixth century (Vetti villa), while until the tenth century we have only sporadic use of the hilltop site of Montereggi (Arbeid and Berti 2009, 406). We also know that in the sixth century, we have much evidence of the Arno flooding, even in the Vetti villa, where a series of clay and sand layers are dated to this period (Cantini 2017, 12–17). It is also possible that, right between the sixth and the ninth centuries, following a general trend of worsening climate (Caporali and others 2005, 180), a massive flood cut a new canal in the sediment of the ancient meander bar.

This river-cutting mode is called 'cutoff chute'. It occurs when a meandering lobe reduces its path by cutting a new canal along the sediment bar that is located within the lobe itself; this type of cutoff takes on significant importance in meander-form rivers characterized by a reasonably limited sinuousness, as in the case of the Arno (Van Dijk and others 2012, 15) (Fig. 3.7).

[GM]

The Villa and the River

The reconstruction of Arno's transformations allowed us to analyse the relationship between man-made landscapes and environmental change.

The distance between the villa and the river could have been only 30 metres in late Roman times, or probably less, so the structure may have acted as a river villa with a port. When the villa is abandoned after all the floods and disruption in the area, people start to frequent the neighbouring heights again, although with sporadic traces. The Roman structure and infrastructure are no longer available in a general trend of abandoning the flooded plain to regain the hills. These processes led to the formation of the medieval landscape, characterized by small villages or isolated farms surrounded by spreading wildness. In the Modern Age, new works on the hydrographic network of the area contribute to redefining the landscape of the plain as it appears today.

We have a near and more recent example of a riverine aristocratic rural complex in the Medici's 'villa dell'Ambrogiana' (Montelupo Fiorentino, FI) on the other side of the Arno, which confirms the strategic geographical position of this territory on North Tuscany. The villa was built, reusing a previous structure, between 1587 and 1590, for Ferdinando I de'Medici as a hunting residence and rest and refurbishment place along the road from Florence to the sea. The Duke and his court arrived from the city in a carriage, rested in the villa, and then used boats to reach Pisa. The architectural complex, in fact, had a little harbour on the Arno, integrated into an artificial cave (Sestili 2019, 8; Conforti and Funis 2018, 15–16, 20–21). We have two pictures of the villa that show the close relation between the building and the river: the painting of Giusto of Utens (1599) (Conforti 1978, 21) and the drawing of Giuseppe Zocchi (1744) engraved by Giovanni Battista Piranesi (Zocchi 1744, n. 17) (Fig. 3.8).

We could so define this portion of the Arno valley 'a perfect place for aristocratic villas', where political and economic necessities joined the pleasures of the life in the countryside.

[FC, GM]

Works Cited

Arbeid, Barbara, and Fausto Berti. 2009. 'Capraia e Limite (FI). Montereggi: campagna di scavo 2008', *Notiziario della Soprintendenza per i Beni Archeologici della Toscana*, 4.2008: 406–08

Alderighi, Lorella, Lorenzo Cecchini, and Pino Fenu. 2009. 'Capraia e Limite (Fi). Scavi di emergenza e saggi archeologici preventivi', *Notiziario della Soprintendenza per i Beni Archeologici della Toscana*, 4.2008: 145–48

Berti, Fausto, and Pino Fenu. 2008. 'Capraia e Limite (FI). Montereggi: campagna di scavo 2007', *Notiziario della Soprintendenza per i Beni Archeologici della Toscana*, 3.2007: 523–25

Cantini, Federico (ed.). 2017. 'La villa dei "Vetti" (Capraia e Limite, FI): archeologia di una grande residenza aristocratica nel Valdarno tardoantico', *Archeologia Medievale*, 44: 9–71

Cantini, Federico, Beatrice Fatighenti, and Riccardo Belcari. 2018. 'Le terme della villa dei Vetti: nuovi dati su un grande complesso tardoantico del Valdarno', in *Atti dell'VIII Congresso Nazionale di Archeologia Medievale (Chiesa del Cristo Flagellato [ex Ospedale di San Rocco], Matera, 12–15 settembre 2018)*, ed. by Francesca Sogliani, Brunella Gargiulo, Ester Annunziata, and Vitale Valentino, vol. 2, sez. III (Florence: All'Insegna del Giglio), pp. 90–97

Caporali, Enrica, Massimo Rinaldi, and Nicola Casagli. 2005. 'The Arno River Floods', *Giornale di geologia applicata*, 1: 177–92

Canuti, Paolo, Corrado Cencetti, Massimo Rinaldi, and Paolo Tacconi. 1994. 'The Fluvial Dynamics of the Arno River 2. Historical Evolution of the Arno River Bed', *Memorie società geologica italiana*, 48: 851–64

Conforti, Claudia. 1978. 'Le residenze di campagna dei granduchi. L'Ambrogiana', in *Città, ville e fortezze della Toscana nel XVIII secolo*, ed. by Amelio Fara, Claudia Conforti, and Luigi Zangheri (Florence: Ediz. Della Cassa di Risparmio), pp. 21–22

Conforti, Claudia, and Francesca Funis. 2018. 'Ozi fiorentini e devozione spagnola nella villa dell'Ambrogiana', in *Ecos culturales, artísticos y arquitectónicos entre Valencia y el Mediterráneo en Época Moderna*, ed. by Mercedes Gómez-Ferrer Lonzano and Yolanda Gil Saura (Valéncia: Universitat de Valéncia), pp. 15–43

Guarducci, Anna, and Leonardo Rombai. 1998. 'Il territorio. Cartografia storica e organizzazione spaziale tra tempi moderni e contemporanei', in *Empoli: città e territorio. Vedute e mappe tra '500 e '900*, ed. by Paola Benigni and Giuseppina Carla Romby (Empoli: Eitori dell'Acero), pp. 35–96

Rauty, Natale (ed.). 1974. *Regesta Chartarum Pistoriensium. Vescovado (secoli XI–XII)*, Fonti Storiche pistoiesi, 3 (Pistoia: Società Pistoiese di Storia Patria)

Ricci Lucchi F. 1980. *Sedimentologia Parte III* (Bologna: ìClueb)

Sestan, Ernesto, and Giancarlo Savino. 1973. *Regesta Chartarum Pistoriensium. Altomedioevo. 493–1000*, Fonti Storiche pistoiesi, 2 (Pistoia: Società Pistoiese di Storia Patria)

Sestili, Giulia. 2019. 'Le Ville di Anton Francesco Doni: tra letteratura e pratica artistica', *Bollettino telematico dell'Arte*, 4 June 2019, 869, <www.bta.it/txt/a0/08/bta00869.html>

Van Dijk, Wout M., W. I. Van de Lageweg, and Maarten G. Kleinhans. 2012. 'Experimental Meandering River with Chute Cutoffs', *Journal of Geophysical Research*, 117: 1–15

Zocchi, Giuseppe. 1744. *Vedute delle ville e d'altrui luoghi della Toscana* (Florence: Giuseppe Allegrini)

MARIA GRAZIA CELUZZA, ELENA O. WATSON,
ALEXIS C. GOOTS, MARI I. ISA, JARED S. BEATRICE,
EMILY R. STREETMAN, AND TODD W. FENTON

4. Late Antique and Early Medieval *Rusellae*

*Archaeology and Anthropology of the
Cemetery of the Episcopal Church*

Introduction

This contribution stems from the results of an excavation carried out at *Rusellae* between 1987–1991 as part of the research of the Art and Archaeology Museum of the Maremma. The excavation, for various reasons, did not continue after 1991, nor was it possible to complete its definitive publication; however, research continued, particularly as regards the human remains, for which we present important preliminary results here. The cataloguing of all the finds is also underway, which should permit us to refine the chronology and the definition of the phases. Radiocarbon dating is also underway for a series of burials in specific positions in the stratigraphy or otherwise interesting for their paleopathological or craniometric analyses.

The Church and the Cemetery at *Rusellae*: Historical and Archaeological Considerations

Excavations have been taking place at *Rusellae* almost without interruption for the last seventy years; however, we should recognize that our knowledge of the city's history is still very limited, and it is particularly so

if we consider the phases from the late antique to the final abandonment of the site. The few certain archaeological chronologies we have can be somewhat illuminated only by a tiny group of inscriptions, while documentary sources from the classical period go silent after the second century AD, and medieval documents are extremely rare.

The whole of the monumental area of the city, however, showed traces of occupation defined generically as 'late': to these, the preliminary reports of Clelia Laviosa, long responsible for the archaeological site for the Soprintendenza, dedicate only a few lines.[1] These traces were in general destroyed as the excavations continued, with the exception of a few walls.

In this context the excavations that we present here are particularly relevant. They were carried out on the slopes of the northern hill where the baths of the Imperial period appear to have been reoccupied as a church. From these we can now extract a chronological sequence that

---

1 Published between 1959 and 1971: Laviosa 1959, 1960, 1961, 1963, 1965, 1969, 1971. For a summary of the late antique and post antique phases of *Rusellae*, see Celuzza 2021.

Maria Grazia Celuzza (mgceluzza@gmail.com) Independent Scholar

Elena O. Watson (watso219@msu.edu) Michigan State University

Alexis C. Goots (gootsale@msu.edu) Michigan State University

Mari I. Isa (mari.Isa@ttu.edu) Texas Tech University

Jared S. Beatrice (beatricj@tcnj.edu) The College of New Jersey

Emily R. Streetman (erstreetman@gmail.com) Independent Scholar

Todd W. Fenton (fentont@msu.edu) Michigan State University

Archaeological Landscapes of Late Antique and Early Medieval Tuscia: Research and Field Papers, ed. by Riccardo Rao and Alessandro Sebastiani, MEDITO 3 (Turnhout 2023), pp. 65–87

Figure 4.1. *Rusellae*, the area of the church inside the Roman bath building, after the excavations in 1942 (Archivio Direz. Regionale dei Musei della Toscana, n. 9919, reproduced with permission).

puts events into a more solid framework, even if this is not yet definitive. The excavation was not easy: the building, already excavated in emergency conditions between 1933 and 1942 (Fig. 4.1), had undergone in 1970 a complete and radical conservation that had entailed trenching along the walls and the reconstruction of their summits.[2] The chronological indicators that we have now thus depend on excavation of the external parts of the edifice.

The baths were abandoned in the fourth century, an event that we can probably relate to the construction of the new baths of *Arzygius* near the Eastern, or 'Roman' gate. These are dated to AD 366 or shortly thereafter (Nicosia and Poggesi 1998, 162–64; Liverani 2017, 249–55). The church occupied the ruins of the building with a basilical plan with three naves. This could be achieved with only minimal adjustments to the original structure. A baptismal font was also created (Celuzza and Fentress 1994; Celuzza and Medri 2019). The study of the pottery from some contexts, although not from the whole of the excavation, has allowed us to date the construction of the church to between the end of the sixth and the seventh centuries.[3] This might still be adjusted, but as we will see, it seems plausible.

Excavation around the church intercepted a vast cemetery (Figs 4.2–4.3) whose extension is not yet clear: so far 170 tombs have been found, dating to between the end of the sixth and seventh centuries (dating based on the associated finds) through to the eleventh–twelfth centuries (dating based on stratigraphy and radiocarbon) (Celuzza, Cencetti, and Pacciani 2002; Celuzza 2021).

The construction of the church imposed various changes on the surrounding area: the paved road of the Imperial period that led to the baths was abandoned and replaced by a similar route laid over the destruction layers, terraced by a wall in *opus africanum*. The next phase of the building includes an important reworking

---

2 *Rusellae* 1977, 118–19; for the history of the excavations and conservation, see Celuzza and Fentress 1994; Celuzza and Medri 2019, 353; Celuzza, Milletti, and Zifferero 2021.

3 Vaccaro 2011, 40–71; contra: Sebastiani 2017.

4. LATE ANTIQUE AND EARLY MEDIEVAL *RUSELLAE* 67

Figure 4.2. *Rusellae*, the church and the cemetery after the excavations 1987–1991 (aerial photograph P. Nannini, SABAP-SI, reproduced with permission).

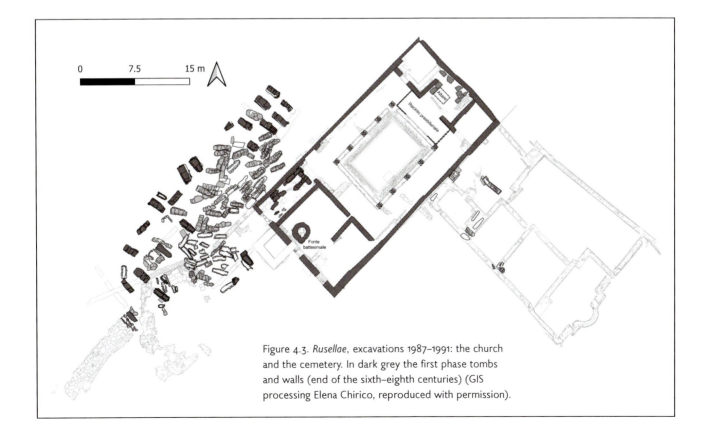

Figure 4.3. *Rusellae*, excavations 1987–1991: the church and the cemetery. In dark grey the first phase tombs and walls (end of the sixth–eighth centuries) (GIS processing Elena Chirico, reproduced with permission).

Figure 4.4. Museo Archeologico e d'Arte della Maremma, inscribed pluteus and small pillars from *Rusellae* (eighth century) (photo courtesy Museo Archeologico e d'Arte della Maremma, reproduced with permission).

of the liturgical furniture (Fig. 4.4), dated to the eighth century and recently attributed to the late phase of the Lombard kingdom.[4] This was followed in the eleventh century by the construction of a tower abutting the facade and accessible only from inside the church.[5] The layer that seals the cemetery is dated by two coins, respectively belonging to the eleventh and to the end of the twelfth, or beginning of the thirteenth, centuries.[6]

We are thus dealing here with a complex of remarkable importance that is also unique in the territory where churches as early as this one is unknown: close to *Rusellae* we can find only the little cemetery church at Campo Alberguccio excavated by Laviosa, undated and ignored by the bibliography, and the much later Romanesque church at Mosconcino-la Canonica.[7] (Fig. 4.5)

If we widen our gaze to the surrounding territory, we note that already in Late Antiquity *Rusellae* appears to have been surrounded by cities in crisis or already abandoned. In the third century the presence of *curatores rei publicae* at Cosa, Heba, and Vetulonia is a symptom of the financial problems and urbanistic decline of those cities. Later these towns, together with nearby Saturnia, were reduced to villages or simply abandoned, often with successive reoccupations that were anything but urban: Cosa, where a village with church and cemetery occupied the Roman forum in the sixth century, is a case in point (Fentress 2003, 75–86). None of these became the seat of a diocese except for Sovana, whose first documented bishop is found, however, in the seventh century.[8]

In contrast, *Rusellae* had a bishop, Vitalianus, by at least AD 499, and perhaps by 495, and was a bishopric.[9] The church built into the ruins of the baths must thus, as far as we know, be the episcopal church. The gap in time between the first record of the institution of the diocese and the archaeological date of the construction of the church can be seen as fairly normal: the place of worship for the community and the structures indispensable for its functions could have been held in other buildings — in other words, 'almeno inizialmente, non pare esservi un nesso automatico fra ruolo episcopale della città e costruzione della cattedrale. I limiti, quantitativi e qualitativi, della documentazione archeologica non consentono spesso conclusioni definitive, ma in non pochi casi esiste un evidente divario cronologico fra costituzione della diocesi e costruzione della cattedrale'.[10] All this must be particularly underlined as there is a

---

4 The decorated elements of the presbyterial screen are published by Ciampoltrini 1991a, 61–63; 1991b, 47. A pluteus carries the signature *Magester Iohannes* (Saladino 1980, 239; Celuzza 2017, 101–02); the most recent treatment of these elements is that of Betti (2021, 77, 81–83; 2022), who develops the analysis of Ciampoltrini and dates the reliefs to the eighth century, linking them to the work of Lucca workshops at the beginning of the century.
5 The tower is dated by the radiocarbon dating of a tomb cut into the construction deposits: the burial (US 1103) dates to cal AD 1038–1179 (91 per cent probability; D-AMS 034478).
6 Celuzza and Fentress 1994; the coins are published in De Benetti and Catalli 2013, 208, nn. 492–93.

7 Campo Alberguccio: Laviosa 1969, 606–07; Celuzza 2021. In this church ionic capitals from the basilica of *Rusellae* were reused (unpublished); Mosconcino-la Canonica: De Marinis and Poggesi 1991; Nicosia and Poggesi 1998, 178–83. A list of churches noted from documents for the period 700–1199 is found in Citter and Arnoldus Huyzendveld 2007, 145, table 4.9.
8 On the *curatores rei publicae* at Cosa, Heba, and Vetulonia, Jacques 1984; Celuzza and Fentress 1994, 612–14; Fentress 2003, 67–69. On Sovana: Kurze 2001; Citter 2007a. On Cosa: Fentress 2003. On late and post-antique Populonia, the fundamental study is now Gelichi 2016. On Luni and its cathedral, with parallels to *Rusellae*, see Lusuardi Siena 1987. See also Cambi 2005, 80–87.
9 MGH, *Auctores Antiquissimi* XII, 12, 400 and 406; Ceccarelli Lemut and Sodi 1994, 22; Polock 1996, 199; Kurze 2001, 325 and 340.
10 'At least initially there doesn't seem to have been an automatic linkage between the episcopal role of the city and the construction of a cathedral. The limits, quantitative and qualitative, of the archaeological documentation often do not permit definitive conclusion, but in many cases there is a clear hiatus between the creation of the diocese and the construction

Figure 4.5. Location of the church of *Rusellae* and the churches in the nearest surroundings (image after Google Earth, processed by the authors).

deeply rooted local tradition, repeated and restated in numerous recent studies, that places the episcopal church elsewhere — outside the walls, in a place to which the toponym *Rusellae* had migrated as well, at a moment which differs depending on who is writing (Ronzani 1996, 157–60). That place is generally identified with the castle of Poggio Mosconcino, at the foot of which are found the ruins of the large Romanesque church mentioned above, Poggio Mosconcino-la Canonica.[11]

reply by the two historians (Ceccarelli Lemut and Sodi 1995). A complete and balanced summary of the sources and the various positions is found in Ronzani 1996, while a brief summary can be found in Rizzitelli 1999.

The church on the hill of *Rusellae*, which we here interpret as the episcopal church, is said never to have had such a function, or only in an initial phase: for these scholars the episcopal church must be identified with one of the pieve known from the area in a much later period, such as *plebs S. Marie de Civita*, the *plebs de Maschona*, *plebs S. Marie de Rusellis*. The *Plebs S. Marie de Civita* or *Plebs de Civita* appears for the first time in a document of 1188 (Kehr 1908, n. 12, 261) and later in the tithes of 1276–1277 (Guidi 1932, 141–44), where we also find the *Plebs S. Maria de Rosellis*. The *Plebes de Maschona* is found in the tithes of 1302–1303 (Giusti and Guidi 1942, 185–90). The identification of the episcopal church with the pieve of S. Maria of Civita is already found in many popular publications, such as, for example, Citter 1996 and Marrucchi 1998, and has recently received a Wikipedia entry.

of the cathedral': Cantino Wataghin, Gurt Esparaguerra, and Guyon 1996, 27–35, explores this in part; the citation is on p. 27; see also Castiglia 2018.

11 To understand the local debate, see the reply by a local historian (Burattini 1994) to the volume on the diocese of *Rusellae* by M. L. Ceccarelli Lemut and S. Sodi (1994), and the following

Apart from the few mentions found above it is difficult to define more precisely the Diocese of *Rusellae*: there is little evidence either documentary or archaeological for the Christianization of this part of Tuscia, and much of this is limited to islands. The well-known testimony of Rutilius Namatianus, which dates to the fifth century, mentions the presence of monks on the island of Capraia, where settlement began a century earlier, and on Gorgona in the Tuscan Archipelago (*De Reditu*, I, 439–46; 525–26). On Pianosa as well we find the presence of a Christian community that buried its dead in an extensive catacomb in use between the fourth and the sixth centuries (Bartolozzi Casti 2005; Sodi 2005). For the mainland there is very little evidence: the destruction of the temple at Scoglietto/Alberese can be related to the edict of Theodosius that definitively outlawed pagan cults between AD 380 and AD 392 (Sebastiani 2016, 266–68). Christian burials are found at Serrata Martini (Castiglione della Pescaia), where a gilt-glass vessel with a scene of the sacrifice of Isaac, now lost, was recovered (Chirico and Sebastiani *infra*), while less certain are the records of similar finds at the villa of Santa Liberata on Monte Argentario (Celuzza 2018, 10). Far less plausible is the existence at Pitigliano of a presumed 'tempietto paleocristiano' dated to the third century AD (Becherini 1968). In a review of the evidence for the Christianization of Etruria, Marta Sordi suggests for this period only an inscription from Cosa that describes the emperor Decius as *restitutor sacrorum*, which should indicate indirectly the presence of Christians in the third century, but it is more likely that the epithet is only a generic formula of Imperial propaganda.[12]

If we consider the whole of the settlement at the city of *Rusellae* in the light of the fragile chronology at our disposal, a picture emerges with many analogies to contemporary cities that in later centuries had different destinies, ranging from medieval success to abandonment for better sites. The abandonment of some sectors of the city and the spoliation of materials from the Roman structures beginning as early as the fourth century do not necessarily indicate the end of urban life, and similarly, burial within the walls became standard from the sixth century onwards. Recent scholarship identifies in this latter tendency a weakening of the idea of concepts of 'inside' and 'outside' the city, as if the Christianization of the population and the new era had

dissolved the ancient *pomerium*.[13] At *Rusellae* all of this is much in evidence: if we consider the burials, besides those within and around the church, there are tombs in the buildings to the south of the forum, others around the basilica, in the area of the main east–west road and on the northern hill where excavations are taking place that have not yet been published (Università di Siena); tombs can also be found outside the walls and around the church of Campo Alberguccio.[14]

If we return to the episcopal chronology, it should be noted that after Vitalianus we have no further trace of bishops for more than ninety years. It is impossible to establish whether this silence of the texts is simply due to a lack of documents, or whether there was a real episcopal crisis. This might be a further reason that the church was only built at the end of the sixth or in the early seventh century. The next bishop, Balbinus/Baldinus, is recorded in AD 591, in a context that does suggest that the city was in good health and the diocese stable. Balbinus was sent by Gregory the Great to Populonia, which lacked either a bishop or priests, with the task of ordaining priests and deacons who could reactivate the religious life of the diocese.[15] Populonia had been the victim of raids from the Lombards of Lucca in the '70s of the sixth century, when Saint Cerbonius was bishop. In the next twenty years the whole of Tuscany fell to the Lombards, a situation made official by the treaty between Gregory the Great and king Agilulf. *Rusellae*, like Populonia, became part of the duchy of Lucca.[16]

It is by now clear that Lucca's interest in Populonia centred on the mineral resources of Elba and its hinterland, and that one of the signs of this interest was the possible intervention of the bishop of Lucca in favour of the diocese, renewing its liturgical furnishings (Gelichi 2016, 349, 360–61).

---

12 Sordi 1996, 13–20, in part. 14 citing Marelli 1984. Manacorda 1979, 92 points out that the name Decius is uncertain, while Fentress (2003, 69 and n. 181) suggests that it is unlikely that the epithet had to be linked to the rebuilding of a temple.

13 Castiglia 2016, 360; Chavarrìa Arnau and Giacomello 2014, 213; 2015, 129–31; Gelichi 2016, 339. On the relationship between burials and public property, La Rocca 1986.

14 Campo Alberguccio n. 7; for burials at the base of the city walls, Campana in this volume. Innumerable small tombs that relate to dispersed settlements are found at *Rusellae*, Terme-Casa Passerini, and in the localities of Grancia, Benelli, Casette di Mota, Poggi di Mota, Ajali, and Grosseto, to stick within an area 10 km from the city. Chirico 2019, 115 with previous bibliography for Passerini. For other finds: Maetzke 1959; von Hessen 1971. For Grosseto: von Hessen 1975; Citter 2007b, 430; Celuzza 2017, 249–50. Other small cemeteries on the north bank of the Lacus Prilius: Citter 1995, 203–04, n. 25; Vaccaro 2005. This settlement has been compared to the model of the 'diffused city': Citter and Vaccaro 2003; Cantini and Citter 2010; see also the observations of La Rocca (1994) and Gelichi (2016, 337–39).

15 Gregory the Great, *Epistulae* 1.15; Ceccarelli Lemut and Sodi 1994, 22; Polock 1996, 199; Gelichi 2016, 343–44. Balbinus participated at the synod of 595 (Polock 1996).

16 Kurze in Kurze and Citter 1995, 160–67; Gelichi 2016, 344–45. See also Pazienza 2016.

What could have been the interests of Lucca in *Rusellae*? It is possible that the town, just as in the preceding Etruscan and Roman periods, was important specifically for its strategic position. Despite the attraction of the territory from the point of view of its woodlands on the slopes of Monte Amiata, of the salt from the lagoons, or of the possibility of controlling the ores of the Colline Metallifere, it is probable that Lucca's motivation for the conquest of *Rusellae* lies elsewhere.[17] *Rusellae* controlled the coast: the Lacus Prilius, the via Aurelia along the coast and the roads running from the coast towards the interior, particularly towards Chiusi and Siena, and the proximity of the northern frontier of the territory of Rome (Chirico and Citter 2018). In this context the dating to the Lombard rather than the Carolingian period of the furnishings of the episcopal church might suggest euergitism on the part of the bishop of Lucca analogous to that seen in Populonia (although it is here that the disappearance of the internal stratigraphy of the church is particularly unfortunate).[18] The presence on the site of at least one distinguished Lombard individual is shown by the presence of a tomb in the cemetery of the church dated to the middle of the seventh century and containing arms and a bejewelled belt buckle (US 1284, fig. 10–11).

The life of the city seems to have continued without interruption beyond the Lombard period. A document from Lucca of AD 715 cites an administrative district headed by *Rusellae* (*fines rosellanos*: CDL I, n. 19, 67, and 72; Kurze 2001, 340), while the sequence of bishops, apart from a hard-to-understand gap of ninety years between Balbinus (AD 595) and Theodorus (AD 649), is continuous until AD 886.[19] Another period of silence follows between this and AD 967, when the bishop Radaldus is mentioned. In AD 935, according to Orlando Malavolti, a Saracen raid struck *Rusellae*, but this is uncorroborated either by texts or by archaeology.[20] Up to now, without the completion of the stratigraphy of the church, we can state that use of the cemetery continued until the end of the twelfth or the beginning

of the thirteenth century, petering out after the transfer of the bishopric to Grosseto in 1132.[21]

[MGC]

Anthropological Discussion

Anthropology Introduction and Background

The human skeletal remains excavated from the *Rusellae* cemetery provide vital insight into the lives of the community interred there and contribute to an understanding of broader health conditions and sociocultural events occurring in the region during the early Middle Ages. This chapter discusses the findings of anthropological research questions that add to the archaeological narrative of *Rusellae*. First, was malaria present at *Rusellae* during the early Middle Ages, and if so, how prevalent was it? Second, who lived at *Rusellae*, what was the ancestry of the individuals interred in the *Rusellae* cemetery, and does this indicate more migration in this region during the Middle Ages than previously thought? The demographic profile representing the proportions of sex and age cohorts interred in this cemetery is also presented.

Malaria

Before its eradication in the late nineteenth century, malaria had a profound impact on the Maremma region, afflicting generations of people in this coastal area. Malaria has drastically influenced the history of the Maremma, and of Italy in general, as it has been cited as the cause for significant mortality and morbidity and as a contributing factor for the abandonment of regional settlements. The reputation of this disease in the Maremma marshes was well known during the Renaissance, when the deaths of several members of the Medici family were attributed to the virulent *Plasmodium falciparum* malarial infection contracted during a hunting trip there — a finding which has since been confirmed via immunodetection methods (Fornaciari and others 2010). Before this period, however, there is a void in the regional history of malaria prior to the transfer of the diocesan seat from *Rusellae* to Grosseto in AD 1138. Therefore, one of the goals of the present study was to examine the *Rusellae* skeletal sample for paleopathological indication of malaria in order to infer its potential presence and impact on the community

---

17   On the boundaries of the territory of *Rusellae* in the classical period: Celuzza 2013. For its strategic importance and that of wood and salt: Citter 2007a, 239, 242; Citter in Chirico and Citter 2018, 108, 113. On the ownership by *Rusellae* of a part of the Amiata in this period, there are various opinions: bibliography in Citter 2007a, 239. On the territory of the diocese and the Colline Metallifere: Ceccarelli Lemut and Sodi 1994, 10–15.

18   Betti 2021, 81–83; 2022. For the euergetic intervention at Populonia: Gelichi 2016, 361.

19   Valerianus 680, Gaudiosus 715, Raupertus 826, Otto 850, anonymus 886: Ceccarelli Lemut and Sodi 1994, 23; Polock 1996; Kurze 2001.

20   Malavolti 1559, 23r; Schneider 1914/1975, 125, n. 100 considers Malavolti's account unfounded; Celuzza and Fentress 1994, 613.

---

21   Coins: De Benetti and Catalli 2013, 208, nn. 492–93; the papal bull relative to the shift in the seat of the diocese is published by Kehr 1908, 260, n. 8.

between approximately the end of the sixth and the twelfth centuries.

Malaria is posited to have spread northward across Italy between 500 BC and AD 1000 (Sallares and others 2004). During this expansion, *P. falciparum*, *P. vivax*, and *P. malariae* parasites, and the *Anopheles* mosquitoes responsible for transmitting these parasites, were introduced and subsequently dispersed throughout human environments, facilitated by anthropogenic events (Sallares and others 2004; Marciniak and others 2018). Based on historical interpretations, malaria presumably spread to western central Italy between 400 and 100 BC, extending along the Tuscan coast during the third and second centuries BC (Sallares and others 2004). The introduction of malaria in the region was likely expedited by maritime transport from Sardinia, Sicily, and northern Africa. Several documentary accounts allude to the presence of malaria in the region in antiquity (Sallares and others 2004). Pliny the Younger, for example, described the Maremma as a pestilential region in the first century AD. During the summer of AD 467, Gallic politician Sidonius Apollinaris recorded contracting an illness consistent with malaria while travelling through Umbria near Tuscany, which he characterized as a diseased land (Sallares 2002).

To assess physical indication of malaria in Italy's history, paleopathological approaches have been applied to archaeological skeletal assemblages from central western sites. Near Lugnano, Umbria, an infant cemetery dating to the mid-fifth century AD at the villa of Poggio Gramignano has been associated with malaria. Skeletal remains from this site exhibiting indicators consistent with inherited anemia, such as thalassemia or sickle cell anemia, indirectly suggest the presence of malaria (Soren and others 1995, 1999), as these genetic conditions that confer some protection against malaria are believed to have developed and spread concomitantly with the disease (Sallares and others 2004). Archaeological characteristics from the cemetery are interpreted as signifying an epidemic event of *P. falciparum* malaria (Soren and others 1995; Soren 2003), the presence of which was confirmed by DNA analysis (Sallares and Gomzi 2001). Within the Maremma region, skeletal observations of potential thalassemia are described at the Roman villa Settefinestre near Cosa dating between the fourth and sixth centuries AD (Fornaciari and Mallegni 1985). Remains excavated from Cosa dating primarily to the eleventh century AD display skeletal lesions interpreted as an indication of possible malarial infection or one of the inherited anemias that give some degree of protection against malaria (Gruspier 2003).

Although these osteological interpretations indirectly suggest malaria, the application of such paleopathological methods is complicated by a lack of skeletal manifestation specific to malarial infection and

disputes regarding the etiologies behind some lesions used in these assessments. In early paleopathological inquiry on malaria, Angel (1964, 1966, 1977) attributed porous, hypertrophic lesions on archaeological crania ('porotic hyperostosis') to hemolytic anemia resulting from genetic conditions that provide some resistance to malaria and thus suggested that the lesions were indirectly indicative of malaria within populations as discussed above; however, this explanation was challenged, and the cranial lesions were subsequently attributed to iron-deficiency anemia (Carlson and others 1974; El-Najjar and others 1976; Hengen 1971; Holland and O'Brien 1997; Stuart-Macadam 1992). Walker and colleagues (2009) have since contended that the likely etiologies for the cranial porosities are megaloblastic anemia and hemolytic anemia, the latter of which occurs in malarial infection and hereditary conditions that confer a degree of resistance to malaria. Although the debate is ongoing surrounding these cranial lesions (McIlvaine 2015; Oxenham and Cavill 2010), a correlation between lesions appearing in the orbits ('cribra orbitalia') and malarial infection has been observed (Gowland and Western 2012). This correlation supports the connection between skeletal lesions, malaria, and malaria-induced anemia.

An analytical method recently proposed by Smith-Guzmán (2015) provides a more diagnostic course to inferring the potential prevalence and impact of malaria in past populations. Using an epidemiological approach, Smith-Guzmán investigated the prevalence of certain paleopathological lesions in two modern skeletal samples — one consisting of individuals from Uganda, where malaria is holoendemic and affects virtually the entire population, and the other comprising individuals from the United States, where malaria has been eradicated. From comparing these two samples, Smith-Guzmán (2015) developed a paleopathological method more specific to malaria that was used in the present study.

Ancestry Estimation

Recently, anthropological interest has grown significantly regarding migration and biological distance throughout the Roman Empire. Studies using craniometric, ancient DNA (aDNA), and stable isotope analyses have shown that the Roman Empire was biologically heterogeneous and that migration, either voluntary or forced, was a normal component of life across the empire (Hens and Ross 2017; Killgrove and Montgomery 2016; Leach and others 2009). Additional studies of group composition and migration during the Lombard period have demonstrated a consistent heterogeneity within cemetery samples and have produced evidence of long-distance migration during this era (Amorim and others 2018; Vai and others 2019). However, there are few biological distance analyses of post-Lombard cemeteries in Italy and throughout Europe in general; therefore, perspectives surrounding migration in the Carolingian Era and the subsequent early Middle Ages are largely drawn from historical and archaeological data and lack biological investigation.

Several burials in the *Rusellae* cemetery are of particular interest with respect to cultural and ancestral heterogeneity at the site. First, the grave of Individual 82–1284 contains Lombard-style funerary objects, including a Lombard sword and a belt dating to the second half of the seventh century AD (Celuzza and others 2002; Celuzza 2021). Further, during initial analysis of the human crania excavated from *Rusellae*, substantial variation was observed in craniofacial morphology throughout the cemetery, potentially indicating the presence of individuals of non-European ancestry in the sample. For example, Individual 82–1103, an adult female (cal AD 1033–1166), exhibited cranial morphology consistent with African ancestry, including a wide intraorbital breadth, a wide and low nasal aperture, alveolar prognathism, and post-bregmatic depression. Building on the potential presence of individuals of non-European ancestry identified through cranial morphology, this study applied craniometric analyses to further explore the ancestry of individuals interred in the *Rusellae* cemetery.

Overall, the cemetery at *Rusellae* offers a unique window into the history of the Maremma region between the late antique and early medieval periods. This study presents the prevalence of skeletal lesions suggestive of malaria to shed light on this endemic disease, includes ancestry estimation for the skeletal sample to explore ancestral heterogeneity at *Rusellae*, and summarizes demographic information from the skeletal sample. The results will provide awareness of health conditions and contribute to an understanding of the population history at the site during the early Middle Ages.

Materials and Methods

Only burials representing discrete individuals were included in this study's sample, and thus comingled remains from contexts with uncertain provenance were excluded. The skeletal remains comprising the *Rusellae* sample represent 195 individuals. Of this total sample, 132 individuals are associated with a period of the cemetery's use, with 25 individuals from Phase I (*c.* end of sixth and seventh centuries) and 107 individuals from Phase II (*c.* eighth to twelfth centuries). Both phase subsamples consist of comparable proportions of sex and age groups. For each individual, the following analyses were conducted as the completeness of the

remains allowed: estimated biological sex and age at death, paleopathological lesions suggestive of malaria, and estimated ancestry.

Estimating Sex and Age

Biological sex and age at death were estimated using standard anthropological criteria provided by Buikstra and Ubelaker (1994). Estimation of sex was based on the ossa coxae, skull, and postcranial measurements. Postcranial measurements were compared to male/female reference points generated from measurements previously taken on individuals within the *Rusellae* sample whose sex had been estimated from the cranium (Celuzza and others 2002). Adult age estimates were made from the pubic symphysis (Brooks and Suchey 1990), auricular surface (Lovejoy and others 1985), and sternal rib end (İşcan and others 1984, 1985). Subadult age estimation was conducted primarily with methods based on dental development and eruption (Moorrees and others 1963; Smith 1991; Ubelaker 1989). If dentition was unavailable, epiphyseal fusion and diaphyseal lengths were used to estimate age (Schaefer and others 2009). A demographic profile of the *Rusellae* cemetery sample was constructed from prevalence data on sex and age groups, expressed as the total number of individuals placed within each category recommended by Buikstra and Ubelaker (1994).

Malaria

To evaluate the presence of malaria, this study used the method developed by Smith-Guzmán (2015), who proposed a suite of five skeletal lesions as possible indicators of malaria: cribra orbitalia, humeral cribra, femoral cribra, spinal porosity, and periosteal reaction. The presence of these lesions was assessed following Smith-Guzmán's (2015) descriptions and scored as either present, absent, or unscorable.

To investigate the prevalence of the pathological lesions suggestive of malaria, frequency data were compiled for the overall sample. Frequencies of each lesion were calculated as the number of individuals exhibiting the lesion in relation to the number of individuals without the lesion. The frequencies of skeletal indicators observed in the *Rusellae* sample were compared with those provided by Smith-Guzmán (2015) taken from two modern samples — the one endemic for malaria and the one that is non-endemic (i.e., malaria-free). This comparison was conducted to assess whether the frequencies of lesions at *Rusellae* were more similar to a population that had high rates of malaria or one in which malaria was absent.

In addition to investigating the prevalence of these lesions, an algorithm of diagnostic criteria developed by Smith-Guzmán (2015) was used to infer how many and which individuals may have been infected with malaria. In summary, if an individual exhibits femoral cribra, humeral cribra, or cribra orbitalia and also demonstrates spinal porosity or periosteal reaction, then the individual is scored as 'positive diagnosis' for malaria. If the individual does not display an appropriate combination of these lesions, malaria is considered absent for the individual (scored as 'negative diagnosis'). This process was carried out for every individual with the necessary elements present to arrive at a 'positive' or 'negative' diagnosis. For example, if an individual only had the elements present to score femoral cribra and periosteal reaction, they would receive a 'positive diagnosis', despite lacking the bones necessary to score the other lesions. The overall frequency of individuals scored as 'positive diagnosis' was calculated. In cases when the observable lesions did not result in a 'positive diagnosis', but the missing markers could have produced a positive outcome, the individual did not receive a diagnosis. Because this could generate overestimation of the frequency of 'positive diagnoses', a more conservative overall prevalence was then produced only using individuals scorable for all five lesions. Of the total subsample that was sufficiently preserved for this algorithm to be performed, the results were then divided by phase to investigate temporal trend of infection.

The subsample used in the diagnostic outcome algorithm was also separated by sex and age cohorts to assess patterns of exposure and disease transmission. In regions of stable endemic malaria transmission, environmental conditions are conducive to continuous mosquito life cycles and year-round presence of malaria (Carter and Mendis 2002). The groups at the greatest risk for infection in these areas include young children and pregnant women who have lower immunity levels (Aufderheide and Rodríguez-Martin 1998; Carter and Mendis 2002). Unstable endemic malaria transmission is characterized by generally constant presence of malaria; however, the rate of infection oscillates with changes in the epidemiological environment (Carter and Mendis 2002). If there is a period of interrupted contact between mosquito vectors and humans, the duration of non-contact can result in decreased acquired immunity; therefore, this type of transmission can have severe consequences for all age and sex groups and produce periodic epidemics. During epidemics, a population experiences a significant increase in transmission and there is a lack of immunity across the population (Carter and Mendis 2002). By examining the demographic profiles of the affected sample from *Rusellae*, one can generate inferences about the endemicity of malaria during the use of the cemetery (Smith-Guzmán 2015).

Ancestry Estimation

Craniometric biological distance analyses allow practitioners to understand group similarity and dissimilarity by using cranial measurements as a proxy for genetic relatedness (Hefner and others 2016). When an individual's cranial measurements are compared with several reference samples using multivariate statistical analyses, that individual's affinity to each of these reference groups can be ascertained, and the individual can be classified into one of the reference groups with an associated level of statistical certainty.

In the present study, spatial coordinate data and interlandmark distances were recorded for each cranium using a MicroScribe® G2 3D digitizer (Immersion Corporation, San Jose, CA, USA) and the program 3Skull (Ousley 2014). Of the total adult sample, a subset of 22 sufficiently complete crania were used in the craniometric linear discriminant analysis (LDA) to explore ancestry throughout the cemetery. Then, a cranium of interest, Individual 82–1103, was investigated individually using FORDISC 3.0 (Jantz and Ousley 2005) to make more specific assessments about their ancestry. For both the group and individual analyses, the W.W. Howells African (Egypt, Teita, Dogon, Bushman, and Zulu) and European (Berg, Zalavar, and Norse) craniometric data sets were used as reference samples (Howells 1973).

The first analysis explored the overall ancestry of individuals interred in the cemetery. An LDA was performed in R version 3.5.3 (R Core Team 2013[22]) using Howells' (1973) three European and five African reference samples. Twenty-two measurements were utilized in the analysis, following Jantz and Ousley (2005). Only adult crania that were free of obstructive pathology and deemed complete or nearly complete were selected for this analysis (n = 22). Missing data from the mostly complete crania were imputed using the k-Nearest Neighbor method (Kenyhercz and Passalacqua 2016). The individuals in this subsample were classified into one of the eight reference samples and were subsequently considered as being most similar to African groups or most similar to European groups.

For the second analysis, Individual 82–1103 was analysed using FORDISC 3.0 software to estimate the individual's ancestry (Jantz and Ousley 2005). As noted previously, Individual 82–1103 was identified as potentially having African ancestry based on cranial morphology. The cranium was mostly complete, so no data imputation was performed. FORDISC 3.0 reports results in terms of posterior and typicality probabilities.

---

22 See bibliography for a complete list of statistical software packages used.

The posterior probability presents the probability of group membership, assuming that the unknown is a member of one of the reference groups. By contrast, the typicality probabilities do not assume the unknown is a member of one of the reference groups. Typicality probabilities characterize how 'typical' an individual is of the reference sample based on biological distance and variation within and among the reference groups.

Demographic Profile

The majority of individuals excavated from the *Rusellae* cemetery were adults, with relatively equal representation of males and females (Table 4.1). This proportion of male and female individuals is expected in an otherwise conventional population and communal cemetery. Of the adult individuals, the majority represented the middle adult age group, followed by the young adult and old adult age groups; however, based on the number of adults present, there are fewer subadults than expected within the cemetery assemblage. This under-representation of subadults suggests the use of mortuary space outside of the excavated cemetery and/or poor preservation of subadult skeletal material. A distinct absence of subadult individuals is observed in contemporary cemetery sites, in which young subadults comprise a much smaller proportion of the cemetery group than anticipated based on infant mortality rates during the Middle Ages (Barbiera and Dalla-Zuanna 2009; Gruspier 2003). Areas of subadult burials at a distance from cemeteries have also been observed in other late Roman and post-Roman sites (Carroll 2011).

Results and Discussion: Malaria

Results

The frequencies of each lesion in the *Rusellae* sample were compared to Smith-Guzmán's (2015) malaria-endemic and malaria-free samples (Fig. 4.6). The *Rusellae* sample

Table 4.1. Demographic profile of the *Rusellae* skeletal sample, separated by age and sex.

Age	Male	Female	Indeterminate	Total
Infant (0–3 years)	0	0	15	15
Child (3–12 years)	0	0	17	17
Adolescent (12–20 years)	3	0	7	10
Young adult (20–35 years)	16	22	1	39
Middle adult (35–50 years)	43	25	2	70
Old adult (>50 years)	10	10	0	20
Adult (>20 years)	7	11	4	22
Unknown	1	1	0	2
Total	**80**	**69**	**46**	**195**

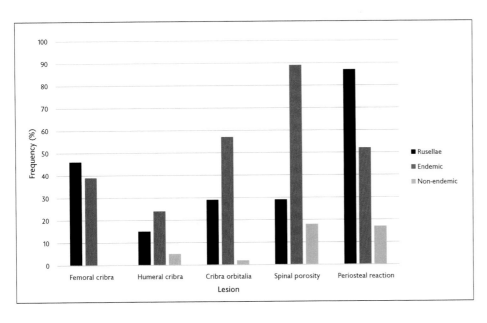

Figure 4.6. Frequencies of lesions in the *Rusellae* sample compared to Smith-Guzmán's (2015) endemic and non-endemic samples (figure by the authors).

exhibited a similar frequency of femoral cribra (46 per cent) compared to the malaria-endemic sample (39 per cent). The frequencies of humeral cribra (15 per cent) and cribra orbitalia (29 per cent) at *Rusellae* were intermediate between the endemic and non-endemic samples. The prevalence of spinal porosity in the *Rusellae* sample (29 per cent) was lower than that observed in the endemic sample and more closely resembled the frequency in the non-endemic sample. Finally, the prevalence of periosteal reactions observed in the *Rusellae* sample (87 per cent) was substantially higher than both endemic and non-endemic samples.

Of the total sample, eighty individuals could be assessed for the potential presence of malaria using a subset of the lesions in the algorithm presented by Smith-Guzmán (2015). Within this subsample, fifty-three individuals (66 per cent) met the algorithmic criteria for a 'positive diagnosis' and thus demonstrated signs of possible infection. Thirty-six individuals were scorable for all five lesions, and half met the 'positive diagnosis' criteria. Therefore, a conservative estimate of 50 per cent demonstrated signs of infection.

Individuals with 'positive' and 'negative' diagnoses were divided into phase, sex, and age cohorts (Table 4.2). Because not all burials were associated with a phase, the phase-specific counts are reduced. Some individuals from both Phase I and Phase II were scored as 'positive diagnosis' and the frequencies were approximately equal; however, the Phase I scorable sample is smaller than the Phase II scorable sample. Individuals from both sexes displayed signs of possible infection, and the frequencies of 'positive diagnoses'

in the male and female groups were similar. Across age groups, a 'positive diagnosis' of malaria was more frequent in younger individuals (i.e., subadults and young adults) than older age groups (i.e., middle and old adults).

Discussion

The results of the paleopathological analysis provide support for the presence of malaria at *Rusellae* during the early Middle Ages. In comparing the frequency of these skeletal indicators between *Rusellae* and two other samples — one endemic for malaria and the other malaria-free (Smith-Guzmán 2015) — the *Rusellae* sample more closely resembled the endemic sample; however, there were also deviations in the prevalence of individual lesions. Of particular interest from this comparison is the similar frequency of femoral cribra (Fig. 4.7) in the *Rusellae* sample and the sample that experienced high levels of malarial infection, with *Rusellae* demonstrating a slightly higher frequency. This parallel between *Rusellae* and the endemic sample supports the potential presence of malaria at *Rusellae*, especially as Smith-Guzmán (2015) reports no femoral cribra in the malaria-free sample. Although there has been some variation in the terminology and etiology assigned to this skeletal lesion, femoral cribra is a distinct and recognized paleopathological lesion seemingly unrelated to specific physical activities (Radi and others 2013).

The frequencies of humeral cribra, cribra orbitalia, and spinal porosity at *Rusellae* fell in-between the endemic and non-endemic samples. A discussion of

Table 4.2. Number and frequency of individuals scored as 'positive diagnosis' and 'negative diagnosis' for malaria, separated by phase, sex, and age groups.

		'Positive Diagnosis'	'Negative Diagnosis'	Total	Frequency of 'Positive Diagnosis'
Phase	**Phase I**	5	3	8	63%
	Phase II	38	19	57	67%
	Total	43	22	65	
Sex	**Male**	25	14	39	64%
	Female	16	13	29	55%
	Total	53	27	80	
Age	**Infant (0–3 years)**	3	0	3	100%
	Child (3–12 years)	6	0	6	100%
	Adolescent (12–20 years)	5	1	6	83%
	Young adult (20–35 years)	18	5	23	78%
	Middle adult (35–50 years)	16	18	34	47%
	Old adult (>50 years)	5	3	8	63%
	Total	53	27	80	

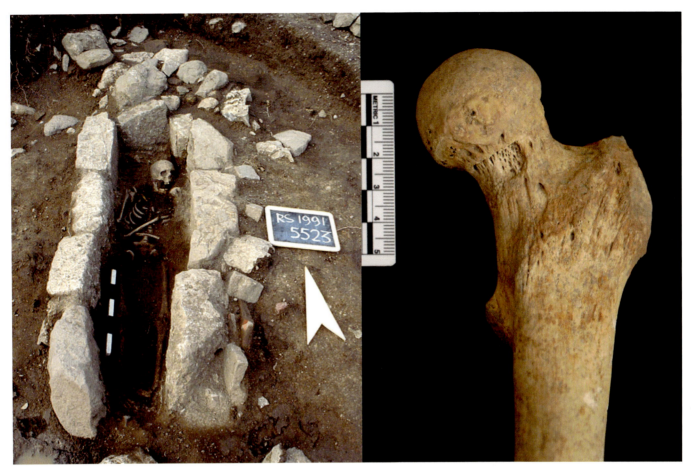

Figure 4.7. Individual 5523, *in situ* (left) and anterior view of proximal left femur displaying femoral cribra (right) (photos by the authors).

these findings is somewhat limited by an incomplete understanding of the biological processes behind these lesions; however, differences could be related to variations in the lesions' expression within the disease's pathogenesis, age-related factors, or differences in duration of infection. It is possible that there are individuals who were infected and did not live long enough to manifest these skeletal markers (Wood and others 1992), as well as individuals whose skeletal lesions could have become resorbed over time with acquired immunity (Smith-Guzmán 2015). Finally, the substantially higher rates of periosteal reactions demonstrated in the *Rusellae* sample could be influenced by other infectious diseases or trauma that result in inflammatory reactions (Ortner 2003).

In employing Smith-Guzmán's (2015) algorithm to investigate how many and which individuals were potentially infected with malaria, 66 per cent, or conservatively 50 per cent, of the scorable individuals met the diagnostic criteria for malaria and therefore were possibly infected with the disease. The high predicted prevalence of malaria in the sample supports its presence at *Rusellae* in the early Middle Ages and, while the frequency is not ubiquitous, it indicates widespread affliction. When separated by phase, individuals from both Phase I and Phase II exhibited signs of infection, suggesting that malaria was present at *Rusellae* during the early and later periods of the cemetery's use. The frequencies of individuals with a 'positive diagnosis' were similar between both phases, indicating some temporal consistency; however, Phase I is represented by few individuals.

The results of this study therefore suggest that the community interred in the *Rusellae* cemetery experienced the deleterious health effects of malaria during the early Middle Ages. The morbidity and mortality of malarial infection depends on multiple variables, including the virulence of the parasite species, level of acquired immunity, presence of genetic polymorphisms conferring protection, and malaria's propensity to coinfect with other conditions and diseases (Carter and Mendis 2002). An individual's experience in a malarial region is also related to the type of transmission specific to their region.

Results of the diagnostic outcome algorithm indicate that both males and females experienced similar risk of infection and all age groups demonstrated signs of infection. These findings suggest that individuals regardless of age and sex were exposed to and at risk of malarial infection. Among age cohorts, the frequency was higher in younger individuals compared to older age groups, which is consistent with the greater risk of infection in the young (Aufderheide and Rodríguez-Martin 1998; Carter and Mendis, 2002). The under-representation of infants precludes assessing the extent of infant mortality at *Rusellae*, but there is not an apparent heightened mortality among reproductive-age females that would indicate consistently stable transmission (Carter and Mendis 2002; Smith-Guzmán 2015). Although the observed lesions cannot be definitively attributed to acute or chronic infection at this time, the presence of these markers in middle and old adults and qualitative observations of resorption in the lesions indicate individuals might have been living with malarial infection. This pattern may propose some degree of endemicity as opposed to strictly epidemic transmission. In endemic areas, infection as adults may not be fatal, but health and life expectancy are negatively affected (Sallares 2002) and repeated infection substantially lowers longevity (Carter and Mendis 2002).

The patterns of hypothesized infection from *Rusellae* dating to the early Middle Ages are consistent with those observed in modern Maremma and inferred from late antique Rome. Malaria in the Maremma region remained hyperendemic until its eradication (Boccolini and others 2012), and a level of immunity could be gradually acquired for those who survived into adulthood after recurrent infection (Sallares 2002). This epidemiological pattern occurs when malarial transmission is seasonally intense and all age groups are at risk of infection (Baird and others 2002), as the immunity acquired by adults can decrease during a period of low transmission. The epidemiological pattern observed in Grosseto during the mid-nineteenth century is comparable to the mortality trends inferred from funerary epigraphs from late antique Rome (*c.* fourth to fifth centuries), as the increase of adult deaths during late summer and early autumn is consistent with seasonal increases in malarial transmission (Scheidel 2009, 2015; Shaw, 1996). Similar circumstances may have been present in the Maremma during the fourteenth century, when Dante Alighieri describes the region's deleterious health conditions during July and September in his Divine Comedy (Sabbatani and others 2010). Lower transmission during the rest of the year can be attributed to decreased mosquito activity and malarial parasite development due to lower temperatures (Sallares and Gomzi 2001), even though *Anopholese labranchiae* mosquitoes — the probable vector in the region (Sallares 2002) — do not hibernate (Weiland 2011).

Finally, the ecological conditions in the landscape surrounding *Rusellae* during the early Middle Ages were likely conducive to support mosquito vector populations and, thus, transmission to human hosts. With the decline of the Roman Empire, countryside marshes and coastal swamps are theorized to have expanded from an inability to maintain waterway infrastructure and rises in sea levels (Fornaciari and Mallegni 1985; Fornaciari and others 2010), thus increasing areas for mosquito breeding. During the early Middle Ages, a coastal lagoon extended inland to the north-west of Grosseto (Bellotti and others 2004). This lagoon would have provided viable conditions for sustaining *A. labranchiae* populations, which thrive in stagnant brackish water (Newfield 2017). The abundance of these mosquito vectors in the Maremma was observed prior to eradication of malaria in the region with numerous breeding sites along the coast (Boccolini and others 2012). Although the site of *Rusellae* is located on top of a hill, the elevation would not have been high enough to escape inoculation from mosquitoes (Weiland 2011).

Results and Discussion: Ancestry Estimation

Results

Of the twenty-two individuals analysed in the discriminant function, seven (32%) showed closer affinity to one of the African groups (Zulu, Teita, and Egypt), while fifteen (68%) showed closer affinity to one of the European groups (Berg, Norse, and Zalavar) (Fig. 4.8). The first axis of the LDA (Fig. 4.8) primarily separates the African and European groups, with the exception of Egypt. The second axis separates the Berg and Bushman groups from each of the other reference samples. The accuracy of the LDA in this case is limited by the representativeness of the reference samples. Although the Howells dataset provides a geographically and temporally broad comparative collection, the results must be understood as indicating a greater or lesser degree of similarity to one of the reference groups, as opposed to a specific group identification (Fig. 4.8).

Results from the individual FORDISC 3.0 analysis of Individual 82–1103 suggest that the initial cranial morphological analysis is consistent with the metric analysis. The present FORDISC 3.0 analysis used the same eight reference groups as the previous analysis. In an eight-group DFA using nineteen measurements, Individual 82–1103 strongly clusters with the Egyptian female sample with a posterior probability of 0.805 and an F typicality of 0.800.

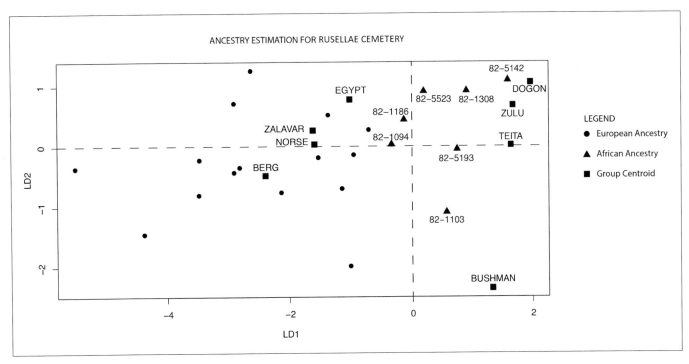

Figure 4.8. Linear discriminant analysis (LDA) for ancestry at the *Rusellae* cemetery depicting individuals classified as European (circle) and African (triangle), with group centroids of the Howells dataset (squares) (figure by the authors).

Discussion

The results suggest that *Rusellae* was a biologically heterogeneous site, with a high degree of craniometric variation represented within the cemetery. Fundamentally, the results show that *Rusellae* was likely a city comprising individuals not only from the Italian peninsula but from elsewhere in the Mediterranean. Additionally, these results are consistent with other studies that have found evidence for the presence of African individuals in Roman Britain (Leach and others 2009; Leach and others 2010; Redfern and others 2016) and Roman Italy (Killgrove and Montgomery 2016). The present study, however, contributes data on the possible presence of individuals of African ancestry in Tuscany during the Lombard and post-Lombard periods, which has yet to be studied from a biological and craniometric perspective.

Individual 82-1103 (Fig. 4.9), dating to cal AD 1033–1166, provides particularly strong evidence for the presence of individuals of African ancestry at *Rusellae*, as the gross morphology and craniometric results indicate a high likelihood that this individual is of African ancestry. The date for this individual roughly corresponds to the abandonment of the site and is in the last phase of interments, indicating the presence of individuals with African ancestry, even in the later phases of occupation. More broadly, approximately 32 per cent of the craniometric subsample shows a closer affinity to African reference samples than European reference samples, indicating a potentially large proportion of individuals with African ancestry at *Rusellae* throughout the use of the cemetery. Although contacts between Italy and the provinces of Africa throughout the empire and after the fall of the empire are well-documented archaeologically and historically, the late evidence of people with African ancestry in Rusellae could also be linked to completely different events that we are not presently able to reconstruct.

Individual 82-1284 (Figs 4.10–4.11) also provides archaeological evidence of differing cultural practices at *Rusellae*. This individual was buried with Lombard-style grave goods including a sax and a belt dating to the second half of the seventh century AD (Celuzza and others 2002; Celuzza 2021). Given the Germanic style of this burial, it is possible that Individual 82-1284 migrated from central Europe to *Rusellae* with the Lombard tribes between the sixth and eighth centuries; however, one cannot rule out the possibility that this individual was a native person who adopted burial traditions of the hegemonic invading group. Grave goods are recognized as not always having a direct relationship with ethnic identity, and researchers propose an interdisciplinary approach to exploring the interaction between genetic ancestry, cultural affiliation, and burial practices (Geary and Veeramah 2016).

The movement of people after the fall of Rome, whether voluntary or involuntary, produced a highly

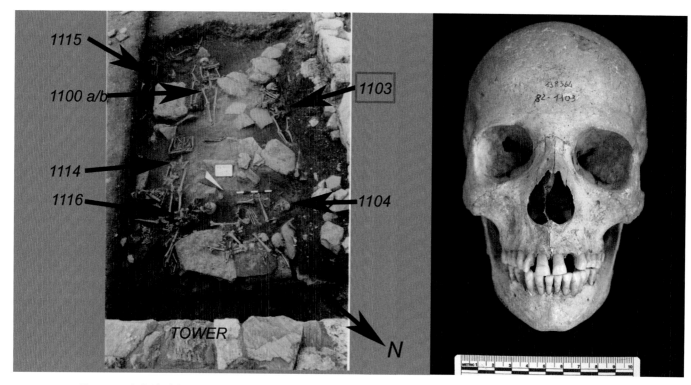

Figure 4.9. Individual 82–1103, *in situ* (left) and anterior view of the skull (right) (photos and processing by the authors).

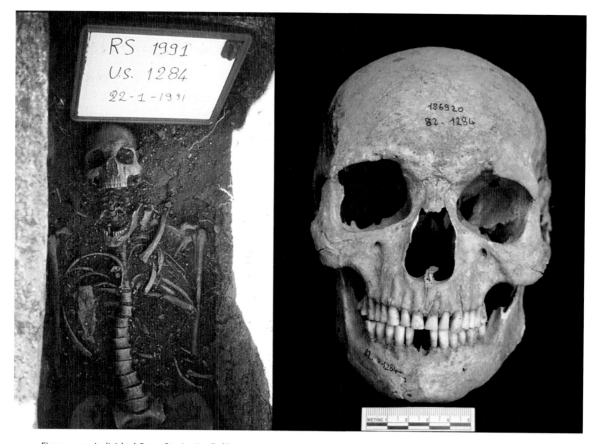

Figure 4.10. Individual 82–1284, *in situ* (left), anterior view of the skull (right), and associated grave goods (bottom) (photos by the authors).

Figure 4.11. Museo Archeologico e d'Arte della Maremma, Individual 82–1284, associated grave goods (photo courtesy Museo Archeologico e d'Arte della Maremma, reproduced with permission).

variable degree of ancestral backgrounds throughout the former Roman Empire. This variation is seen most clearly in areas that are major population centres of the Mediterranean, including coastal cities in southern and western Italy, which for centuries, were the primary connection between the Christian and Muslim Mediterranean (Horden and Purcell 2000). *Rusellae*'s position as a node between the coast and the interior of Italy situated the city as inherently more likely to experience migration. This phenomenon of coastal cities exhibiting greater diversity than inland cities has been demonstrated in the Roman era (Emery and others 2018) and appears to continue throughout the occupation of *Rusellae*. Therefore, while this study is among the first to identify individuals of African ancestry in early medieval Tuscany, it should perhaps not come as a surprise that a relatively coastal city would present such findings.

[EOW, ACG, MII, JSB, ERS, TWF]

Future Directions

Although much of the cemetery is associated with broad phases, a more granular chronology is lacking across the burials. Additional radiocarbon dating beyond Individual 82–1103 is planned as more definitive dates will contribute to conclusions regarding malaria as well as the nature of craniometric variation at *Rusellae*.

To verify the presence of malaria, future work will entail confirmatory testing of the malarial parasite (e.g., aDNA or immunological testing). Because the specific parasite species historically present in Italy would result in different clinical manifestations of malaria, determining the type would be of interest in considering the health experiences of this community and the temporospatial distribution of these disease variants in history. Assessing the type of malarial infection may also provide additional context for the manifestation of the skeletal lesions of focus, as the method employed in this study was developed from a population infected primarily with *P. falciparum* (Smith-Guzmán 2015).

Additional analyses that would contribute to understanding migration at *Rusellae* include stable isotope and aDNA studies. Stable isotopes have successfully been used to identify nonlocal migrants in a number of Roman-era cemeteries (Emery and others 2018; Killgrove and Montgomery 2016; Prowse and others 2007). Similarly, aDNA has been used to explore genetic variation within a sample, with outliers potentially indicating migrants to the site and genetic admixture implying a simultaneous cultural admixture (Vai and others 2019).

One limitation of this study is the appropriateness of the reference samples used in estimating ancestry. Currently, there is no data set of cranial measurements for 'Medieval Italians', and given the nature of migration throughout the Mediterranean, a homogenous data set of this type is unlikely to exist. Ancestry estimation is limited, therefore, to the broad categorization of people from *Rusellae* as consistent with African or European ancestry based on a worldwide data set. Until further reference samples are identified, or stable isotope or aDNA studies are undertaken, more specific assertions about geographic origin cannot be made. Future analyses of the *Rusellae* sample will include additional reference groups, such as a medieval Nubian data set, other Lombard cemeteries throughout Italy and central Europe, and contemporary Tuscan cemeteries. By using more representative reference samples, the classifications derived from the LDA will provide more reliable evidence of either European or African ancestry and may allow for a distinction between central European and Italian origin.

Acknowledgements

Funding for this research was graciously provided by the Research Scholars Award from the College of Social Science, the Department of Anthropology, and the Graduate School of Michigan State University. The authors are grateful to the following people for their invaluable contributions and support: Dr Elena Chirico, Dr Elizabeth Fentress, Professor Sauro Gelichi, Dr Elsa Pacciani, Dr Alessandro Riga, Dr Alessandro Sebastiani, Dr Caitlin Vogelsberg, and the staff at the Museo Archeologico e d'Arte della Maremma, Grosseto. The authors thank DirectAMS laboratory for their radiocarbon dating service.

Works Cited

Amorim, Carlos Eduardo G., Stefania Vai, Cosimo Posth, Alessandra Modi, István Koncz, Susanne Hakeneck, Maria Cristina La Rocca, Balász Mende, Dean Bobo, Walter Pohl, and others. 2018. 'Understanding 6th-Century Barbarian Social Organization and Migration Through Paleogenomics', *Nature Communications*, 9: 1–11

Angel, J. Lawrence. 1964. 'Osteoporosis: Thalassemia?', *American Journal of Physical Anthropology*, 22: 369–74

——. 1966. 'Porotic Hyperostosis, Anemias, Malarias and Marshes in the Prehistoric Eastern Mediterranean', *Science*, 153: 760–63

——. 1977. *Anemias of Antiquity: Eastern Mediterranean, Porotic Hyperostosis: An Enquiry*, Paleopathology Association Monograph No. 2 (Detroit: Paleopathology Association), pp. 1–5

Aquino, Jakson, Dirk Enzmann, Marc Schwartz, Nitin Jain, and Stefan Kraft. 2018. descr: Descriptive Statistics. R package version 1.1.4. <https://CRAN.R-project.org/package=descr>

Aufderheide, Arthur C., and Conrado Rodríguez-Martin. 1998. *The Cambridge Encyclopedia of Human Paleopathology* (Cambridge: Cambridge University Press)

Baird, J. Kevin, Michael J. Bangs, Jason D. Maguire, and Mazie J. Barcus. 2002. 'Epidemiological Measures of Risk of Malaria', *Methods in Molecular Medicine*, 72: 13–22

Barbiera, Irene, and Gianpiero Dalla-Zuanna. 2009. 'Population Dynamics in Italy in the Middle Ages: New Insights from Archaeological Findings', *Population and Development Review*, 35.2: 367–89

Bartolozzi Casti, Gabriele. 2005. 'La catacomba di Pianosa', in *Da Populonia a Massa Marittima: i 1500 anni di una diocesi, Atti del convegno*, ed. by Anna Benvenuti (Florence: Editrice la Mandragora), pp. 67–96

Becherini, Luigi. 1968. 'Il tempietto paleocristiano di Pitigliano', *Bollettino della Società Storica Maremmana*, XVII: 141–45

Benvenuti, Anna. 2005 (ed.). *Da Populonia a Massa Marittima: i 1500 anni di una diocesi, Atti del convegno* (Florence: Editrice la Mandragora)

Betti, Fabio. 2021. '*Ursus magester* e gli altri. Le sottoscrizioni di artefici nella scultura altomedievale in Italia centrale: analisi comparativa e contesto storico', in *Domus sapienter staurata. Scritti di storia dell'arte per Marina Righetti*, ed. by Anna Maria D'Achille, Antonio Iacobini, and Pio Francesco Pistilli (Cinisello Balsamo: Silvana Editoriale), pp. 75–86

Betti, Fabio. 2022. 'La bottega di Magester Iohannes a Roselle nel contesto della produzione scultorea di età tardolongobarda in Italia', in *L'arredo liturgico fra Oriente e Occidente (V–XV secolo). Frammenti, opere e contesti*, ed. by Fabio Coden (Cinisello Balsamo: Silvana Editoriale), pp. 228–36

Bellotti, Piero, Claudio Caputo, Lina Davoli, Silvio Evangelista, Eduardo Garzanti, Francesco Pugliese, and Publio Valeri. 2004. 'Morpho-Sedimentary Characteristics and Holocene Evolution of the Emergent Part of the Ombrone River Delta (Southern Tuscany)', *Geomorphology*, 61: 71–90

Boccolini, Daniela, Luciano Toma, Marco di Luca, Francesco Severini, M. Cocchi, A. Bella, A. Massa, F. Mancini Barbieri, Gioia Bongiorno, Luca Angeli, and others. 2012. 'Impact of Environmental Changes and Human-Related Factors on the Potential Malaria Vector, *Anopheles labranchiae* (Diptera: Culicidae), in Maremma, Central Italy', *Population and Community Ecology*, 49.4: 833–42

Brooks, Sheilagh, and Judy Suchey. 1990. 'Skeletal Age Determination Based on the Os Pubis: A Comparison of the Aesádi-Nemeskéri and Suchey-Brooks Methods', *Human Evolution*, 5.3: 227–38

Buikstra, Jane E., and Douglas H. Ubelaker (eds). 1994. *Standards for Data Collection from Human Skeletal Remains* (Fayetteville: Arkansas Archaeological Survey)

Burattini, Vittorio. 1994. 'Chiose storiche 1994', *Rivista Diocesana Grosseto*, 29: 169–92

—— (ed.). 1996. *La Cattedrale di Grosseto e il suo popolo 1295–1995, Atti del convegno* (Grosseto: I Portici)

Cambi, Franco. 2005. 'Cosa e Populonia. La fine dell'esperienza urbana in Etruria e la nascita delle due Toscane', *Workshop di archeologia classica: paesaggi, costruzioni, reperti*, 2: 71–90

Cantini, Federico, and Carlo Citter. 2010. 'Le città toscane nel V secolo', in *Le trasformazioni del V secolo. L'Italia, i barbari, l'Occidente romano*, ed. by Paolo Delogu and Stefano Gasparri (Turnhout: Brepols), pp. 409–35

Cantino Wataghin, Gisella, Josep Maria Gurt Esparraguera, and Jean Guyon. 1996. 'Topografia della *Civitas Christiana* tra IV e VI secolo', in *Early Medieval Towns in West Mediterraneum, Atti del convegno*, ed. by Gian Pietro Brogiolo (Mantova: Società Archeologica Padana), pp. 17–41

Carlson, David S., George J. Armelagos, and Dennis P. van Gerven. 1974. 'Factors Influencing the Etiology of Cribra Orbitalia in Prehistoric Nubia', *Journal of Human Evolution*, 3: 405–10

Carroll, Maureen. 2011. 'Infant Death and Burial in Roman Italy', *Journal of Roman Archaeology*, 24: 99–120

Carter, Richard, and Kamini N. Mendis. 2002. 'Evolutionary and Historical Aspects of the Burden of Malaria', *Clinical Microbiology Reviews*, 15.4: 564–94

Castiglia, Gabriele. 2016. 'Lucca e Siena a confronto: trasformazioni urbane nella *Tuscia Annonaria* dall' età classica alla fine dell'altomedioevo', *Mélanges de l'École française de Rome – Moyen Âge*, 128.1 <https://mefrm.revues.org/2870>

——. 2018. 'Le *ecclesiae episcopales* nelle città toscane tra tardo antico ed alto medioevo. Sviluppi monumentali e relazioni con la topografia urbana', *Hortus Artium Medievalium*, 24: 106–20

Ceccarelli Lemut, Maria Luisa, and Stefano Sodi. 1994. *La Diocesi di Rusellae-Grosseto dalle origini al XIII secolo*, Quaderni Stenoniani, 2 (Pisa: Pacini)

——. 1995. 'Storia generale e storia locale. Osservazioni metodologiche su una recente controversia relativa alla storia antica e medievale della Diocesi di Rusellae-Grosseto', *Bullettino Senese di Storia Patria*, 102: 395–410

Celuzza, Mariagrazia. 2013. 'Il territorio di Rusellae', in *Rusellae: le monete dagli scavi archeologici 1959–1991 e dal territorio, Collezioni numismatiche in Italia: documentazione dei complessi*, ed. by Massio De Benetti and Fiorenzo Catalli (Arcidosso: Effigi), pp. 256–59

——. 2017. *Museo Archeologico e d'Arte della Maremma. Museo di Arte Sacra della Diocesi di Grosseto*, II ed. (Arcidosso: Effigi)

——. 2018. 'Un paesaggio con rovine sul mare: la *Domitiana positio*', *L'Argentariana* 6: 3–10

——. 2022. 'Roselle', in *Una terra di mezzo. I Longobardi e la nascita della Toscana, Catalogo della mostra*, ed. by Chiara Valdambrini (Milan: Silvana Editoriale), pp. 259–63

Celuzza, Mariagrazia, Sandra Cencetti, and Elsa Pacciani. 2002. 'Scavi nel cimitero della più antica cattedrale di Rusellae', in *Antropologia del Medioevo: biologia e cultura, Atti del convegno*, ed. by Elsa Pacciani, Rosa Boano, and Margherita Micheletti (Arezzo: LP Grafiche), pp. 77–87

Celuzza, Mariagrazia, and Elizabeth Fentress. 1994. 'La Toscana centro-meridionale: i casi di Cosa-Ansedonia e Rusellae', in *La storia dell'altomedioevo italiano (VI–X secolo) alla luce dell'archeologia, Atti del convegno internazionale*, ed. by Riccardo Francovich and Ghislaine Noyé (Florence: All'Insegna del Giglio), pp. 601–14

Celuzza, Mariagrazia, and Maura Medri. 2019. '*Rusellae* (Rusellae, GR). Le Terme alle pendici della collina nord', in *Le Terme Pubbliche nell'Italia Romana (II secolo a.C. – fine IV d.C.), Atti del Convegno*, ed. by Maura Medri and Antonio Pizzo (Rome: TRE Press), pp. 351–66

Celuzza, Mariagrazia, Matteo Milletti, and Andrea Zifferero. 2021. 'Rusellae and its Territory. From the Etruscan to the Roman City', in *Archaeological Landscapes of Roman Etruria: Research and Field Papers*, ed. by Alessandro Sebastiani and Carolina Megale, MediTo – Archaeological and Historical Landscapes of Mediterranean Central Italy, 1 (Turnhout: Brepols), pp. 45–51

Chavarria Arnau, Alexandra, and Federico Giacomello. 2014. 'Riflessioni sul rapporto tra sepolture e cattedrali nell'alto medioevo', *Hortus Artium Medievalium*, 20: 209–20

——. 2015. 'Sepolture e cattedrali in Italia settentrionale: il dato archeologico', *Rivista di Archeologia Cristiana*, XCI: 129–66

Chirico, Elena. 2019. 'Bagno di Rusellae: Podere Passerini e le c.d. Terme Leopoldine, una possibile ricostruzione archeologica', in *Oltre il Duomo, Catalogo della Mostra*, ed. by Barbara Fiorini (Arcidosso: Effigi), pp. 107–16

Chirico, Elena, and Carlo Citter. 2018. 'I beni pubblici e della corona dall'Impero Romano ai Longobardi: il caso di Rusellae (Grosseto)', in *Città e campagna: culture, insediamenti, economia (secc. VI–IX), II Incontro per l'Archeologia barbarica*, ed. by Caterina Giostra (Mantova: Società Archeologica Padana), pp. 97–120

Ciampoltrini, Giulio. 1991a. 'Annotazioni sulla scultura di età carolingia in Toscana', *Prospettiva* 62: 59–66

——. 1991b. '*Pulchrius ecce micat nitentes marmoris decus*. Appunti sulla scultura di età longobarda nella Toscana meridionale', *Prospettiva*, 64: 4–48

Citter, Carlo. 1995. 'Il rapporto fra Bizantini, Germani e Romani nella Maremma toscana attraverso lo studio della dinamica del popolamento – il caso rosellano', in *Acculturazione e mutamenti. Prospettive nell'archeologia medievale del Mediterraneo:*

VI ciclo di lezioni sulla ricerca applicata in archeologia, ed. by Riccardo Francovich and Enrica Boldrini (Florence: All'Insegna del Giglio), pp. 201–22

——. 1996. *Guida agli edifici sacri* (Siena: Nuova Immagine)

——. 2007a. 'Gli edifici religiosi tardo antichi e altomedievali nelle diocesi di Rusellae e Sovana: il dato archeologico e i problemi in agenda', *Archeologia Medievale*, XXXIV: 239–45

——. 2007b (ed.). *Archeologia urbana a Grosseto, II. Edizione degli scavi urbani 1998–2005* (Florence: All'Insegna del Giglio)

Citter, Carlo, and Antonia Arnoldus Huyzendveld. 2007 (eds). *Archeologia urbana a Grosseto, I. La città nel contesto geografico della bassa valle dell'Ombrone* (Florence: All'Insegna del Giglio)

Citter, Carlo, and Emanuele Vaccaro. 2003. 'Le costanti dell'urbanesimo altomedievale in Toscana (secoli IV–VIII)', in *Atti del III convegno nazionale della S.A.M.I.*, ed. by Paolo Peduto and Rosa Fiorillo (Florence: All'Insegna del Giglio), pp. 309–13

De Benetti, Massimo, and Fiorenzo Catalli. 2013 (eds). *Rusellae: le monete dagli scavi archeologici 1959–1991 e dal territorio*, Collezioni numismatiche in Italia: documentazione dei complessi (Arcidosso: Effigi)

De Marinis, Giuliano, and Gabriella Poggesi. 1991. 'Rusellae, Poggio di Mosconcino', *Studi e Materiali* VI: 343–45

Dowle, Matt, and Arun Srinivasan. 2019. data.table: Extension of 'data.frame'. R package version 1.12.8. <https://CRAN.R-project.org/package=data.table>

El-Najjar, Mahmoud Y., Dennis J. Ryan, Christy G. Turner, and Betsy Lozoff. 1976. 'The Etiology of Porotic Hyperostosis Among the Prehistoric and Historic Anasazi Indians of Southwestern United States', *American Journal of Physical Anthropology*, 44: 477–87

Emery, Matthew V., Robert J. Stark, Tyler J. Murchie, Spender Elford, Henry P. Schwarcz, and Tracy L. Prowse. 2018. 'Mapping the Origins of Imperial Roman Workers (1st–4th Century CE) at Vagnari, Southern Italy, Using 87Sr/86Sr and Delta 18O Variability', *American Journal of Physical Anthropology*, 166: 837–50

Fentress, Elizabeth. 2003. *Cosa V: An Intermittent Town, Excavations 1991–1997*, Memoirs of the American Academy in Rome, Suppl. 2 (Ann Arbor: The University of Michigan Press)

Fornaciari, Gino, and Francesco Mallegni. 1985. 'Le ossa umane', in *Settefinestre: una villa schiavistica nell'Eturia romana, 2*, ed. by Andreina Ricci (Modena: Edizioni Panini), pp. 275–77

Fornaciari, Gino, Valentina Giuffra, Ezio Ferroglio, Sarah Gino, and Raffaella Bianucci. 2010. '*Plasmodium falciparum* Immunodetection in Bone Remains of Members of the Renaissance Medici Family (Florence, Italy, Sixteenth Century)', *Transactions of the Royal Society of Tropical Medicine and Hygiene*, 104: 583–87

Fox, John, and Sanford Weisberg. 2019. *An {R} Companion to Applied Regression*, Third Edition (Thousand Oaks: Sage) <https://socialsciences.mcmaster.ca/jfox/Books/Companion/>

Francovich, Riccardo, and Ghislaine Noyé. 1994 (eds). *La storia dell'altomedioevo italiano (VI–X secolo) alla luce dell'archeologia, Atti del convegno internazionale* (Florence: All'Insegna del Giglio)

Geary, Patrick J., and Krishna R. Veeramah. 2016. 'Mapping European Population Movement Through Genomic Research', *Medieval Worlds*, 4: 65–78

Gelichi, Sauro. 2016. 'Prima del monastero', in *Un monastero sul mare. Ricerche archeologiche a San Quirico di Populonia*, ed. by Sauro Gelichi and Giovanna Bianchi (Florence: All'Insegna del Giglio), pp. 337–71

Giusti, Martino, and Pietro Guidi. 1942. Rationes decimarum Italiae. Tuscia II. *La decima degli anni 1295–1304* (Città del Vaticano: Biblioteca Apostolica Vaticana)

Gowland, Rebecca L., and A. G. Western. 2012. 'Morbidity in the Marshes: Using Spatial Epidemiology to Investigate Skeletal Evidence for Malaria in Anglo-Saxon England (AD 410–1050)', *American Journal of Physical Anthropology*, 147: 301–11

Gruspier, Katherine. 2003. 'The Human Skeletal Remains', in *Cosa V: An Intermittent Town, Excavations 1991–1997*, ed. by Elizabeth Fentress (Ann Arbor: The University of Michigan Press), pp. 353–61

Guidi, Pietro. 1932. Rationes decimarum Italiae. Tuscia I. *La decima degli anni 1274–1280* (Città del Vaticano: Biblioteca Apostolica Vaticana)

Harrell Jr., Frank E., and Charles DuPont. 2019. Hmisc: Harrell Miscellaneous. R package version 4.3-0. <https://CRAN.R-project.org/package=Hmisc>

Hastie, Trevor, Robert Tibshirani, Friedrich Leisch, Kurt Hornik, and Brian D. Ripley. 2017. mda: Mixture and Flexible Discriminant Analysis. R package version 0.4-10. <https://CRAN.R-project.org/package=mda>

Hefner, Joseph T., Marin A. Pilloud, Jane E. Buikstra, and Caitlin C. M. Vogelsberg. 2016. 'A Brief History of Biological Distance Analysis', in *Biological Distance Analysis: Forensic and Bioarchaeological Perspectives*, ed. by Marin A. Pilloud and Joseph T. Hefner (London: Elsevier), pp. 3–22

Hengen, Otto P. 1971. 'Cribra Orbitalia: Pathogenesis and Probable Etiology', *Journal of Human Evolution*, 22: 57–75

Hens, Samantha M., and Ann H. Ross. 2017. 'Cranial Variation and Biodistance in Imperial Roman Cemeteries', *International Journal of Osteoarchaeology*, 27: 880–87

von Hessen, Otto. 1971. *Primo contributo all'archeologia longobarda in Toscana: le necropoli* (Florence: Olschki)

———. 1975. *Secondo contributo all'archeologia longobarda in Toscana. Reperti isolati e di provenienza incerta* (Florence: L.S. Olschki)

Holland, Thomas D., and Michael J. O'Brien. 1997. 'Parasites, Porotic Hyperostosis, and the Implications of Changing Perspectives', *American Antiquity*, 62.2: 183–93

Horden, Peregrine, and Nicholas Purcell. 2000. *The Corrupting Sea: A Study of Mediterranean History* (Malden: Blackwell)

Howells, William W. 1973. *Cranial Variation in Man: A Study by Multivariate Analysis of Patterns of Differences among Recent Human Populations*, Papers of the Peabody Museum of Archaeology and Ethnology, 67 (Cambridge: Peabody Museum)

Işcan, M. Yaşar, Susan R. Loth, and Ronald K. Wright. 1984. 'Age Estimation from the Rib by Phase Analysis: White Males', *Journal of Forensic Sciences*, 29.4: 1094–104

———. 1985. 'Age Estimation from the Rib by Phase Analysis: White Females', *Journal of Forensic Sciences*, 30.3: 853–63

Jacques, François. 1984. *Le privilège de liberté. Politique impériale et autonomie municipale dans les cités de l'Occident romain* (Rome: École française de Rome)

Jantz, Richard L., and Stephan D. Ousley. 2005. FORDISC 3. Knoxville, TN: University of Tennessee

Kassambara, Alboukadel, and Fabian Mundt. 2019. factoextra: Extract and Visualize the Results of Multivariate Data Analyses. R package version 1.0.6. <https://CRAN.R-project.org/package=factoextra>

Kehr, Paul Fridolin. 1908. *Italia Pontificia*, vol. III (Berlin: n.pub)

Kenyhercz, Michael W., and Nicholas V. Passalacqua. 2016. 'Missing Data Imputation Methods and their Performance with Biodistance Analyses', in *Biological Distance Analysis: Forensic and Bioarchaeological Perspectives*, ed. by Marin A. Pilloud and Joseph T. Hefner (San Diego: Academic Press), pp. 181–94

Killgrove, Kristina, and Janet Montgomery. 2016. 'All Roads Lead to Rome: Exploring Human Migration to the Eternal City through Biochemistry of Skeletons from Two Imperial-Era Cemeteries (1st–3rd c. AD)', *PLoS ONE*, 11.2: 1–30

Kuhn, Max, Jed Wing, Steve Weston, Andre Williams, Chris Keefer, Allan Engelhardt, Tony Cooper, Zachary Mayer, Brenton Kenkel, R Core Team, and others. 2019. caret: Classification and Regression Training. R package version 6.0–84. <https://CRAN.R-project.org/package=caret>

Kurze, Wilhelm. 2001. 'Rusellae-Sovana', in *Vescovo e città nell'Alto Medioevo: quadri generali e realtà toscane, Atti del convegno*, ed. by Giampaolo Francesconi (Pistoia: Società Pistoiese di Storia Patria), pp. 321–53

Kurze, Wilhelm, and Carlo Citter. 1995. 'La Toscana', in *Città, castelli, campagne nei territori di frontiera (secoli VI–VII), Atti del V Seminario sul tardoantico e l'alto medioevo in Italia centro-settentrionale*, ed. by Gian Pietro Brogiolo (Mantova: Società Archeologica Padana), pp. 159–81

La Rocca, Cristina. 1986. 'Dark Ages a Verona: edilizia privata, aree aperte e strutture pubbliche in una città dell'Italia settentrionale', *Archeologia medievale* XIII: 31–78

———. 1994. '*Castrum vel potius civitas*. Modelli di declino urbano in Italia settentrionale durante l'Alto Medioevo', in *La storia dell'altomedioevo italiano (VI–X secolo) alla luce dell'archeologia, Atti del convegno internazionale*, ed. by Riccardo Francovich and Ghislaine Noyé (Florence: All'Insegna del Giglio), pp. 545–54

Laviosa, Clelia. 1959. '*Rusellae*. Relazione preliminare della prima campagna di scavi', *Studi Etruschi*, XXVII: 3–40

———. 1960. '*Rusellae*. Relazione preliminare della seconda campagna di scavi', *Studi Etruschi*, XXVIII: 289–337

———. 1961. '*Rusellae*. Relazione preliminare della terza campagna di scavi', *Studi Etruschi*, XXIX: 31–45

———. 1963. '*Rusellae*. Relazione preliminare della quarta campagna di scavi', *Studi Etruschi*, XXXI: 39–62

———. 1965. '*Rusellae*. Relazione preliminare della quinta e della sesta campagna di scavi', *Studi Etruschi*, XXXIII: 23–54

———. 1969. '*Rusellae*. Relazione preliminare della settima e dell'ottava campagna di scavi', *Studi Etruschi*, XXXVII: 577–609

———. 1971. '*Rusellae*. Relazione preliminare della nona e della decima campagna di scavi', *Studi Etruschi*, XXXIX: 521–56

Lê, Sébastien, Julie Josse, and François Husson. 2008. 'FactoMineR: An R Package for Multivariate Analysis', *Journal of Statistical Software*, 25.1: 1–18, <10.18637/jss.v025.i01>

Leach, Stephany, Mary Lewis, Carolyn Chenery, Gundula Müldner, and Hella Eckardt. 2009. 'Migration and Diversity in Roman Britain: A Multidisciplinary Approach to the Identification of Immigrants in Roman York, England', *American Journal of Physical Anthropology*, 140: 546–61

Leach, Stephany, Hella Eckardt, Carolyn Chenery, Gundula Müldner, and Mary Lewis. 2010. 'A Lady of York: Migration, Ethnicity and Identity in Roman Britain', *Antiquity*, 84: 131–45

Liverani, Paolo. 2017. 'Rusellae tardoantica e l'ultima attestazione dell'*ordo Rusellanorum*', in *Epigrafia e società dell'Etruria romana, Atti del Convegno*, ed. by Giovanni Alberto Cecconi, Andrea Raggi, and Eleonora Salomone Gaggero (Rome: Quasar), pp. 237–60

Lovejoy, C. Owen, Richard S. Meindl, Thomas R. Pryzbeck, and Robert P. Mensforth. 1985. 'Chronological Metamorphosis of the Auricular Surface of the Ilium: A New Method for Determination of Adult Skeletal Age at Death', *American Journal of Physical Anthropology*, 68: 15–28

Lusuardi Siena, Silvia. 1987. 'Luni paleocristiana ed altomedievale nelle vicende della sua cattedrale', *Quaderni del Centro Studi Lunensi*, 10–12 (1985–1987): 289–320

Maetzke, Guglielmo. 1959. 'Necropoli barbariche nel territorio grossetano', *Notizie degli scavi*: 66–88

Malavolti, Orlando. 1559. *Dell'historia di Siena* (Siena)

Manacorda, Daniele. 1979. 'Considerazioni sull'epigrafia della regione di Cosa', *Athenaeum*, 57: 73–97

Marciniak, Stephanie, D. Ann Herring, Alessandra Sperduti, Hendrik N. Poinar, and Tracy L. Prowse. 2018. 'A Multi-Faceted Anthropological and Genomic Approach to Framing *Plasmodium falciparum* Malaria in Imperial Period Central-Southern Italy (1st – 4th c. CE)', *Journal of Anthropological Archaeology*, 49: 210–24

Marelli, Ugo. 1984. 'L'epigrafe di Decio a Cosa e l'epiteto di *restitutor sacrorum*', *Aevum*, 58: 52–56

Marrucchi, Giulia. 1998. *Chiese medievali della Maremma grossetana. Architettura e decorazione religiosa tra la Val di Farma e i Monti dell'Uccellina* (Empoli: Editori dell'Acero)

McIlvaine, Britney Kyle. 2015. 'Implications of Reappraising the Iron-Deficiency Anemia Hypothesis', *International Journal of Osteoarchaeology*, 25: 997–1000

Moorrees, Coenraad F., Elizabeth A. Fanning, and Edward E. Hunt Jr. 1963. 'Age Variation of Formation Stages for Ten Permanent Teeth', *Journal of Dental Research*, 42.6: 1490–502

Nicosia, Francesco, and Gabriella Poggesi (eds). 1998. *Rusellae. Guida al parco archeologico* (Siena: Nuova Immagine Editrice)

Newfield, Timothy P. 2017. 'Malaria and Malaria-Like Disease in the Early Middle Ages', *Early Medieval Europe*, 25.3: 251–300

Ortner, Donald J. (ed.). 2003. *Identification of Pathological Conditions in Human Skeletal Remains* (San Diego: Academic Press)

Ousley, Stephan D. 2014. 3Skull. Version 1.76

Oxenham, Marc Fredrick, and Ivor Cavill. 2010. 'Porotic Hyperostosis and Cribra Orbitalia: The Erythropoietic Response to Iron-Deficiency Anaemia', *Anthropological Science*, 118.3: 199–200

Pazienza, Anna Maria. 2016. 'Una regione periferica del Regno? La Tuscia in età longobarda', in *I Longobardi oltre Pavia: conquista, irradiazione, intrecci culturali*, ed. by Giancarlo Mazzoli and Giuseppe Micieli (Milan: Cisalpino), pp. 33–52

Polock, Marlene. 1996. 'La diocesi di Grosseto, già di Rusellae, fino al 1198', in *La Cattedrale di Grosseto e il suo popolo 1295–1995, Atti del convegno*, ed. by Vittorio Burattini (Grosseto: I Portici), pp. 195–208

Prowse, Tracy L., Henry P. Schwarcz, Peter Garnsey, Martin Knyf, Roberto Macchiarelli, and Luca Bondioli. 2007. 'Isotopic Evidence for Age-Related Immigration to Imperial Rome', *American Journal of Physical Anthropology*, 132: 510–19

R Core Team. 2013. R: A Language and Environment for Statistical Computing. R Foundation for Statistical Computing, Vienna, Austria. <www.R-project.org/>

Radi, Nico, Valentina Mariotti, Alessandro Riga, Stefania Zampetti, Chiara Villa, and M. Giovanna Belcastro. 2013. 'Variation of the Anterior Aspect of the Femoral Head-Neck Junction in a Modern Human Identified Skeletal Collection', *American Journal of Physical Anthropology*, 152: 261–72

Ram, Karthik, and Hadley Wickham. 2018. wesanderson: A Wes Anderson Palette Generator. R package version 0.3.6. <https://CRAN.R-project.org/package=wesanderson>

Redfern, Rebecca C., Darren R. Gröcke, Andrew R. Millard, Victoria Ridgeway, Luci Johnson, and Joseph T. Hefner. 2016. 'Going South of the River: A Multidisciplinary Analysis of Ancestry, Mobility and Diet in a Population from Roman Southwark, London', *Journal of Archaeological Science*, 74: 11–22

Revelle, William. 2018. psych: Procedures for Personality and Psychological Research, Northwestern University, Evanston, Illinois, USA, <https://CRAN.R-project.org/package=psychVersion=1.8.12>

Rizzitelli, Claudia. 1999. 'Rusellae', in *Archeologia urbana in Toscana. La città altomedievale*, ed. by Sauro Gelichi (Mantova: Società Archeologica Padana), pp. 105–16

Ronzani, Mauro. 1996. 'Prima della cattedrale: le chiese del vescovato Rusellae-Grosseto dall'età tardo-antica all'inizio del secolo XIV', in *La Cattedrale di Grosseto e il suo popolo 1295–1995, Atti del convegno*, ed. by Vittorio Burattini (Grosseto: I Portici), pp. 157–94

Rusellae. 1977. *Rusellae: gli scavi e la mostra, Catalogo della mostra permanente* (Pisa: Pacini)

Sabbatani, Sergio, Roberto Manfredi, and Sirio Fiorino. 2010. 'Malaria Infection and Human Evolution: Infections in the History of Medicine', *Le Infezioni in Medicina*, 1: 56–74

Sallares, Robert. 2002. *Malaria and Rome: A History of Malaria in Ancient Italy* (Oxford: Oxford University Press)

Sallares, Robert, and Susan Gomzi. 2001. 'Biomolecular Archaeology of Malaria', *Ancient Biomolecules*, 3: 195–213

Sallares, Robert, Abigail Bouwman, and Cecilia Anderung. 2004. 'The Spread of Malaria to Southern Europe in Antiquity: New Approaches to Old Problems', *Medical History*, 48: 311–28

Saladino, Vincenzo. 1980. 'Iscrizioni latine da Rusellae III', *Zeitschrift für Papyrologie und Epigraphik*, 40: 229–48

Schaefer, Maureen, Sue Black, and Louise Scheuer. 2009. *Juvenile Osteology: A Laboratory and Field Manual* (London: Academic Press)

Scheidel, Walter. 2009. 'Disease and Death in the Ancient City of Rome', *Princeton/Stanford Working Papers in Classics*, <www.princeton.edu/~pswpc/pdfs/scheidel/040901.pdf> [accessed 15 December 2019]

——. 2015. 'Death and the City: Ancient Rome and Beyond', *Princeton/Stanford Working Papers in Classics*, <http://dx.doi.org/10.2139/ssrn.2609651> [accessed 20 December 2019]

Schneider, Fedor. 1914/1975. *L'ordinamento pubblico nella Toscana medievale. I fondamenti dell'amministrazione regia in Toscana dalla fondazione del regno longobardo alla estinzione degli Svevi, 568–1268*, ed. by Fabrizio Barbolani di Montauto (Florence: Grafiche F.lli Stianti)

Sebastiani, Alessandro. 2016. 'New Data for a Preliminary Understanding of the Roman Settlement Network in South Coastal Tuscany. The Case of Alberese (Grosseto, IT)', *Res Antiquae*, 13: 243–72

——. 2017. 'From Villa to Village. Late Roman to Early Medieval Settlement Networks in the *ager Rusellanus*', in *Encounters, Excavations and Argosies: Essays for Richard Hosged*, ed. by John Moreland, John Mitchell, and Bea Leal (Oxford: Archaeopress), pp. 281–90

Shaw, Brent D. 1996. 'Seasons of Death: Aspects of Mortality in Imperial Rome', *The Journal of Roman Studies*, 86: 100–38

Smith, Holly B. 1991. 'Standards of Human Tooth Formation and Dental Age Assessment', in *Advances in Dental Anthropology*, ed. by Mark A. Kelley and Clark Spencer Larsen (New York: Wiley-Liss), pp. 143–68

Sievert, Carson. 2018. plotly for R. <https://plotly-r.com>

Smith-Guzmán, Nicole E. 2015. 'The Skeletal Manifestation of Malaria: An Epidemiological Approach Using Documented Skeletal Collections', *American Journal of Physical Anthropology*, 158: 624–35

Sodi, Stefano. 2005. 'Le origini del monachesimo insulare nell'Arcipelago Toscano', in *Da Populonia a Massa Marittima: i 1500 anni di una diocesi, Atti del convegno*, ed. by Anna Benvenuti (Florence: Editrice la Mandragora), pp. 97–109

Sordi, Marta. 1996. 'Ipotesi sull'origine del Cristianesimo in Etruria', in *La Cattedrale di Grosseto e il suo popolo 1295–1995, Atti del convegno*, ed. by Vittorio Burattini (Grosseto: I Portici), pp. 13–20

Soren, David. 2003. 'Can Archaeologists Excavate Evidence of Malaria?', *World Archaeology*, 35.2: 193–209

Soren, David, Todd Fenton, and Walter Birkby. 1995. 'The Late Roman Infant Cemetery Near Lugnano in Teverina, Italy: Some Implications', *Journal of Paleopathology*, 7.1: 13–42

——. 1999. 'The Infant Cemetery at Poggio Gramignano: Description and Analysis', in *A Roman Villa and a Late Roman Infant Cemetery*, ed. by David Soren and Noelle Soren (Rome: L'Erma di Bretschneider), pp. 477–530

Stuart-Macadam, Patricia. 1992. 'Anemia in Past Human Populations', in *Diet Demography and Disease, Changing Perspectives on Anemia*, ed. by Patricia Stuart-Macadam and Susan Kent (New York: Aldine), pp. 151–70

Ubelaker, Douglas H. 1989. 'The Estimation of Age at Death from Immature Human Bone', in *Age Markers in the Human Skeleton*, ed. by M. Yaşar İşcan (Springfield: Charles C. Thomas), pp. 55–70

Vaccaro, Emanuele. 2005. 'Il sepolcreto di età longobarda presso La Pescaia nel quadro delle evidenze insediative e funerarie della valle del Bruna', in *Roccastrada e il suo territorio. Insediamenti, arte, storia, economia*, ed. by Roberto Farinelli and Giulia Marrucchi (Empoli: Editori dell'Acero), pp. 21–26

——. 2011. *Sites and Pots: Settlement and Economy in Southern Tuscany (AD 300–900)*, BAR Series 2191 (Oxford: Archeopress)

Vai, Stefania, Andrea Brunelli, Alessandra Modi, Francesca Tassi, Chiara Vergata, Elena Pilli, Martina Lari, Roberta Rosa Susca, Caterina Giostra, Luisella Pejrani Baricco, and others 2019. 'A Genetic Perspective on Longobard-Era Migrations', *European Journal of Human Genetics*, 27: 647–56

van Buuren, Stef, and Karin Groothuis-Oudshoorn. 2011. 'mice: Multivariate Imputation by Chained Equations in R', *Journal of Statistical Software*, 45.3: 1–67, <www.jstatsoft.org/v45/i03/>

Venables, Bill, and Brian Ripley (eds). 2002. *Modern Applied Statistics with S*, Fourth Edition (New York: Springer)

Walker, Phillip L., Rhonda R. Bathurst, Rebecca Richman, Thor Gjerdrum, and Valerie A. Andrushko. 2009. 'The Causes of Porotic Hyperostosis and Cribra Orbitalia: A Reappraisal of the Iron-Deficiency Anemia Hypothesis', *American Journal of Physical Anthropology*, 139: 109–25

Wei, Taiyun, and Viliam Simko. 2017. R package 'corrplot': Visualization of a Correlation Matrix (Version 0.84). Available from <https://github.com/taiyun/corrplot>

Weihs, Claus, Uwe Ligges, Karsten Luebke, and Nils Raabe. 2005. 'klaR Analyzing German Business Cycles' in *Data Analysis and Decision Support*, ed. by Daniel Baier, Reinhold Decker, and Lars Schmidt-Thieme (Berlin: Springer), pp. 335–43

Weiland, Jonathan. 2011. 'Malaria in Etruria', *Etruscan Studies*, 14.1: 97–106

Wickham, Hadley. 2007. 'Reshaping Data with the reshape package', *Journal of Statistical Software*, 21.12: 1–20, <www.jstatsoft.org/v21/i12/>

Wickham, Hadley, Mara Averick, Jennifer Bryan, Winston Chang, Lucy D'Agostino McGowan, Romain François, Garrett Grolemund, Alex Hayes, Lionel Henry, Jim Hester, and others 2019. 'Welcome to the tidyverse', *Journal of Open Source Software*, 4.43: 1686, <https://doi.org/10.21105/joss.01686>

Wood, James W., George R. Milner, Henry C. Harpending, and Kenneth M. Weiss. 1992. 'The Osteological Paradox: Problems of Inferring Prehistoric Health from Skeletal Samples', *Current Anthropology*, 33.4: 343–70

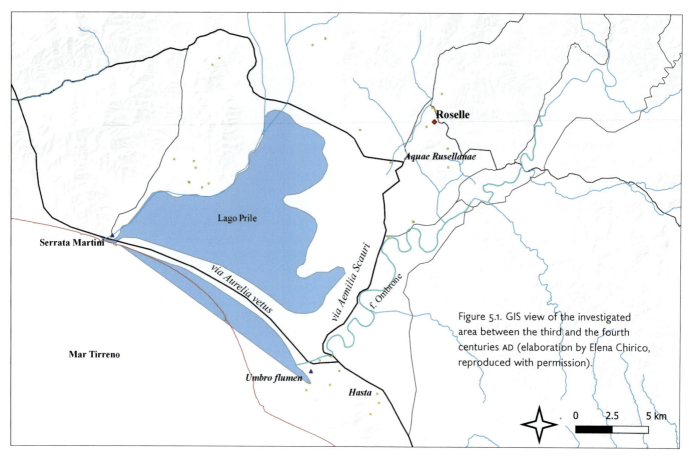

Figure 5.1. GIS view of the investigated area between the third and the fourth centuries AD (elaboration by Elena Chirico, reproduced with permission).

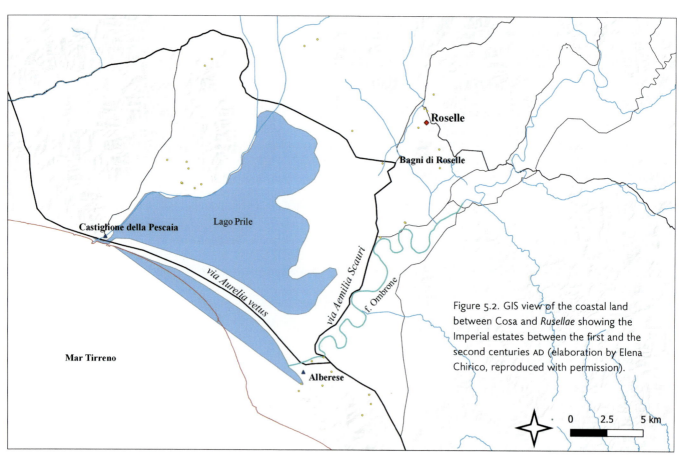

Figure 5.2. GIS view of the coastal land between Cosa and *Rusellae* showing the Imperial estates between the first and the second centuries AD (elaboration by Elena Chirico, reproduced with permission).

ELENA CHIRICO AND ALESSANDRO SEBASTIANI

5. The Coastal *ager Rusellanus* between the Fourth and Sixth Centuries AD

Introduction

This chapter details the settlement networks that came into being along the coastal area of the *ager Rusellanus* between the time of Constantine and the Lombard conquest in AD 590. The timeframe in question first saw the constitution of *Tuscia* and then, from the second half of the fourth century AD, of *Tuscia Suburbicaria*. The investigated area corresponds to the strip of land found between the modern town of Castiglione della Pescaia (Roman *Salebro*) and Alberese, which in the Imperial period was administrated by the city of *Rusellae* (Fig. 5.1).

Our aim is to describe the developments and changes in this region through an assessment of the known Roman infrastructure within the landscape and of the central places built along the main routes (whether terrestrial, riverine, or maritime) that acted as marketplaces and aggregation poles for local communities. The chapter focuses on three main settlement areas: Alberese, Bagni di Roselle, and Castiglione della Pescaia. These settled nuclei were connected through an articulated network represented by the *via Aurelia vetus*, the *via Aemilia Scauri*, the Ombrone river, and the Tyrrhenian Sea. Recent studies on the geology of the area have shown that the coastline was some five kilometres east of the modern shore, while the actual plain between Grosseto and Castiglione was occupied by the now drained *Lacus Prilis* (Arnoldus-Huyzendveld 2007; Arnoldus-Huyzendveld and Citter 2015; Luti and others 2000). Moreover, data collected during the excavations carried out by the Alberese Archaeological Project (Sebastiani 2016b, 2017; Sebastiani and others 2015), the analysis of some of the settlements investigated by the Soprintendenza, such as the *mansio* of Hasta (Poggesi 2004, 113–16), the Roman villa at Sterpeto/San Martino (Vaccaro 2011, 251), and the great bathhouse complex

at Bagni di Roselle (Chirico 2019b, 2021), together with the reassessment of the archival documentation of the Roman villa estate at Paduline/Serrata Martini (Ademollo 1880; Cygielman 2014) enrich our understanding of this zone, providing a view of a much more intricated and sophisticated settlement network than previously postulated.

The investigated area's strategic position along the Tyrrhenian coast was one of the key factors determining its economic success. The settlements in question were all an integral part of the supply network for the capital city between the late first and early second centuries AD; it is in this period that the area became part of the Imperial estate, the first southern nucleus of which started under the reign of Nero with the public acquisition of the coastal area between Cosa and Talamone along with the islands of Giglio and Giannutri (Ciampoltrini and Rendini 2005; Sebastiani 2016b, 265–66) (Fig. 5.2). The Imperial acquisition coincided with a very large-scale infrastructure program during the reigns of Trajan and Hadrian, which within a few decades, led to the creation of an efficient system of ports north of Rome, essential in ensuring the regular supply of the Roman *annona*. At one extreme of this supply line lay the Roman villa at Paduline/Serrata Martini, which served as an essential connection with the *Portus Cosanus* and the islands of Giglio and Giannutri (Rendini 2008, 2016).

Further south, supply routes were structured around Imperial residences and cabotage ports located at the mouth of various rivers such as *Umbro flumen* at Alberese (Chirico 2019c; Sebastiani and others 2016). It is argued here that this economic and settlement network persisted into the late Roman period, adapting itself to the unique political and socio-economic transformations of the later Empire, while a moment

Elena Chirico (chiricoelena@gmail.com) Independent Scholar

Alessandro Sebastiani (as424@buffalo.edu) University at Buffalo (SUNY)

Archaeological Landscapes of Late Antique and Early Medieval Tuscia: Research and Field Papers, ed. by Riccardo Rao and Alessandro Sebastiani, MEDITO 3 (Turnhout 2023), pp. 88–105
BREPOLS PUBLISHERS   DOI 10.1484/M.MEDITO-EB.5.133995

of fraction and discontinuity can be recognized in the later sixth century AD, when large portions, if not the entirety, of all local settlements were abandoned and never reoccupied.

In what follows, we provide an overview of the settlement network characterizing the coastal area of the *ager Rusellanus* between the fourth and sixth centuries AD, highlighting the continuity and changes that occurred in the occupational sequences of its various central places.

Settlements in the Fourth Century AD

In the fourth century AD, the *ager Rusellanus* was an essential access point for goods moving across the Tyrrhenian Sea trade routes, featuring an articulated road system linking the coast and the hinterland, as well as the area between *Rusellae* and its various landing places. The maritime ports at Serrata Martini and at *Umbro flumen* were also connected with the inland through the *via Aurelia vetus*, while the *via Aemilia Scauri* ran through the hinterland, guaranteeing connectivity between *Umbro flumen*, Bagni di Roselle, and *Rusellae*. A vast array of public infrastructure, including several *mansiones* such as *Hasta*, *Aquae Rusellanae*, and Sterpeto/San Martino, served to further integrate the network. These important stopover points facilitated the movement of agrarian goods, lumber,[1] products of pastoralism, and livestock for breeding to the main city. Furthermore, from the third century AD onward, the Tyrrhenian ports assured the continuous supply of wine, olive oil, garum, objects, and common vessels from the provinces, especially from Tunisia, Baetica, Lusitania, central Italy, and northern *Tuscia*.

The Area of Alberese

Umbro flumen: The port structures have not been documented, while the building connected to a *mansio/positio* at Prima Golena was discovered thanks to an aerial photograph showing a square plan typical of such structures (Fig. 5.3). The aerial photograph additionally shows the passage of the *via Aurelia vetus* a few metres from the building. The consular road headed towards Castiglione della Pescaia was located some miles north of Prima Golena, while the inland *via Aemilia Scauri*,

located across the Ponte del Diavolo, was recorded in the *Catasto Leopoldino* at the last bend taken by the Ombrone river before reaching *Rusellae*. Excavations at Prima Golena are still in progress, with only a portion of the building having been uncovered and the material studies still ongoing, but a preliminary sketch can be provided. A late antique occupation of the site is documented by two rooms whose materials date to between the fourth and late fifth centuries AD. The first room, situated in a portion of the building previously used as a central courtyard, is interpreted a kitchen due to the presence of two hearths, burnt ash layers, and various burnt ceramics, jars, tableware, and some oil lamps of local production attested throughout the *ager Rusellanus* during the fourth century AD. The second room is more difficult to interpret and features a raised *opus spicatum* floor, creating a sort of platform. A system of channels in the room indicates some form of production activity that is currently unspecifiable. The *mansio*, or a portion of it, therefore seems to taken on a more utilitarian character in this century, perhaps in relation to the nearby manufacturing district at Spolverino, located on the last bend of the Ombrone river and connected to a riverine harbour (Chirico 2019c).

Spolverino: The manufacturing district constitutes a small portion of a larger production-port facility built along the Ombrone river in the direction of *Rusellae* (Sebastiani 2014, 2016a, 2016b). The investigated area contained a series of contiguous rectangular or quadrangular rooms, used as workshops and differentiated in their primary production (Fig. 5.4). An analogous settlement at La Giuncola, another productive settlement along the Ombrone river, presents a similar plan, including a series of contiguous, modularly organized rooms, with a similar material record and chronological horizon (Chirico and Sebastiani Forthcoming). The manufacturing district was enlarged and reorganized to host several workshops between the late third and early fourth centuries AD, a range suggested by the material finds. Two stamped bricks further specify the chronology of this intervention, or part of it, to the age of Maxentius.[2] A glass and metal workshop, the latter focusing on the recycling and production of lead bullion, were built (Sebastiani 2016a; Sebastiani and Derrick 2016, 2020) and were served by a common kitchen, an arrangement similar to that documented at Prima Golena. A later intervention is recorded between the second half of the fourth and middle of the fifth centuries AD when a room is set up for the

---

1   Lumber trade and exchange is recorded in Livy (Ab Urbe Condita, 28.45.18) for the Republican era. Given the proximity of the location to Mount Amiata and the ongoing commercial routes through the middle valley of the Ombrone river, we can assume that this activity persisted into the Imperial period. The navigability of the lower section of the river has been recently determined in Ghisleni and others 2011.

2   CIL XV 1570a: Officina summae rei officina Domitiana AD 278–312.

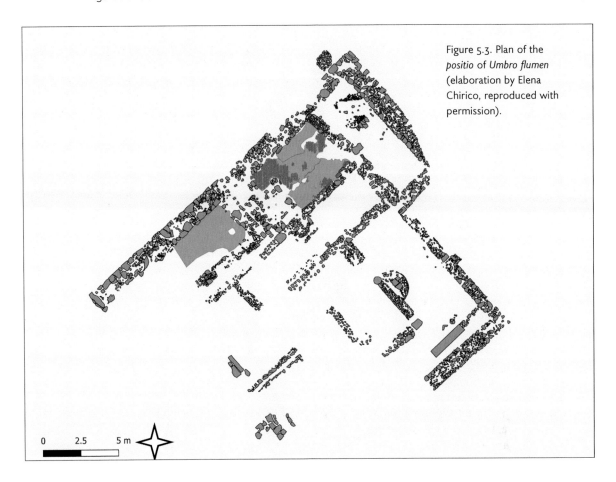

Figure 5.3. Plan of the *positio* of *Umbro flumen* (elaboration by Elena Chirico, reproduced with permission).

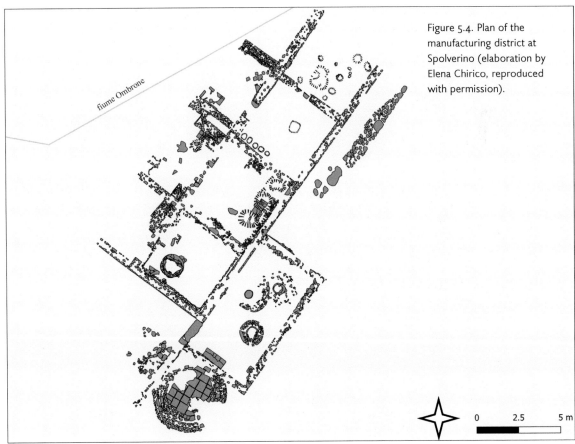

Figure 5.4. Plan of the manufacturing district at Spolverino (elaboration by Elena Chirico, reproduced with permission).

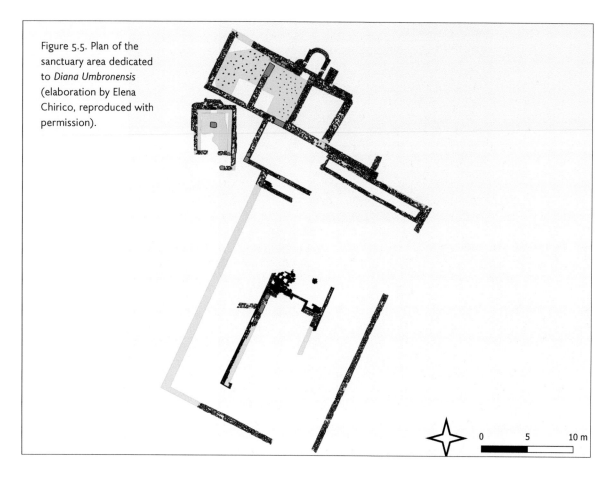

Figure 5.5. Plan of the sanctuary area dedicated to *Diana Umbronensis* (elaboration by Elena Chirico, reproduced with permission).

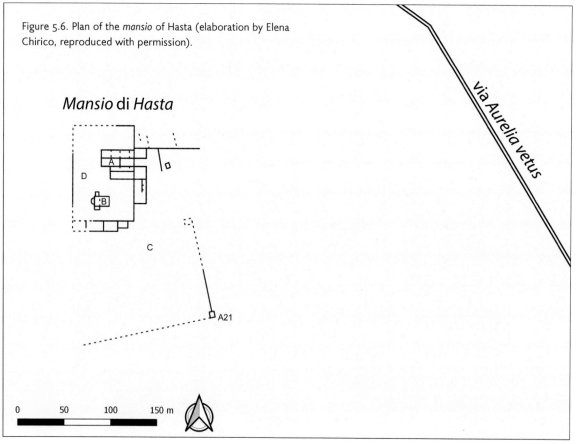

Figure 5.6. Plan of the *mansio* of Hasta (elaboration by Elena Chirico, reproduced with permission).

conservation of foodstuffs, with amphorae and vessels partially inserted at the ground level.

Scoglietto: Contrary to the building and production investment documented at Spolverino and *Umbro flumen*, at Scoglietto the temple of *Diana Umbronensis* had been rebuilt in the early third century AD but had already fallen into a state of neglect by the beginning of the next century (Chirico and Colombini 2015) (Fig. 5.5). A small necropolis was installed within its ruins, where a single *in situ* burial was identified, preserving a *nummus* of Constantine II dated to AD 348. Meanwhile, the remains of eight other possible inhumates were recovered in the filling levels of the cistern.[3] At the end of the century, the temple was reduced to ruins and subsequently dismantled, as suggested by large blocks of masonry and a layer of marble chips. A fragment of a statue head could be distinguished in this context, recovered at the entrance of the temple and interpreted as evidence for the possible destruction of the cult statue. Despite the destruction of the temple, the ancient cult continued to survive for a few decades before being completely forgotten; the significant number of fourth- to fifth-century AD oil lamps recovered around the structure are interpreted as a symbol of the ongoing devotion of some worshippers (Brando 2015).

Vacchereccia: Not far from Scoglietto, at Vacchereccia, the field survey carried out by Emanuele Vaccaro in the territory of Alberese recorded a farm occupied between the fourth and early sixth centuries AD, as suggested by the recovery of fragments of African Red Slip Ware D (Hayes 71, 76, and 91), imitations of Hayes 61 bowls with red slip and plain ware, containers from Tunisia, and an example of an amphora from Empoli (Vaccaro 2011, 255–56).

Montesanto: Located along the *via Aurelia vetus*, the Villa of Podere Montesanto was built during the first century AD and continued to be used until at least the fourth century (Poggesi 2004, 116–19; Vaccaro 2011, 257). A rescue excavation carried out by the Soprintendenza in the 1990s brought to light twenty-one parallel walls, tentatively interpreted as functional spaces but perhaps having served as corridors or passages between different rooms. The materials recovered consist mostly of *terra sigillata* in use between the first and third centuries AD. Meanwhile, a field survey in the lower terrace of the site documented a later occupation running until the sixth

century AD, with materials ranging from African Red Slip Ware A, C, and D, Tunisian and Spanish amphorae, fine ware imitating Hayes 61, and cooking ware often found within the territory and the city of *Rusellae*.

Hasta: The *Tabula Peutingeriana* registers the *mansio* of Hasta along the *via Aurelia* (IV, 3). The structure was identified in 1987 just outside of the modern village of Alberese, in the locality of Le Frasche, during agricultural works which brought about the near total destruction of the complex (Poggesi 2004, 113–16; Sebastiani 2015, 14). Newspapers from the period record the havoc wreaked on the villa, 'chopped up' by tractors that devastated the Roman building for months on end, churning up marble slabs, mosaic fragments, pipes, vessels, nails, human bones, remains of painted plaster, and coins. Aerial photographs captured some years before the destruction of the building allow for a reconstruction of the layout of the *mansio*, which was definitively destroyed during agricultural work in 1993. On this occasion, the intervention of the Soprintendenza per i Beni Archeologici della Toscana secured the partial recuperation of materials, including masonry blocks and structural features, along with a ground survey whose data are presented here. The *mansio* sat around 300 m from the *via Aurelia vetus*, which it faced on its western side. It took the form of a courtyard structure organized within a rectangular enclosure occupying an area of almost 6.58 m² (around 0.65 ha). Inside, another enclosure was perhaps delimited at its four corners by small lookout towers (Fig. 5.6). Room A21 constitutes the most probable evidence for a lookout tower; given the building's proximity to the roadway and the dangers this carried, it seems logical to imagine a system of three other small towers, together providing for total surveillance from the structure. The *mansio* was organized along a vast courtyard (C), inside of which must have been stalls, structures for storage, *tabernae*, service rooms, and workshops. The enclosure contained two structures, A and B, separated by an open area (D), which perhaps functioned as a garden. Structure A, in the north-west part of the garden D, constituted the central nucleus of the *mansio*. Structure B took the form of a thermal installation likely composed of an *apodyterium/frigidarium*, a *tepidarium*, and a *caldarium*. Planimetric analysis, along with consideration of the material evidence and building techniques, suggest that the *mansio*, built in a location previously frequented between the second and first centuries BC, was occupied between the age of Domitian/early second century AD and the late fifth to early sixth centuries AD. The recovery of numerous brick stamps associated with urban and Imperial workshops, meanwhile, points to the building's connection with the various public interventions occurring in this period, including the

---

3   The human remains retrieved in the cistern at Scoglietto were mixed with rubble, a sign of a profanation of their original depositions that had happened already in the fourth century AD. For further details see Aniceti 2015.

restructuring of ports and Imperial residences between Talamone and Cosa and in the islands of Giglio and Giannutri. In the course of the fourth century AD, Hasta was subjected to a programme of remodelling evidenced by various windowpanes created with the so-called 'cylinder' method, a technique with origins in the third and in exclusive use by the fourth centuries AD. Material finds confirm the occupation of the *mansio* until the late fifth to early sixth centuries AD, testifying to the full insertion of the surrounding territory into the Mediterranean exchange network and thus its dependence on imports, especially from Tunisia but also from Baetica and Lusitania for oil and garum. Meanwhile, in the period under consideration, the presence of amphorae from Empoli point to the consumption of Italian wine.

Farms: *c.* 600 m south of the *mansio*, one of the three farmhouses identified during the field study continued to be occupied. The structure, built in the third century AD, likely housed labourers working the *fundus* associated with the *mansio* of Hasta.

Podere Passerini: The complex known as Podere Passerini-Terme Leopoldine at Bagni di Roselle constituted an important piece of public infrastructure supporting the delivery and utilization of water during the periods of Trajan and Hadrian (Chirico 2019b, 2021). Thermal structures here were partially built upon the mineral springs that flowed from the south-west slopes of Poggio di Moscana, whose course was altered by the flood of 1966, but which remain active today. Based upon the properties of the water, analysed several times up to the 1980s, the site can be identified as the *Aquae Rusellanae* that, in the late sixteenth century, Phillip Clüver associated with the medieval toponym of *Bagni di Roselle*.

The settlement occupied a footprint of nearly 62,000 m² and was situated along a road connected with the *via Aemilia Scauri* heading toward *Rusellae* (Fig. 5.7). Its plan featured at least two entrances, the first of which (entrance A) was accessed via the road. The only documentation of the building's layout dates to 1823, when part of the ancient structure emerged during the construction of the so-called *Terme Leopoldine*. This plan documents a large, circular room (A1) around which two smaller, rectangular rooms of different dimensions (AA2 and AA3) were situated. According to descriptions of the excavation, a round basin (noted as *il cratere*) flanked by five *silani* styled as lions was discovered in room A1. The corridors AA4 and AA5 led to a series of rooms (D, D1), some of which were artificially heated, others of which functioned as *apodyteria* or rooms for massages and relaxation; others still might have been *tabernae*. The entire settlement was organized within an

enclosure. Three hypothetical spaces (D, D1, and D2) were arranged side by side around a vast, porticoed courtyard. The descriptions claim that the small spaces off the side of the so called *cratere* (D and D1) were heated artificially. D2, on the other hand, might have contained *tabernae*, shops, and perhaps workshops. These various sectors were linked by long and spacious corridors, such as A5, which connected the thermal sector with the area located toward the Villa Passerini (discovered and excavated by the Passerini family itself, which purchased the plot of land from the diocese in 1839). Most of the building was uncovered between 1863 and 1865. The detailed excavation descriptions of Santi, together with the plans of Passerini, provide a basis for at least a partial reconstruction of the settlement's evolution. Later investigations, including those of the former Soprintendenza Archeologica between 1994 and 2004, provide an enriched view of the building's history from the late first century AD to the medieval period.

The Passerini building develops over three levels. The excavated portion (corresponding with the first floor) was accessed by the entrance A7, which was embellished with a Cipollino marble colonnade in composite and Corinthian orders. The open space A8, likely a peristyle, lay on axis with A7. Five small rooms of various dimensions were situated around A8, perhaps sleeping chambers or service rooms. The courtyard A14 opened to the south of A7 and featured two symmetrical, square wings (AA16 and AA17). These might have been associated with spaces for dining, as suggested by the identification of one of the rooms, featuring a vaulted roof, as a *triclinium*. Other living and reception rooms, service spaces, and perhaps a few *cubicula* (most of which would have been found on the upper floor) were likely arranged to the north of A7. The various rooms documented were decorated with marble, plaster, and black-and-white mosaic pavements. The complex's residential core was probably flanked by a productive sector, suggested by two rooms discovered during surveys in 2003 featuring *cocciopesto* pavements and walls dressed in simple white plaster. Fragments of coarse-ware ceramics, two amphora walls, and a few human bones were documented in these spaces.

The structure at Podere Passerini served as the residential and administrative centre of the thermal springs. Markets were organized around the complex, strategically placed at the intersection of several roads not far from *Rusellae*, where we can imagine retail businesses taking place. Two inscriptions found in the necropolis, located near the so-called mill where three *alla cappuccina* burials were discovered without grave goods, suggest that the complex was a state-owned property managed by freedmen acting in the capacity of *procuratores*. The tombs here were covered with repurposed *tegulae*, one of which possessed a

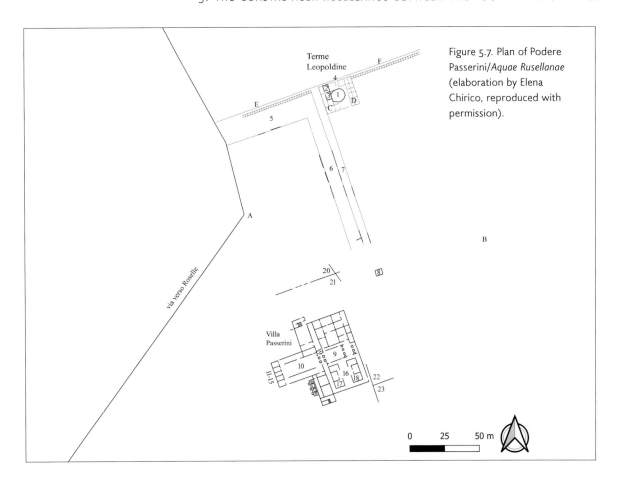

Figure 5.7. Plan of Podere Passerini/*Aquae Rusellanae* (elaboration by Elena Chirico, reproduced with permission).

stamp of the *officinator* of Plotina Pompeia, wife of Trajan. Meanwhile, two of the funerary inscriptions recall descendants of slaves freed by Hadrian and the Antonines: Aelius Agrippinus and Aurelia Saturnina (late second/early third century AD) and Vibius Romulus and Vibia Priscilla (late third/early fourth century AD). The complex was significantly restored between the late third and early fourth centuries AD, a chronological range suggested by a third-century AD capital, the marble lion heads decorating the so-called *cratere* (which inspired the erroneous identification of the structure until the mid-twentieth century as the baths of Diocletian), and by a white marble sculptural group inspired by the myth of Bacchus. Known as the *Bacco fanciullo*, the sculpture dates to between the late third and early fourth centuries AD and is conserved at the British Museum, where it has been recently studied (Guerrini 2019).

Paduline-Serrata Martini: Evidence for the port connected with the Imperial villa is limited to the underwater foundations at the mouth of the Bruna river, formed by dolia cut in half and then filled with pozzolana and stacked together. Geophysical survey conducted around 100 m north-east of the site at Paduline revealed a kind of natural bend in the river, interpreted as a canal or part of the coastline of the ancient *Lacus Prilis*. Flanking this feature were the main structures of the villa along with a section of road interpreted as a diverticulum of the *via Aurelia vetus*, portions of which were discovered in the port zone of Serrata Martini and on various occasions up to the 1960s. The villa thus flanked both the Tyrrhenian Sea and the *Lacus Prilis*, connected with the coastal area by the *via Aurelia vetus* and with the inland and *Rusellae* by the *via Aemilia Scauri*. Earthworks during the sixteenth century and again between 1776 and the 1950s, during cycles of work on an artificial canal connected with the Bruna river, greatly impacted the structure. Excavations for the *Collettore* canal in the twentieth century cut the settlement into two parts, the one to the north taking the name of Paduline and the other the name of Serrata Martini. The two settlement nuclei might have been originally connected by long and broad corridors, like in other Imperial residences. Paduline's overall plan was recorded for the first time by engineers working on the *Catasto Leopoldino*, labelled as *ruderi*. The excavation of Paduline undertaken by the Soprintendenza Archeologica between the late 1980s–1990s investigated the part of the residential core built between the late first and early second centuries AD (Fig. 5.8). This sector was attributed to Hadrian

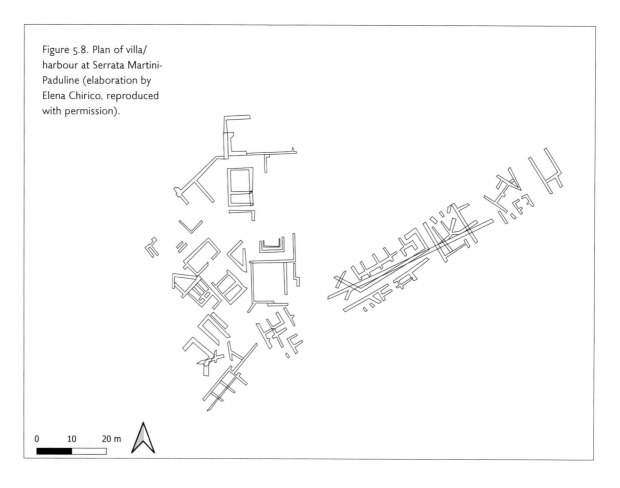

Figure 5.8. Plan of villa/harbour at Serrata Martini-Paduline (elaboration by Elena Chirico, reproduced with permission).

on the basis of various statues which were recovered, including of the emperor himself, of his wife Vibia Sabina, and two of Diana (favoured deity of Hadrian). More likely, the villa was completed by Hadrian but begun between the last years of Domitian's reign and first years of Trajan's. A late antique phase is documented in the port area of Serrata Martini, which was first investigated in the late nineteenth century, revealing a *caldarium*, *frigidarium*, and parts of a necropolis for the laborers connected with the Imperial residence and port. The excavation reports note *alla cappuccina* tombs, while other tombs were documented in the 1960s and then again during the SBAT excavations in 1998, all unfortunately lacking grave goods. Datable elements included a few brick stamps from the late Flavian period, a *dupondius* of Domitian, and most importantly, the North African amphorae reutilized for the burials themselves (Africana A2, Africana 1/Keay III, late second to early third centuries AD). These suggest a chronological horizon for the tombs ranging from between the late first and early third centuries AD up through the entire fifth century (a final chronology that is indicated by radiocarbon analysis conducted on some of the inhumated remains). Further evidence of the late antique phase is provided by ceramic materials recovered in the rubbish heaps of the baths, documenting a long occupation stretching from the late Republic (second to first centuries AD) until the late sixth century AD (Vaccaro 2011, 105–10), along with various objects described in the nineteenth-century reports, including a few coins of Constans II, two axes or hatchets from the Lombard period, and a fragment of gilded glass.

The gilded glass fragment is of particular importance (Fig. 5.9). Lost during the Second World War but documented by a photograph and drawing preserved in the Museo Archeologico e d'Arte Sacra della Maremma (Ademollo 1880, 12), it dates to the last quarter of the fourth century AD, constituting the oldest evidence thus far of a Christian presence in the pagan necropolis. The original report describes the object as a fragment of the bottom of a vessel depicting the sacrifice of Abraham or Isaac and featuring an inscription in gold letters, helping to date the fragment to the Gothic War/Byzantine period. The production of gilded glass, also known as funerary glass for its frequent memorializing/decorative use around grave niches, began in the third century AD and reached peak popularity in the fourth century, before going out of use during the sixth. Fourth-century AD examples depict both pagan and Christian scenes, the latter often inspired by Old Testament episodes such as the cycle of Jonah, Moses' miracle of the fountain, and (as is the case in the example from Serrata Martini) Abraham's sacrifice of Isaac. The Serrata Martini fragment is comparable to an example preserved at the Vatican Museums dating to the last quarter of the fourth century AD (Zanchi Roppo 1969, 197–98, n. 233, fig. 53, inv. 755). It can be partially reconstructed despite its broken state: two figures appear within a circular cornice frame, the left a nude youth beneath a tree with his hands bound behind his back, the right a figure whose face has been lost and is recognizable only by a mantel. The inscription is incomplete, running along the inside of the cornice frame and, unlike in the Vatican example, is written in Latin but with Greek letters. Ferrua interprets the phrase as '[άνιμα] δουλκις πιε ζηση[ς]' (drink and live, oh sweet spirit) (Ferrua 1974, 331), a common formula used on gilded glass objects. Corollary examples were recovered at the Villa of Faragola inscribed on three sixth-century AD lamps, reinterpreting a customary salutation used during banquets within a funerary context, perhaps in relation to the *refrigerium* ritual and indirectly to the symbolic banquet of the underworld. In recent years, studies have cast light on Rome's important role as a production centre of incised glass and its influence on popular iconography in the west. The Serrata Martini glass would have arrived from Rome via a sea landing documented further south at Santa Liberata on Monte Argentario, identified as *Domitiana positio* by the Itineraries and where various fragments of gilded glass have been recovered. This location is mentioned by the name *Insula Matidia* in a document attributed to Pope Silvester (AD 314–335) listing the various holdings donated by Constantine to the basilica of Saints Peter and Marcellinus at Rome.[4] Serrata Martini, meanwhile, does not appear on this list, pointing to a more fleeting situation. The *curtis* of La Piscaria, corresponding with the castle constructed from the seventh century AD forward and thus after the abandonment of the port village at Serrata Martini, is cited as *patrimonium Sancti Petri* in a diploma of Louis the Pious dating to AD 814 (Citter 2007b, 136). The transfer of the property into Lombard hands as a fiscal property seems to have taken place after the conquest, perhaps as part of a conciliatory policy after their conversion to Christianity.

The overview just provided is enriched by various data collected in the zone since the 1960s, which documents a notable stability of settlement patterns between the fourth and fifth centuries AD in areas such

Figure 5.9. Drawing of the gilded glass from Serrata Martini/Paduline (elaboration by Elena Chirico, reproduced with permission).

as the western bank of the *Lacus Prilis*. Sites such as the medium-large farm of *Fattoria Badiola* document an occupation lasting between the Etruscan-Roman period up to the fifth century AD. The Villa of Poggio Franco, meanwhile, ranges from the second century BC to the fifth century AD. Other sites were reoccupied between the fourth and fifth centuries AD, exploiting the lake's fishing and salt resources. The Villa of Le Mortelle, for example, was reoccupied between the fifth and mid-sixth centuries AD after an abandonment in the mid-Imperial period. The Villa of Fosso Cortigliano was reoccupied between the fourth and fifth centuries AD (Curri 1978, 135–43; Vaccaro 2011, 248–49). In the hinterland of *Rusellae*, the villas at Aiali (Vaccaro and others 2009), Casette di Mota (Vaccaro 2011, 250), and Sterpeto-San Martino (Vaccaro 2011, 251) continued to be occupied without interruption, but it is not known whether these settlements contracted; probable changes of use in these sites, meanwhile, are not always easily verifiable.

To conclude, the transformations described in several settlements between the late third and fourth centuries AD suggest a more dynamic situation in this territory than has been assumed in the past. The restorations

---

4 *Insula Matidiae — quod est mons Argentarius —* the promontory containing the Villa of Santa Liberata and the Villa of the Marucci was donated to the basilica of Saints Marcellinus and Peter (Liber Pontificalis, I, 183, ed. by Duchesne, 1955).

documented at *Aquae Rusellanae* and indicated at *Hasta* suggest a continuity of residential life and of the administrative, economic, and social organization of public power. It hardly seems a coincidence that during the precise period when the birth of the *cursus publicus* is documented at the beginning of the fourth century AD, both the state-owned properties and the various *mansiones* and stopover points throughout the rest of the peninsula were restored in an analogous manner (Corsi 2000, 2016; Kolb 2016; Lemcke 2013). These developments allowed for the tightening of state control over roads and led to the transformation of road stations into mechanisms of, to use the words of Cristina Corsi, centralized control. Such a role may have been bestowed upon such large settlements as *Aquae Rusellanae* or the *mansio* of *Hasta*, residences of the Imperial *procuratores*. Meanwhile, restoration interventions in the area of *Umbro flumen* and Spolverino (even if further research is still necessary into the former) indicate a public investment in a production-oriented infrastructure. The abandonment of the temple of *Diana Umbronensis* in Scoglietto, moreover, can be considered an effect of spiritual transformations during the rise of Christianity rather than of economic or socio-political contraction. Perhaps following the Theodosian provisions of AD 391–392 (which ordered the destruction of all sanctuaries, the death penalty for the exercising of pagan rites, and the confiscation of properties, prohibited altars, votive offerings, torches, crowns, and anything else related to pagan cults) the structure was symbolically demolished. The anti-pagan strategy of Theodosius is clear evidence that the eradication of paganism, especially in the countryside and among the lower strata of the population, was no easy task. At Scoglietto, for example, devotion to the cult persisted for decades before definitively stopping, as evidenced by various oil lamps of North African production left around the dismantled religious structure. The presence of a Christian burial in the port of Serrata Martini only strengthens this hypothesis. Its inclusion in a pagan burial ground should come as no surprise in a century that began with Constantine and a phase of ostensibly tolerant religious coexistence, in which religious identities were still being defined and negotiated, and ended with the loss of that coexistence during the reign of Theodosius.

Settlements in the Fifth Century AD

The fifth century AD can be considered the beginning of the end, marked by a series of events that strained the peninsula and squarely impacted *Tuscia*, whose territories suffered especially from Gothic raids after AD 405 and in AD 413. The state of crisis is reflected by the Imperial tax relief provided to the areas most affected by the invasions. The testimony of Rutilius[5] records that the province received such provisions for five years as a result of the *hostium incursio* in 418 and again in AD 422.[6] Elsewhere, the AD 432 Vandal conquest of Carthage led to the sudden interruption of tax revenues in Rome and eventually to the sack of Genseric in AD 455. This event might be considered the most resonant sign of crisis leading up to the collapse of the western part of the empire (Arthur 1991; Brown 2014, 417; Wickham 2003a, 9–10, 2003b, 2005, 2009, 29).

A state of crisis is archaeologically reflected by the abandonment of many settlements and the change in function of others in reaction to the needs of a weakened system. Material analysis, especially of the ports of *Umbro flumen* and Serrata Martini, confirms the image arising from other studies in which imports from North Africa did not cease immediately with the conquest of Carthage but continued until the end of the century. In other words, the fall of Carthage determined neither the decline of North African trade with the West nor the end of North African supplies for Rome; nonetheless, a significant, selective decrease in settlements is evident starting with the beginning of the fifth century AD. Imports were limited to *Rusellae*, the port areas, central places such as *Hasta*, Sterpeto-San Martino, Casette di Mota and to some sites around the urban centre.

The transformations of the fifth century AD are marked in Alberese by the abandonment of the Roman infrastructure. The landing of *Umbro flumen* and the district of Spolverino were abandoned by the end of the century, while a new type of housing is documented starting with the middle of the century: the cave (Fig. 5.10).

Spolverino: In the second half of the fifth century AD, the manufacturing district began to decline. The metallurgical atelier remained in use until the end of the century, but the kitchens and the room for storing food were abandoned. The only new activity identified is the installation of a lime kiln within which various fragments of marble were recovered, including an almost complete mortarium.

Umbro flumen: Ceramic materials indicate the abandonment of the *mansio* between the end of the century and the beginning of the sixth century AD.

---

5 Codex Th. XI, 28, 7; Rutilius, *De Reditu Suo*, I, 35–45; Cambi and Carandini 2002.

6 Codex Th. XI, 28, 6; XI, 28, 12; Sirago 1985.

5. THE COASTAL *AGER RUSELLANUS* BETWEEN THE FOURTH AND SIXTH CENTURIES AD   99

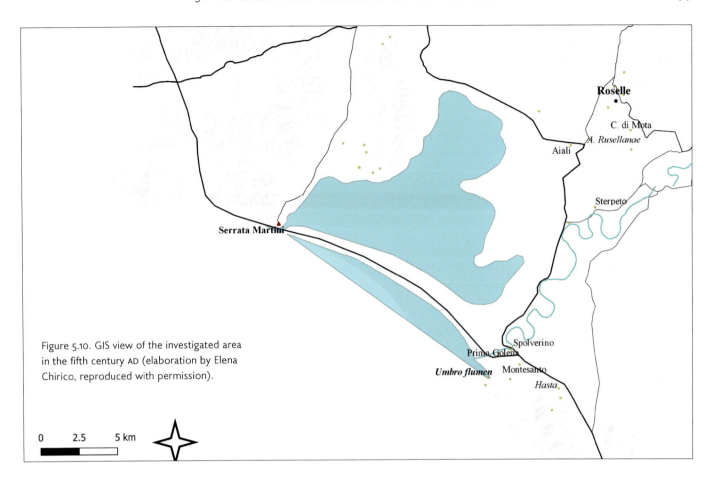

Figure 5.10. GIS view of the investigated area in the fifth century AD (elaboration by Elena Chirico, reproduced with permission).

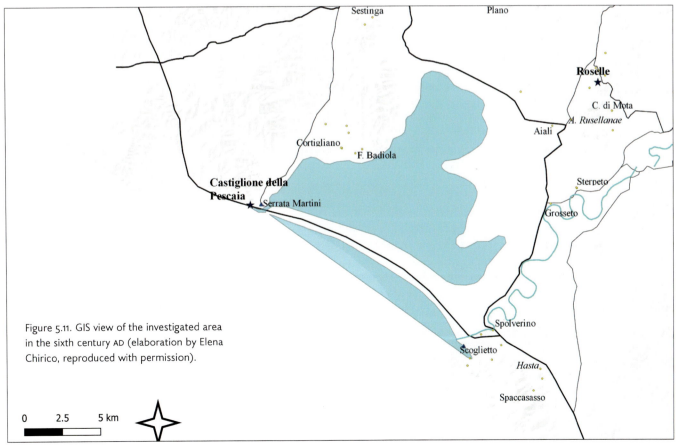

Figure 5.11. GIS view of the investigated area in the sixth century AD (elaboration by Elena Chirico, reproduced with permission).

Grotta Scoglietto: In the cave of Scoglietto below the ancient temple of Diana, which was occupied by a necropolis featuring amphora burials dating between the second century and mid-fifth to mid-sixth centuries AD, a residence and a space for exchange and commerce were constructed. The late antique occupation is documented by imports from North Africa along with local ceramics for domestic use. An important commercial role is attested by sixty-six coins datable between the second half of the third and the beginning of the fifth century AD. Two bronze coin weights, equivalent to the *solidus aureus* and the *tremissis* (*exagia*, dated between fifth and seventh centuries AD) were also recovered (Chirico 2019a, 133; De Benetti 2007a; Vaccaro 2007; 2008, 242).

Spaccasasso: In a remote area of the Uccellina Mountains is another cave with traces of occupation during the same years, between the mid-fifth and mid-sixth centuries AD. The cave was interpreted as the home of a family specializing in the exploitation of forest resources and perhaps in pig breeding. Retail exchange activities associated with the cave were also hypothesized based upon the discovery of a steelyard counterweight (*stadera*). The cave's remote position, however, was not favourable to trade. The presence of just three coins dated between the second half of the third and the fourth centuries AD, a small number compared to the Scoglietto cave, suggests an alternative identification of the cave as a dwelling for a small group of brigands operating along the *via Aurelia vetus*. Evidence of banditry is documented in the area between Cosa, Heba, and Talamone between the third and early sixth centuries AD, especially near roads (Chirico 2019a, 134–35; De Benetti 2007b; Vaccaro 2007, 234–35; 2008, 242; 2011, 25, 85, 103, 104).

Field survey indicates an unclear form of occupation for each site in question. *Hasta* and Montesanto continue to be occupied until the end of the century, along with the port district of Serrata Martini, the villas of Sterpeto-San Martino, Aiali, Casette di Mota in the hinterland of *Rusellae*, and perhaps *Aquae Rusellanae* (although evidence for this site in particular is lacking). It is very likely that these central places lost their essential functions during the fifth century AD, following the fate of the public institutions that had generated them.

Settlements in the Sixth Century AD

Because the Gothic occupation did not bring about obvious changes in the state administrative machinery, it is effectively invisible archaeologically. The situation was markedly different, however, during the Byzantine phase, particularly during the years of conflict that ended with a brief period of Byzantine domination. At the beginning of the sixth century AD, a major shift in agrarian systems is evident throughout the territory in question, with nearly all its villas and infrastructure abandoned and reoccupied by small nuclei of necropolises (Fig. 5.11).

Hasta: Among the finds that came to light during construction works in 1987 were various human bones, suggesting the presence of a small cemetery on the site of the ancient *mansio*, similar to what is documented in Scoglietto and Spolverino.

Scoglietto: The ancient promontory was occupied by a community whose presence is indicated by a hut of the *Grubenhäuser* type built among the ruins of the Severian temple. Ceramic materials along with a Byzantine *denarius* dating to the middle of the sixth century AD suggest a general chronology. The house appears to have been destroyed by a fire in the middle of the century, perhaps in association with the Byzantine reconquest of the Tyrrhenian coast documented more clearly in nearby Cosa.

Spolverino: At the beginning of the sixth century AD, a necropolis consisting of four burials without grave goods and reutilizing preexisting structures was installed within the ruins of the district (Sebastiani 2014).

Grosseto: During excavations in the city centre, a gold *a cestello* earring from the second half of the sixth century AD was found *c.* 100 m from the site of the seventh century AD town (Fig. 5.12). The earring, together with a few fragments of sixth-century AD vessels, possibly points to rather stable occupation in the area a few decades before the first substantial evidence of the medieval village appears (Celuzza 2017, 249).

Badia Vecchia-Sestinga: The recovery of a horde containing thirty gold coins dating to the Byzantine period suggests an important occupation, if unclear in nature, of the settlement (Curri 1978, 112, n. 392). The third-century AD epigraph recalling the *Res Publica* of Vetulonia was found in this area (CIL XI, 7257; (Celuzza and Fentress 1994, 612; Citter 2007a, 457, n. 13).

Fosso Cortigliano: A small necropolis consisting of four burials, two of which were destroyed by agricultural activities, was found among the ruins of the villa (Curri 1978, 135–43). The tombs were made of reused materials, mostly *tegulae*, and contained two male individuals between 40–45 years old. Fragments relating to the skull of a child were recovered in one of the tombs of these two adults. The lack of grave goods hinders

Figure 5.12. Golden earring *a cestello* from Grosseto (courtesy of Museo Archeologico e Arte Sacra della Maremma, reproduced with permission).

Figure 5.13. Lead stamp with the representation of the *menorah* from Sterpeto-San Martino (photo by Paolo Nannini – SABAP, reproduced with permission).

a clear chronological definition. Based on materials recovered during the field survey conducted by Vaccaro (2011, 248–49), the tombs can be dated to between the villa's abandonment in the fifth century and the seventh century AD.

Fattoria Badiola: In the early sixth century AD, a small necropolis was placed within the ruins of the villa. Four burials were excavated in 1974, two of which were in a destroyed state (Curri 1978, 75). The tombs did not contain grave goods, but the recovery of a late sixth- to early seventh-century AD bronze hair clip, decorated with concentric circles and bearing similarities to an artefact found in the Byzantine *castrum* of San Antonino, suggests a general date (Vaccaro 2011, 23, no. 41). In this period, the area around the site was occupied by small settlements, likely connected to the cemetery in the ruins of the villa and exploiting the fishing and salt resources of the *Lacus Prilis*.

Castiglione della Pescaia: At the end of the sixth century AD, the port district of Serrata Martini was abandoned. The settlement moved to the nearby highlands, which were later occupied by the castle of Castiglione, the future *curtis* of La Piscaria mentioned in the pontifical sources from the first half of the eighth century AD onwards. A small burial ground of about ten graves was found on the western side of the hill during excavations in the 1980s (Citter 1995, 208; 2007b, 138). The occupation of the area as far back as the second half of the sixth century AD is only vaguely confirmed by a *tremissis* of Tiberius II (578–582) or of Flavius Mauricius Tiberius (582–602). The necropolis can be dated to the early seventh century AD based on the recovery of a small flask with combed, slipware decoration and red streaks dating to the period, along with the grave goods in two tombs, one of a female and one of a male, datable to the second half of the seventh century AD (Vaccaro 2011, 91).

San Martino de Plano: Near Braccagni, the village of San Martino de Plano stands in stark contrast to what occurred in the central places of the Roman period, where we witness the contraction of the inhabited area and the abandonment of infrastructure between the fifth and sixth centuries AD. The settlement, located on the eastern side of the *Lacus Prilis* and founded in the Republican age with the construction of a farm and a few houses, saw a major expansion between the fifth and early seventh centuries AD (Cygielman and others 2009; Vaccaro 2011, 15–16, 22–23, 28–29, 31–32). Material finds document the site's full access to overseas trade routes arriving from Tunisia, North Africa, and the eastern Mediterranean. Various tombs were recovered in the village's necropolis, most without grave goods. The exception is the tomb of a female individual, evidently a person of rank who lived between the fifth and sixth centuries AD, buried with a pair of gold pendant earrings, three bronze globular hairpins, an amber necklace, a bracelet also likely of amber, and a headdress. It is probable that the woman's dress was decorated with glass beads and gold thread.

Sterpeto-San Martino: A small necropolis is documented within the Villa of Sterpeto. The tombs lacked grave goods, but their similarity with the nearby graves at Casette di Mota suggests a date between the sixth and seventh centuries AD (Maetzke 1959, 82). During a recent survey conducted by the Soprintendenza Archeologica, a rectangular lead stamp (5.6 × 3.8 cm) was found — so far unpublished — with an image representing the menorah, a symbol of Jewish and Christian art particularly widespread in the sixth century AD (Fig. 5.13). Similar stamps, usually in terracotta or bronze, were used to mark food and drinks and featured a common iconography. The menorah was commonly imprinted on oil lamps, amulets, gems, medallions, and ritual objects produced mostly in North Africa. In Italy, a seven-stemmed menorah appears in a medallion on an architectural fragment from Catania. The Sterpeto stamp, on the other hand, is made of lead, suggesting a different use (e.g., as a weight).

Aiali: A small necropolis was installed in the ruins of the villa and documented during recent studies conducted by Vaccaro, Ghisleni, and Campana (2009). The few excavated tombs lacked grave goods but were generically dated to the Lombard age based on their formal characteristics, which included large stone slab coverings (Maetzke 1959, 85).

Casette di Mota: The Villa of Casette di Mota was abandoned at the end of the sixth century AD. Its necropolis, made up of 10 burials, dates to between the late sixth and early seventh centuries AD. This chronology is suggested by the presence of a female burial featuring a rich collection of grave goods, including bronze leaf fibula, a knife, earrings in copper or bronze wire with droplet pendants in glass, two rings in bronze wire, glass beads, and gold *a cestello* earrings bearing similarities to contemporaneous objects identified in Luni (Maetzke 1959, 83–84).

Podere Passerini: The situation recorded at *Aquae Rosellana* is relatively more complex. The presence of a necropolis is suggested by excavation descriptions from the second half of the nineteenth century and confirmed by the discovery of human bones during surveys in 2003. The earlier descriptions report that the building was destroyed by fire; the settlement may have been abandoned, like most other Roman *mansiones* and infrastructure points, between the mid- to late fifth century AD, or it may have been destroyed by fire during the Gothic invasions, the Gothic War, or the Middle Ages (Saracen raids are documented in the area after AD 935). Surprisingly, no small necropolis was identified at *Aquae Rusellanae*, unlike in the other contexts analysed. Instead, 300 or more skeletons were recovered, each holding an instrument more like a spade than a weapon and with coins placed under back of the head. The descriptions mention coins depicting a Lombard cross and others from the Middle Ages. It is possible that *Aquae Rusellanae* hosted the burials of a smaller community before receiving such an exceptional number of graves. The tombs were concentrated in the vestibule A7, the peristyle A8, and in a *galleria*, presumably the corridor A15. This suggests that the numerous burials were purposefully installed within the rooms of Villa Passerini, perhaps due to a dramatic event (e.g., a massacre, epidemic, or natural disaster) necessitating such a large number of burials in a short timeframe.

Final Remarks

In conclusion, the landscape of the early sixth century AD appears decidedly sparser than that of the Roman age. The first signs of imbalance and disruption had manifested themselves in the second half of the fifth century AD. Between the end of this century and the Gothic War, the Roman-era organization of the countryside met, it is safe to say, its definitive end.

The Byzantine victory did not mark a return to the past. Possible elements of institutional continuity notwithstanding, remarkable transformation must have been the defining characteristic of this period. This is especially evident when taking into consideration the relationship between rural and urban areas, which were complicated by the addition of a third element: the *castrum*, a fortified residential form that became the dominant model of settlement. These small fortifications, often on hilltops, emerged as the new military and civil reference points of the territory. They were often equipped with ports or a landing-places, as in the case of Castiglione della Pescaia (which, during phases of conflict, reutilized the Roman landing of Serrata Martini) or occupied various strategic positions along important roads, such as in the case of *Rusellae*.

With Justinian's resumption of the *Imperium*, Byzantine generals legitimately inherited and settled in the ancient properties of the *res Caesaris*, a process confirmed by Procopius' observations on the immense imperial and private estates of *Tuscia*. Procopius also informs us that, at the end of the conflict, the countryside continued to be inhabited by farmers and Byzantine commanders who, welcomed by the population, took possession of various lands in *Tuscia*.

Between the mid-fifth century and mid-sixth century AD, a new and different organization of the countryside emerged with the development of novel settlement types: caves and huts. The countryside continued to be inhabited, but settlement patterns were structured differently. Abandoning nuclear forms, settlements now took on a scattered distribution, even as they remained quite widespread. The frequent appearance of small burial grounds composed of no more than ten graves and installed within Roman ruins, for example, points to a sparse but extensive occupation of the countryside. The Scoglietto hut, which partially exploits the structures of the abandoned temple, serves as a prime example of such sites, where the only evidence of the population often takes the form of tombs.

It is our opinion that the apparent poverty of these settlement forms does not indicate a razing of the system nor an absence of social differentiation but translates into a change in ownership, needs, and values. During this period, the material expression of social status was in a process of immense change across the West, stemming from the adoption of more modest ways of life, even among the senatorial aristocracies, which some scholars have linked to the process of Christianization. Burials (and other cultic forms of buildings) became the language of representation for the new elite occupying the highest social strata in the wake of the western Empire's disintegration.

Works Cited

Ademollo, Alfonso. 1880. *Scavi della Serrata Martini presso Castiglione della Pescaia. Relazione del Dott. Alfonso Ademollo, Regio Ispettore degli Scavi e Monumenti della Provincia di Grosseto*

Aniceti, Veronica. 2015. 'I resti umani individuati nella cisterna a Scoglietto. Analisi preliminari', in *Diana Umbronensis a Scoglietto. Santuario, Territorio e Cultura Materiale (200 a.C. – 550 d.C.)*, ed. by Alessandro Sebastiani, Elena Chirico, Matteo Colombini, and Mario Cygielman, Archaeopress Roman Archaeology, 3 (Oxford: Archaeopress), pp. 298–305

Arnoldus-Huyzendveld, Antonia. 2007. 'Le trasformazioni dell'ambiente naturale della pianura grossetana. Dati geologici e paleo-ambientali', in *Archeologia urbana a Grosseto. I. La città nel contesto geografico della bassa Valle dell'Ombrone. Origine e sviluppo di una città medievale nella 'Toscana delle città deboli'. Le ricerche 1997–2005*, ed. by Carlo Citter and Antonia Arnoldus-Huyzendveld, Biblioteca del Dipartimento di Archeologia e Storia delle Arti – Sezione Archeologica, 16 (Florence: All'Insegna del Giglio), pp. 41–62

Arnoldus-Huyzendveld, Antonia, and Carlo Citter. 2015. 'Lo scoglietto nel paleo-paesaggio della piana Di Grosseto', in *Diana Umbronensis a Scoglietto. Santuario, Territorio e Cultura Materiale (200 a.C. – 550 d.C.)*, ed. by Alessandro Sebastiani, Elena Chirico, Matteo Colombini, and Mario Cygielman, Archaeopress Roman Archaeology, 3 (Oxford: Archaeopress), pp. 1–11

Arthur Paul. 1991. 'Naples: A Case of Urban Survival in the Early Middle Ages?', *Mélanges de l'Ecole Française de Rome*, 103: 759–84

Brando, Massimo. 2015. 'La suppellettile da illuminazione', in *Diana Umbronensis a Scoglietto. Santuario, Territorio e Cultura Materiale (200 a.C. – 550 d.C.)*, ed. by Alessandro Sebastiani, Elena Chirico, Matteo Colombini, and Mario Cygielman, Archaeopress Roman Archaeology, 3 (Oxford: Archaeopress), pp. 114–43

Brown, Peter, 2014. *Per la cruna di un ago. La ricchezza, la caduta di Roma e lo sviluppo del Cristianesimo, 350–550 d.C.* (Turin: Einaudi)

Cambi, Franco, and Andrea Carandini (eds). 2002. *Paesaggi d'Etruria. Valle dell'Albegna, Valle d'Oro, Valle del Chiarore, Valle del Tafone – Progetto di Ricerca Italo-Britannico seguito allo Scavo di Settefinestre* (Rome: Edizioni di Storia e Letteratura)

Celuzza, Maria Grazia, 2017. *Museo Archeologico e d'Arte della Maremma. Museo di Arte Sacra della Diocesi di Grosseto. Guida* (Arcidosso: Effigi)

Celuzza, Maria Grazia, and Elizabeth Fentress. 1994. 'La Toscana Centro-Meridionale: i casi di Cosa-Ansedonia e Roselle', in *La Storia dell'altomedioevo italiano (VI–X Secolo) alla luce dell'archeologia. Atti del Convegno (Certosa di Pontignano – Siena 1992)*, ed. by Riccardo Francovich and Ghislaine Noyé, Biblioteca di Archeologia Medievale, 11 (Florence: All'Insegna del Giglio), pp. 601–14

Chirico, Elena. 2019a. 'Il brigantaggio in Maremma in età tardoantica', in *Antico e non Antico. Scritti multidisciplinari offerti a Giuseppe Pucci*, ed. by Valentino Nizzo and Antonio Pizzo (Milan: Mimesis Edizioni), pp. 125–36

——. 2019b. 'Podere Passerini e le c.d. Terme Leopoldine a Bagni di Roselle: una possibile ricostruzione archeologica', in *Oltre il Duomo di Grosseto*, ed. by Barbara Fiorini (Arcidosso: Effigi), pp. 106–17

——. 2019c. 'Prima Golena (Alberese, GR): Umbro Flumen una *mansio-positio* a servizio della viabilità', *Bollettino di Archeologia Online*, X.1–2: 85–96

——. 2021. 'Aquae Rusellanae: Il complesso termale a Bagni di Roselle (GR, Italia)', *Journal of Fasti Online*, 514: 1–22

Chirico, Elena, and Matteo Colombini. 2015. 'Età Severiana – Tarda Età Imperiale (fine del II secolo d.C. – metà del IV secolo d.C.)', in *Diana Umbronensis a Scoglietto. Santuario, Territorio e Cultura Materiale (200 a.C. – 550 d.C.)*, ed. by Alessandro Sebastiani, Elena Chirico, Matteo Colombini, and Mario Cygielman, Archaeopress Roman Archaeology, 3 (Oxford: Archaeopress), pp. 54–59

Chirico, Elena, and Alessandro Sebastiani. forthcoming. 'Ritrovamenti archeologici in Loc. La Giuncola (Grosseto). Nuovi dati sul popolamento romano nell'area di Alberese', *Bollettino di Archeologia Online XI*

Ciampoltrini, Giulio, and Paola Rendini. 2005. 'Il sistema portuale dell'ager Cosanus e delle Isole del Giglio e di Giannutri', in *Le strutture dei porti e degli approdi antichi*, ed. by R. Turchetti (Pisa: Soveria Mannelli), pp. 127–50

Citter, Carlo. 1995. 'Siti, approdi, viabilità da Alberese a Castiglione della Pescaia: dalla preistoria all'età Moderna', in *Il Forte di San Rocco. Una struttura militare nel sistema difensivo del litorale toscano del secolo XVIII*, ed. by Serafina Bueti (Grosseto: Laboratorio cartotecnico e stampa Archivio di Stato), pp. 131–49

——. 2007a. 'Il caso di Grosseto nel quadro dell'urbanesimo medievale in Toscana alla luce dell'archeologia', in *Archeologia urbana a Grosseto. II. Edizione degli scavi urbani 1998–2005*, ed. by Carlo Citter, Biblioteca del Dipartimento di Archeologia e Storia delle Arti – Sezione Archeologica, 16, 2 vols (Florence: All'Insegna del Giglio), II, pp. 444–62

——. 2007b. 'La tarda Antichità e il Medioevo', in *Archeologia urbana a Grosseto. I. La città nel contesto della bassa Valle dell'Ombrone*, ed. by Carlo Citter and Antonia Arnoldus-Huyzendveld, Biblioteca del Dipartimento di Archeologia e Storia delle Arti – Sezione Archeologica, 16, 2 vols (Florence: All'Insegna del Giglio), I, pp. 134–51

Corsi, Cristina. 2000. *Le strutture del cursus publicus in Italia. Ricerche topografiche ed evidenze archeologiche*, BAR International Series, 875 (Oxford: British Archaeological Reports)

——. 2016. 'Luoghi di strada e stazioni stradali in Italia tra età tardoantica e altomedioevo', in *Statio Amoena. Sostare e vivere lungo le strade romane*, ed. by Patrizia Basso and Enrico Zanini Archaeopress Archaeology (Oxford: Archaeopress), pp. 53–70

Curri, Claudio B. 1978. *Forma Italiae: Regio VII, Volumen IV: Vetulonia* (Florence: Olschki)

Cygielman, Mario. 2014. 'Serrata Martini (Castiglione della Pescaia – GR). Una necropoli dimenticata', in *Amore per l'antico. Dal Tirreno all'Adriatico, Dalla Preistoria al Medioevo e oltre. Studi di antichità in ricordo di Giuliano de Marinis*, 2 vols, ed. by G. Baldelli and Fulvia Lo Schiavo (Rome: Scienze e Lettere), I, pp. 221–32

Cygielman, Mario, Emanuele, Emanuele Vaccaro, Giuliana Agricoli, and Mariaelena Ghisleni. 2009. 'Grosseto. Braccagni, Vocabolo San Martino', *Notiziario della Soprintendenza ai Beni Archeologici della Toscana*, 4: 259–77

De Benetti, Massimo. 2007a. 'I reperti numismatici dalla Grotta dello Scoglietto (Alberese – Grosseto)', *La Preistoria nelle Grotte del Parco Naturale della Maremma*, ed. by Carlo Cavanna, Atti del Museo di Storia Naturale della Maremma, 22: 99–116

——. 2007b. 'Spaccasasso (GR): Ritrovamenti monetali e un contrappeso da stadera', *La Preistoria nelle grotte del Parco Naturale della Maremma*, ed. by Carlo Cavanna, Atti del Museo di Storia Naturale della Maremma, 22: 243–48

Ferrua, Antonio. 1974. 'ZESES è ZHCHIC o ZHCAIC?', *Aerimi*, 48: 329–34

Ghisleni, Mariaelena, Emanuele Vaccaro, Kim Bowes, Antonia Arnoldus, Michael MacKinnon, and others. 2011. 'Excavating the Roman Peasant I: Excavations at Pievina (GR)', *Papers of the British School at Rome*, 79: 95–145

Guerrini, Claudia, 2019. 'Roselle Terme: dalla Maremma a Londra, la vicenda collezionistica della statua del "Bacco Fanciullo" dall'area di Podere Passerini', in *Oltre il Duomo*, ed. by Barbara Fiorini (Arcidosso: Effigi), pp. 116–21

Kolb, Anne. 2016. 'Mansiones and Cursus Publicus in the Roman Empire', in *Statio Amoena. Sostare e vivere lungo le strade romane*, ed. by Patrizia Basso and Enrico Zanini, Archaeopress Archaeology (Oxford: Archaeopress), pp. 3–9

Lemcke, Lukas. 2013. *Imperial Transportation and Communication from the Third to the Late Fourth Century: The Golden Age of the Cursus Publicus* (Ottawa: University of Waterloo)

Luti, R, Pier Luigi Aminti, L. Donati, and Enzo Pranzini. 2000. 'Ricerche sul territorio di Roselle per l'individuazione degli approdi esistiti dall'età etrusca a quella moderna', *Science and Technology for Cultural Heritage*, 9.1–2: 15–65

Maetzke, Guglielmo. 1959. 'Grosseto – Necropoli "barbariche" nel territorio grossetano', *Notizie degli Scavi*, 13: 66–88

Poggesi, Gabriella. 2004. 'I rinvenimenti di età romana nel territorio di Alberese: Le Frasche e Montesanto', in *La villa romana di Nomadelfia. Aspetti dell'insediamento rurale nel territorio rusellano*, ed. by Mario Cygielman (Arcidosso: Effigi), pp. 113–19

Rendini, Paola. 2008. *I monumenti antichi dell'Isola di Giannutri. Venti anni di attività della Soprintendenza per i Beni Archeologici della Toscana (1989–2008)* (Siena: Nuova Immagine)

——. 2016. 'La villa romana di Giglio Porto (Isola Del Giglio). La decorazione Pparietale', in *Pitture murali nell'Etruria romana. Testimonianze inedite e stato dell'arte. Atti della Giornata di studi sulla gipsoteca di arte antica*, ed. by Fulvia Donati (Pisa: Edizioni ETS), pp. 65–74

Sebastiani, Alessandro. 2014. 'Spolverino (Alberese – GR). The 4th Archaeological Season at the Manufacturing District and Revision of the Previous Archaeological Data', *Journal of Fasti Online*, 320: 1–13

——. 2015. 'Le indagini archeologiche di età romana nel territorio di Alberese', in *Diana Umbronensis a Scoglietto. Santuario, Territorio e Cultura Materiale (200 a.C. – 550 d.C.)*, ed. by Alessandro Sebastiani, Elena Chirico, Matteo Colombini, and Mario Cygielman, Archaeopress Roman Archaeology, 3 (Oxford: Archaeopress), pp. 12–22

——. 2016a. 'Glass and Metal Production at Alberese. The Workshops and the Manufacturing District of Spolverino', *European Journal of Post-Classical Archaeologies*, 6: 53–70

——. 2016b. 'New Data for a Preliminary Understanding of the Roman Settlement Network in South Coastal Tuscany. The Case of Alberese (Grosseto, IT)', *Res Antiquae*, 13: 243–72

——. 2017. 'From Villa to Village. Late Roman to Early Medieval Settlement Networks in the Ager Rusellanus', in *Encounters, Excavations and Argosies. Essays for Richard Hodges*, ed. by John Moreland, John Mitchell, and Bea Leal (Oxford: Archaeopress), pp. 281–90

Sebastiani, Alessandro, Elena Chirico, and Matteo Colombini. 2016. 'Grosseto Località Alberese: Indagini nel sito marittimo di età romana nell'area di Prima Golena', *Notiziario della Soprintendenza ai Beni Archeologici della Toscana*, 11: 451–54

Sebastiani, Alessandro, Elena Chirico, Matteo Colombini, and Mario Cygielman. 2015. *Diana Umbronensis a Scoglietto. Santuario, Territorio e Cultura Materiale*, Archaeopress Roman Archaeology, 3 (Oxford: Archaeopress)

Sebastiani, Alessandro, and Thomas Derrick. 2016. 'Note on the Glass Workshops and Glass Assemblage from Spolverino (Alberese – GR)', *Journal of Glass Studies*, 58: 279–86

——. 2020. 'A Regional Economy of Recycling over Four Centuries at Spolverino (Tuscany) and Environs', in *Recycling and the Ancient Economy*, ed. by Chloe Duckworth and Andrew Wilson (Oxford: Oxford University Press), pp. 359–82

Sirago, V. A. 1985. 'Italia e Roma nell'ideologia e nella realtà storica del IV secolo', *Quaderni*, 4: 1–26

Vaccaro, Emanuele. 2007. 'L'occupazione tardoantica delle grotte dello Scoglietto e di Spaccasasso (Alberese – Grosseto)', *La Preistoria nelle grotte del Parco Naturale della Maremma*, ed. by Carlo Cavanna, Atti del Museo di Storia Naturale della Maremma, 22: 227–41

——. 2008. 'An Overview of Rural Settlement in Four River Basins in the Province of Grosseto on the Coast of Tuscany (200 B.C.–A.D. 600)', *Journal of Roman Archaeology*, 21: 225–47

——. 2011. *Sites and Pots: Settlement and Economy in Southern Tuscany (AD 300–900)*, BAR International Series, 2191 (Oxford: British Archaeological Reports)

Vaccaro, Emanuele, Mariaelena Ghisleni, and Stefano Campana. 2009. 'The Site of Aiali from the Late Republican Period to the Middle Ages in the Light of Surface Potter Analysis', in *Seeing the Unseen. Geophysical and Landscape Archaeology*, ed. by Stefano Campana and Salvatore Piro (London: CRC Press), pp. 303–24

Wickham, Chris. 2003a. 'Per uno studio del mutamento socio-economico di lungo termine in Occidente durante i secoli V-VIII', *Quaderni di Dottorato* 1.1: 3–22

——. 2003b. 'Studying Long-term Change in the West', in *Theory and Practice in Late Antique Archaeology*, ed. by William Bowden and Luke Lavan (Leiden: Brill), pp. 385–403

——. 2005. *Framing the Early Middle Ages. Europe and the Mediterranean, 400–800* (Oxford: Oxford University Press)

——. 2009. *The Inheritance of Rome. A History of Rome from 400 to 1000* (London: Allen Lane)

Zanchi Roppo, Franca. 1969. *Vetri paleocristiani a figure d'oro conservati in Italia*, Studi di Antichità Cristiane (Bologna: Patron)

LUISA DALLAI AND LORENZO MARASCO

6. The nEU-Med Project

Archaeology of a Coastal District in Tuscany during the Early Middle Ages

Introduction: Context and Methodologies

The archaeological investigation carried out at the early medieval site of Vetricella (Scarlino — Grosseto, Tuscany) and in the adjacent Cornia and Pecora river valleys, with its multidisciplinary approach, represents the core of a wider European Research Project (ERC Advanced) entitled *nEU-Med*: 'Origins of a new economic union (seventh–twelfth centuries): resources, landscapes and political strategies in a Mediterranean region' (Bianchi and Hodges 2018, 2020).

The project, developed between 2015 and 2021, aimed at reconstructing, through the archaeological record and from a Mediterranean perspective, the times and means through which a sample portion of the mid-Tyrrhenian Italian landscape, part of the so-called 'Colline Metallifere' district in southern Tuscany, passed from the 'crisis' of the post-classical period to the economic revival of the twelfth century (Hodges 2018). The historical landscape that emerged in Tuscany from that very process took on the form of municipal cities and commercial networks, the latter especially through maritime trade (see, for instance, the growth of Pisa and its leading role in the eleventh and twelfth centuries), revealing a territory strongly enmeshed in the complex but homogenous set of relations that constituted the western Mediterranean.

By comparing recent historiographical hypotheses with previously established ones (Franceschi 2017), the ERC nEU-Med project sought to identify the material traces pointing to a long-term process already taking place in the eighth–ninth centuries and that gradually, through new stimuli occurring in the tenth and eleventh centuries, led to that aforementioned development. Over

a five-year period, the research attempted to answer historical and methodological questions, including: what territorial transformations stimulated or were in some way tied into changes in social and settlement structures? Which proxies and multidisciplinary approaches can be used to acquire the information necessary for a more accurate historical-environmental reconstruction? The research project has tried to find these answers by investigating a key territory, part of the wider northern Maremma region, through a series of methodological approaches. The study area comprises the valleys crossed by the Cornia and Pecora rivers (respectively, the Val di Cornia and Val di Pecora) and the adjacent coastline that constitutes the Gulf of Follonica. These broad plains, now intensively cultivated, were characterized in antiquity by lagoons and marshlands, intertwined with fertile lowlands suitable for cereal crops. Behind the plains rise the hills of the Colline Metallifere, rich in forests and mineral resources, in particular mixed sulphides of lead, copper and silver, as well as iron hydroxides (Fig. 6.1A,C).

The whole territory experienced massive economic growth from the onset of the Etruscan period, the result of intense mining exploitation linked to the inland ore deposits and nearby iron oxides mined on the Island of Elba; at the same time, the territory provided other strategic resources, particularly salt. During this period, the territorial organization also saw the emergence of important cities such as Populonia to the north, and Vetulonia and *Rusellae* to the south. The widespread use of local natural resources (i.e., salt, cereals, woodland, minerals) during the Roman period led this territory

Luisa Dallai (luisa.dallai@unisi.it) Università di Siena

Lorenzo Marasco (lorenzo.marasco@gmail.com) Università di Siena

Archaeological Landscapes of Late Antique and Early Medieval Tuscia: Research and Field Papers, ed. by Riccardo Rao and Alessandro Sebastiani, MEDITO 3 (Turnhout 2023), pp. 107–125

BREPOLS ❧ PUBLISHERS

DOI 10.1484/M.MEDITO-EB.5.133996

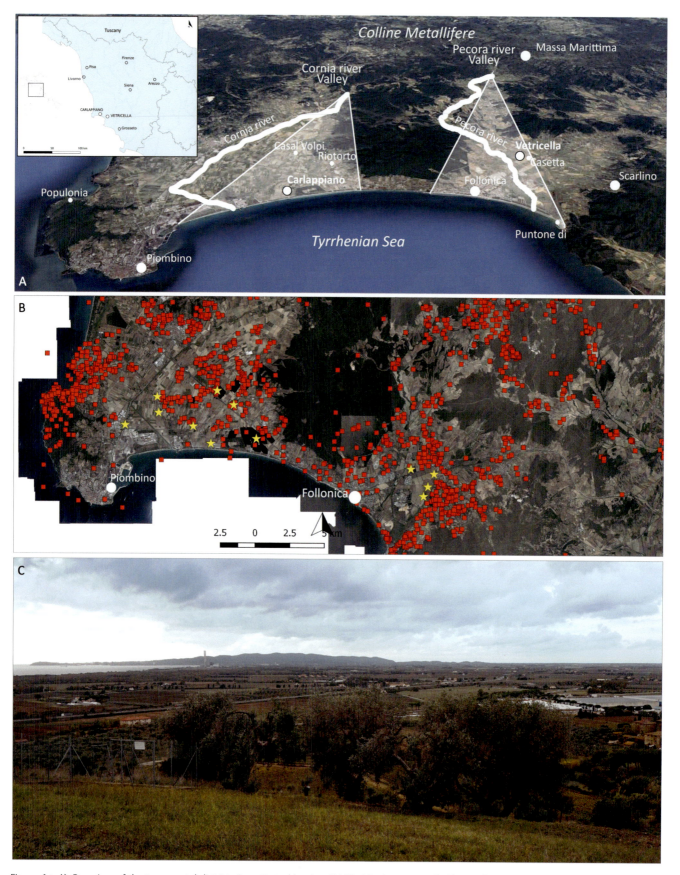

Figure 6.1. A) Overview of the two coastal districts investigated by the nEU-Med Project research. B) Distribution of the main archaeological survey areas (squares), location of the geognostic cores (stars), and multidisciplinary surveys (grids). C) Panoramic view of the coastal plain between Piombino and Follonica (photos by the authors).

to be rightfully included among the most significant commercial districts in the Mediterranean, thanks to the presence of strategic roadways, such as the *via Aurelia*, and maritime stoppage points. From the middle of the third century BC, with the re-organization of the road system, ports such as *Portus Scabris*, located in the vicinity of Scarlino, *Falesia*, probably in the southern portion of the promontory of Populonia, and Baratti, to the north of the same promontory, provided connection points between land and sea routes (Cambi 2002).

This territory and the crucial role played by its strategic resources over a long period of time have given rise to a series of historical-archaeological investigations that highlighted its outstanding potential for the analysis of settlement, mining, and metallurgical dynamics in pre-industrial times: a long tradition of studies carried out by universities and institutions through excavations, territorial surveys, landscape reconstruction, and historical-documentary research. The coastal lowlands, in particular, have been the focus of research projects centred on the diachronic reading of the historical landscape (Fedeli 1983; Cucini 1985) (Fig. 6.1B). These were followed by more in-depth studies in the lower Val di Cornia, as part of the survey project on the ancient city and diocese of Populonia (Botarelli and Cambi 2004–2005; Cambi, Cavari, and Mascione 2009; Dallai 2016), and in the Pecora valley (Marasco 2013).

The result of this season of research illustrated population trends in the coastal plain area, highlighting a discontinuity in territorial occupation that occurred from antiquity to the Middle Ages, accompanied also by a number of thematic approaches to the study of the historical environment, often centred on the question of the actual extent of the coastal lagoon areas stretching across the plain (Isola 2009; Pieruccini and Susini 2020).

Previous historical models put forward for this territory hypothesized that a change in settlement layout took place at the start of the early medieval period, with the decline of the pre-existing Imperial structures and the spontaneous establishment of hilltop villages on the fringes of the coastal plains (Francovich and Hodges 2003). The institutional vacuum left by the collapse of the Roman organizational system would have contributed to the development of most of these newfound settlements into centres (known as *curtes*) capable of self-sufficient economic management and production control, later developing into aristocratic castles.

The ERC nEU-Med project audited the vast amount of previously collected data, integrating it with new results acquired from archaeological and environmental investigations in selected areas of the Cornia and Pecora valleys. Thanks to a strongly multidisciplinary approach, the archaeological record was interpreted in

relation to the changing landscape; in these changes, both the environmental dynamics and the action of the human communities that interacted with the environment in different periods were identified. In order to reconstruct the diachronic transformations of the context, the project promoted the use of integrated survey methodologies (archaeological, geological, geochemical, archaeobotanical, geophysical), remote sensing tools (LiDAR and photogrammetry) and geoarchaeological analyses. Through the combination of multiple sources and a 'multi-scalar' approach, which included intra-site and spatial surveys, the study gathered new data that allowed to follow the evolution of the Holocene landscape of the coastal plain, define the extent of the wetlands and chart the most important aspects of the forest landscape (Buonincontri and others 2020; Pieruccini and others 2021). Lastly, the distal and coastal portions of the Val di Pecora and Val di Cornia underwent a campaign of deep mechanical coring (Pieruccini and Susini 2020): through the analysis of twelve continuous cores 5 to 10 metres in length, their sedimentological/stratigraphic study, palaeobiological and geochemical analysis and radiocarbon dating, the picture of the coastal context of the two valleys has finally assumed more well-defined limits. Extensive excavations in two key contexts (Carlappiano in Val di Cornia and Vetricella in Val di Pecora) have made it possible to collect data of considerable interest, identifying the key resources of the territory and understanding the mechanisms of their management and valorization between the early and late Middle Ages (Dallai and others 2018; Bianchi 2022). The site of Vetricella, in particular, offered for the first time the opportunity to extensively investigate the management centre of a large public *curtis* (see Hodges in this book).

[LD, LM]

Studying the Lower Cornia Valley: New Sources for Reinterpreting the Historical Landscape

The Val di Cornia has long been at the centre of diachronic and thematic studies promoted by Riccardo Francovich in the 1990s and continued by the University of Siena in the following decades. The multidisciplinary research carried out by the nEU-Med project has revitalized the study of this territory, fostering a strongly integrated methodological approach featuring archaeology, geoarchaeology, geochemistry, and archeobotany (Dallai and others 2018; Pieruccini and others 2018; Pieruccini and Susini 2020).

Today, the lower Cornia valley is an intensely cultivated territory, but for centuries the flatland area

Figure 6.2. Archaeological excavation at Carlappiano (Piombino, Livorno). A) Detail of the anthropic anomaly with the three excavation areas; Area 2000 is circled in red. B) Detail of the anomaly from the 1938 IGM flight. C) The thirteenth-century drainage system. D) The drainage channel after a week of heavy rain during the excavation campaign. E) Remains of one of the walls bounding the open areas for brine crystallization (photos by the authors).

adjacent to the dunes flanking the coastline of the gulf of Follonica was partly a marsh, reclaimed between the nineteenth and twentieth centuries (Pellegrini 1984). The main hydrographic element of the plain is the Cornia river, which originates from the heights near Campiglia Marittima and originally flowed into the ancient lagoon of Piombino (Censini and others 1991; Federici and Mazzanti 1995) (Fig. 6.1A).

In this complex coastal area, the reconstruction of the main features of the historical landscape has traditionally relied on archaeological, documentary, cartographic, and photographic sources. Among these, historical cartography, including cadastral maps, has played a central role. Since the late eighteenth century, in fact, both the Cornia and Pecora floodplains have been represented in thematic cartographies, some of which were made specifically to represent areas subject to seasonal or continuous flooding; in these, the extent of the alluvial areas subject to land reclamation activities is described in detail (Bartoli 2017).

An image of the reclaimed plain, not yet subject to the intense infrastructural and settlement development that characterizes it today, can be obtained from historical aerial photographs dating to the first half of the twentieth century (IGM flight 1938, 1940; GAI 1954). In this crystallised landscape, still untransformed by the profound settlement and infrastructural changes that characterize it today, details of great importance for the reconstruction of the historical landscape are clearly identifiable; among the main ones, there is the hydrographic network, still partially recognizable in the form of paleochannels. Along with traces of watercourses, a number of anomalies are clearly marked, originating either from erosion and transformation processes operated by water across the plain, or of anthropic origin (Poggi 2021); anomalies of the latter type define the case of Carlappiano, a site excavated as part of the research promoted by the ERC nEU-Med project (Fig. 6.2A,B) (Dallai and others 2018).

On these grounds, the reconstruction of settlement dynamics of the coastal territory would lead one to hypothesize a seaside plain occupied by relatively deep and extensive lagoon areas, with a more or less significant impact on the environment, settlement network, and road system, according to the historical period (Fedeli 1983; Isola 2009). Presently, thanks to the resumption of research and the integration of new methods of analysis, it is possible to better define, and in some cases correct, these reconstructions, providing a more detailed morphological layout of the plain.

New proxies and datasets have been produced by the nEU-Med project in order to achieve this result. In 2017 and 2018, fieldwork campaigns were conducted in select sample areas of the Cornia and Pecora valleys (Dallai and Volpi 2019). At the same time, the coring campaign provided the first records documenting the changes that occurred in the physical palaeoenvironments along the Northern Mediterranean in the Late Holocene (Fig. 6.1B). In addition to a more detailed characterization of the sedimentary facies, twenty-four radiocarbon readings as well as significant biological evidence were obtained from the cores, all of which crucial for understanding the environmental context and long-term evolution of the plain (Pieruccini and Susini 2020), especially with regard to dimensional variation in the inland lagoon areas. As far as the subject of this contribution is concerned, i.e., the Val di Cornia and in particular the lagoon of Torremozza located in its eastern portion, all the recently acquired environmental and archaeological proxies have led us to hypothesize that in historical times the lagoon did not differ significantly in terms of size from how it was represented in the cadastral cartography of the early nineteenth century (as shown in Fig. 6.4C). The following pages will discuss this hypothesis through unconventional datasets, such as geochemical data. These were obtained through detailed mapping of large territorial samples: over 400 hectares in the Val di Cornia and 140 in the Val di Pecora, with a total of circa 12,000 onsite pXRF measurements, used as additional evidence. Photogrammetric analysis carried out via drone flights and the acquisition of LiDAR images of the wooded areas located on the hills surrounding the lower Cornia and Pecora river valleys complete this set of new strategies adopted by the project to reconstruct and better understand past landscape settings.

The Coastal Environment and the Site of Carlappiano

All the illustrated methodologies and their combined use were applied to a specific sample area of the lower Cornia valley, located near the mouth of what was once the Cornia river (today known as Corniaccia) on the dune of Carlappiano, where the project carried out one of its two main field excavations (Dallai 2018).

From an environmental point of view, the most recent reconstructions based on geoarchaeological data obtained through manual and mechanical core drills, along with geological and archaeological cross sections, confirm that Carlappiano was established on one of the coastal sand ridges separating the ancient marshland from the sea; early evidence of settlements on these raised dry areas date to the Middle Bronze Age (Federici and Mazzanti 1992, 196; Fedeli 1983, 65–74).

Mechanical coring (core number five), carried out a short distance from the site (Fig. 6.4C), intercepted dune sediments at a depth of between 1 and 3 metres below ground level. Radiocarbon readings indicate that

Figure 6.3. Archaeological excavation at Carlappiano (Piombino, Livorno). A) Detail of the anthropic anomaly with the three excavation areas; Area 3000 is circled in red. B) General view of Area 3000 during excavation with the wall foundations ascribed to the warehouses. C) 3D reconstruction of the Carlappiano saltworks in their environmental context (courtesy of Dr M. Buono, University of Siena).

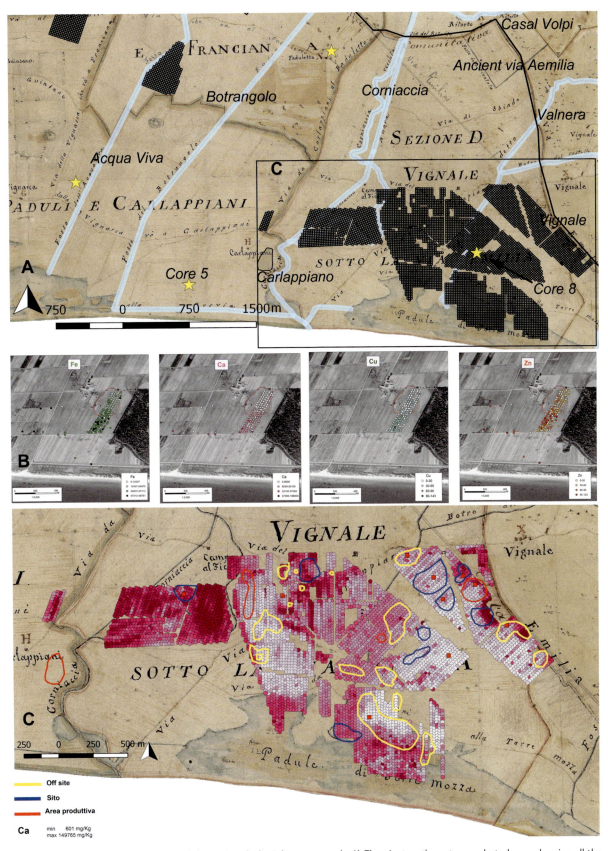

Figure 6.4. The lower Cornia valley and the ERC multidisciplinary research. A) The nineteenth-century cadastral map showing all the sites mentioned in the paper: Carlappiano, Vignale, Casal Volpi, the Botrangolo, Valnera, and Corniaccia rivers; in black the route of the Roman road. The stars indicate the location of the nEU-Med cores; the grids correspond to the areas of the multidisciplinary survey. B) Chemical values obtained from the pXRF survey on the Carlappiano anomaly for diagnostic elements Fe-Iron; Ca-Calcium; Cu-Copper; Zn Zinc. C) Site locations and pXRF Ca values plotted in a GIS system on the nineteenth-century cadastral map marking the ancient lagoon limits (photos by the authors).

the dune had already formed in the fourth millennium BC; since then, the main geomorphological features of this part of the plain (i.e. the sand dune separating the sea from the nearby plain) have not changed substantially (Pieruccini and Susini 2020).

The silt and clay layers deposited on the dune testify to an environment no longer subject to high-energy events linked to marine dynamics, but rather evolving towards a more sheltered alluvial plain, with shallow and relatively still waters. From the manual core drilling and trenches carried out in the excavation areas at Carlappiano, it was possible to trace the profile of the dune in the area that would later be settled. The site in fact benefits from a 'high ground' morphology, where the sandy ridge appears between -50 and -160 cm from the current ground level.

A mixed deciduous broadleaf forest, which probably benefited from the better-drained soil offered by the sandy ridge, left traces of fuelwood identified from anthracological analyses carried out on data gathered during the excavation, showing the predominant use of *Q. cerris*, *Q. pubescens*, *Ulmus*, and *O. carpinifolia* (Buonincontri and others 2018).

Prior to the excavation, study of the aerial photos revealed the existence of a marked sub-circular anomaly, probably of anthropic origin (Fig. 6.2B); field survey confirmed the presence of a considerable concentration of archaeological material, mainly brick and pottery sherds, along with some slag and mineral fragments. In addition, magnetometric analysis showed both linear and dipole anomalies within the limits of the circular feature (Dallai 2018).

The interdisciplinary research strategy adopted for this area also included a preliminary archaeological survey combined with a first set of pXRF readings carried out on site with a portable instrument; readings were taken following a regular grid pattern, the same used for the geophysical surveys (Volpi 2018). Following the results obtained from the geophysical and geochemical proxies, as well as the *intra situ* archaeological survey, three different excavation areas were set up, allowing researchers to define the nature and chronology of the site (Fig. 6.2A). The material evidence recorded at Carlappiano refers to an articulated complex of channels, buildings, and open spaces that can be traced back to the production of salt. Thanks to archaeological research, the importance of this specific production cycle that took place in the coastal territory and the Gulf of Follonica in particular has been documented from the Final Bronze Age onwards (Aranguren and others 2014; Sevink and others 2020); its importance has also been considered in relation to other forms of large-scale production, such as fish processing in the later Etruscan-Roman period (Carusi 2018). Moreover, data gathered from the archaeological survey, together

with the specific location of the site, suggest that the last phase of the production sequence, namely the crystallization of the brine, took place at Carlappiano; the repeated accumulation of salt over time could also be the cause of the depletion of chemical elements recorded by the pXRF readings within the area enclosed by the circular feature (Fig. 6.4B) (Dallai 2018, 45–47).

The strong public control exercised, at least from the eighth century onwards, over coastal areas such as the lower Val di Cornia and Val di Pecora, rich in natural resources, is emphasized in early medieval historical sources (Tomei 2020). At that time, the Cornia valley in particular was part of a vast fiscal property identified by the toponym *Franciano*. Until the eleventh century and prior to the crisis that invested the March of Tuscany, fiscal control over the lower Cornia and Pecora valleys, as well as the coastal areas characterized by analogous forms of production, remained tight. When, in August 1094, half of the *curtis* of *Franciano* passed from the Aldobrandeschi family to the monastery of San Quirico of Populonia, the saltworks appeared as the first entry in the list of resources and rights acquired by the monks, evidently constituting a particularly valuable asset; the archaeological survey at Carlappiano has identified this historical phase and part of the related structures, referable to a chronological timespan set between the twelfth and thirteenth centuries.

Saltworks, as is known, are not imposing structures and therefore offer relatively limited material traces from an archaeological point of view. Excavations in Area 2000 at Carlappiano, however, have brought to light portions of a canal (Fig. 6.2C,D) and walls enclosing open areas (Fig. 6.2E) where, in all probability, salt was collected and left to dry, while in Area 3000 archaeological work uncovered the remains of structures (most likely warehouses) for storing the product (Fig. 6.3).

A long canal connected the production area to a much larger ditch, clearly identifiable from aerial photographs (in particular the 1938 IGM flight) and early nineteenth-century cartography. The ditch enclosed a large portion of the dune and, by means of a channel, joined it to the original Corniaccia river. The presence of this articulated canal system ensured the drainage of the area, while allowing it to be replenished with a freshwater supply, essential in the final stages of production. Freshwater was in fact added to control the saturation level of the saline solution and prevent the precipitation of chloride and magnesium sulphates.

The Hydrographic Network and the Lagoon at Torremozza

The portion of plain enclosing the dune of Carlappiano and the hills towards the village of Riotorto is characterized by an articulated inland riverine system, whose waters are channelled towards the coast by three main streams, the Botrangolo, the Valnera, and the Corniaccia, all toponyms that feature in the cartography of 1821 (Pieruccini and Susini 2020, 162, fig. 1). Today, the courses taken by these streams correspond in part to their historical routes, the result of land reclamation carried out at the beginning of the nineteenth century: the rectilinear and non-natural forms of the Botrangolo and Valnera rivers are depicted in the 1821 cadastral cartography, whereas the Corniaccia river shows a double course, testifying to an ongoing embankment process. In time, the river produced a significant number of intertwining meanders before reaching the sea at the site of San Martino; traces of fluvial ridges formed near the river mouth are visible in historical aerial photographs and nineteenth-century cadastral cartography.

The fundamental role played by these watercourses in the geomorphological stability of this part of the plain, affecting both settlement dynamics and production processes, is testified to by the choices related to the road system taking place over the centuries. All routes, in fact, including those dating to the nineteenth century, avoid crossing the plain in the stretch between Vignale (to the south) and Casal Volpi (to the north), an area subject to seasonal flooding, as indicated on the cadastral map, following instead a more inland road.

The palaeochannels and meanders clearly visible from the aerial photographs (in particular 1938 IGM flight and 1954 GAI flight) testify not only to these complex waterway dynamics, but also to the great energy produced by the merging of different watercourses and the consequent accumulation of sediments. This picture is again confirmed by data from one of the geognostic cores (core number 8) carried out in the very heart of the plain that was thought to be covered by water (Fig. 6.4A). The core showed a complete absence of facies related to marshy environments or still-water, providing layers of medium to large sized pebbles and gravels, indicating the presence of high-energy river dynamics.

Likewise, the stratigraphic sequence from the site of Carlappiano showed the occurrence of river flooding, visible especially in the excavation matrix, the largest of these events, dated between the thirteenth and fourteenth centuries, leading to the abandonment of the site and its production activities (Dallai 2018, 45).

In conclusion, the data collected so far has shown that part of the plain behind the dune of Carlappiano was never a lagoon but rather an area subject to meandering or seasonal flooding, a riverbed-like environment around which, and on its safer and drier slopes, Late antique and early medieval settlements, including Vignale, were established.

So what would the real extent of the lagoon have actually been, especially during the medieval period? Can its limits be more clearly defined by combining settlement patterns with other environmental proxies? Once again, it is through a multidisciplinary approach, and in particular through a combined archaeological and physico-chemical survey, that we can answer these questions.

A 20 × 20 m GIS grid system was applied over the entire area indicated in the nineteenth-century cadastral map as the boundary between dryland surfaces and wetlands, i.e., between the ancient dune and the lagoon. Following this regular pattern, XRF measurements were taken directly on site using a portable field instrument for a total of over 8000 readings (Dallai and Volpi 2019). This was accompanied by the systematic recording of archaeological evidence and bibliographical data, analysed in a GIS environment, which allowed the creation of an extremely detailed cartography, useful for a precise reconstruction of the area. Likewise, the management of geochemical readings in the same database system made it possible to observe the spatial distribution and concentration of key elements: some of these (in particular Ca-calcium, Fe-iron, K-potassium) have a specific diagnostic value, linked to water dynamics and the nature of the soil; their variation may therefore correspond to different soil types or human activities.

For the purpose of our research, it was of fundamental importance to compare sandy soils, characterized by a lower concentration of elements, with clay-silt soils, richer in calcium and iron. While the former represent raised dune areas, clay and silt soils are indicative of areas potentially subject to water stagnation. Superimposing the different values on the nineteenth-century cadastral cartography it is possible to follow the lagoon boundaries represented in the cadastre. These show a substantially stable landscape in which the extent of the ancient lagoon does not appear to differ much from what was recorded before the nineteenth-century reclamation. This result is also in line with the settlement pattern recorded in the areas surrounding the lagoon (Fig. 6.4C).

[LD]

The Coastal Lowland of the Pecora River: A New Season of Research

Like the neighbouring Val di Cornia, the Pecora river valley and the plain below the castle of Scarlino have been at the centre of systematic archaeological research thanks to the work carried out by Riccardo Francovich since the 1980s (Francovich 1985). His research, and the subsequent reconstruction hypotheses of a post-Classical landscape, have been of fundamental importance in the field of Medieval Archaeology, both in Tuscany and throughout Italy (Francovich and Hodges 2003).

Numerous studies have repeatedly focused on the secular transformations and landscape dynamics taking place in this wide lowland expanse facing the Tyrrhenian Sea and the Island of Elba, crossed by the Pecora river flowing from the hills near Massa Marittima (the district of the Colline Metallifere). These works have traced a long historical narrative, focusing in particular on the Etruscan and Roman periods, and the transition to the Middle Ages, which is also the subject of this study (Cucini 1985; Marasco 2013). A key role in the construction of the historical landscape was played by the ancient lagoon environment, consisting of a large inland saltwater basin, separated from the sea by an ancient coastal ridge and still referred to in early written sources as the Lake of Scarlino (Marasco 2018, 58–63). Repeated field surveys recorded a continuous occupation of the former lake area throughout the Classical period (Fig. 6.1B), consisting of settlements and production sites linked to the natural resources of the coastal plain. In particular, significant salt production activities and intense metallurgical processing are attested from the Protohistoric period and during the subsequent Etruscan and Roman periods (Aranguren and others 2014). The exceptional productive vitality of the area is determined not only by the natural morphology of the territory, an extensive coastal area with easily navigable gulf and large inland lake, but also by its proximity to the hinterland mining districts of Massa Marittima and the Island of Elba (Fig. 6.5A).

Furthermore, an important commercial network developed in this territorial setting, taking on the form of roadways that followed the coast and lake, or maritime routes with landing places such as the aforementioned *Portus Scabris*, an important Roman-period harbour located at Puntone di Scarlino (Vaccaro 2018). Consequently, during the Classical period, the archaeological evidence reveals a landscape consisting of an inhabitable and economically active plain, rich in organized farming areas and made more fertile by a complex network of water channels.

Despite evidence of decline during the second and third centuries AD, the late antique period still offers a picture of continuity for some of the main sites (villas and farms) and minor farming nuclei. Considering also the continuous evidence of ironworking that took place along the causeway near the coastal dunes and the still active *Portus Scabris*, as well as the nearby Roman villa of Puntone di Scarlino, it can be stated that the socio-economic fabric at the end of the fifth century was still quite solid, albeit in changed forms.

Archaeological evidence has shown that a radical change in the region's settlement pattern occurred in the early Middle Ages. It is precisely in this area, in fact, that the first evidence contributing to the Tuscan model of early medieval settlement, linked to the phenomenon that saw the relocation of communities to hilltop sites and their subsequent development into castles from the tenth century onwards, was first identified (Francovich 2008).

With the end of the Roman period, the coastal plain, previously occupied by villas and farms (one of the last sites was frequented until the beginning of the seventh century), was thought to have been abandoned, the population retreating to the nearby hills. Here archaeology has documented traces of numerous early medieval villages, assuming the material form of castles at the turn of the millennium. The early Middle Ages saw the gradual affirmation of important noble families (the most notable in this area being the Aldobrandeschi) who also asserted their control through these fortified structures.

The nEU-Med project reconsidered this historical landscape, reassessing and improving the model for the post-Classical period with the support of new methodologies and a multidisciplinary approach (Bianchi and Hodges 2018). After a first season of research carried out between 2006 and 2013 (Marasco 2012, 715–17), from 2016 the newly launched project integrated previous data in order to advance new historiographic hypotheses.

Starting from the site of Vetricella, an exceptional early medieval context located in the centre of the already-described Pecora river plain, an integrated study was carried out to reconstruct the geomorphological structure of the landscape and the anthropic activities that involved settlement dynamics and resource exploitation.

Geomorphological surveys were carried out between 2016 and 2018 to understand the changes taking place in the Pecora valley and the Lagoon of Scarlino (Pieruccini and others 2018; Pieruccini and Susini 2020). Through the analysis of exposed sections, explorative trenches and geognostic coring, it was possible to reconstruct the historical environment of the area, trace the original course of the Pecora during the early Middle Ages and map the fluctuations of the lagoon through the deposits of material carried downstream by the river.

In addition, these studies have also revealed traces of anthropic activities for the creation of new landscape forms after the end of the Roman period, transformations that can be traced back to the eighth–ninth centuries, with an increase from the mid-tenth century onwards, and apparently aimed at acquiring new spaces for the exploitation of local resources (Buonincontri and others 2020).

Survey activities conducted since 2008 in the lowland area around what was once the lagoon have revealed traces of a system of previously unidentified early medieval settlements, possibly connected to the

6. THE NEU-MED PROJECT 117

Figure 6.5. The lower Val di Pecora and the site of Vetricella. A) Location of the main features of the historic landscape. B) The site of Vetricella before the first excavation campaign. C) UAV orthophoto of the excavation at the end of the 2018 campaign (elaborated by Giulio Poggi, nEU-Med team).

Figure 6.6. A–B) Period plans of the first and second occupation at Vetricella (Periods 1 and 2). C) Examples of a possible forge and kiln from Period 1. D) Test trenches carried out in the enclosing ditches (photos by the authors).

newly discovered site of Vetricella (Marasco 2013). The latest fieldwork activities and the new multidisciplinary approach employing remote sensing and geomorphological survey, as well as chemical soil analysis by way of pXRF (Dallai, Marasco, and Volpi 2018; Dallai, Volpi, and Carli 2020), have allowed researchers to identify Vetricella as a central place connected to a complex network of economic resources and landscape management.

Archaeological evidence dates the highpoint of this system between the late ninth and early eleventh century, as a direct expression of royal power.

Vetricella and its Historical Phases in Territorial Context

The site of Vetricella was first discovered in the summer of 2005 through aerial survey, when clear circular crop marks were first recorded (Fig. 6.5B). The exceptional shape of these features, consisting of three concentric circles enclosing a slightly raised mound, was initially interpreted as a *seigneurial* fortification complex (Marasco 2009).

The considerable material evidence recovered during the excavation as well as the data garnered from the surrounding landscape, which prompted a more in-depth review of the currently known written sources, finally revealed the presence of another type of authority on the plain (Fig. 6.5C,D). Vetricella has now been interpreted as the centre of a royal estate, the ancient *curtis* of *Valle*, first mentioned in the 937 dotary of Hugh of Arles to his future wife Berta and her daughter Adelaide (Bianchi and Collavini 2018, 151). The nEU-Med project has in fact identified activities involving public authority, directly related to the management of royal possessions in the area of the Pecora Valley and around Vetricella, dating between the eighth and eleventh centuries (Bianchi and Hodges 2020; Marasco and Briano 2020).

The first traces of occupation at the site date back to the seventh–eighth centuries, when evidence of wooden structures and burnt surfaces were recorded in a number of sectors (Fig. 6.6A,C). Although these contexts have only been partly investigated and are often heavily altered by subsequent activities, they can nevertheless be interpreted as an early phase of occupation characterized by metallurgical activities (identified as Period 1 in the stratigraphic sequence).

It is in the second period that the most exceptional traces of the role exercised by public authority become clear (Fig. 6.6B,D). Around the middle of the ninth century, an imposing project was carried out for the establishment of a fortified lowland centre, characterized by a defensive system made up of three concentric ditches (two of which measure between 4 and 8 metres in width and about 2 metres in depth; Susini and Pieruccini 2020) enclosing a slightly raised central mound crowned by a tower-like structure (building A).

A direct connection can be noted between the *curtis* of Valli, the other public properties attested in early medieval written sources, and the coeval archaeological context of Vetricella, the latter undergoing a significant structural change in accordance with building traditions typical of northern Europe in the Carolingian period (Marasco 2013, 66). Little, however, can be said about the exact function of this complex, other than that of territorial control, as few occupation levels have been preserved (most were recovered in the form of secondary deposits within the two innermost ditches).

The role of Vetricella as a possible central place in a wider economic network has also been hypothesized in accordance with the quantity and types of materials recovered during the excavations (in particular the large number of numismatic, ceramic, and metal finds). These indicate a clear role of the site in the management and administration of production activities related to food and metal resources, especially from the early tenth century onwards.

This interpretation of Vetricella, based on excavation data, is further supplemented by the results of multidisciplinary surveys carried out in the area around the site where, from the ninth-tenth century, a series of settlement nuclei were established, attested by numerous ceramic fragments and remains of metallurgical activities (Marasco 2018, 61–63; Dallai, Marasco, and Volpi 2018, 100–02). A number of these archaeological contexts have been subject to more in-depth analysis through geophysical prospections, pXRF surveys, and stratigraphic investigations, the latter through exploratory trenches. An example is provided by a context located approximately 800 metres from Vetricella and identified by a large area with a significant dispersal of ceramic fragments, skeletal remains, and metal slag (the context is referred to as Podere Casetta). This site has been interpreted as a large settlement nucleus (perhaps a village) established a short distance from the remains of a late Roman (fourth–fifth c. AD) farm, and characterized by the presence of a masonry structure and burial area dated to the second half of the tenth century. The stratigraphic investigation, albeit limited, confirmed the initial hypothesis, recognizing a complex settlement environment coeval with the nearby fortified centre of Vetricella and probably connected to it by an evident spatial relationship.

Overall, the line of research promoted by the nEU-Med project facilitated the recognition of the continued existence of an entire landscape system around Vetricella, characterized by minor watercourses, today either buried or channelled, as well as portions of surveyed land on which material traces and chemical elements indicative of a structured anthropic presence have been recorded. As previously mentioned, the project has also documented evidence of landscape alteration during the tenth century, aimed at the creation of new cultivated surfaces while increasing production output (Buonincontri and others 2020).

As a central place, Vetricella reached its maximum development after the mid-tenth century during the Ottonian age (Period 4.1 and 4.2), when a considerable change in the site's layout took place, characterized by new constructions and the dismantling of earlier structures (Fig. 6.7A,B). The most relevant archaeological evidence for this period consists of a closely knit sequence of construction activities and two overlapping building contexts, dated to between the last decades of the tenth and the beginning of the eleventh century. The use of lime mortar appears for the first time to reconstruct the base of the tower and cover a portion of the innermost ditch, now almost completely sealed to create a homogenous flooring area. In the second phase of Period 4, a stone and mortar cobbling was also set directly over the inner ditch (Fig. 6.7D).

The analysis of the structures used for the production of mortar further underlined the historical relevance of Vetricella and the possible network of relations in which it was enmeshed. These are two mortar mixers (an example can be seen in Fig. 6.7C), which constitute a technological solution already attested in various other tenth-century sites across Tuscany and whose link with transalpine building traditions has already been noted (Bianchi 2011).

Most of the constructive activities of Period 4.1 took place in the last thirty years of the tenth century, as stratigraphic evidence and chronological data provided by radiocarbon readings clearly indicate. A new defensive system formed by a wooden palisade, which evidently replaced the no longer functional ditches, and the establishment of a small burial area (presently consisting of 52 graves) are part of the transformations undergone by the site. The position of the burials in association with a smaller building, in all likelihood a small oratory made of perishable material (building B), reveals a radial pattern seemingly in relation to the central tower structure (Viva 2020). Radiocarbon analyses carried out on several of the burials confirmed a chronology set between the end of the tenth and the beginning of the eleventh century. The chronological correspondence of these burials with the previously described cemetery area at the nearby coeval site of Podere Casetta should be noted (Fig. 6.5A), testifying to a localized community around Vetricella, linked to its function as a central place.

The changes that occurred during this period are also testified by a significant increase in material data, both in the form of deposit levels and finds, which evidently reflect those same changes in the site's layout that were accompanied by major economic investments. Thousands of artefacts were recovered during the excavation of Period 4 deposits, many of which are residues attributable to earlier periods but that nevertheless testify to the long-term role of the site in the management of resources and the storing of produce. The recording of hundreds of grain storage jars, animal bone remains — attesting to the breeding of pigs and horses — and numerous iron finds connected to different forms of activities, along with twenty-one coins (dating between the tenth and early eleventh centuries), all contribute in pointing to the importance of Vetricella in the economic-productive system of the surrounding territory.[1]

Further stratigraphic data also seem to show the moment of significant historical transformation that occurred between the tenth and eleventh centuries, on the threshold of an historical and political upheaval that led to a drastic change in the actors involved. It is possible to recognize a direct link between the decline recorded at the site after the mid-eleventh century and the diminishment of public authority in Tuscany in the same period, with the resulting exponential growth of castles and territorial aristocracies. Likewise, archaeo-logical analysis conducted in the lower Val di Pecora has recorded the abrupt disappearance of the previously illustrated system of small settlement nuclei, reflected also in the total absence of twelfth-century archaeological material. The last two periods of occupation attested at Vetricella (Periods 5 and 6) still feature the central tower structure (dismantled during the twelfth century) and wooden enclosures, although lacking consistent stratigraphic deposits.

In conclusion, the study of the coastal plain of Scarlino and the Pecora River has allowed scholars to analyse under new lenses a medieval landscape that had been only partially considered in previous historical models, providing new insights thanks to the work carried out at Vetricella. A landscape that, as we have seen, was not only populated by hilltop settlements, but also by different-sized nuclei scattered across the lowlands, perhaps part of a wider network set in a territory in which environmental elements such as the wide coastal seaboard, large inland lake, flat marshland areas, and cultivated fields, as well as the proximity of important mining resources, were all decisive factors in its settlement history. In spite of previous historical narratives, archaeological evidence shows a non-marginal

---

1 For a detailed analysis of the numerous artefacts recovered from the Vetricella site, see contributions dedicated to specific classes of materials in Bianchi and Hodges 2020.

Figure 6.7. A–B) Period plans of the fourth phase of occupation at Vetricella, divided into two sub-phases (Period 4.1 and Period 4.2). C) Detail of the first mortar mixer, located to the south of the tower. D) Aerial view of the stone and mortar cobbling set directly over the innermost ditch (photos by the authors).

plain where resources were still considered key elements in the early Middle Ages, despite marked differences with the earlier Roman period.

[LM]

Conclusions

At the end of this brief review it is possible to put forward some concluding remarks.

From a methodological point of view, it is useful to emphasize how, thanks to a multidisciplinary approach, the integration of different sources and the merging of different fields of specialization, even for an area that has seen such extensive study as southern Tuscany, it is possible to gather new data, useful for the reconstruction of the historical landscape, especially the medieval one. In this regard, the case study offered by the Val di Cornia, and in particular the dune of Carlappiano and the area of Torre Mozza, is exemplary. Thanks to the newly acquired data, a much more detailed picture of the local environmental context has been drawn, in which the lagoon areas do not appear so markedly different, in historical times, from what was documented in the first half of the nineteenth century.

The multidisciplinary approach (archaeological, geoarchaeological, geochemical, palynological and micropaleontological) adopted by the project has also proved fundamental in advancing new reconstructive hypotheses in relation to the fluvial dynamics of the largest of the plain's watercourses, the Cornia river, and the strong impact it had on both the coastal dunes, the roads crossing the plain and the settlement network. The use of the same multidisciplinary approach in the Val di Pecora allowed to understand the strong connections between certain specific environmental contexts and the development of the human landscape, a relationship that, during the medieval period, was no longer the cause of the abandonment of the lowland areas and related productive activities, but rather an element of precise administrative policy strategies. The correct reconstruction of the historic landscape also permitted to better comprehend the archaeological data acquired from the excavations carried out at the site of Vetricella in relation to its territorial context.

In conclusion: the ERC nEU-Med project, and in particular the study of the coastal plains of the Pecora and Cornia rivers, offered the opportunity to analyse an evolving landscape under a new lens, focusing on the settlement and resource exploitation dynamics of the medieval period, better defining the environmental characteristics of the landscape while at the same time highlighting its settlement and production potential. Thanks to the evaluation of the environmental proxies and their inclusion in a solid historical-archaeological framework, the survey also revealed the specific peculiarities, and thus the strengths, of the two plains between Late Antiquity and the Middle Ages: to the north, the wide Cornia valley, with its shallow inland waters, was particularly suited to the production of salt, a resource that had a long history in this area, crucial also in the medieval period, as the excavation of Carlappiano has clearly shown. Further south, the Val di Pecora, with its deep lagoon and landing points, a natural outlet for the mineral resources from the hinterland and main collector of those from the nearby Island of Elba, offered the opportunity to investigate for the first time the material traces of the central site of a large royal *curtis*, through the excavation of Vetricella. As early as the eighth century, the role of the two plains appears anything but marginal; on the contrary, the environmental, settlement and trade context reconstructed thanks to nEU-Med proves to be functional to precise economic strategies. In particular, the control of specific well-established cycles of production (first and foremost salt and iron) is probably at the root of the long permanence of these territories within the royal fisc, as historical documents, first and foremost the dotary of Hugh of Arles, testify.

The excavation of Vetricella, in particular, highlighted the role played by the site as a collector of different resources from a vast hinterland, albeit in a profoundly ruralized context (Hodges in this volume).

It is precisely the exceptional nature of Vetricella, together with the recent study of the surrounding territory, that tells us a new story characterized by profound landscape transformations and an effective exploitation of its economic potential, which began as early as the Carolingian period and where the main protagonists were kings and the public authority (Marasco and Briano 2020; Bianchi 2022).

[LD, LM]

Works Cited

Aranguren, Bianca Maria, Maria Rosaria Cinquegrana, Alberto De Bonis, Vincenza Guarino, Vincenzo Morra, and Marco Pacciarelli. 2014. 'Le strutture e lo scarico di olle del Puntone Nuovo di Scarlino (GR) e i siti costieri specializzati della protostoria mediotirrenica', *Rivista di Scienze Preistoriche*, 64: 227–58

Bartoli, Cinzia. 2017. 'La cartografia storica come strumento di conoscenza del territorio e delle sue dinamiche. Alcune considerazioni sull'applicazione dei dati geo-storici nell'ambito della ricerca archeologica nel golfo di Piombino e Follonica', *Trame nello Spazio*, 7: 61–67

Benvenuti, Marco, Giovanna Bianchi, Jacopo Bruttini, Mauro Buonicontri, Laura Chiarantini, Luisa Dallai, Gaetano Di Pasquale, Alessandro Donati, Francesca Grassi, and Valentina, Pescini. 2015. 'Studying the Colline Metallifere Mining area in Tuscany: An Interdisciplinary Approach', in *IES Book of the 9th International Symposium on Archaeological Mining History (Trento, 5–8th June 2014)* (Valkenburg aan de GeuL: Silvertant Erfgoedprojecten), pp. 261–87

Bianchi, Giovanna. 2011. 'Miscelare la calce tra lavoro manuale e meccanico. Organizzazione del cantiere e possibili tematismi della ricerca', in *Dopo la calcara: la produzione della calce nell'altomedioevo*, ed. by Giovanna Bianchi, Archeologia dell'Architettura, 16 (Florence: All'Insegna del Giglio), pp. 9–18

Bianchi, Giovanna. 2022. *Archeologia dei beni pubblici. Alle origini della crescita economica in una regione mediterranea (secc. IX–XI)* (Florence: All'Insegna del Giglio)

Bianchi Giovanna, and Simone Maria Collavini. 2018. 'Public Estates and Economic Strategies in Early Medieval Tuscany: Toward a New Interpretation', in *Origins of a New Economic Union (7th-12th Centuries). Preliminary Results of the nEU-Med Project: October 2015–March 2017*, ed. by Giovanna Bianchi and Richard Hodges, Biblioteca di Archeologia Medievale, 25 (Florence: All'Insegna del Giglio), pp. 147–62

Bianchi, Giovanna, and Richard Hodges (eds). 2018. *Origins of a New Economic Union (7th-12th Centuries). Preliminary Results of the nEU-Med Project: October 2015–March 2017*, Biblioteca di Archeologia Medievale, 25 (Florence: All'Insegna del Giglio)

——. 2020. *The nEU-Med Project: Vetricella, an Early Medieval Royal Property on Tuscany's Mediterranean*, Biblioteca di Archeologia Medievale, 28 (Florence: All'Insegna del Giglio)

Bianchi, Giovanna, and Luisa Dallai. 2019. 'Le district minier des Collines Métallifères (Toscane, Italie) durant la période médiévale. L'exploitation des ressources et les implications politiques et économiques', in *Les métaux précieux en Méditerranée médiévale. Exploitations, transformations, circulations*, ed. by Nicolas Minvielle Larousse, Giovanna Bianchi, and Marie Christine Bailly Maître, Bibliothèque d'Archéologie Méditerranéenne et Africaine, 27 (Aix en Provence: Presses Universitaires de Provence), pp. 29–40

Botarelli, Lucia, and Franci Cambi. 2004–2005. 'Il territorio di Populonia fra il periodo etrusco tardo e il periodo romano. Ambiente, viabilità, insediamenti', in *Populonia. Scavi e ricerche dal 1998 al 2004*, ed. by Gilda Bartoloni, Scienze dell'Antichità. Storia archeologia antropologia, 12 (Rome: Quasar), pp. 23–43

Buonincontri, Mauro Paolo, Gaetano Di Pasquale, and Marta Rossi. 2018. 'The Ancient Plan Landscape by means of the Anthracological Remains', in *Investigations at Carlappiano. New archaeological Findings in Anthropic and Natural Landscapes*, ed. by Luisa Dallai, in *Origins of a New Economic Union (7th-12th Centuries). Preliminary Results of the nEU-Med Project: October 2015–March 2017*, ed. by Giovanna Bianchi and Richard Hodges, Biblioteca di Archeologia Medievale, 25 (Florence: All'Insegna del Giglio), pp. 42–43

Buonincontri, Mauro Paolo, Pierluigi Pieruccini, Daide Susini, Carmine Lubritto, Paola Ricci, Fabian Rey, Willy Tinner, Daniele Colombaroli, Ruth Drescher-Schneider, Luisa Dallai, Lorenzo Marasco, Giulio Poggi, Giovanna Bianchi, Richard Hodges, and Gaetano Di Pasquale. 2020. 'Shaping Mediterranean Landscapes: the Cultural Impact of Anthropogenic Fires in Tyrrhenian Southern Tuscany during the Iron and Middle Ages (800–450 BC / AD 650–1300)', *The Holocene*, 30.10: 1420–37

Cambi, Franco. 2002, 'I confini del territorio di Populonia: stato della questione', in *Materiali per Populonia*, ed. by Franco Cambi and Daniele Manacorda (Florence, All'Insegna del Giglio), pp. 9–29

Cambi, Franco. 2009. 'Populonia. Ferro, territorio e bacini di approvvigionamento fra il periodo etrusco e il periodo romano', in *Materiali da costruzione e produzione del ferro. Studi sull'economia populoniese fra periodo etrusco e romanizzazione*, ed. by Franco Cambi, Fernanda Cavari, and Cynthia Mascione (Bari: Edipuglia), pp. 221–30

Cambi, Franco, Fernanda Cavari, and Cynthia Mascione (eds). 2009. *Materiali da costruzione e produzione del ferro. Studi sull'economia populoniense fra periodo etrusco e romanizzazione* (Bari: Edipuglia)

Carusi, Cristina. 2018. 'Intorno alla produzione di sale a Populonia e nell'ager cosanus: due casi di studio a confronto', in *Materiali per Populonia 8*, ed. by Valeria Acconcia and Claudia Rizzitelli (Pisa: ETS), pp. 303–12

Censini, Gianfranco, Armando Costantini, Antonio Lazzarotto, Michele Maccantelli, Renato Mazzanti, Fabio Sandrelli, and Enrico Tavarnelli. 1991. 'Evoluzione geomorfologica della pianura di Piombino in Toscana', *Geografia Fisica e Dinamica Quaternaria*, 14: 45–62

Cucini, Costanza. 1985. 'Topografia del territorio delle valli del Pecora e dell'Alma', in *Scarlino I. Storia e territorio*, ed. by Riccardo Francovich (Florence: All'Insegna del Giglio), pp. 147–335

Dallai, Luisa. 2016. 'Paesaggio e risorse: il monastero di San Quirico di Populonia, la pianura ed il promontorio di Piombino', in *Un monastero sul mare. Ricerche a San Quirico di Populonia (Piombino, LI) / A Monastery by the Sea. Archaeological Research at San Quirico di Populonia (Piombino, LI)*, ed. by Giovanna, Bianchi and Sauro Gelichi, Biblioteca di Archeologia Medievale, 24 (Florence: All'Insegna del Giglio), pp. 89–108

—— (ed.). 2018. 'Investigations at Carlappiano. New Archaeological Findings in Anthropic and Natural Landscapes', in *Origins of a New Economic Union (7ᵗʰ-12ᵗʰ Centuries). Preliminary Results of the nEU-Med Project: October 2015–March 2017*, ed. by Giovanna Bianchi and Richard Hodges, Biblioteca di Archeologia Medievale, 25 (Florence: All'Insegna del Giglio), pp. 29–56

Dallai, Luisa, and Vanessa Volpi. 2019. 'Nuovi approcci allo studio del paesaggio storico: il progeto ERC nEUMed e le indagini multidisciplinari condotte nella bassa Val di Cornia', *Archeologia medievale*, 49: 179–95

Dallai, Luisa, Lorenzo Marasco, and Vanessa Volpi. 2018. 'Progetto ERC nEU-Med: pXRF e magnetometria, uno studio integrato del paesaggio antropico in Val di Cornia e Val di Pecora', in *Atti dell'VIII Congresso Nazionale di Archeologia Medievale. Vol. 2, Sez. III – Paesaggio e Territorio*, ed. by Francesca Sogliani, Brunella Gargiulo, Ester Annuniata, and Valentino Vitale, SAMI (Florence: All'Insegna del Giglio), pp. 98–103

Dallai Luisa, Vanessa, Volpi, and Isabella Carli. 2020. 'Archaeological and Geochemical Surveys in the Pecora Valley: the First Results', in *The nEU-Med Project: Vetricella, An Early Medieval Royal Property on Tuscany's Mediterranean*, ed. by Giovanna Bianchi and Richard Hodges, Biblioteca di Archeologia Medievale, 28 (Florence: All'Insegna del Giglio), pp. 143–58

Fedeli, Franco. 1983. *Populonia. Storia e territorio* (Florence: All'Insegna del Giglio)

Federici, Paolo Roberto, and Renato Mazzanti. 1995. 'Note sulle pianure costiere della Toscana', *Memorie della Società Geografica Italiana*, 5: 65–70

Franceschi, Franco. 2017. 'La crescita economica dell'Occidente medievale: un tema storico non ancora esaurito. Introduzione', in *Atti del XXV Convegno Internazionale di Studi, Centro Italiano di Studi di Storia e d'Arte (Pistoia, 14–17th May 2015)* (Rome: Viella), pp. 1–24

Francovich, Riccardo (ed.). 1985. *Scarlino I. Storia e territorio* (Florence: All'Insegna del Giglio)

——. 2008. 'The Beginning of Hilltop Villages in Early Medieval Tuscany', in *The Long Morning of Medieval Europe*, ed. by Jennifer Davis and Michael McCormick (London: Routledge), pp. 55–82

Francovich, Riccardo, and Richard Hodges. 2003. *Villa to Village. The Transformation of the Roman Countryside in Italy, c. 400–1000* (London: Duckworth)

Hodges, Richard. 2018. 'Towards a New Mediterranean Narrative for Early Medieval Tuscany', in *Origins of a New Economic Union (7th-12th Centuries). Preliminary Results of the nEU-Med Project: October 2015–March 2017*, ed. by Giovanna Bianchi and Richard Hodges, Biblioteca di Archeologia Medievale, 25 (Florence: All'Insegna del Giglio), pp. 11–18

Isola, Carlo. 2009. 'Le lagune di Populonia dall'antichità alle bonifiche', in *Materiali da costruzione e produzione del ferro. Studi sull'economia populoniese fra periodo etrusco e romanizzazione*, ed. by Franco Cambi, Fernanda Cavari, and Cynthia Mascione (Bari: Edipuglia), pp. 163–70

Jan, Sevink, Wieke de Neef, Luca Alessandri, Rutger L. van Hall, Burkart Ullrich, and Peter A. J. Attema. 2020. 'Protohistoric Briquetage at Puntone (Tuscany, Italy): Principles and Processes of an Industry based on the Leaching of Saline Lagoonal Sediments', *Geoarchaeology*: 1–18, DOI: 10.1002/gea.21820

Marasco, Lorenzo. 2009. 'Un castello di pianura in località Vetricella a Scarlino (Scarlino Scalo, GR): indagini preliminari e saggi di verifica', in *Atti dell'VIII Congresso Nazionale di Archeologia Medievale. Vol. 2, Sez. III – Paesaggio e Territorio*, ed. by Pasquale Favia and Giuliano Volpe, SAMI (Florence: All'Insegna del Giglio), pp. 326–31

——. 2012. 'Una "motta" medievale in Toscana: nuovi dati sull'assetto di una pianura costiera maremmana tra alto medioevo e secoli centrali', in *Villaggi, comunità e paesaggi medievali*, ed. by Paola Galetti, Incontri di studio, 10 (Spoleto: CISAM), pp. 709–18

——. 2013. 'La Castellina di Scarlino e le fortificazioni di terra nelle pianure costiere della Maremma Settentrionale', in *Fortificazioni di terra in Italia: motte, tumuli, tumbe e recinti*, ed. by Aldo Angelo Settia, Lorenzo Marasco, and Fabio Saggioro, Archeologia Medievale, 40 (Florence: All'Insegna del Giglio), pp. 57–68

—— (ed.). 2018. 'Investigations at Vetricella: New Archaeological Findings in Anthropic and Natural Landscapes', in *Origins of a New Economic Union (7ᵗʰ-12ᵗʰ Centuries). Preliminary Results of the nEU-Med Project: October 2015–March 2017*, ed. by Giovanna Bianchi and Richard Hodges, Biblioteca di Archeologia Medievale, 25 (Florence: All'Insegna del Giglio), pp. 57–80

Marasco, Lorenzo, and Arianna Briano. 2020. 'The Stratigraphic Sequence at the Site of Vetricella (Scarlino, Grosseto): A Revised Interpretation (8th-13th Centuries)', in *The nEU-Med Project: Vetricella, an Early Medieval Royal Property on Tuscany's Mediterranean*, ed. by Giovanna Bianchi and Richard Hodges, Biblioteca di Archeologia Medievale, 28 (Florence: All'Insegna del Giglio), pp. 9–21

Pieruccini, Pierluigi, Mauro Paolo Buonincontri, Davide Susini, Carmine Lubritto, and Gaetano Di Pasquale. 2018. 'Changing Landscapes in the Colline Metallifere (Southern Tuscany, Italy): Early Medieval Palaeohydrology', in *Origins of a New Economic Union (7th-12th Centuries). Preliminary Results of the nEU-Med Project: October 2015–March 2017*, ed. by Giovanna Bianchi and Richard Hodges, Biblioteca di Archeologia Medievale, 25 (Florence: All'Insegna del Giglio), pp. 19–28

Pieruccini, Pierluigi, and Davide Susini. 2020. 'The Holocene Sedimentary Record and the Landscape Evolution along the Coastal Plains of the Pecora and Cornia Rivers (Southern Tuscany, Italy): Preliminary Results and Future Perspectives', in *The nEU-Med Project: Vetricella, an Early Medieval Royal Property on Tuscany's Mediterranean*, ed. by Giovanna Bianchi and Richard Hodges, Biblioteca di Archeologia Medievale, 28 (Florence: All'Insegna del Giglio), pp. 161–68

Pieruccini, Pierluigi, Davide Susini, Mauro Paolo Buonincontri, Giovanna Bianchi, Richard Hodges, Carmine Lubritto, and Gaetano Di Pasquale. 2021. 'Late Holocene Human-induced Landscape Changes in Calcareous Tufa Environments in Central Mediterranean Valleys (Pecora River, Southern Tuscany, Italy)', *Geomorphology*, 383, 107691, <https://doi.org/10.1016/j.geomorph.2021.107691>

Pellegrini, Lucia. 1984. *La bonifica della Val di Cornia al tempo di Leopoldo II (1831–1860)* (Pontedera: Bandecchi e Vivaldi)

Poggi, Giulio. 2021. 'Evoluzione del paesaggio storico e dinamiche uomo-ambiente: sistemi di fonti, Remote Sensing e multi-proxies ambientali (Pianura costiera del Fiume Cornia, Toscana Meridionale, Italia)' <10.25434/poggi-giulio_phd2021>, PhD Thesis

Sevink, Jan, Wieke de Neef, Luca Alessandri, Rutger L. van Hall, Burkart Ullrich, and Peter A. J. Attema. 2020. 'Protohistoric Priquetage at Puntone (Tuscany, Italy): Principles and Processes of an Industry Based on the Leaching of Saline Lagoonal Sediments', *Geoarchaeology*: 1–18, DOI: 10.1002/gea.21820

Susini, Davide, and Pierluigi Pieruccini. 2020. 'Preliminary Geoarchaeological Results from the Intermediate Ring-shaped Ditch at the Archaeological Site of Vetricella (Scarlino, Grosseto)', in *The nEU-Med Project: Vetricella, an Early Medieval Royal Property on Tuscany's Mediterranean*, ed. by Giovanna Bianchi and Richard Hodges, Biblioteca di Archeologia Medievale, 28 (Florence: All'Insegna del Giglio), pp. 29–32

Tomei, Paolo. 2020. 'Il sale e la seta. Sulle risorse pubbliche nel Tirreno settentrionale (secoli V–XI)', in *La transizione dall'antichità al medioevo nel Mediterraneo centro-orientale*, ed. by Giovanni Salmeri and Paolo Tomei, Studi Di Archeologia e Storia del Mondo Antico e Medievale, 4 (Pisa: ETS), pp. 21–38

Vaccaro, Emanuele. 2018. 'Long-distance Ceramic Connections: Portus Scabris (Portiglioni-GR), Coastal Tuscany and the Tyrrhenian Sea', in *Origins of a New Economic Union (7th-12th Centuries). Preliminary Results of the nEU-Med Project: October 2015–March 2017*, ed. by Giovanna Bianchi and Richard Hodges, Biblioteca di Archeologia Medievale, 25 (Florence: All'Insegna del Giglio), pp. 81–100

Viva, Serena. 2020. 'Burials from the Cemetery at Vetricella (Scarlino, Grosseto): Anthropological, Paleodemographic and Paleopathological Analysis', in *The nEU-Med Project: Vetricella, an Early Medieval Royal Property on Tuscany's Mediterranean*, ed. by Giovanna Bianchi and Richard Hodges (Florence: All'Insegna del Giglio), pp. 105–20

Volpi, Vanessa. 2018. 'The Contribution of Geochemical Prospection to the Interpretation of Excavation Data', in *Investigations at Carlappiano. New archaeological Findings in Anthropic and Natural Landscapes*, ed. by Luisa Dallai, in *Origins of a New Economic Union (7th-12th Centuries). Preliminary Results of the nEU-Med Project: October 2015–March 2017*, ed. by Giovanna Bianchi and Richard Hodges, Biblioteca di Archeologia Medievale, 25 (Florence: All'Insegna del Giglio), pp. 43–44

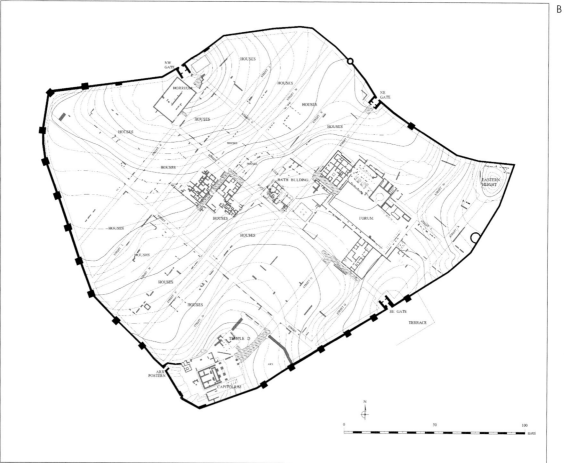

Figure 7.1. Cosa, the site (© Cosa Excavations, reproduced with permission).

ANDREA U. DE GIORGI, MICHELLE HOBART,
MELISSA LUDKE, AND RUSSELL T. SCOTT

7. Cosa during Late Antiquity

Despite its small size, the Latin colony of Cosa has produced a staggering amount of archaeological and historical information, while also occupying a prominent place in the discussion of Roman urbanism in southern Etruria.[1] A wealth of studies, a majority of which appear in the Memoirs of the American Academy in Rome, have illustrated the site's monuments and their cultural significance (Fig. 7.1),[2] and this information continues to attract scholarly attention, especially as regards Cosa's built environment and material culture.[3]

Overall, the narrative of its settlement in the midst of political and presumably environmental vicissitudes that have led to its now popular characterization as 'intermittent town' is well known.[4] The record of research and publication was begun more than seventy years ago under the leadership of Frank E. Brown, who was also responsible for the creation of a touristic itinerary and a designated on-site museum that was something of a novelty in Italy at that time. His work has unpacked a great deal of Cosa's rich history.[5] The field work at Cosa also spearheaded a flurry of research in the territory of the city and its immediate environs, not least the *Portus Cosanus*, its maritime outlet.[6] Thanks to Doro Levi's early reconnaissance work and the seminal investigations of American and Italian teams in the 1970s in the Valle

d'Oro, the fertile district adjacent to the town site, this area became a locus of fundamental discussions about the nature of the Roman villa system, its economy, and, ultimately, duration.[7]

This impressive scholarly legacy has stood the test of time, yet only tangentially has it addressed the epochs that followed Cosa's heyday in the Republican and Early Imperial periods. We owe it to Elizabeth Fentress that the post-classical modifications of the city and their historical framework finally took centre stage, highlighting the diversity of community settlement. Current research now addresses the causes that hindered, and in turn, accelerated the transformation of Cosa's built environment from the second century AD onward.[8] Its environmental limitations, and, not least, endemic lack of water, have been foregrounded in the study of the site's evolution and ecology.[9] No matter how complex the procurement and conservation of water might have been, this did not bar human occupation on the promontory, as shown by sophisticated water harvesting, retention, and delivery systems over the centuries. In this context, the current excavation of a bath establishment west of the forum gives new evidence for sophisticated water management on site and for Cosa's occupation beyond the high Empire.

Nevertheless, how Cosa fared during Late Antiquity and the early Middle Ages remains to be brought into

---

1   We would like to express our gratitude to the editors, the reviewers, and everyone at Brepols. Also, special thanks to Jacque Collins-Clinton who read an early version of the paper.

2   Scott 2019, 21–29.

3   Mogetta 2019, 241–68.

4   Fentress was the first to coin the term in 2003.

5   The scholarship on archaeological fieldwork at Cosa is vast; for a recent summary, see De Giorgi 2019.

6   McCann 1987.

---

7   Dyson 2005; Carandini and others 2002; Castagnoli 1956, 149–65; Dyson 1978, 251–68; Rathbone 1981, 10–23. Also of importance is the trail blazing survey of Doro Levi in the area of Monte Nebbiello, le Forane, and la valle del fosso Radicata, see Levi 1927.

8   Scott and others 2021, 201–18.

9   De Giorgi 2018, 3–26.

Andrea U. De Giorgi (adegiorgi@fsu.edu) Florida State University

Michelle Hobart (michelle.hobart@cooper.edu) Cooper Union University

Melissa Ludke (mludke@msu.edu) Florida State University

Russell T. Scott (dscott@brynmawr.edu) Bryn Mawr College

Archaeological Landscapes of Late Antique and Early Medieval Tuscia: Research and Field Papers, ed. by Riccardo Rao and Alessandro Sebastiani, MEDITO 3 (Turnhout 2023), pp. 126–140

BREPOLS ❧ PUBLISHERS   DOI 10.1484/M.MEDITO-EB.5.133997

sharper focus, particularly the phases of abandonment and repopulation that punctuated life there in the post-classical age. The settlement strategies devised in response to historical and environmental challenges in particular continue to offer exciting possibilities for more nuanced investigation.

Early Visits, Empty Cityscapes, and Settlement in Post-Classical Cosa

Upon his 1842 visit to Cosa, George Dennis was not particularly impressed, save for his bewilderment in front of the ramparts.[10] As a result, his description of the Cosa ruins teems with the malaise of evoking an ancient city turned into a haven for criminals. Inadvertently or not, Dennis's description reprised the trope of the desolate city abandoned to rodents, originally found in the AD 417 travelogue of Rutilius Claudius Namantianus, and a recurring image in the scholarly treatment of Cosa.[11] What has not been sufficiently stressed, however, is that Namatianus' *De Reditu Suo* stands out for its poetic achievements, less so for ethnographic merits.[12] His disquiet over the Visigothic invasions contributed to the generally gloomy aura of the poem, which essentially dealt with a world that was changing in fundamental ways. Empty cityscapes, with or without rodents, served the verse well.

Textual references aside, the archaeological record of Cosa during Late Antiquity is at variance with his view of a vanished city in the fifth century. To be sure, the data offers a picture of a community that by all measures had shrunk markedly from its heyday. It was destitute, but nevertheless alive to the opportunities that the site could offer. How this community and its anchorage at the *Portus Cosanus* could potentially still be integrated into the network of interregional maritime connections remains to be determined. It is indeed a considerable distance between *Portus Pisanus* and Ostia, and an anchorage like that of Cosa may have

been serviceable during the fifth to seventh centuries.[13] The evidence is tenuous, but there are ways to move the discussion forward.

An early analysis by F. Bisconti sought to illustrate the vitality of the post-classical epoch at Cosa.[14] In particular, he compiled a list of buildings in the *Forum* and on the *Arx* that were plausibly occupied from the third century onward. Comprehensive though this catalogue of sites may be, it produces, however, a picture of settlement that remains inert and does not include the presumed *statio* at Succosa, the twin community that lies less than one km east of Cosa, as the crow flies (Fig. 7.2). Attested by the *Tabula Peutingeriana*, its physical remains have yet to be tested and incorporated within the context of the late antique, Byzantine, and early medieval narrative of area settlement.[15] In connection with the ongoing discussion about comparative settlement patterns in Tuscany and central Italy in the Early Middle Ages, several post-excavation narratives by Elizabeth Fentress and her colleagues have also furthered the discussion of Cosa's continuity of occupation after the Severan age, with broader cultural trends.[16] The question of the elusive Byzantine settlement at the site and its evolution, however, needs to be taken up again.

Rethinking the Post-Roman Settlement after Twenty Years: The State of the Question

The recent revival of archaeological excavations of the Roman bath complex near the Forum, here presented, as well as a reassessment of legacy data, make it now possible to enlarge our sense of Cosa's late antique occupation. In what follows, we highlight new methodological and material guidelines. The physical evidence for post-Roman settlement is a matter of dispute, with pottery and small finds being the most reliable source. Arguably, for the treatment of this epoch and the dating of the material, Stephen Dyson's *Cosa: The Utilitarian Pottery* remains a benchmark. It provides a cross section of daily life in the shrinking community and gestures at the range of exchanges and interactions that the town had with the Mediterranean at large. It needs to be stressed, however, that the relevant ceramic material analysed by Dyson was collected from a cistern in the forum, turned as it were into a rubbish pit. The evidence thus confirms that the reservoir went

---

10 Dennis 1848, 276. He wrote: 'Within the city, all is ruin — a chaos of crumbling walls, overturned masonry, scattered masses of bare rock, and subterranean vaults, "where the owl peeps deeming it midnight," — all overrun with shrubs and creepers, and acanthus in great profusion. The popular superstition may be pardoned for regarding this as the haunt of demons; for ages it was the den of bandits and outlaws, and tradition, kept alive by the natural gloominess of the spot, has thus preserved, it may be, the remembrance of their atrocities.'

11 Rut. Nam. *de red.* 285–90: 'Dicuntur cives quondam migrare coacti muribus infestos deservisse lares.' See for instance McCann 1987, 27. Also Fentress and Cirelli 2012, a contribution to a volume on extinct cities; Celuzza 2015.

12 Clarke 2014, 89–107.

13 Sami 2021, 257.

14 Bisconti 1985, 63–77.

15 Fentress and others 2003.

16 Fentress and Cirelli 2012.

Figure 7.2. Cosa, the territory and Succosa (Richard Talbert and Andrea U. De Giorgi, reproduced with permission).

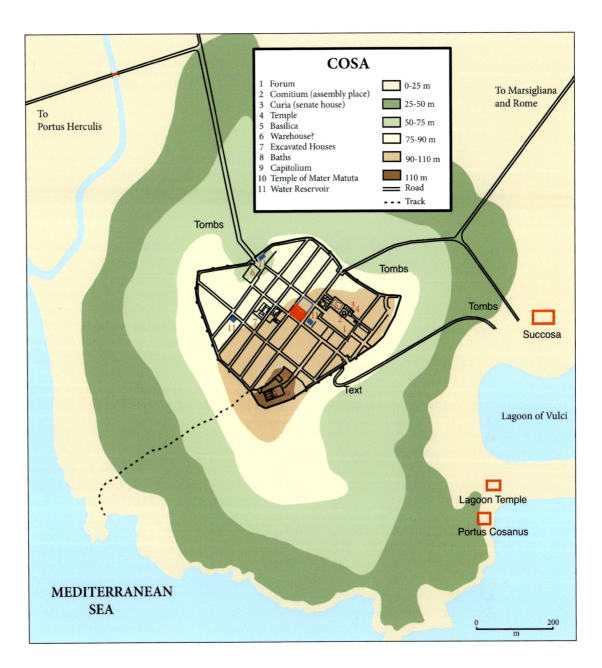

out of use between the sixth and seventh centuries.[17] Unfortunately, the excavation data in the forum casts modest light on the type of village that occupied this space following the Severan era, as we shall see below.

Another yardstick in our analysis is that after two hundred years of apparent abandonment, Cosa was occupied again between the ninth and tenth centuries. The presence of two small cemeteries, within the perimeter of the city walls, confirms that early medieval settlers re-occupied both the *Arx* and the bottom of the hill of the Eastern Height between the ninth and the thirteenth centuries. These settlements were dated by coins and skeletal evidence.[18] Not much more physical evidence survives: small huts have left scant traces on the Eastern Height because, as on the *Arx*, during World War II the area was transformed into an artillery position, with consequent destruction of the preexisting remains. To sum up: in the ebb and flow of occupation it is a matter of fact that a medieval community is attested on the *Arx*, the Eastern Height, and in the *Forum*. The reprise of the archaeological datasets, however, enables a more finely grained reading of the story.

---

17 Cerri and others 2003, 269–319, with revisions of Dyson's dating.

18 Fentress and others 2003, 106–07.

Figure 7.3. Cosa: The medieval wall on the Arx (photo by Andrea U. De Giorgi).

The Excavation Datasets

Starting with the fifth century AD, Cosa underwent outright decline. The analysis of the material culture and the reassessment of the early excavations highlight the increasing reduction in human presence within the city walls. For instance, the mithraeum and the shrine of Liber pater were in use during the early fifth century, only to be abandoned around the middle of the century when the latter plausibly underwent disruption, as scatters of materials outside the building attest.[19] At that time, most public buildings of the *Forum*, if not all, were also abandoned. Yet, the strongest argument for continuity comes from accumulations of late antique material retrieved from the large forum cistern already mentioned and other areas within the walls and republished in the *Cosa V* volume (Fentress and others 2003). The questions at issue are thus the reduction of the post-Roman community and the putative Byzantine revival both in the *Forum* and on the *Arx*.

Previously, the establishment of a purported fortified settlement under a Byzantine officer was described in conjunction with the analysis of the materials excavated earlier by Brown and by the 1997 expedition. Also, the discovery of slingshots has been interpreted as part of the equipment used by the Byzantine infantry, but the dating of this weaponry is problematic.[20] (In that same vein, soap stone, or *pietra ollare*, can also be found in periods as late as the ninth and tenth centuries). Nevertheless, the illustration of the reconstructed sixth century Byzantine Arx at Cosa appears in several publications and has gone unchallenged; its hypothetical presence must therefore be reassessed against the background of historical and material data that has emerged in the last twenty years. A 1991 *PBSR* study set the path for the archaeological exploration and study of post-Roman Cosa.[21] In particular, its analysis showed the site's integration in maritime networks reaching as far as the Black Sea, Syria, and, in the west, the Narbornnese region. These frameworks, however, were not explored to the fullest.

It needs to be stressed that the preliminary dating of the post-Roman materials of the Arx is based on two archaeological contexts; one opened in 1990 (Arx II, 4, 14 with late ARS), and the rest, the majority, from unstratified material on the Arx, collected by Brown's team between 1948 and 1950.[22] This distinction between Brown's collections and those later published in *Cosa V* is key, inasmuch as the dating for this area relies mostly on the surface materials, and no record seems to survive of where exactly these were found. In other words, with the archaeologists seeking to reach the Republican and Imperial layers, much of the 'later' record was presumably overlooked or inaccessible under the World War II installations — thirty years would have to elapse for medieval archaeology to become a discipline in its own right.[23] Fortunately, Brown's exploration collected examples of early medieval 'Forum Ware' and much of the thirteenth century medieval glazed pottery published in *Cosa V*; also, a few key fragments that dated the Byzantine wall were found in the 'construction trench'.[24] These fortuitous finds were pivotal in advancing the subject of Byzantine life at Cosa. While the depth of Brown's clearing of the area of Temple D, the edge of the Arx compound, and the overall stratigraphy remain a matter of dispute, the presence of a long stretch of a well-built medieval wall north of Temple D confirms the validity of the historical accounts and, overall, helps us make sense of the abundant late medieval pottery from the Arx surface collection (Fig. 7.3).

---

19 Collins Clinton 1977. See in particular the inscribed table support, pp. 15, 56–57 no. 9, fig. 30. This may have been used originally in an earlier Bacchic setting. Also, two female heads that were found in 1967 on the threshold of the shrine entrance: nos 2 and 3, pp. 50–52. Collins-Clinton made clear in her book that the sculptures were reused from other contexts or places, see p. 24. As for the mithraeum's use in the fifth century, of relevance is the evidence of north African lamps and copies, nos 1066–1067; 1079; 1084. See Fitch and Goldman 1994.

20 Rihill 2009.
21 Fentress and others 1991.
22 Fentress and others 1991.
23 Hobart 2023.
24 Fentress and others 1991; Fentress and others 2003.

In the late 1990s Fentress moved her exploration from the *Arx* to the *Forum* to study previously excavated areas within the civic buildings. Here new trenches were opened with a view toward finding the 'late ovens' north of the *Curia*, which had previously been cleared down to solid foundations. The discovery of fragments of maiolica raises the issue of medieval, rather than 'Byzantine' finds. Interestingly, Brown's investigations of the *Forum* were still legible in the 90s, thanks to the recognizable signature of spoil heaps and trenches. More importantly, there was also a sequence of phase maps spanning the Republican period from 180 BC on to the fourth and fifth centuries AD, to be exact AD 330–415 (Fig. 7.4). The late dating was based on Dyson's pottery studies, which in the 70s defined the last periodization of the history of the site and had not yet been revised. Whether medieval materials were also part of the equation is unknown.

The Forum Bath

Excavation of two bath suites adjacent to the *Forum* of Cosa was conducted by Florida State University and Bryn Mawr College during the month of June from 2013 to 2019 and resumed in the Spring of 2022. The complexes, located in grid squares VI/VII–D, were incompletely plotted in the initial survey of the town site made during the first years of the excavations by the American Academy in Rome under Brown and described as the remains of a single small bath of unknown size and likely Republican date.[25] The later work has distinguished two baths, one of Augustan date in the upper half of the block, accessed from Street O, the other of late Hadrianic/early Antonine date. It also identified a significant post-antique robbing phase of the area that apparently served building operations that were in course on the *Arx* and perhaps elsewhere in the early fourteenth century.

The soundings in both areas, painstakingly negotiating olive trees and unmovable fallen vaulting, have brought to light assemblages that attest to activities at the site spilling into the fourth and fifth centuries AD, with some tenuous traces of sixth century materials, as well as of the fourteenth century (Fig. 7.5).[26] Central Sounding 1 (CS1), in particular, offers a compelling sample of ARS 'D' and African cooking wares, among others, that bear on questions about the occupation of the site. CS 1 (stratigraphic units 18000, 180111,

---

25 Brown 1951; Brown, Richardson, and Richardson 1994. Cf. Oleson 1984; McCann 1987, 98–128.
26 The materials were studied and catalogued by Massimo Brando, Christina Cha, and Rebecca Frank.

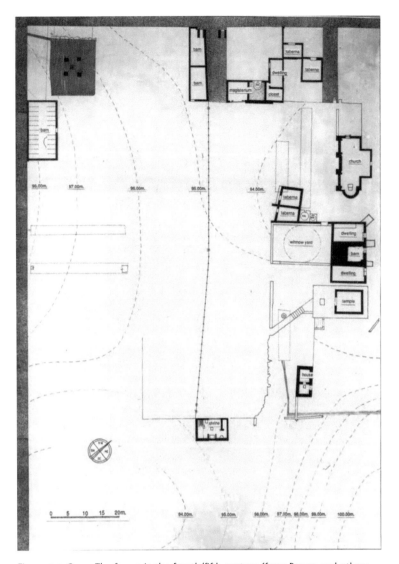

Figure 7.4. Cosa: The forum in the fourth/fifth century (from Brown and others 1994, fig. 79, 248).

18012, and 18013) has also produced ample material evidence for fifth century usage: several late Roman cups – Hayes 3 (fifth c. AD), DSP (Derivées des sigillées paléochretiennes) sherds (fourth–fifth c. AD), Painted common ware (fourth–fifth c. AD), ARS D (fourth–fifth c. AD), African cooking ware (fourth–fifth c. AD), African cooking ware – casserole (second–fourth c. AD), late Roman C cup – Hayes 3 (fifth c. AD), and ARS D bowl – Hayes 61 (fifth c. AD). Other soundings have also corroborated these trends, such as in Elevated Cistern 2 (EC 2) (stratigraphic units 21090), with ceramics from the middle of a fourth to the fifth c. AD cut into a *cocciopesto* floor, as well as a sample of African cooking ware (second to fourth c. AD), African cooking ware pan – Atl.t. CVI, 10/Bonifay Type 1/Hayes 23B (mid third–mid fourth c. AD) and EC 3 (stratigraphic unit 25022), with evidence of ARS D (fifth c. AD), African

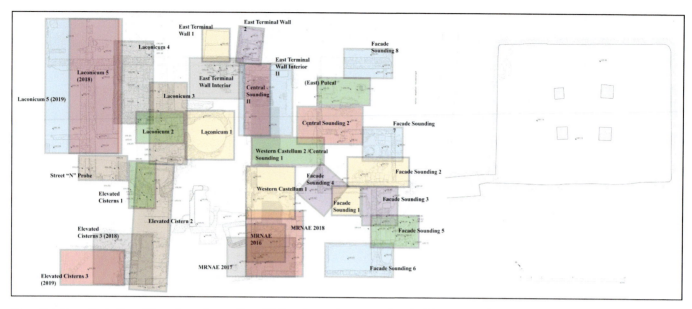

Figure 7.5. Cosa, the bath and its sectors of excavations (© Cosa Excavations, reproduced with permission).

cooking ware (fourth–fifth c. AD), and African cooking ware – Atl.t. CIV, 7 (end of fourth-beg. of fifth c. AD). Also, we recorded Sparse-Glaze pottery (tenth–eleventh c. AD) in Central Sounding 2 (CS 2) (stratigraphic unit 28017 – medieval) in a level above a *cocciopesto* floor, along with African cooking ware pans – Atl.t. CVI, 10/Bonifay Type 1/Hayes 23B (mid-third to the mid-fourth c. AD). Sector Laconicum 5 (Lac5) (stratigraphic unit 2903) had much evidence for the fifth century to the beginning of the sixth century AD based on the latest datable pottery. In this context, we identified an ARS D bowl – Hayes 91 tarda/Bonifay Sigillee Type 51 (mid sixth c. AD), Painted common ware (fifth c. AD), African cooking ware (casserole) – Atl.t. CVII, 6 (end of fourth–beg. of fifth c. AD), African cooking ware – Hayes 196A (end of fourth–beg. of fifth c. AD), African cooking pan – Atl.t. CVI, 10/Bonifay Type 1/Hayes 23B (mid third-mid fourth c. AD), African cooking ware – Atl.t. CIV, 7 (end of fourth–beg. of fifth c. AD), African cooking pot – Atl.t. CVII, 6 (end of fourth–beg. of fifth c. AD), African cooking ware – Bonifay type 9C/Hayes 185 (third–fourth c. AD), and Amphora – Kapitan 2 (third to fourth c. AD). Lastly, Central Sounding 3 (CS3) (stratigraphic unit 30012) contained African cooking ware – casserole (second–fourth c. AD), ARS C (third–fourth c. AD), and ARS D – stamp Atlante 397 (fifth–sixth c. AD). Of course, with the excavation still under way, these indications are provisional.[27]

Whether the imperial bath no longer functioned as a bath but provided space in the better built rooms of the bathing suite for activities that also took advantage of a well and its water lifting mechanism, we are not yet able to determine.[28] Nevertheless, it may be suggested that by the middle of the sixth century the site's spoliation was advanced, with its decorative apparatus and marble revetments targeted for lime production. Mosaic floors, too, were not spared in the process, with the occasional piling of entire slabs after lifting (Fig. 7.6). Further, the discovery of a massive marble *labrum* in sector EC 2, propped in a way that would facilitate its demolition, ultimately attests to practices that may have been key to the production of lime for the medieval walls on the *Arx* (Fig. 7.7).

The Late Roman and Medieval Coinage

Over the course of the excavations at Cosa, approximately 326 late Roman and medieval coins have been uncovered from the second through fourteenth centuries AD (Fig. 7.8).[29] This number also includes the illegible and partially legible coins from all of the excavations that are datable based on weight and depth/thickness. According to T. V. Buttrey, Cosa's former numismatist, the coinage record of the site's first phase of excavation, from 1948 to 1970, matched the identified chronological patterns of occupation, in which the coins recovered

---

27 This evidence tallies with the ceramics from the Shrine of Liber, see Collins Clinton 1977, 71–83, especially the cooking ware, nos 61–63.

28 For a preliminary discussion of the bath and its functioning, see De Giorgi 2018.

29 Buttrey 1980, 32–36; Buttrey 2003, 250–59.

Figure 7.6. Cosa, the bath: slabs of mosaic floors lifted and left *in situ* (© Cosa Excavations, reproduced with permission).

Figure 7.7. Cosa, the bath: *labrum* prepared for demolition (© Cosa Excavations, reproduced with permission).

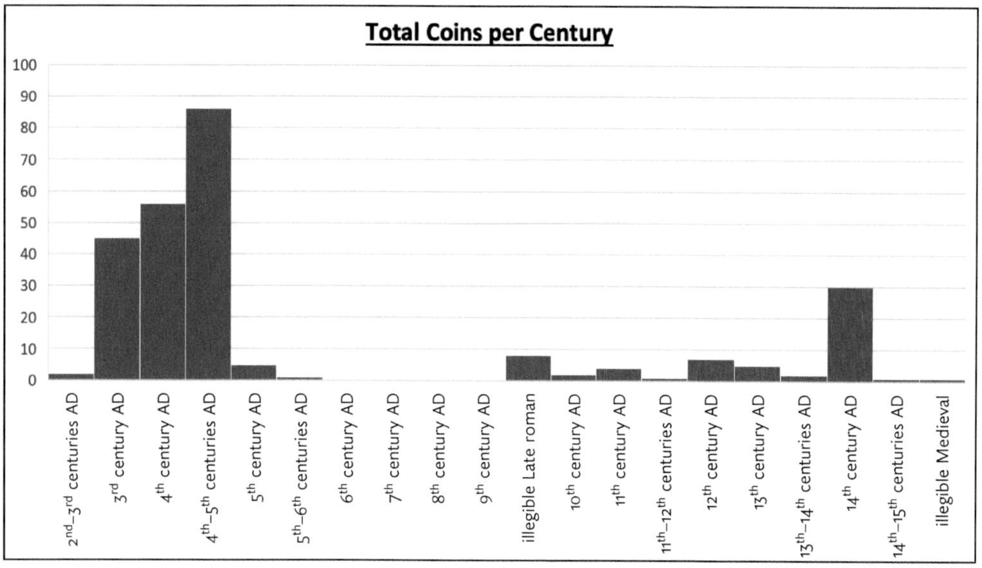

Figure 7.8. Cosa, the 1948–2019 coin finds. Graph of coin distribution at Cosa by century (figure by authors).

an absence of coin circulation at the site, and thus an absence of occupation, but could actually be a misrepresentation of late Roman currency circulation at Cosa based on the lack of lost coins.

Once the coin finds reappear in the archaeological record, at least in areas around the Eastern Height, *Arx*, and *Forum*, only two coins actually date to the tenth century, while a majority of the 1948–1970 coins are between the eleventh and twelfth centuries. What is more, a majority of the 1990–1997 coins date to the thirteenth and fourteenth centuries, largely due to the presence of a small hoard that may have once been inside a purse, since disintegrated, which was dropped into a cistern near the *Arx*. Archaeologists associated this small hoard with the Sienese attack of Ansedonia in 1329, during which it was buried, based on the *terminus post quem* of John XXII *denari*.[33] Be that as it may, the remaining coins included in the hoard are largely from the Papal States. The Papal States were also well represented among the excavation finds of 1948–1970, indicating some activity at the site during the medieval period, corroborated by other finds discovered during the 1990–1997 excavations. As with the small hoard discovered during the 1990–1997 excavations, the tenth to twelfth century coins found during the 1948–1970 excavations appear to be mainly associated with the church on the *Arx* and nearby burials.[34]

Overall, the coins discovered during the 1948–1997 excavations contained a variety of denominations and were predominantly silver and bronze, no gold coins having yet been discovered at Cosa overall. After the mid-third century AD, there is also an influx of *antoniniani* at the site until Diocletian's reform, which had previously been dominated by *asses* and *sestertii*. The coins of the medieval period are similar with respect to small change denominations and metals, as there were no gold coins present, but only silver *denari* and bronze small change. The absence of gold coins at the site does not mean of course that no gold coins were ever present in the city, but due to their high value, they were less likely to be left behind while the site was occupied.[35]

present a trend of continuity from the third century BC into the fifth century AD. A hiatus follows until the tenth century when coin finds are spotty, until a resurgence in the fourteenth century. Later, under the direction of Fentress, Buttrey published the Greco-Roman coins, while Alessia Rovelli analysed the medieval coins. During the 1990–1997 excavations, fewer coins were discovered in comparison to the previous campaigns. In particular, there was a marked decrease after the second century AD with only three coins dating to the fourth, and fifth or sixth centuries.[30] For the medieval coins, there were fewer finds discovered during the 1948–1970 excavations with twenty-one coins total for the tenth through fourteenth centuries, compared to the forty-one total coins from the 1990–1997 excavations.[31]

Based on the 'gap' in the coinage between the sixth and tenth centuries, and the possible presence of a hoard, presumably some kind of offering, associated with the late Roman shrine to Liber Pater in the *Forum*, which was the source for a majority of the third and fourth century coins found during the course of the 1948–1970 excavations, Buttrey concluded that the totals from the two excavations combined reflect the supposed depopulation of Cosa that remained until the intermittent settlement of the medieval period.[32] He had some misgivings about the scarcity of coins from the sixth century, however, given the reliable archaeological evidence supporting occupation of the *Forum* and *Arx* during that period; namely that the lack of coins from the sixth century may not accurately reflect

---

30 Buttrey 2003, 250–59.
31 Rovelli 2003, 260–65.
32 Buttrey 2003, 251–52.

33 Rovelli 2003, 260.
34 Buttrey 1980, 34. See especially the coins from the shrine of Liber Pater.
35 Kent 1988, 201–17.

As for spatial distribution, the coins were scattered throughout the excavation areas of the site, but with some concentrations based on location. Since the earlier excavations focused on particular sectors of the site, such as the houses, and the monuments of the *Forum*, the coins either come from these locations, or from portions of the road, such as the so-called Via Sacra that leads up to the *Arx*. As a result, a majority of the late antique and medieval coin finds come from public areas still serviceable during the latter periods of the city's occupation, such as the 'Capitolium' on the *Arx* and the *Forum* basilica.[36] In addition, late antique coins were found in cisterns, and other water features throughout the site. Incidentally, the coins recently excavated from the bath complex cohere with these trends, with a number of second and third century coins, some of which were concentrated in discrete areas of the bath, as well as some illegible coins from Late Antiquity and at least one legible medieval coin. As many of these coins were relatively worn in condition upon discovery, several can only be determined as late Roman or late antique based on weight and thickness, rather than by any other identifying features. Further, at least two of these coins appear to have been flattened at some point, with one also halved, which appears to possibly be medieval in date. It may be that at least some areas of the bath were utilized in some way during Late Antiquity, even if not as a bath.

About fifteen of the coins discovered in the bath appear to date to the late Roman or medieval periods, among which five are legible, about three to four partially legible, and four illegible, with weight and thickness as interpreting criteria. Of these coins, only one definitively dates to the time of the Crusader kings, while among the legible late Roman coins, there is one each of Septimius Severus, Severus Alexander, Maximinus Thrax (but, with his son Maximus' portrait), Gordian III, and Philip I. These coins all appear to be worn and bronze in colour, but several, based on their weight, could originally have been plated. Among the partially legible coins, a few may be Constantinian in date due to the size, weight, and partially identifiable features on the coins, while a couple contain a radiate profile, but are otherwise illegible. One of these coins, a *denarius*, shows a reverse that may have been associated with Caracalla and issued by Septimius Severus, but the obverse is too worn to make a definitive identification. The remaining illegible late antique coins from the bath appear to have a range of 0.5 g–6.9 g in weight and 0.10 cm–0.30 cm in thickness, and all are either bronze, or plated. Interestingly, mid to late Roman Imperial coins have a roughly equal representation

Figure 7.9. Coin of Gordion III. AD 241–244 (© Cosa Excavations, reproduced with permission).

Figure 7.10. Coin of Philip I. AD 244–249 (© Cosa Excavations, reproduced with permission).

within the bath in terms of identifiable coins compared to identifiable earlier periods, which is consistent with the bath's architectural phasing.

The late Roman coins from the bath area appear to be mostly concentrated in three main locations, other than some stray finds throughout the complex: the north-eastern sector, the south-west sector, and the south-east sector. In the north-eastern sector, which is the hot area of the bath complex, the late Roman coins are clustered in what may have been a corridor to the north near a wall, albeit within different strata and contexts. One coin of Gordian III was from a layer of collapse that covered a stratum containing burning (Fig. 7.9). Approximately five coins then came from this burn layer that covered a *cocciopesto* surface, among which was the one Septimius Severus coin and a coin of Commodus, which makes the three remaining illegible coins likely to be of similar later second century AD dates. These coins are also consistent with the second century construction date of the nearby walls. Since this burn layer was also associated with a larger stratum of collapse and accumulated building material, the coins could potentially have originated from within the collapsed architecture, especially due to the presence traces of mortar on their surface.[37] A possible reason

---

36 Buttrey 1980, 61–78.

37 A number of other coins from the bath complex have been discovered with mortar still adhering to their surface, some of which also came from directly within architecture, indicating that some of these coins were potentially associated with the bath's construction and were from among the significant layers of its collapse.

for this interpretation is the presence of a third century coin of Philip I (Fig. 7.10), found directly beneath this burn layer on top of a *cocciopesto* surface, which likely was lost prior to the final collapse of the roof and upper portions of the walls.

On a surface in a room within the south-west area of the bath, which likely was the bath's *apodyterium*, four coins were found, among which was a Severus Alexander *sestertius*, a partially legible possible *nummus*, and two largely illegible coins other than a possible portrait, but likely also of third century date. The Severus Alexander *sestertius* was also found in close proximity to an illegible coin, which, based on weight, appears to be another *sestertius*, from what appears to be a third to eighth century disposal area. The possible *nummus* came from the same stratigraphic layer, but further to the south in the room. Similarly, the area in which the late Roman coins were found within the south-eastern sector of the complex is also associated with a late antique disposal area within rooms of the former bath. Three illegible late Roman coins of probably second to third century date based on weight and thickness were found to the south of two marble slabs repurposed as rudimentary steps set into a surface in order to accommodate a slight slope to the north. All three coins were also discovered on or close to the surface, perhaps indicating that this area was in use during the third century AD.

Each area of the bath in which these coins were discovered contains a wealth of evidence supporting multiple phasing, including from the second through sixth centuries AD. Many of the second and third century coins were recovered from areas of the bath that were either constructed or in use during these time periods, while coins either from the same periods, or later, were found in the upper area of the bath where there is the most evidence for a systematic dumping of architectural bath material. The coins then do support the hypothesis that this area was being repurposed, reused and/or spoliated at a later date.

In conjunction with the coins discovered during the earlier excavations of Cosa, the numismatic evidence from the bath complex adds to our understanding of the late antique period of the city as a whole. While the total number of late Roman and medieval coins discovered in the city is rather low compared with the Republican and early Imperial periods of the site, they do demonstrate a continued use of certain areas of the city, the site of the bath included. This picture of Cosa during Late Antiquity differs slightly from previous conceptions of the city's habitation and abandonment; rather than a complete desertion of the site, the coins' trends dovetails with other evidence that shows sporadic settlement. The numismatic evidence from the previous and new excavations thus contributes to an enlarged perspective on the city's chronology,

in which Cosa continued to be occupied longer than previously believed, albeit with a reduced population that still made use of coin.[38]

Catalogue of coins

1. C18.125. Septimius Severus. AD 195–196. As. Tyana, Cappadocia. 9.3 g. 22.17 mm. [T]YANEWN T P T IER K ACY K (Greek transliterated) Herakles l. SNG Tübingen 4709.
2. C19.140. Severus Alexander. AD 222–231. Sestertius. Rome. 18.5 g. 28 mm. [SA]LVS PV[BLICA] S C Salus seated l. RIC IV 608.
3. C15.108. Maximinus Thrax. AD 236–238. Sestertius. Rome. 23.9 g. 33 mm. MAXIMUS CAES G[ERM] Bust of Maximus r. PRINCIPI [IVVENTVTIS S C] Maximus standing l. holding spear and baton. RIC IV max 13.
4. C18.159. Gordian III. AD 241–244. Sestertius. Rome. 19 g. 30.22 mm. [LI]BERTAS A[VG] S C Libertas l. RIC IV 318.
5. C18.157. Philip I. AD 244–249. Sestertius. Rome. 23.2 g. 28.82 mm. LAET [FV]NDA[TA S C] Laetitia l. holding sceptre and pileus. RIC IV 175.
6. C15.77. Baldwin III. 1143–1163. Denier. Jerusalem. 1.1 g. 19 mm. DE IERUSALEM Tower of David. Metcalf 1995, Sch 3.21–22.
7. C18.113. Illegible. 6.9 g. 23.01 mm.
8. C18.127. Illegible. *c.* third century AD. Flattened AE2 or AE3? Caracalla/Septimius Severus? 3.3 g. 22.81 mm. Portrait r. with military cuirass and radiate crown.
9. C18.143. Illegible. Antoninianus. *c.* second–third century AD. 2.1 g. 14.24 mm.
10. C19.157. Partially legible. Nummus. *c.* second–third century AD. 0.5 g. 11.8 mm.
11. C19.177. Illegible. 2.6 g. 19.7 mm.

Cosa, the Gothic War, and Historiography

The Justinianic *Renovatio Imperii* extolls the continuity of the Roman Empire, rather than lamenting its swan song. Of course, the text is imbued with propaganda to conceal the paradox of the anarchic fragmentation of the fifth century, amid invasions, battles, plagues, while it seeks to rebuild the pillars of the Roman provinces. Justinian, the key figure in the early sixth century, is described as the one who established 'new' territorial boundaries and secured economic supplies to satisfy demands with those geographic areas with which Byzantium was principally trading, such as the Balkans, Syria, Palestine, and North Africa. Admittedly, Roman

---

38 Sebastiani 2017, 281–90.

historiography plays a critical role in glorifying the last efforts of the declining Empire and carving in stone the new Byzantine presence all over the Mediterranean. But not all regions and islands were reached by the Empire. In Italy, Byzantine presence and culture are associated mostly in the south of the peninsula with the exception of the north-east, the Ravenna exarchate.

The historiography of the Gothic War and the defensive role played by the Byzantine army is often explained moreover as a phenomenon that involved most of the Italian peninsula. However, the events played out differently with a great variety of outcomes. Tuscany's coast and interior, as well as Rome, suffered a long series of invasions and the Gothic War ended with the Lombards occupying quite a sizeable sector of Italy (AD 568). Enrico Zanini's survey pointedly titled 'Italie Bizantine,' discusses the balkanization of the peninsula at that time. Strikingly, the only site for the whole of Tuscany is sixth century Byzantine Cosa.[39] Once again, the issue at stake is whether there are enough concrete elements to suggest a Byzantine presence at Cosa. That Tuscany was occupied by Lombards for two centuries (sixth and eighth) is generally accepted, yet there is still an entrenched assumption that ties the history of Tuscany to Rome and conjures up a Byzantine presence, no matter how tenuous the evidence is. More fundamentally though: what is a Byzantine settlement? Much ink has been spilled on the subject, but the defining criteria of a Byzantine town still evade us. While he is mainly concerned with southern Italy, Paul Arthur has nevertheless suggested some guidelines:[40]

1. The site has to be a central place
2. It must have an autonomous or semi-autonomous local administration
3. It maps out public works and attracts jobs
4. It has a self-sufficient economy based on agricultural production and distribution, while also generating *surplus*
5. It displays economic diversity
6. It showcases a hierarchical class system
7. It stimulates demographic growth thanks to the factors above.

It is quite apparent that sixth century Cosa did not meet any of these parameters. Not even the establishment of a Byzantine fortification, or a *centro direzionale*, seems to fit the material evidence (one cannot of course discount the possibility that plans to establish a Byzantine enclave came to naught due to a variety of circumstances).[41] Although cogent, these questions

lead to a cul-de-sac and the only evident trace from the cityscape of late antique Cosa is the increasing dismantling of a Roman town and, with it, every form of centralized control, giving way to private initiatives. As already mentioned, seafaring must be also taken into account: the Cosa seaboard was still part of the cabotage system connecting Rome to France. The villa at the Tagliata may have served as a lay-by, but the period also witnessed the rise of the *Portus Fenigliae*, once *Portus Cosanus* was in disuse. Few harbours of larger dimensions were left, and *Portus Scabris* is a good case in point, illustrating as it does the materials circulating during the sixth and seventh centuries.[42] Were any of these sites Byzantine? In all likelihood they were not, trading as they were on a minor scale on the routes of old, with a reduced demography and the low-profile that enabled evading taxes and tolls.

At Cosa and in Tuscany the Byzantine fortified settlement has also been explained with the presence of North African pottery. ARS, in particular, is typically used as proxy to show ties with the centralized power, during a period when trade was greatly reduced. The few fragments that come from the *Arx* — Hayes 88 and 99 — and others from the *Forum* cistern, dating to the fifth–early sixth century, show a paucity of material that is also reflected in the currency, with a total of seven coins: six from Brown's earlier unstratified excavations dated to the sixth century and one published in *Cosa V*.[43] The 'good evidence for occupation' both in the *Forum* and on the *Arx* during the sixth century did not contradict but actually confirmed the continuity of Cosa during the Byzantine period, though not as a Byzantine presence.[44] Although the argument for the Byzantine presence at Cosa is circular and not grounded in substantial evidence, it has received wide acceptance. Tunisian imports and other wares from different areas of the Mediterranean indicate that merchants were trading and moving along the coast when cabotage stops replaced the ancient harbours. Nevertheless, the existence of an unfinished, defensive infrastructure on the *Arx* compound is not sufficient evidence for a Byzantine fort. Nor can Byzantine infantry be put there based on the continuity of *trade*.

The small finds from the bath excavations replicate the material trends highlighted by *Cosa V*, albeit proposing a wider range of typologies. The pottery is still under study and briefly listed here: black-glaze, no later than the first century AD and *sigillata Italica*,

---

39 Zanini 1998.
40 Arthur 1995 and 2004.
41 Zanini 1998.

42 For an updated synthesis of the northern central Italian Tyrrenic coast economic activities, landscape of the coast, and the interior different cultures, see Sebastiani Megale 2021. See also Vaccaro 2018 and Ciampoltrini and Rendini 2004.
43 Dyson 1976; Fentress and others 2003, 269–319; Buttrey 2003, 251.
44 Fentress and others 2003.

which dates from the later first to the end of the second century, along with some *derivata sigillata*. Imported red painted ware documents trade with Southern Italy in the fourth and fifth centuries. By and large, the largest amount of late antique pottery comes from North Africa with cooking pots, amphorae, and African Red Slip ware, with materials dating as late as the mid-sixth century (Hayes 91). Finally, Kapitan 2 amphorae show that rare and precious goods were still imported to Cosa between the third and fourth centuries. Arriving from either Samos or the Aegean islands, this type of amphora is found not only all over the Mediterranean, including the northern British coasts, but also in Russia and Pannonia. Ultimately, they attest to the site's continuing integration in sea routes. Lastly, only one piece of early medieval Sparse Glaze has been identified thus far.

Although this survey is still provisional, it appears as though the materials from the bath area display a wide spectrum of forms and types. Further, some were found in sealed stratigraphic contexts, all the while revealing a degree of pottery use that is apparently at variance with the intermittent occupation model that is suited to the other areas of the town that have been examined.

The Post Roman Cemeteries at Cosa

Three clusters of burials at Cosa can be assigned to the late antique and early medieval epochs. The first is located outside the *Forum*, behind the Basilica (that is in grid square IX D of the Brown excavations) and late antique, while the other two are early medieval. The older of the two is located at the bottom of the Eastern Height, also outside the *Forum* and possibly re-used as the sacred space of Temple B. The skeletons dated by C-14 to the ninth century have been analysed and studied.[45] Further, the community belonging to this burial site has been associated with the earliest defensive post, possibly a timber tower, built on the Eastern Height and protected by the ditch that surrounded the corner of the city. Lastly, the third cemetery was on the *Arx* on the southern exterior of the Capitoline Temple. All of the skeletons were removed during the 1960s and no sign of the cemetery is visible; only some elements of the church walls associated with it remain. This last burial site was dated to the ninth century by coins, but most likely was used throughout the medieval period.[46]

Conclusions

It is a profitable time to discuss urbanism in Tuscany and Italy during Late Antiquity and the Early Middle Ages. The current flurry of scholarly inquiries and paradigms raise questions both about the granularity of the available data and set the discussion of the realities of small, elusive communities like that at Cosa against broader cultural trends. From its magnificent plateau on the Ansedonia promontory, Cosa still poses an investigative challenge to determine the agencies, large or small, that relentlessly modified its built environment, not only during the colony's seminal years, but especially as frequentation began to dwindle down after the second century AD. Reevaluation of legacy data along with the analysis of new evidence opens new interpretive possibilities for the site. The assumption that the history of Cosa's settlement is known in all of its complexity invites reconsideration, as new material realities come to the fore. It is plain that at least three areas of the town were occupied in the medieval period — the *Forum*, and the bath in its environs, where a coin of Baldwin III (1143–1163), minted in Jerusalem, was recently found, the Eastern Height and the Arx. At this time, the stone tower on the Eastern Height was built presumably by the powerful family of the Aldobrandeschi who were the lords, *comites*, of most of Southern Tuscany. But because the archaeological record may remain modest in future, the traces and character of a medieval presence will need other forms of documentation or reading.

To conclude, it is important to stress that Cosa has a long and prolific history of successful excavation that has trained generations of archeologists and set the foundation for models of Roman urbanism. Frank Brown's *Cosa, the Making of a Roman Town* is now a classic and continues to be used as a benchmark in Roman archaeology. Fortunately, Brown also had the foresight to carefully record everything Roman and non-Roman that he saw, thus allowing new generations of archaeologists to study all eras of occupation within the walls. That perspective, along with innovative approaches to exploration of the site, can produce new information to be set against that from ongoing archaeological initiatives elsewhere in Italy. As for future initiatives at Cosa, it may, for example, be hoped that, on the Arx, the foundation trench of the later walls will be investigated to better understand the nature of the purported Byzantine fortification. On a larger scale, it might also be possible to survey the built environment with a view toward mapping the different types of concrete work. The 2013–2020 geophysical survey has already contributed to a whole re-reading of the occupation of the town, but questions within the city and its connectivity still loom large.

---

45 Fentress and others 2003, 353–62.
46 Buttrey 2003.

Works Cited

Arthur, Paul. 1995. 'Il Particolarismo Napoletano Altomedievale: Una Lettera Basata Sui Dati Archeologici', *Mélanges de l'École française de Rome*, 107: 17–30

——. 2004. 'Alcune Considerazioni Sulla Natura Delle Città Bizantine', in *Le Città Italiane Tra La Tarda Antichità e l'alto Medioevo. Atti Del Convegno (Ravenna, 26–28 Febbraio 2004)*, ed. by Andrea Augenti (Florence: All'Insegna del Giglio), pp. 27–36

Augenti, Andrea. 2010. *Città e porti dall'Antichità al Medioevo* (Rome: Carrocci Editore)

Baldassarri, Monica. 2011. 'Cosa – Ansedonia,' in 'Strutture portuali e comunicazioni marittime nella Toscana medievale alla luce della fonte archeologica (VIII inizi XIII secolo)', in *Sistemi portuali della Toscana mediterranea*, ed. by Monica Baldassarri (Pisa: Pacini Editore), pp. 81–116

Bisconti, Fabrizio. 1985. 'Tarda Antichità Ed Alto Medioevo Nel Territorio Orbetellano: Primo Bilancio Critico', in *Atti Del V Congresso Nazionale Di Archeologia Cristiana* (Rome: La Nuova Italia), pp. 63–77

Brown, Edward. 1951. *Cosa I: History and Topography*, Memoirs of the American Academy in Rome, 20 (Rome: American Academy in Rome)

Brown, Frank, Emeline Richardson, and Lawrence Richardson. 1994. *Cosa III. The Buildings of the Forum: Colony, Municipium, and Village*, Supplements to the Memoirs of the American Academy in Rome, 37 (Ann Arbor: The University of Michigan Press)

Buttrey, Theodore V. 1980. *Cosa: The Coins*, Memoirs of the American Academy in Rome, 34 (Rome: American Academy in Rome)

——. 2003. 'The Greek and Roman Coins', in *Cosa V: An Intermittent Town. Excavations 1991–1997*, ed. by Elizabeth Fentress, Supplements to the Memoirs of the American Academy in Rome (Ann Arbor: The University of Michigan Press), pp. 250–59

Cambi, Franco. 2005. 'Cosa e Populonia. La fine dell'esperienza urbana in Etruria e la nascita delle due Toscane', *Workshop di Archeologia Classica*, 2: 71–90

——. 2021. 'The Tuscan Coast in the Classical Period – Research Project: Towards a New Landscape Archaeology', in *Archaeological Landscapes of Roman Etruria. Research and Field Papers*, ed. by Alessandro Sebastiani and Carolina Megale (Turnhout: Brepols), pp. 27–38

Carandini, Andrea, Franco Cambi, Mariagrazia Celuzza, and Elizabeth Fentress. 2002. *Paesaggi d'Etruria: valle dell'Albegna, valle d'Oro, valle del Chiarone, valle del Tafone. Progetto di ricera Italo Britannico seguito allo scavo di Settefinestre* (Rome: Edizioni di Storia e Letteratura)

Castagnoli, Ferdinando. 1956. 'La centuriazione di Cosa', *Memoirs of the American Academy in Rome*, 24: 147, 149–65

Celuzza, Maria Grazia. 2015. 'Ancora Su Rutilio Namaziano e l'archeologia Delle Coste Tirreniche', in *Diana Umbronensis a Scoglietto. Santuario, Territorio e Cultura Materiale (200 a.C. – 550 d.C.)*, ed. by Alessandro Sebastiani, Elena Chirico, Matteo Colombini, and Mario Cygielman, Archaeopress Roman Archaeology, 3 (Oxford: Archaeopress), pp. 367–74

Cerri, Laura, Sergio Fontana, and Elisa Gusberti. 2003. 'La Ceramica Della Casa Di Diana e Della Forum Cistern', in *Cosa V: An Intermittent Town. Excavations 1991–1997*, ed. by Elizabeth Fentress, Memoirs of the American Academy in Rome, Supplementary Volumes, 2 (Ann Arbor: The University of Michigan Press), pp. 269–319

Ciampoltrini, Giulio, and Paola Rendini. 1988. 'L'Agro Cosano tra tarda antichità e alto medioevo segnalazioni e contributi', *Archeologia Medievale*, 15: 519–34

——. 2004. 'Ports and Trade in the Ager Cosanus and on Giglio Island from the Mid to Late Imperial Age', in *Close Encounters: Sea- and Riverborne Trade, Ports and Hinterlands, Ship Construction and Navigation in Antiquity, the Middle Ages and in Modern Time*, ed. by Marinella Pasquinucci and Timm Weski, BAR International Series, 1283 (Oxford: British Archaeological Reports), pp. 85–91

Clarke, Jacqueline. 2014. 'The Struggle for Control of the Landscape in Book 1 of Rutilius Namatianus', *Arethusa*, 47.1: 89–107

Collins-Clinton, Jacquelyn. 1977. *A Late Antique Shrine of Liber Pater at Cosa*, Études Préliminaires Aux Religions Orientales Dans l'Empire Romain, 64 (Leiden: Brill)

——. 2000. 'The Neronian Odeum at Cosa and Its Sculptural Program: A New Julio-Claudian Dynastic Group', *Memoirs of the American Academy in Rome*, 45: 99–130

De Giorgi, Andrea U. 2018. 'Sustainable Practices? A Story from Roman Cosa (Central Italy)', *Journal of Mediterranean Archaeology*, 31.1: 3–26

——. 2019. 'The Colonial Landscape of the Middle Republic: The State of the Question', in *Cosa and the Colonial Landscape of Republican Italy (Third and Second Centuries BCE)*, ed. by Andrea U. De Giorgi (Ann Arbor: The University of Michigan Press), pp. 1–20

Dennis, George. 1848. *Cities and Cemeteries of Etruria* (London: John Murray)

Dyson, Stephen L. 1976. 'Cosa: The Utilitarian Pottery', *Memoirs of the American Academy in Rome*, 33: 3–175

——. 1978. 'Settlement Patterns in the Ager Cosanus: The Wesleyan University Survey, 1974–1976', *Journal of Field Archaeology*, 5.3: 251–68

——. 2005. 'Successes and Failures at Cosa (Roman and American)', *Journal of Roman Archaeology*, 18: 615–20

Fentress, Elizabeth. 1994. 'Cosa in the Empire: The Unmaking of a Roman Town', *Journal of Roman Archaeology*, 7: 209–22

Fentress, Elizabeth and others. 2003. *Cosa V: An Intermittent Town, Excavations 1991–1997*, Supplements to the Memoirs of the American Academy in Rome (Rome: American Academy in Rome)

Fentress, Elizabeth, and Enrico Cirelli. 2012. 'After the Rats: Cosa in the Late Empire and Early Middle Ages', in *Urbes Extinctae: Archaeologies of Abandoned Classical Towns*, ed. by Andrea Augenti and Neil Christie (Farnham: Ashgate), pp. 97–113

Fentress, Elizabeth, Teresa Clay, Michelle Hobart, and Matilda Webb. 1991. 'Late Roman and Medieval Cosa I: The Arx and the Structure near the Eastern Height', *Papers of the British School at Rome*, 59: 197–230

Fitch, Cleo Rickman, and Norma Wynick Goldman. 1994. *Cosa: The Lamps*, Memoires of the American Academy in Rome, 39 (Rome, American Academy in Rome)

Hobart, Michelle (ed.). 2023. *Medieval Landscapes of Southern Etruria: Archaeology at Capalbiaccio*, MediTo – Archaeological and Historical Landscapes of Mediterranean Central Italy, 2 (Turnhout: Brepols)

Levi, Doro. 1927. 'Escursione archeologica nell'Agro Cosano', *Studi Etruschi*, 1: 477–85

Kent, John P. C. 1988. 'Interpreting Coin Finds', in *Coins and the Archeologist*, ed. by John Casey and Richard Reece (London: Seaby), pp. 201–17

Mannsperger, Dietrich. 1998. *Sylloge Nummorum Graecorum: Phrygien – Kappadokien – Römische Provinzprägungen in Kleinasien*, Vol. 6 (Münzsammlung: Universität Tübingen)

Mattingly, Harold, Edward A. Sydenham, Robert A. G. Carson, R, and Carol H. V. Sutherland. 1923–1981. *The Roman Imperial Coinage* (London: Spink, 1923–1981)

McCann, Anna Marguerite. 1987. *The Roman Port and Fishery of Cosa: A Center of Ancient Trade* (Princeton: Princeton University Press)

Metcalf, David M. 1995. *Coinage of the Crusades and the Latin East in the Ashmolean Museum, Oxford* (London: Royal Numismatic Society: Society for the Study of the Crusades and the Latin East)

Mogetta, Marcello. 2019. 'Monumentality, Technological Innovation, and Identity Construction in Roman Republican Architecture: The Remaking of Cosa, Post-197 BCE', in *Size Matters – Understanding Monumentality Across Ancient Civilizations*, ed. by Federico Buccellati, Sebastian Hageneuer, Sylvia van der Heyden, and Felix Levenson, Historie, 146 (Bielefeld: Transcript), pp. 241–68

Oleson, Joseph P. 1984. *Greek and Roman Mechanical Water-Lifting Devices: The History of a Technology* (Toronto: Toronto University Press)

Rathborne, Dominic W. 1981. 'The Development of Agriculture in the "Ager Cosanus" during the Roman Republic: Problems of Evidence and Interpretation', *Journal of Roman Studies*, 71: 10–23

Rihill, Tracey. 2009. 'Lead "Slingshot" (Glandes)', *Journal of Roman Archaeology*, 22: 146–69

Rovelli, Alessia. 2003. 'The Medieval Coins', in *Cosa V: An Intermittent Town. Excavations 1991–1997*, ed. by Elizabeth Fentress, Supplements to the Memoirs of the American Academy in Rome (Ann Arbor: The University of Michigan Press), pp. 260–65

Sami, Denis. 2021. 'The Network of Interregional Roads and Harbours', in *A Companion to Byzantine Italy*, ed. by Salvatore Cosentino, Brill's Companions to the Byzantine World (Leiden: Brill), VIII, pp. 255–78

Scott, Russell T. 2019. 'Cosa: How Perfect! How Come?', in *Cosa and the Colonial Landscape of Republican Italy (Third and Second Centuries BCE)*, ed. by Andrea U. De Giorgi (Ann Arbor: University of Michigan Press), pp. 21–29

Scott, Russell T., Andrea U. De Giorgi, Richard Posamentir, and Christina Cha. 2021. 'Cosa Excavations: New Interpretative Frameworks', in *Archaeological Landscapes of Roman Etruria. Research and Field Papers*, ed. by Alessandro Sebastiani and Carolina Megale, MediTo – Archaeological and Historical Landscapes of Mediterranean Central Italy, 1 (Turnhout: Brepols), pp. 207–18

Sebastiani, Alessandro. 2017. 'From Villa to Village. Late Roman to Early Medieval Settlement Networks in the Ager Rusellanus', in *Encounters, Excavations and Argosies. Essays for Richard Hodges*, ed. by John Moreland, John Mitchell, and Bea Leal (Oxford: Archaeopress), pp. 281–90

Sebastiani, Alessandro, and Carolina Megale (eds). 2021. *Archaeological Landscapes of Roman Etruria. Research and Field Papers*, MediTo – Archaeological and Historical Landscapes of Mediterranean Central Italy, 1 (Turnhout: Brepols)

Vaccaro, Emanuele. 2018. 'Long-Distance Ceramic Connections: Portus Scabris (Portiglioni-GR) Coastal Tuscany and the Tyrrenian Sea', in *Origins of a New Economic Union (7th-12th Centuries): Preliminary Results of the nEU-Med Project, October 2015-March 2017*, ed. by Giovanna Bianchi and Richard Hodges (Florence: All'Insegna del Giglio), pp. 81–100

Zanini, Enrico. 1998. *Le Italie Bizantine. Territorio, Insediamenti Ed Economia Nella Provincia Bizantina d'Italia (VI–VIII Secolo)* (Bari: Edipuglia)

RICHARD HODGES

8. Cityness

A Chimera in Early Medieval Tuscany

Italian conservatism maintained classical core ideals, and thus, by extension, the concept of urban living for its elites, through the greatest economic crises in the history of the peninsula. These ideals were still operative in the period of economic revival and acute political decentralization, which can be clearly seen in the eleventh century at latest (Wickham 2005, 655–56).

'Cityness', to use the evocative word coined by Chris Wickham (2005, 595) to define a later first-millennium urban mentality, is a complex concept that should allude to more than the sum of the historical and archaeological sources combined, but it fails to do this. 'Cityness' has had a strong ideological element in much of history. For the Romans, it simply constituted culture, *civilitas*; it would have been a major step for the 'civilized', 'civilian' aristocrat to think that s/he could live without it. Thus, when city-dwelling became less common for the powerful in some parts of the post-Roman world, a major cultural shift took place. More generally, in every region of the former empire, the definitions of 'cityness' changed considerably from its Roman origins; the ideological pull that cities had for aristocracies shifted accordingly. We cannot always pin this down in our documentary sources, for they are not dense enough, but the new spatial patterns that new ideas of the city generated can be seen in the archaeology' (Wickham 2005, 595). It is an appropriate historical analysis, but the very name of the concept has obfuscated an issue in which many archaeologists and historians have confused it with urban continuity.

The central problem is that Wickham interprets 'cityness' principally through the lens of the aristocracy, their continuing pre-eminence in society, and the documentary sources. His interpretation of the written sources is made by peering through a modern secular prism. It is an interpretation that finds particular favour

in Italy, where twelfth-century medieval (lay) communes have been interpreted as a cornerstone in the rise of the medieval European community. These communes, 'embodied by the driving and creative bourgeois forces of society' (Boone 2012, 331) — their 'cityness' being institutionally different from those circumstances in Byzantium — are traditionally regarded as the platform on which, not to put too fine a point on it, the modern European project was constructed. 'Cityness', in sum, has obfuscated an episode of post-classical history in which towns in the ancient and high medieval sense played almost no part.

This essay is a contribution to the debate about post-classical urban sites in early medieval Tuscany and asks, incidentally, why Italian archaeologists have resisted confronting the material evidence before them.

A Temple Society

If European civilization is built on that of Rome, it now appears obvious that the Rome involved was not that of Augustus, Cicero, and classical urbanism, but that of Constantine, Augustine, the Justinianic Code, and the Church. The Roman empire had evolved through several different institutional iterations before it entered a final chapter now well documented by numerous archaeological excavations in the Mediterranean region. The unequivocal evidence for the end of the ancient city is before us, and so is an explanation that is well supported by the textual histories. This has been brilliantly set out by Peter Brown in a series of studies. His model goes as follows: public benefaction, an age-old tradition in ancient cities, was suddenly upended. Gifts to churches were thought to join this world to the celestial world beyond. Supporting churches, the clergy, and the poor steadily emerged as a rite of passage to this boundless world beyond. Between AD 370–430, this new Christian

---

Richard Hodges (r.hodges@aur.edu) American University of Rome

Archaeological Landscapes of Late Antique and Early Medieval Tuscia: Research and Field Papers, ed. by Riccardo Rao and Alessandro Sebastiani, MEDITO 3 (Turnhout 2023), pp. 141–147

BREPOLS ❧ PUBLISHERS

DOI 10.1484/M.MEDITO-EB.5.133998

worldview did not pass without controversy. The fifth century was marked by increasing pressures on the secular elite, who resisted the ideals of the ambitious bishops. In the latter part of the century, however, as the Roman state steadily weakened, the Church inexorably accumulated wealth — especially moveable and landed wealth — altering the very axes of society. The collapse of traditional aristocracies left the church in a prime position. 'It was an age of managerial bishops and their clerical staffs' Brown has written (2012, 530). Western Roman aristocrats, faced with economic stresses brought on by the larger fiscal circumstances, opted to redefine the future: 'Led by a clergy made ever more starkly different from themselves in culture and lifestyle, the laity sought out new ways to place their wealth beyond the grave for the salvation of their souls' (Brown 2012, 530). In a society that knew all about the main social effects of friendship and patronage, the emergence of men and women who claimed intimate relations with invisible patrons meant far more than the rise of a tender religiosity of personal experience, and more than the groping of lonely men for invisible companionship. It meant that yet another form of power was available for the inhabitants of a Mediterranean city (Brown 2012). Salvation of souls, especially in sixth-century cities, in terms of gift-giving became the driving ambition of Christian society and was to remain so for the coming centuries.

If we trust the material record, it focuses our attention upon a massive social upheaval in later Roman towns that presaged economic collapse. Towns that had been populated by rich houses in the fourth and fifth centuries, in the aftermath of Constantine's revolution, were suddenly filled with churches by the sixth century (Brown 2012, 521–22). The shifting pendulum meant that investment in sustaining the economy was forsaken for well-documented ideological reasons. After a generation during the earlier sixth century of over-investment in conspicuous consumption dedicated to salvation, there was no countervailing investment. Coupled with military expenditure, over-taxation had a deadening impact all around the Mediterranean regions (Sarris 2006, 174–75). The archaeology has been staring us in the face for a generation. From the mid-sixth to the later seventh centuries came the inexorable ruralization of great and small classical cities and the abandonment of the countryside.

Michael McCormick, unlike Chris Wickham (2005; see however, Wood 2007), intuitively recognized the symptoms of this spectacular urban transformation but not its cause: 'A scholarly Rip Van Winkle who went to sleep over his late Roman or early medieval dissertation twenty years ago would scarcely recognize the age which recent research has unveiled. New methods and tools have sprung up and invite new questions.

Together, the new insights and new tools open large new vistas to the historian. The time is ripe for trying new approaches to old problems' (McCormick 2001, 3). The cause, McCormick has since hypothesized, was due to events: to neither invasions nor migrations but to environmental change brought on by such triggers as a massive volcanic eruption and the bubonic plague of the Justininiac period (McCormick and others 2012; Harper 2017; for contrary positions see, however, Moreland 2018; and Sessa 2019). McCormick correctly identifies the point of inflection in the Mediterranean region in the central decades of the sixth century (Hodges 2021a) but omits to recognize that, exactly at this time in the mid-Justinianic period, the Merovingian North Sea region and western British Isles including Ireland were at a point of expansion not contraction. In both regions the volcanic dust and plague have been recorded, but the resilience of the local tribes in and around the British Isles begs the question of why the Mediterranean world failed to display similar resilience (Moreland 2018).

Ian Wood has championed Brown's thesis, showing its importance until the mid- to later Merovingian era and its revival under the Carolingians (2018). He has christened this the period of a temple society. Wood's term gives prominence to the long reach of Christianity, as well as to the importance of the clergy at its operational heart. Salvation rather than market ethics mattered most. Gift-giving was now of paramount importance, as were countergifts as a means of exchange. Once grasped, Wood's definition provides a cosmological framework for describing the fate of Roman towns, the continuity of great former metropolises like Rome as places, and of course the near desertion of numerous ancient cities. No less important it raises critical questions about the transformation of this temple society in the mid- to later tenth and eleventh centuries into a feudal society, during which time there occurred the beginnings of — mostly periodic — markets initially at places associated with Christian cults.

Why have we ignored this elephant in the room? Why has 'cityness' been pursued along with secular continuity as opposed to highlighting the essential clerical nature of the urban form after *c.* AD 500? This is what Bryan Ward-Perkins (2005, 174) concluded:

> a shared Christian heritage has good historical credentials as the basis for a common culture and identity, but is awkward for present-day reasons: Christianity, with its many sectarian squabbles, is now as divisive as it was once unifying; and adopting it as a badge of 'Europeanness' would, of course, definitely exclude all non-Christians from the club. Furthermore, linking Europe with Christianity, might give the Pope ideas above his

station, would be disturbingly 'American', and would certainly clash with liberal and left-wing European traditions of secularist politics.

Controversial though he is, Ward-Perkins may be right, yet this obviates the significance of Brown's thesis echoed cogently by Wood and confirmed by the expanding archaeological record for the sixth to tenth centuries. Ward-Perkins fails to highlight an imagined community in which Latin Christendom took its ideological bearings from Rome, albeit through Europe's tribal prisms of what Brown describes as micro-Christendoms (2003).

Polyfocal Places

During the seventh- to ninth-century episode, old urban centres, if they were still occupied, were managed by a coalition or collection of small but separated entities largely dominated by relic churches surrounded by ruins and gardens. Place names and sometimes even their status (usually associated with a bishopric) invariably survived; however, the physical presence of such places was entirely different from their ancient topography. They did not operate as cities or towns in the ancient or medieval sense but as polyfocal places — essentially ruralized places — in a non-market environment.

In topographical terms these were polyfocal places — *città ad isole* (Wickham 2005, 652–53; or *disabitato*: Delogu 2017, 107) — as opposed to towns or even villages. These places comprised disparate, unconnected ('spatial destructuring': Wickham 2005, 652–53) communities occupying a common location defined as a place in antiquity, as opposed to unitary settlements integrated by public works (and infrastructure) managed by a civic authority such as existed in antiquity and, once again, from the eleventh century onwards. Their commonality was secured through their shared beliefs and the ranked systems of gift-giving.

For the archaeologist working with material sources wherein size (measures) matters, these places resembled an archipelago of islands or oases comprising principally of churches, monasteries, and aristocratic residences that, with their few dependencies in this flat hierarchical society, formed a coalition of settlements within otherwise largely deserted urban landscapes principally characterized in modern archaeological terms by sterile black earth created by open fields or gardens (Santangeli Valenziani 2011).

Rome is the quintessential polyfocal place of this era until the renewal of the urban fabric in the later eleventh and twelfth centuries. Brown (2003, 429) colourfully describes the early medieval eternal city as follows: '[it] would have struck visitors as a dream-like temple city as vast as Angkor Wat.' It became what Richard

Krautheimer (1980, 143) described as 'merely … a respectable county seat.' Using the *Liber Pontificalis*, Paolo Delogu has interpreted ninth-century Rome, for example, as essentially a papal city, inhabited by aristocrats and dependent economically upon subsistence strategies rather than the extensive commercial strategies of the Roman or Byzantine empires (Delogu 2007, 105; 2010, 256; 2017).

Excavations in Rome's Piazza Venezia, like those at the Cripta Balbi, show the spectacular scale of Rome's monumental dereliction by the later seventh century as well as the maintenance of small-scale industrial activity dedicated to maintaining the constellation of churches (Molinari, Santangeli Valenziani, and Spera 2015). Drawing upon evidence recorded in the *Liber Pontificalis*, Delogu has shown how, under Popes Hadrian and Leo, many churches and monasteries were refurbished at the end of the eighth century (Delogu 1988). Despoliation of ancient buildings for materials, as well as the making of lime mortar, is the principal archaeological index of this episode coinciding with the Carolingian renovation (Santangeli Valenziani 2015). Under Pope Paschal I, in the second decade of the ninth century, new monasteries and churches were erected for the first time in centuries (Goodson 2010). This investment was in support of increased pilgrimage and, in all likelihood, judging from the spike in donations of silver and gold to Rome's churches, increased secular patronage for purposes of private salvation. The revival of secular settlement would appear to occur in the period after this, characterized principally by green-glazed Forum Ware pitchers dated to the mid- to later ninth century. Small *curtis*-like nuclei occupied Rome's abandoned insulae close to the arteries within the ancient city that connected the circuit of pilgrimage churches. Settlements of this kind were located within the ruined Forum of Rome, Trajan's Markets, and the Largo Argentina, Rome (Brogiolo 2011, 175; Santangeli Valenziani 2011). Evidence of artisanal and rural peasant communities are notably absent. Rome was unexceptional. The archaeology of Lucca, Naples, and Ravenna, let alone Benevento, Otranto, and Salerno, as far as we can tell, was similar. In each old centre churches dominated the fabric of ruination. Secular settlement before the later ninth century was largely small-scale and often made use of ancient buildings as opposed to new settlements.

Polyfocal communities with their distinctive attributes constitute a definable stage in the process of medieval Italian urbanization and indeed a widespread European settlement form in the early Middle Ages (Blair 2018). Polyfocal towns were administrative central-places first and foremost where exchange, if it existed, was anchored in cosmological terms around the church with its inalienable relics. These places were nodes in highly contracted exchange networks, where the circulation of goods was restricted and the use of coin was minimal (Rovelli 2009, 75). These characteristics governed what Wickham has called 'cityness'; plainly these reveal urban communities that were essentially quite unlike ancient or medieval cities.

Ancient towns that had been transformed into polyfocal places in which the church was a pre-eminent presence occur throughout western Europe between the seventh and ninth centuries. Once-celebrated ancient centres like Canterbury, Mainz, Marseilles, or Tours were mere shadows of their former antique forms in this period. None possessed urban characteristics, though their inhabitants may have thought of themselves as city dwellers. The slow revival of such places has attracted the attention of Frans Theuws. He has explained the later Merovingian decline of the once major Roman city of Maastricht — along with the other Meuse towns (that famously fascinated the Belgian historian, Henri Pirenne) — as the product of the departure of its bishop, in this instance to Liège (2007). Its continuity as a place, he contends, rests upon its revival by the Church as a meeting place. In the case of Maastricht, festivals around saint's days were held, with the church of Saint-Servatius serving as a transactional force, periodically bringing strangers together: 'Maastricht was not just a meeting place like many others but a special one due to the presence of the saint' (Theuws and Kars 2017, 388). Ancient centres like Maastricht differed significantly from, for example, the large urban (non-place, largely undocumented) centres known as emporia (around the North Sea region) where the Church was notably absent (Theuws 2004). Transactional places in the seventh to tenth centuries, nonetheless, sustained a level of regional engagement that differed from their roles in antiquity and that differed again from their roles in the High Middle Ages. Perhaps it was because of this regional continuity (masking a clear functional discontinuity) that these polyfocal communities, with their specific, invented and imaginary histories, provided the bases for the revival of towns in the tenth and eleventh centuries?

Early Medieval Tuscany without its Towns

Tuscany had no towns in the early Middle Ages. This much is clear from the archaeological evidence. Tuscany possessed ancient places that were called towns or cities in the texts of this period but were polyfocal communities — principally monasteries and royal or aristocratic households occupying old, ruined townscapes. Lucca was a typical illustration of a ruined city with an important Lombard palace as

well as several monasteries. This coalition of separate elements lent it regional and occasionally international status. It even possessed a mint, but the mint was not for a coin-using economy; its purposes were much more restrictive, hence the rarity of its issues. Pisa (Meo 2013) and Florence (Cantini and Bruttini 2013), once rich riverine ports until the seventh century, were similarly reduced to polyfocal communities serving primitive rural economies. Pisa in particular continues to fascinate, given its high medieval history. The archaeology charted by Antonino Meo (2013, 2018) shows that the eleventh-century port evolved from a small, riverside village that may date from the ninth century. Like Venice, it perhaps owes its origins to a liminal political status on or beyond the bounds of the Tuscan march, which established its eventual role as a trading community once Mediterranean-wide trade revived slowly in the tenth century.

Vetricella (discussed by Marasco in this volume) was in many ways the successor of the ancient cabotage port of *Portus Scabris*, close to the Tyrrhenian entrance of the Follonica lagoon. The ample ceramics from *Portus Scabris* show its coastal and Mediterranean commerce decline in the sixth century and cease in the early seventh century (Vaccaro 2018). Early and high medieval ceramics are miniscule in number from the port as elsewhere in Tuscany (Vaccaro 2011, 2015) and Italy (Cirelli and others 2015). Plainly, with the collapse of its hinterland, the trading village disappeared. This contrasts, for example, with Comacchio at the mouth of a lagoon connecting to the Po river. In this case, the village continued to function and even grew in size to a population of perhaps a thousand by AD 700/730, thanks to its role as an intermediary for small-scale Byzantine trade from the Aegean and Sicily (Gelichi, Negrelli, and Grandi 2021). *Portus Scabris* had no such hinterland in the fluvial corridor leading to the Colline Metallifere. Its successor settlement was at Vetricella, an inland coastal landing place for impermanent exchange, approximately where the lagoon intersected with the *via Aurelia* (Hodges 2020b). At this point between the seventh and mid-ninth centuries, Elba iron ore was smelted in small-scale furnaces alongside which were anomalous post-built structures. Only around 850 was a royal fisc established here, probably overseeing large metalworking operations connected to a point of inflection in commodity production in the Tuscan march.

Ancient Populonia with its early medieval elite settlement nestling in the ruins may have been one of the centres served by Vetricella's iron-working operations (see Gelichi 2017). Populonia was in effect a hilltop polyfocal settlement, similar to Cosa (Cirelli and Fentress 2012), *Rusellae* (Celuzza and others, *infra*), and Siena (Cantini 2007) — all ancient places with long histories that ended as urban settlements in the early seventh century but remained properties of new clerical and tribal communities. In the largely abandoned ancient hilltop town of *Rusellae* above Grosseto, a bishop built a church and residence within the ruins of a bath overlooking the *via Aurelia* in southern Tuscany. Burial was a key aspect of such places, as donors sought salvation. This was also a strategic investment in a transactional place on a pilgrim route to Rome, most probably a result of Rome's revival as an international centre.

As Vetricella was responding to new demands for metal, Pope Leo created *Leopolis* at Centocelle close to Tarquinia (Romana Stasolla, *infra*). This was an altogether different investment as it was on an *ex-novo* site, without major ancient history. According to the *Liber Pontificalis*, it was close to the northern limits of the papal state overlooking the southern reaches of the Tuscan march. Excavations and surveys of Centocelle show it to have been a heavily fortified, hilltop bastion overlooking the Tyrrhenian pilgrim route, the *via Aurelia*. With two gates, the main road, however, ran directly to a new bishop's palace, his church and baptistery. In form it resembles Carolingian royal fortified residences (Noyé 2013; Renoux 2015; Untermann 2015) rather than a productive town with a grid of streets (including a central broad street), workshops, and other amenities. Perhaps it was a papal notion of a town, a transformative copy of Frankish places like Frankfurt and perhaps Paderborn. Was Centocelle also constructed in expectation of a revival of Byzantine maritime commerce? Elsewhere, in southern Italy, an Ionian commercial network appears to date from the mid-ninth century, concurrent with an increase in trans Adriatic Sea trade around the northern Adriatic region (Hodges 2021b). Centocelle was never to thrive. The rebirth of towns was slow to occur in this region. When it did, at places like Massa Maritima and Tarquinia spanning the mid- to late eleventh century, the impact on rural settlement is crystal clear, as Giovanna Bianchi has shown (2010).

Conclusion

This model for post-classical towns in Italy begins with a point of inflection in the sixth century when the Church and its espousal of salvation slowly eliminated the Mediterranean economy. This approach is not a traditional one. The emphasis is not upon the more intransigent and fundamentalist aspects of late antique religion but on syncretism and flexibility (Ward-Perkins 2005, 180). This is not a revival of 'archeologia cristiana' with its painstaking reconstruction of authoritative texts. The religious figures who determine this point of inflection were charismatic ascetics and intellectuals who imposed their ideas upon popes and managerial

bishops. The archaeology may not excavate the mindsets of these individuals, but it shows two very clear trends: the desertion and ruination of Italian ancient cities after the sixth century, and the lingering place of churches in the ruralizing of places that invariably retain their ancient names. This was to change in the later eighth century, as pilgrimage to Rome and the Holy Land put increased emphasis upon investment in cults and accommodating visitors. Local donors were also drawn once more to supporting these churches until the tectonic plates in society moved in the mid-ninth century. The earthquake in Italian society involved the diffused impact of the Carolingian reforms that began to be adopted at all levels of society (Davis 2015). This was, in effect, Marc Bloch's first feudal revolution. It brought agrarian reform: secondary products, storage, and massively increased redistribution of agrarian and material goods. The archaeology of Vetricella and its hinterland running from the Tyrrhenian Sea to the Colline Metallifere details the impact of materialism at a local level as clearly as do modern stratigraphic excavations in Rome. The wishful thinking that this materialism continued unabated from antiquity is not based upon tight chronological evidence: it is based upon a desire to demonstrate continuity invoking a peasantry tied somehow to an urbanism that simply is not supported by coin-dated levels, carbon 14 dates, or archaeomagnetic dates. No less clear now is that, in Tuscany, as in other regions, rural redistribution centres like Vetricella (in the case of iron-working) or Donoratico (in the case glazed tableware vessels) were the first post-classical places to provide agrarian communities with material goods — not emergent towns. Places like Pisa and, further afield, Rome revived as the Mediterranean economy did in the late tenth and earlier eleventh centuries (Hodges 2021b). By the mid-eleventh century, in time, rural market towns like Massa Marittima took shape, replacing the earlier redistribution estates. It was this last transition — Bloch's second feudal age — that provided the platform for the twelfth-century explosion of urban living in Tuscany and elsewhere (Hodges 2020b).

The poverty of dated archaeological levels for the period between 600–1000 in Tuscany (and Italy generally) has permitted archaeologists to pursue slavishly the historical paradigms. Towns existed, we are told, because the textual sources tell us they did. Well, the evidence is before us now. The archaeology shows an indisputable ruralization of ancient towns and with this the evidence of churches occupying the ancient ruins. This continuity of place should not distract us from the parameters of change evident in the mosaic of archaeological information. The 'continuity' of the church in fact itself obfuscates much, as is fully apparent in the complex topographical history of San

Vincenzo al Volturno as a reference point (Hodges 2014, 2018, 2020a).

Why, then, have Italian archaeologists resisted the interpretation of their data? What does it tell us about the generation of archaeologists raised since the 1970s on modern techniques? Is it not still the case that the discourse has become trapped by issues of identity as opposed to connectivity? Steeped in regionalism, defined by the uneven contemporary political economies of modern Italy, there has been a resistance to placing the medieval archaeology (and the changing role of the principal arbiter of the age, the Church) within *la longue durée* or within a global (European or Mediterranean) context. This is an obvious paradox. After fifty years of modern archaeological research, Tuscany boasts some of the best-studied landscapes and townscapes of medieval Europe. It is time to break free of the academic chains of regionalism and demonstrate to historians — most of whom are especially receptive — the stages by which medieval urban Tuscany emerged from the primitive aftermath of the collapse of a Mediterranean temple society and its polyfocal legacies.

Works Cited

Bianchi, Giovanna. 2010. 'Dominare e gestire un territorio. Ascesa e sviluppo delle "signorie forti" nella Maremma Toscana del Centro nord tra X e metà XII secolo', *Archeologia Medievale*, XXXVII: 93–104

Blair, John. 2018. *Building Anglo-Saxon England* (Princeton: Princeton University Press)

Boone, Marc. 2012. 'Cities in Late Medieval Europe: the Promise and the Curse of Modernity', *Urban History*, 39: 329–49

Brogiolo, Gian-Pietro. 2011. *Le origini della città medievale* (Mantua: Società Archeologica Padana)

Brown, Peter. 2003. *The Rise of Western Christendom. Triumph and Diversity, AD 200–1000* (Oxford: Blackwell)

——. 2012. *Through the Eye of the Needle. Wealth, the fall of Rome and the Making of Christianity in the West, 350–55 AD* (Princeton: Princeton University Press)

Cantini, Federico. 2007. 'Siena in the Early Middle Ages. New Data from the Excavations at Santa Maria della Scala', *Early Medieval Europe*, 15: 290–314

Cantini, Federico, and Jacopo Bruttini. 2013. 'Tra la città e il fiume. L'area degli Uffizi tra tarda antichità e Medioevo', in *Archeologia a Firenze. Città e Territorio*, ed. by Valeria D'Aquino, Guido Guarducci, Silvia Neucetti, and Stefano Valentini (Oxford: Archaeopress), pp. 269–304

Cirelli, Enrico, and Elizabeth Fentress. 2012. 'After the Rats: Cosa in the Late Empire and Early Middle Ages', in *Vrbes Extinctae. Archaeologies of Abandoned Classical Towns*, ed. by Neil Christie and Andrea Augenti (Farnham: Ashgate), pp. 97–114

Cirelli, Enrico, Francesca Diosono, and Helen Patterson (eds). 2015. *Le forme della crisi. Produzioni ceramiche e commerci nell'Italia centrale tra Romani e Longobardi (III–VIII d.C.)* (Bologna: Ante Qvem)

Davis, Jennifer R. 2015. *Charlemagne's Practice of Empire* (Cambridge: Cambridge University Press)

Delogu, Paolo. 1988. 'The Rebirth of Rome in the 8th and 9th Centuries', in *The Rebirth of Towns in the West AD 700–1050*, ed. by Richard Hodges and Brian Hobley (London: CBA), pp. 32–42

——. 2007. 'Rome in the Ninth Century: the Economic System', in *Post-Roman Towns, Trade and Settlement in Europe and Byzantium. Vol. 1. The Heirs of the Roman West*, ed. by Jennifer Henning (Berlin: De Gruyter), pp. 105–22

——. 2010. 'Giampiero Bognetti, storico della civiltà', in *Le Origini del Medioevo*, ed. by Paolo Delogu (Rome: Jouvence), pp. 365–81

——. 2017. 'The Popes and their Town in the Time of Charlemagne', in *Encounters, Excavations and Argosies. Essays for Richard Hodges*, ed. by John Mitchell, John Moreland, and Bea Leal (Oxford: Archaeopress), pp. 105–15

Gelichi, Sauro. 2017. 'Prima del monastero', in *Un monastero sul mare. Ricerche e archeologia a San Quirico di Populonia (Piombino, LI)*, ed. by Giovanna Bianchi and Sauro Gelichi (Florence: All'Insegna del Giglio), pp. 333–67

Gelichi, Sauro, Claudio Negrelli, and Elena Grandi. 2021. *Un emporio e la sua cattedrale. Gli scavi di piazza XX Settembre e Villaggio San Francesco a Comacchio* (Florence: Insegna del Giglio)

Goodson, Caroline. 2010. *The Rome of Pope Paschal I. Papal Power, Urban Renovation, Church Building and Relic Translation, 817–824* (Cambridge: Cambridge University Press)

Harper, Kyle. 2017. *The Fate of Rome. Climate, Disease and the End of an Empire* (Princeton: Princeton University Press)

Hodges, Richard. 2014. 'Landscape and Society: The Making of San Vincenzo's Mediterranean Valley', in *Living in the Landscape*, ed. by Katherine Boyle, Ryan Rabett, and Chris Hunt (Cambridge: McDonald Institute), pp. 267–85

——. 2018. 'Trade and Culture Process in a 9th-century Monastic Statelet: San Vincenzo al Volturno', in *Migration, Integration and Connectivity on the Southeastern frontier of the Carolingian Empire*, ed. by Danijel Dzino, Ante Milošević, and Trpimir Vedris (Leiden: Brill), pp. 268–86

——. 2020a. 'The Primitivism of the Early Medieval Peasant in Italy?', in *Social Inequality in Early Medieval Europe*, ed. by Juan Antonio Quiròs Castillo (Turnhout: Brepols), pp. 165–74

——. 2020b. 'Defining the Archaeology of Bloch's First Feudal age. Implications of Vetricella Phases 1 and 2 for the Making of Medieval Italy', in *Vetricella: An Early Medieval Royal Property in Tuscany's Mediterranean*, ed. by Giovanna Bianchi and Richard Hodges (Florence: All'Insegna del Giglio), pp. 169–84

——. 2021a. 'Seeking Salvation at Byllis in the 6th Century', *Journal of Roman Archaeology*, 34.2: 380–87

——. 2021b. 'The Adriatic Sea AD 500–1100: A Corrupted Alterity?', in *Byzantium, Venice and the Adriatic Sea, c. 700–1453*, ed. by Magdalena Skoblar, British School at Athens Studies in Greek Antiquity, 2 (Cambridge: Cambridge University Press), pp. 15–44

Krautheimer, Richard. 1980. *Rome: A Profile of the City* (Princeton: Princeton University Press)

McCormick, Michael. 2001. *Origin of the Medieval Economy* (Cambridge: Cambridge University Press)

McCormick, Michael, Ulf Büntgen, Mark A. Cane, Edward R. Cook, Kyle Harper, Peter Huybers, Thomas Litt, Sturt W. Manning, Paul Andrew Mayewski, Alexander F. M. More, Kurt Nicolussi, and Willy Tegel. 2012. 'Climate Change during the Roman Empire: Reconstructing the Past from Scientific and Historical Evidence', *Journal of Interdisciplinary History*, 42: 251–73

Meo, Antonino. 2013. *Alle origini del comune di Pisa*, unpublished ms, Pisa

——. 2018. 'Anfore, uomini e reti di scambio sul "mare pisano" (VIII–XII secolo)', *Archeologia Medievale* XLV: 219–38

Molinari, Alessandra, Riccardo Santangeli Valenzani, and Lucrezia Spera (eds). 2015. *L'archeologia della produzione a Roma (secoli V-XV). Atti del Convegno Internazionale di Studi Roma 27–29 Marzo 2014*. Collection de l'Ecole française de Rome, 516 (Bari: Edipuglia)

Moreland, John. 2018. 'AD 536: Back to Nature', *Acta Archaeologica*, 89: 91–111

Noyé, Ghislaine. 2013. 'Per la storia della ricerche archeologica recente sulle fortificazione in terra in Francia e in Italia. Stato delle conoscenze e dei problemi', *Archeologia Medievale*, 40: 15–35

Renoux, Annie. 2015. 'Du palais impérial aux palais royaux et princiers en Francie occidentale (*c.* 843–1100)', in *The Emperor's House: Palaces from Augustus to the Age of Absolutism*, ed. by Michael Featherstone and others (Berlin: De Gruyter), pp. 93–106

Rovelli, Alessia. 2009. 'Coins and Trade in Early Medieval Italy', *Early Medieval Europe*, 17: 45–74

Santangeli Valenziani, Riccardo. 2011. *Edilizia residenziale in Italia nell'altomedioevo* (Rome: Carocci)

——. 2015. 'Calcare ed altre tracce di cantiere, cave e smontaggi sistematici degli edifici antichi', in *L'Archeogia della Produzione a Roma (secoli V–XI)*, ed. by Alessandra Molinari, Riccardo Santangeli Valenzani, and Lucrezia Spera (Rome: École française de Rome), pp. 335–44

Sarris, Peter. 2006. *Economy and Society in the Age of Justinian* (Cambridge: Cambridge University Press)

Sessa, Kristina. 2019. 'The New Environmental Fall of Rome. A Methodological Consideration', *Journal of Late Antiquity*, 12: 211–55

Theuws, Frans. 2004. 'Exchange, Religion, Identity and Central Places in the Early Middle Ages', *Archaeological Dialogues*, 4: 121–38

——. 2007. 'Where is the Eighth Century in the Towns of the Meuse Valley?', in *Post-Roman Towns, Trade and Settlement in Europe and Byzantium. Vol. 1. The Heirs of the Roman West*, ed. by Jennifer Henning (Berlin: De Gruyter), pp. 153–64

Theuws, Frans, and Mirjam Kars (eds). 2017. *The Saint-Servatius Complex in Masstricht. The Vrijthof Excavations (1969–1970). Roman Infrastructure – Merovingian Cemetery – Carolingian Cemetery – Early Town Development* (Bonn: Habelt)

Untermann, Mattias. 2015. 'Frühmittelterliche Pfalzen im östfrankischen Reich', in *The Emperor's House: Palaces from Augustus to the Age of Absolutism*, ed. by Michael Featherstone and others (Berlin: De Gruyter), pp. 107–26

Vaccaro, Emanuele. 2011. *Sites and Pots: Settlement and Economy in Southern Tuscany (AD 300–900)* (Oxford: British Archaeological Reports), pp. 168–231

——. 2015. 'Ceramic Production and Trade in Tuscany (3rd-mid 9th c. AD): New Evidence from the South-west', in *Le forme della crisi. Produzioni ceramiche e commercio nell'Italia centrale tra Romani e Longobardi (III–VIII d.C.)*, ed. by Enrico Cirelli, Francesca Diosono, and Helen Patterson (Bologna: Ante Qvem), pp. 221–27

——. 2018. 'Long-Distance Ceramic Connections: Portus Scabris (Portiglioni-GR) Coastal Tuscany and the Tyrrenian Sea', in *Origins of a New Economic Union (7th-12th Centuries): Preliminary Results of the nEU-Med Project, October 2015-March 2017*, ed. by Giovanna Bianchi and Richard Hodges (Florence: All'Insegna del Giglio), pp. 81–100

Ward-Perkins, Bryan. 2005. *The Fall of Rome and the End of Civilization* (Oxford: The Clarendon Press)

Wickham, Chris. 2005. *Framing the Early Middle Ages* (Oxford: Oxford University Press)

Wood, Ian. 2007. 'Review Article: Landscapes Compared', *Early Medieval Europe*, 15: 223–37

——. 2018. *The Transformation of the Roman West* (Leeds: Arc Humanities Press)

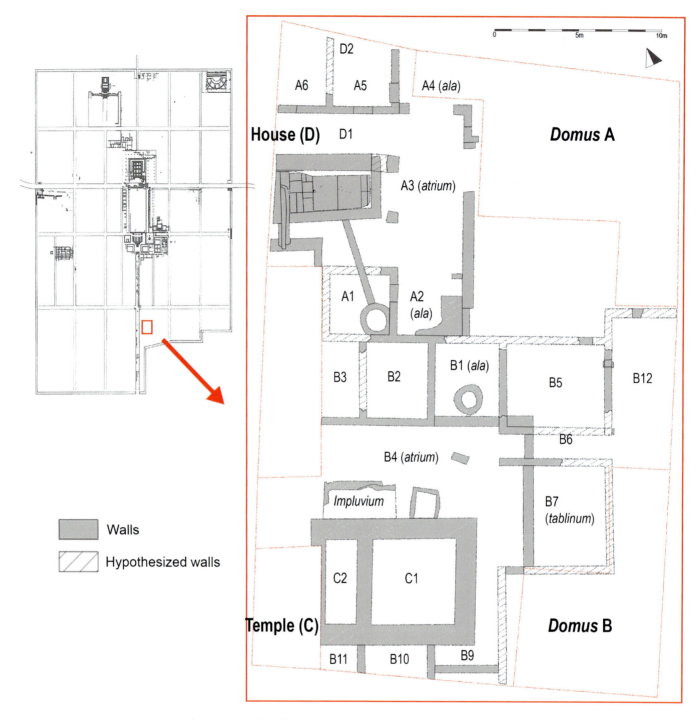

Figure 9.1. Porta Marina excavations. The rediscovered buildings. Drawings by Rocco Marcheschi, reproduced with permission.

SIMONETTA MENCHELLI, STEFANO GENOVESI,
AND ROCCO MARCHESCHI

9. Late Roman Luna in the Light of the Porta Marina Excavations

Introduction

Our excavations carried out in an *insula* in the southernmost part of Luna, near the hypothesized urban wall and Porta a Mare (Sea-Gate) (Menchelli and others 2016, 2018, 2021a) immediately to the east of the *Cardo Maximus*, provide interesting data about the late Roman period which, especially if compared with the results of research in other urban districts, can increase our general knowledge about the city.

The two *domus* identified in this peripheral *insula* (Fig. 9.1a and b, to the north and to the south respectively), built in the second half of the second century BC, underwent major changes and transformations through the centuries, but the area continued to be inhabited — or at least frequented — at least up to the late seventh–early eighth centuries AD.

In the second half of the first century AD, *domus* B, which was the larger of the two and decorated with mosaics and frescoes, was occupied by the construction of a small temple (7.40 m × 9.90 m; Fig. 9.1c), built on its south-western part and, in particular, on the *atrium*.

In the progressive changes of the townscapes, therefore, this previously marginal district must have become more important to the urban plan, as it came to be the site of a temple. This had repercussions from both topographical and social points of view because it transformed from a private/residential area to a public one, a phenomenon that is well documented in various sectors of Luna, particularly in the first century AD.[1]

Regarding *domus* A, at the moment we have no evidence of building transformations in the early to middle Imperial periods, but it is improbable that it could have kept its residential function due to its proximity to the religious building. In any case, in the second–third centuries AD, this district also was likely to have shared in the general prosperity of the city deriving from the exploitations of the Apuanian marble quarries. A well-known epigraph of AD 255 refers to Luna as a *splendida civitas* (CIL XI 1354; Angeli Bertinelli 1983), and indeed the commercialization of the Apuanian marble was still documented in the third century, although it would gradually peter out in the following century, provoking an inevitable crisis in the economic and social structures and, consequently, in the urban plan and its organization.

Especially in its final decades, the fourth century was a period of great transformations: in particular, the Grande Tempio and the Capitolium with its surrounding area were abandoned (Ward-Perkins 1978), maybe as a consequence of an earthquake, which was repeatedly referred to in regard to Luna (Gervasini 2016, 36). These events may be connected to disasters that occurred during the earthquake, but in any case, they are also related to new religious motivations. Indeed, Luna is generally considered a city that underwent an early Christianization: good evidence of this is provided by the election of one of Luna's citizens, Eutichianus, as

---

[1] The nearby *Domus Repubblicana* and *Domus degli Affreschi* were also partially obliterated in the Claudian period for the construction both of the *Forum adiectum* and of the so-called

Tempio di Diana; the plan and dimensions of the latter are very similar to those of the temple located now at Porta Marina (Durante and Gervasini 2000; Gervasini 2016, 37–39).

Simonetta Menchelli (simonetta.menchelli@unipi.it) Università di Pisa

Stefano Genovesi (fefo.genovesi@gmail.com) Università di Pisa

Rocco Marcheschi (rocco.marcheschi@phd.unipi.it) Università di Pisa

Archaeological Landscapes of Late Antique and Early Medieval Tuscia: Research and Field Papers, ed. by Riccardo Rao and Alessandro Sebastiani, MEDITO 3 (Turnhout 2023), pp. 148–162

Figure 9.2. Porta Marina excavations. The late antique phases (drawings by Rocco Marcheschi, reproduced with permission).

Pope in AD 275; moreover, the Edict of Theodosius in AD 380 must have accelerated the anti-pagan movements (Durante 2003, 204).

In regard to our excavations, in the area of the *domus* A, a destruction layer consisting of burned beams and rooftiles deriving from the collapse of the main roof was identified, dating to the fifth century AD, while a *domus* in the northern district of Luna (Durante 2001, 31) and the restored portions of the *Domus degli Affreschi* were abandoned some decades before, in the late fourth century (Cavalieri Manasse and others 1982, 165).

A very significant change, moreover, must have happened in the Porta Marina district when the Temple lost its role and importance, most probably in the last decades of the fourth or in the early fifth century, for the religious reasons mentioned above. Following our stratigraphies, the Temple was the object of a careful removal of its floor, its walls, and all its decorative elements, as we did not find any collapsed building materials and as the only remains of the Temple, which are the foundations of the service rooms under the *cella* and podium, were brought to light immediately under the topsoil.

As is widely known, in Late Antiquity the recovery of construction materials, if one excludes the evidence of the destructuralization process, could be a hint of new building projects with recovery activities regulated by law and organized by local authorities (Marsili 2016). Starting from the late fourth–early fifth centuries, these operations are well documented in various parts of the city, as in the Capitolium area, even if many marble artefacts were not reutilized, or in the Forum (Ward-Perkins 1978, 42–43). Also, the *spolia* from the small Temple at Porta Marina may have been immediately reused in some buildings at Luna,[2] deposited in places suitable for subsequent reuse, or transformed into lime, a process well documented at Luna by a lime-kiln identified in the area of the *Domus degli Affreschi*. (Durante 2001, 23; Petrella 2007).

Abundant construction materials were also necessary for the building activities in the late fourth and the early fifth centuries: as noted elsewhere, the public area north of the Capitolium was occupied by the restorations of the *Domus dei Mosaici* that displays the famous mosaic depicting the *Circus Maximus*, dated to the early fifth century, by a fishpond and related processing activities (Durante 2001, 24; 2003, 208–09)

---

[2] At the moment, there is no evidence of the reuse of the materials from this Temple. One ongoing project aims at reconstructing sculptural ornaments of the buildings at Luna and could provide new data regarding this topic (Cadario and Legrottaglie 2018).

and by a private bathhouse complex in the foundations of which building materials and statues are visible (Ward-Perkins 1978, 38, fig. 11). Yet again in the fourth century, after a number of restorations and with the addition of the later famous, homonymous mosaic, the *Domus di Oceano* was rebuilt according to the needs of a Christian member of the urban elite; finally, in the late fifth century, the *Domus* was transformed into a Paleo-Christian basilica (Lusuardi Siena 2003, 198–99). Evidently, in the fifth century AD, the splendour of the early Imperial period, such as the euergetic activities aiming at the construction and restoration of public works (Angeli Bertinelli 1995), was just a memory.

In the context of social changes due obviously to the disappearance of the Imperial economic interest and financial investment in the marble quarries, there were nevertheless in Luna some members of the ruling elite who were wealthy enough to invest in very rich, private *domus*. In fact, the Luna *candentia moenia* mentioned by Rutilius Namatianus in AD 415, while keeping in mind the author's poetic license, evoke a city that was still shining with its white marble.[3]

As for what we can observe in our excavations, the economic viability of the city in the fifth century is documented by the installation of a workshop, most probably aimed at cleaning fabrics and skins, that occupied part of the *domus* A (Fig. 9.2b) and operated until the mid-sixth century. This workshop, among other things, confirms that the urban infrastructural system was still functioning, bearing witness to an abundant water supply also in this peripheral area, just like the *cloaca maxima* that continued to drain the water from this workshop and from the others attached to the wealthy *domus*.[4]

After their destruction in the fourth century AD (Durante 2003, 205–06), the main road axes — the *cardo maximus* and *decumanus maximus* — also appear to have been continuously restored, and therefore, it is possible to observe some weak elements of continuity, even if quite vague, in the urban plan until the fifth to the early sixth centuries. Similarly, the economic and commercial vitality of the city is documented by the imports of manufacture and goods that continued to arrive from the entire Mediterranean basin through Roman trade routes (Lusuardi Siena 2003, 200; Menchelli forthcoming).

Another helpful element in the debate around changes and continuity within the city is offered by the Christianization process of Luna: as seen above, this caused dramatic developments, mainly with the abandoning or dismantling of the pagan temples; although these sometimes underwent full destruction, they most probably also represented an expression of resilience. The diocese that is documented from AD 465 with the presence of Bishop Felice and the relevant ecclesiastical organization strengthened the cohesion of the urban society and presumably the maintenance of public and private spaces that could be useful for the new needs of the city centre.[5]

A further crucial change took place during the Byzantine period when Luna became the main centre of the *Provincia Maritima Italorum*: the Cathedral was fully renewed thanks to *Gerontius*, a servant of Christ, and further building works were carried out on the northern side of the fortified quadrilateral (the so-called *Cittadella*), built to protect the Cathedral and the entire episcopal complex. The latter also included a female convent, founded by Bishop Venanzio at the end of the sixth century in a house that he owned (Dadà 2006, 341); in this period, a strong and influential Jewish community was also active in Luna (Durante 2003, 203–14).

At the Porta Marina excavations, the Byzantine phase is documented by the construction of a house (D), which was installed on the northern *domus* in the second half of the sixth century AD, by a contemporary well in the area of the southern *domus*, and by the utilization of a structure as a rubbish dump (Menchelli and others 2021a) (Fig. 9.2c). These data enrich the knowledge of private buildings in Luna, until now only based on the 'Byzantine' houses excavated in the Forum in the 1970s and 1980s (Ward-Perkins 1981); moreover, other contemporaneous, humble timber domestic structures were identified in area of the theatre, installed into its large walls that were still standing at that period (Gervasini and Mancusi 2020).

In this period, therefore, the Roman urban plan appears to have been destructuralized by the presence of the *Cittadella*, by the dismantling and the re-utilization of pre-existing buildings, by the removal of materials, and by the fall in the occupation of urban land. Nonetheless, Luna continued to maintain its position as a city, as it was able to carry out many relational activities both with the Byzantine administration and with the ecclesiastical network while remaining a strong reference point for the territory given its strategic location along the main coastal and the Apennine road system as well as the survival of its efficient harbour.

---

3 Rutilius Namatianus II, 63–68; see also Vinchesi 2016, 30–31.

4 See Durante 2003, 206–08; see also Ward-Perkins 1978, 44 in regards to the late Roman drainpipe built in the portico of the Grande Tempio. On the efficiency of the water system as a marker of the general condition of cities in Late Antiquity, see Brogiolo 2016.

---

5 Lusuardi Siena 2003, 197; in general, for the managerial Bishop see Brown 2012.

In fact, as pointed out, the Byzantine houses of Luna excavated in the 1970s and 1980s, despite their humble building techniques, certainly provided materials that could be attributed to activities and lifestyles of some high economic level;[6] for example, the inhabitants of house D, apart from availing themselves of wares and foodstuffs imported from the Mediterranean basin, also enjoyed a 'rich' diet, strongly based on meat, prevalently pork (Reynaert 2018). This is absolutely in line with what has been seen in other contexts of Late Antiquity in Luna (Barker 1977).

After the Lombard conquest in AD 642, the settlement patterns in the city are mainly documented by storage pits built into drystone walls (Lusuardi Siena 2003, 201), by water wells (Durante 2003, fig. 3), and by holes for waste disposal (Johnson 2016), the latter two being clear evidence of the definitive crisis of the Roman infrastructural system. Further evidence from the Lombard period includes deep trenches for recovering materials, present in the main buildings and graves in the Forum area (Ward-Perkins 1981, 92; Durante 2003, 212), in the theatre (Ward-Perkins 1981, 92; Gervasini and Mancusi 2020), and in the privileged burials along the perimetral walls of the Cathedral (Lusuardi Siena 2003, 201).

Regarding the archaeologically documented houses, in the Porta Marina area, building D appears to have been in use in the second half of the seventh century, showing imported materials dated up to the early eighth century, which act as weak evidence of human groups that followed one another over time. A similar chronology can perhaps be envisaged for the houses in the theatre (Gervasini and Mancuso 2020) and for those identified in the south-western corner of the Capitolium, built alongside the eighth- and ninth-century AD street pavement, that constitute further valuable evidence for the early medieval settlement patterns of Luna (Gervasini and Mancusi 2016).

Finally, in the Lombard period and despite the vanishing urban and ruralized plan (see Hodges in this volume), the city of Luna continued to be a centre with a certain political and administrative autonomy exercised by the bishops, the authority of whom finds some clear pieces of evidence in the *Cittadella*, Luna's new topographical centre, and in the coins from the Episcopal Mints. Indeed, Luna as a polyfocal place was able to maintain its strategic role in the road system between the Mediterranean Sea, Northern Italy, and Europe[7] and in the maritime commercial routes, which the Byzantine Empire directed towards the West with increasing difficulty (Menchelli forthcoming; see also Hodges in this volume). Luna, therefore, survived throughout antiquity, and its decline was long and not unidirectional but rather experienced different phases of crisis and resilience, but in the eleventh and twelfth centuries, its area became unhealthy due to coastal landscape changes; consequently, in 1204, the bishopric was transferred to Sarzana, and the place of Luna was definitively abandoned.

In conclusion, Luna could be considered a significant case study in the debate about the urban transformations in Central Western Italy in AD 400–1000. In particular, the Byzantine *Cittadella*, including the Cathedral with the entire Episcopal Complex, provides evidence of the final destructuring of the 'colonial' urban plan and the transition from the Roman to the Christian city.

In the following centuries, the 'managerial' Bishops ran a polyfocal Luna, which, in any case, was still a node in exchange networks. Finally, the city — having no Patron Saints — appears to have been less fortunate than Maastricht (Theuws and Kars 2017). Hence the departure of its Bishops trigged the end of its residual 'urban' life in the early thirteenth century.

[SM]

The Area of *Domus* B after the Abandonment of the Temple (Building C)

During the second half of the first century AD, the southern *domus* (*domus* B) underwent a first transformation due to the construction of a Temple (Building C) in an area previously occupied by the *atrium* and the southern sector of the *domus* (Fig. 9.1). A series of operations redesigned the plan of the rooms along with the northern and eastern sides of the *atrium*. In particular, the inner walls of the rooms were razed to the ground, while the entrances to the *atrium* (Rooms B1, B6, and B7),[8] and the eastern sector (Room B12, presumably the peristyle of the *domus*) were closed. When this thorough refurbishment was completed, the floors were raised using different building materials, consisting of mortar, small fragments of painted plaster,

---

6 Lusuardi Siena 2003, 200. It is also suggested that commercial and productive activities may have been carried out in the houses in the Forum (*case bottega*) (Lusuardi Siena and others 2011). Regarding the humble architecture in Eastern Liguria, see Benente 2017, 205.

7 These routes would remain in use in the following centuries, as shown by the network of the *via Francigena* and other medieval religious itineraries (Durante 2003, 212).

8 Most probably, the construction of the southern wall of Room 1 was related to the erection of the Temple.

Figure 9.3. Aerial view of the area of *domus* B, including the water well and the squared structure resting against the foundations of the Temple (photo by Domingo Belcari, reproduced with permission).

and fragments of schistose stones — all of them deriving from the spoliation of the *domus*.[9]

The Temple probably fell into disuse at the end of the fourth century AD, and this area was affected by important changes that redefined its new destination. As shown by the stratigraphic evidence, this process consisted of an intense and systematic spoliation that led to the removal of the paving, the walls, and the marble decorations of the Temple.

The scant archaeological evidence does not permit any available insights into what happened in the area after the spoliation of the Temple: only a thin stratigraphic deposit is preserved immediately above the foundations of the temple complex, which had been frequently affected by ancient and modern works; therefore, the layers that obliterated the foundations of the Temple did not provide any evidence of either collapse of pre-existing structures, or traces of a new floor. Consequently, regarding the phase following the abandonment of the Temple, the excavation has revealed the absence of any building activities that can reasonably be related to this phase (Fig. 9.2a); moreover, we documented a very scant presence of fifth-century ceramics. These elements suggest that, during this period, the area was characterized by scarce human activities, in contrast to the northern sector of the *insula* where a workshop was installed in the same period.

According to our excavations, during the sixth and seventh centuries AD, building activity resumed in the area, as attested by the construction of some facilities (Fig. 9.2b–c; Fig. 9.3). Indeed, between the end of the fifth and the first half of the sixth centuries, a water well made of drystone walls with large pebbles, a few fragments of schistose stones, and bricks was built in room B1 (Fig. 9.2b; Figs 9.3–9.4).[10]

The construction of the well affected, with its wide circular cut, the mortar floor preparation and the southern wall of room B1, both linked to the building works in the area around the Temple.[11] At the same

---

9 For a more detailed analysis of the activities affecting *domus* B due to the construction of the Temple, see Menchelli and others 2020; 2021.

10 For the chronology, see Menchelli and others 2018, 52, n. 42.
11 As the southern wall of Room B1 was partially destroyed by the construction of the well, most likely all the walls of the room, and perhaps those closest by, were not visible in this phase.

Figure 9.4. Room B1. The water well viewed from east (photo by Paolo Sangriso, reproduced with permission).

time, a new floor — consisting of a thick layer of clay — was laid down all around the well and over a large part of room B1.[12] Finally, a thick layer of large pebbles, few fragments of schistose stones, and broken bricks document the obliteration of the well in the second half of the seventh century AD; most likely, this layer derived from the destruction of the upper part of the well itself.[13]

The well in room B1 shows strong similarities to the *pozzi d'acqua*, which are mainly distributed in the Forum and in its surrounding area, as regards their construction technique and size.[14] These are commonly considered important indicators, despite being of problematic dating, of the continuity of the settlement in Luna, or its changes, during Late Antiquity.[15]

In a small number of cases, it is possible to suppose some kind of correlation, not necessarily exclusive,[16] between the sixth- and seventh-century AD documented houses in Luna and the presence of water wells. One example is represented by the three timber houses discovered on the north-eastern side of the Forum, two (Casa I and II) of which date back to the mid-sixth century AD and one (Casa III) to the first half of the seventh century AD (Ward-Perkins 1979, 1981). These houses might have had access to at least two wells in different periods: one just to their north and the other

---

12 The clay floor layer directly covers both the original floor of *domus* B (second half of second century BC) and the later mortar layer related to the building of the Temple (second half of the first century AD), being affected in the same way by the well's circular cut.

13 A fragment of amphora Keay 8a (second half of the seventh century AD, Bonifay 2004, 141–42), found among the scarce ceramic material coming from this thick layer, is decisive for the dating of the abandonment of the well.

14 An initial list of the water wells (*pozzi d'acqua*) discovered in Luna was provided by Ward-Perkins 1977, 670–71.

15 See Durante 2003, 212, fig. 3 for the dating of the wells from Luna and their distribution in the 'colonial' city.

16 For the purchase of the *usum potei* by several inhabitants living in the same area, see Tjäder 1954, 38–41; see also Gelichi 1994, 161–62.

Figure 9.5. Area of *domus* B. The northern foundations of the Temple and the squared structure viewed from the west (photo by Rocco Marcheschi, reproduced with permission).

in the eastern *porticus* of the Forum. A further example is represented by the well inside the eastern *porticus* of the Capitolium,[17] which may have been used by the houses in the north-eastern corner of the Forum and is dated to the seventh century AD; the life strata of this well are also associated with pits and underground storage facilities (*cantine*).[18]

In addition to the well, our excavations brought to light an underground structure (measuring approximately 1.66 m × 1.75 m) that was built resting against the northern foundations of the Temple (Fig. 9.2b; Fig. 9.5). On the other three sides, its dry-stone walls were made of a few rows of large pebbles and fragments of schistose stones arranged in a single line. This underground structure was used as a dump, and it was progressively filled between the late sixth and the first half of the seventh centuries AD (Fig. 9.2c). At the current state of research, both its dating and its original function are uncertain. As has been seen, from the stratigraphical point of view, this structure is certainly more recent than the Temple, but the preliminary analysis of the archaeological finds does not offer clear evidence for placing its construction during Late Antiquity.

In conclusion, we have very few elements with which to define the different features of the settlement in the southern area of the insula during the fifth century AD. By contrast, for the sixth and the seventh centuries AD, a little more data is available, which indicate that the area was characterized by residential elements, like the well and the waste dump, despite the absence of any remains of houses.

For this phase, therefore, it is possible to postulate the presence of one or more dwellings, probably located around the central courtyard, whose inhabitants most probably had access to the well located here. The houses might have been built with perishable materials, as documented for coeval houses in the north-eastern sector of the Forum, or by exploiting the existing

---

17 For the building peculiarities of the well documented as P.CS.1, see Ward-Perkins 1977, 670.

18 Regarding the houses discovered in the eastern *porticus* of the Capitolium, see Lusuardi Siena 2003, 265, n. 6.

ancient walls, e.g., with the Temple foundations, in accordance with the practices attested in Building D (Genovesi, *infra*).

[RM]

The Area of *Domus* A between the Fifth and the Seventh Centuries AD

During the fifth century AD, a fire destroyed part of the northern *domus*, as documented by fallen charred beams of the roof's truss found on the floor in the north-eastern sector of the *atrium*. After such a disaster, the house was not restored, but it underwent a deep transformation and was converted into a workshop.[19]

A north–south wall, some 0.8 m thick, was built in order to divide the *atrium* area from the eastern sector of the *domus*, apparently not considered part of the newly constructed workshop. The latter, on the contrary, was installed in the rooms close to the *cardo maximus* (Fig. 9.2b; Fig. 9.6). A small, circular cistern was built with an internal diameter of 1.32 m in the *cubiculum* located east of the southern *ala*: this structure had a *cocciopesto* bottom, with a slight slope towards the north. A clay pipe, made by means of overlapping cylindrical tiles, was housed inside a structure consisting of mortar and broken tiles; it exited the cistern northwards and entered a 6.5 m × 2.5 m rectangular tank, which replaced the *impluvium* of the *domus*. The newly built wall, surrounding the bottom of the tank, was made by reutilizing the old marble slabs of the *impluvium* and others that had been recovered from elsewhere, thus exceeding the original size of the *impluvium*. As for the disposal of the dirty water, the rectangular tank continued to use the same sewer of the *impluvium* of the *domus*.

The *atrium* floor level was also raised, by means of a 0.3-m thick clay layer, covered in turn by a *cocciopesto* floor, which is still well preserved in the southern sector of the *atrium*. A quadrangular pillar (0.6 m × 0.6 m) located 0.3 m from the south-eastern corner of the rectangular basin, indicates the construction, within the *atrium* area, of new roofing, at the moment still not identifiable but very different from the *domus'* original one.

The pottery finds from the new floor layer provide significant data about the workshop's chronology. Its construction probably dates back to the final decades of the fifth century AD, as documented by the presence of Tunisian mortar (*Carthage Class* 1, type A), common after the second quarter of the fifth century AD (Bonifay 2004, 252, fig. 138.1), ARS bowls, namely Hayes 67 (fifth century AD, Bonifay 2004, 171, 173, fig. 92, no. 6 and 8) and Hayes 91B types (the central decades of the fifth century AD, Bonifay 2004, 179, fig. 95, type 50), and Keay 62Q amphorae, also from Tunisia and dated between the last third of the fifth and the mid-sixth centuries AD (Bonifay 2004, 137, fig. 74, 3). Another *Carthage Class* 1 type mortar was reused in making the water clay pipe.

In summary, the workshop built in the *atrium* consisted of a set of structures: the circular tank, the pressure pipe, and the rectangular tank. So far, we have no specific data regarding its productive function, even if it is clear that it was connected with washing activities, requiring running water. At the moment, the absolute lack of evidence of the typical small, round wells for the so-called *saltus fullonum* permits us to exclude that the workshop was a *fullonica*, suggesting other hypotheses such as leather washing.[20]

During the second half of the sixth century AD, the area of *domus* A again underwent a phase of profound changes: this part of the *insula* was reorganized, and the new arrangement continued to be used until the late seventh and the early eighth centuries AD, when the whole area was abandoned. The floor of the entire area, over a surface of at least 100 m², was raised by about 0.4 m by means of stockpiling many soil and debris layers that contained huge amounts of building bricks and stones, mortar, *cocciopesto*, and *opus spicatum* floor parts. This building reorganization can be dated by the presence in the layers of the ARS bowl Hayes 99B type (the second quarter of the sixth–mid-seventh centuries AD, Bonifay 2004, 181, fig. 96, 4), of the Keay 62E Tunisian amphorae (Bonifay 2004, 35, 140, figs 74, 11; 2016, 516) and of the Eastern *Late Roman Amphora* 4B2 type (both of these amphorae were traded from the mid-sixth century AD, Pieri 2005, 106–07, tav. 40, 8).

Above this new walking plan, our excavations brought to light a building activity, which once again gave the area of *domus* A a residential function. The building to be identified as a house is located at the north-western corner of the excavation trench; so far two rectangular rooms (D1, D2), covering an overall surface of 30 m², have been identified (Fig. 9.2c).[21]

The walls of this house were built on the *domus* structures, which therefore constituted their base, while the highest part of the walls was probably set in perishable materials, such as mudbricks. The southern perimetral wall of the building, characterized by the remarkable

---

19 This intervention almost completely destroyed the relevant stratigraphies of all the previous periods.

20 On the importance of water in the tanning process, see Fabiani 2018, 380–84. Regarding the structures characterizing a *fullonica*, see Flohr 2013, 23–26.

21 As both of the rooms are still being excavated, their complete plan is not yet known.

Figure 9.6. Area of *domus* A. Aerial view of the *atrium* of the *domus* after the building interventions of the mid-fifth century AD (photo by Domingo Belcari, reproduced with permission).

width of 0.8 m, was instead specifically built as part of this late antique intervention (Fig. 9.7). In fact, it was constructed using a different building technique, with schistose stones and a few broken roof-tiles and bricks, all of them reused from older buildings and bound with yellow clay. Even if it was constructed without mortar, this wall was probably intended to reach a noteworthy height, perhaps because it could have been required for a possible first floor.

The Southern room's main feature is a 0.6 m × 0.6 m fireplace, made of a layer of broken tiles and bricks and surrounded on all sides by schist stones vertically inserted into the floor. The latter was made of mortar mixed with clay and covered an underfloor cavity filled with reused materials (broken bricks and roof-tiles, small stones, and small pottery sherds), while instead, a simple beaten earth floor has been found in the northernmost room (D2) (Fig. 9.2c). The presence of the oven and the differences between the floors of the two rooms most probably reflect their different functions, D1 being part of the living area and D2 being perhaps connected with working or daily activities: the latter could have

Figure 9.7. Area of *domus* A. The southern perimeter wall of the Byzantine house (on the left) and aerial photo of Rooms D1 and D2 (photos by Domingo Belcari and Stefano Genovesi, reproduced with permission).

been designated as a working space, as a warehouse, or as a stable, or much more likely, it could have been used for all these purposes.

Five post holes and the traces of a blackish layer, whose formation can be connected with the decay of a timber axe's plank, provide evidence of a second building in the south-western sector (Fig. 9.2c). This structure — probably entirely made of timber, apart from the roof which was perhaps tiled — covered a surface of 37.1 m² and abutted the perimeter wall between *domus* A and B, still standing in the late sixth century AD. In this same area, excavations have brought to light a large number of fragments of trade amphorae, soapstone cooking pots, bone tools, and glass vessels — mostly small chalices of Isings 111 type (Menchelli forthcoming): this evidence allows us to identify the timber structure as a warehouse, used both for foodstuffs and everyday tools.

The stratigraphies of Porta Marina provide significant evidence of urbanistic — mainly for private buildings — and economic changes in Luna between the fifth and the seventh centuries AD. The building interventions during the mid-fifth century AD dramatically transformed the northern *domus*, which lost its residential function and became an area for a workshop, even if its productive activity still remains uncertain. This change can be seen as clear evidence in Luna for the well-known trend that documents, along with the disappearance of the *domus*, the progressive increase in artisanal activities (Gelichi 1994, 155–59; Brogiolo 2011, 75–76, 181–84; Augenti 2016, 50, 56, 241–43). During the fifth century AD, moreover, we can see the pivotal emergence of the Christian monumental quarter around the cathedral, built in about the middle of the century (Lusuardi Siena 2003, 203–14; Gervasini and Mancusi 2014), and at the same time, the enduring, noteworthy private building activity documented by some very rich *domus* — e.g. the so-called *Domus dei Mosaici* (Durante and Gervasini 2000, 63–67).

As regards Luna, another step in this long process from the Imperial age to Late Antiquity can be dated to the final decades of the sixth century AD. In the area of Porta Marina, the distinctive feature of this phase is the increase in undeveloped sectors: except for the house located in the north-western sector (Rooms D1, D2) and the timber structure abutting the southern perimetral wall of the *domus*, all the available space was in fact used as an open courtyard. A similar process is

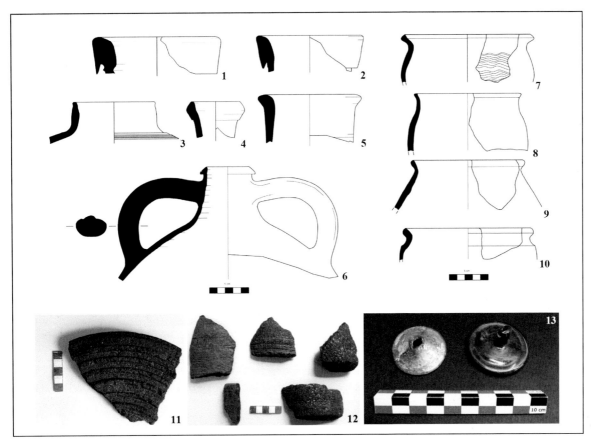

Figure 9.8. Pottery finds and glass vessels from the late sixth–seventh centuries AD. Contexts. 1–2. Tunisian Keay 61 type amphorae; 3. Eastern bag-shaped amphora; 4. Tunsian *spatheion* (type 3C); 5. Tunisian Keay 8A type amphora; 6. So-called 'amphora of Miseno'; 7–10. Cooking pottery; 11–12. Cooking soapstone vessels; 13. Isings 111 type glass chalices (photos and drawings by Stefano Genovesi, reproduced with permission).

archaeologically well known for Italian cities, where the density of buildings within the urban grid progressively decreased: this is one of the distinctive features of urban transformations between the sixth and seventh centuries AD (Brogiolo 2011, 108–23, 165–73, 179–80; Augenti 2016, 39–60), along with the almost definitive disappearance of the late Imperial residential models and the central role of the *insula episcopalis*.

The house of Porta Marina, built at the time of the founding of the Byzantine territories of Liguria such as the *Provincia Maritima Italorum*,[22] provides new evidence in Luna of private building; therefore, by comparing our data with the results of previous excavations, we can now document the coexistence in the city of different housing models, all of them dating back to the sixth–seventh centuries AD.

In fact, the 1970s excavations in the Forum brought to light two houses almost completely made of timber (Ward-Perkins 1979, 1981; Cagnana 1994, 170–72); the best preserved one consists of an outer portico and a single rectangular room (3 m × 10.7 m) covering a surface of 32.1 m². The entire structure was supported by square timber pillars, while two different beaten earth floors document distinct uses of the internal spaces: a small oven located in the eastern sector of the house provides evidence of the latter's productive use, while the western sector was probably a living area.

A very recent study of the excavations in the theatre of Luna, coordinated by the Soprintendenza Liguria (Gervasini and Mancuso 2020), documents the reutilization of the spaces within the *cunei* of the *cavea* as a housing area. Evidently, the theatre was a very suitable place for habitation, due to its huge walls, and was still standing in Late Antiquity. The rim of a *Samos Cistern Type* amphora,[23] found inside an underground silo in the fourth *cuneus*, testifies that the house was

---

22 On the Byzantine civil and military administration of this district, see Zanini 1998.

23 Genovesi and Marcheschi 2020, 123. The filling layer of the silos contained the rim of a *spatheion* 1, dating to the fifth century AD.

still occupied at the very least until the third quarter of the sixth century AD, when the production of these amphorae started.[24]

The house at Porta Marina, with its rectangular rooms utilizing both old and newly built walls, documents the presence in Luna of models well known in other Italian urban centres — mostly located in Romagna, such as Rimini (Brogiolo 2011, 168), Ravenna (Cirelli 2008, 204–05), and Classe (Augenti and others 2009, fig. 2; Augenti 2010, 48–50) — and in Liguria, in the Byzantine fortified site of S. Antonino di Perti (Cagnana 1994, 171; Cagnana 2001). Even if the above-mentioned houses no longer had anything in common with the Roman age *domus*, we are nonetheless allowed by the contemporary written sources to use this term for defining private buildings with stone-based walls,

several rectangular rooms, and an open courtyard with some kind of annex.[25]

We hope that further archaeological investigations in the Porta Marina area will permit the identification of, along with its overall plan, the social and economic importance of the house's owners and their role within the political context of Luna (Fig. 9.8).[26] Finally, regarding private housing, it will be possible, in this advanced stage of research, to attempt to correlate the archaeological data with the information from sixth- to seventh-century AD written sources.

[SG]

---

25 See for the *papyrus* Tjäder 38–41, dating to AD 616–619 (Tjäder 1954, 38–41, 126–38), and other documents of the seventh century (Tjäder 1954, 21, 352–59, 25, 376–80; Rabotti and others 1985, 31, no. 64). See also Gelichi 1994, 161–63; Augenti 2016, 168.

26 The material culture of the Porta Marina context is composed of glass vessels — namely the Isings 111 type chalices and lamps and African Red Slip sherds (Hayes 104C, 105C, 108, 109 types), as well as Tunisian (Keay 61A/D, Keay 61C, Keay 8A, type 3B and C *spatheia*), Eastern (*LRA* 1 and 5–6 types), and Italic (so-called *di Miseno*) amphorae and local cooking pottery and soapstone cooking vases — fully reflected in contemporary contexts of Rome (Paroli and Vendittelli 2004) and highlights the purchase capability of the house's owners throughout the late sixth–seventh centuries AD. See also Menchelli forthcoming.

---

24 Two African Red Slip Ware (production D) sherds, which are the rims of a Hayes 91D type fillet vase (Bonifay 2004, 179, 181, fig. 95; AD 600–700) and of a Hayes 99D type bowl (Bonifay 2004, 181, fig. 96, 10; AD 650–700), were found in the orchestra area. On this amphora, see Arthur 1998; Saguì 2001, 283–94.

Works Cited

Angeli Bertinelli, and Maria Gabriella. 1983. 'L'epigrafia e la colonia romana di Luna: Le strutture politiche e amministrative', *Quaderni Centro Studi Lunensi*, 8: 39–52

——. 1995. 'Il ricordo epigrafico dell'evergetismo a Luna', in *Splendida Civitas Nostra. Studi in onore di Antonio Frova*, ed. by Giuliana Cavalieri Manasse and Elisabetta Roffia (Rome: Quasar), pp. 45–60

Arthur, Paul. 1998. 'Eastern Mediterranean Amphorae between 500 and 700: A View from Italy', in *Ceramica in Italia: VI–VII Secolo, Atti Del Convegno in Onore Di J. W. Hayes*, ed. by Lucia Saguì Biblioteca di Archeologia Medievale, 7 (Florence: All'Insegna del Giglio), pp. 157–84

Augenti, Andrea. 2010. *Città e porti dall'antichità al medioevo* (Rome: Carocci Editore)

——. 2016. *Archeologia dell'Italia medievale*, Grandi Opere (Bari: Laterza)

Augenti, Andrea, Enrico Cirelli, and Davide Marino. 2009. 'Case e magazzini a Classe tra VII e VIII secolo: Nuovi dati dal quartiere portuale (scavi 2002–2005)', in *Atti del V Congresso Nazionale di Archeologia Medievale. Palazzo della Dogana, Salone del Tribunale (Foggia); Palazzo dei Celestini, Auditorium (Manfredonia); 30 Settembre-3 Ottobre 2009*, ed. by Giuliano Volpe and Pasquale Favia (Florence: All'Insegna del Giglio), pp. 138–44

Barker, Graeme. 1977. 'L'economia del Bestiame a Luni', in *Scavi di Luni II. Relazione delle campagne di scavo 1972–1973–1974*, ed. by Antonio Frova (Rome: L'Erma di Bretschneider), pp. 725–30

Benente, Fabrizio. 2017. 'Dark Age Liguria: Analisi di dati editi e problemi aperti per una riflessione sul popolamento della Liguria orientale tra Tarda Romanità e Alto Medioevo', *Archeologia Medievale*, 44: 293–17

Bonifay, Michel. 2004. *Études sur la céramique romaine tardive d'Afrique*, BAR International Series, 1301 (Oxford: British Archaeological Reports)

——. 2016. 'Éléments de typologie des céramiques de l'Afrique Romaine', in *La ceramica africana nella SiciliarRomana*, ed. by Daniele Malfitana and Michel Bonifay (Catania: IBAM), pp. 507–73

Brogiolo, Gian Pietro. 2011. *Le origini della città medievale*, PCA Studies, 1 (Mantova: Società Archeologica Padana)

———. 2016. 'Nuovi temi per la città tardoantica', in *Paesaggi urbani tardo-antichi. Casi a confronto*, ed. by Maria Concetta Parello and Maria Serena Rizzo (Bari: Edipuglia), pp. 17–21

Brown, Peter. 2012. *Through the Eye of the Needle. Wealth, the Fall of Rome and the Making of Christianity in the West, 350–55 AD* (Princeton: Princeton University Press)

Cadario, Matteo, and Giuseppina Legrottaglie. 2018. 'Imagines et ornamenta Lunae. La scultura romana a Luni, materiali e contesti', ed. by Silvia Lusuardi Siena and Giuseppina Legrottaglie, *Quaderni Centro Studi Lunensi*, 11: 63–73

Cagnana, Aurora. 1994. 'Considerazioni sulle strutture abitative liguri fra VI e XIII Secolo', in *Edilizia residenziale tra V e VIII secolo. IV Seminario sul Tardoantico e l'Altomedioevo in Italia centrosettentrionale (Monte Barro, 1993)*, ed. by Gian Pietro Brogiolo (Mantova: Società Archeologica Padana), pp. 169–77

———. 2001. 'Le "case di legno" di S. Antonino: Confronti e ipotesi di restituzione degli alzati', in *S. Antonino. Un insediamento fortificato nella Liguria bizantina*, ed. by Tiziano Mannoni and Giovanni Murialdo (Bordighera: Istituto Internazionale di Studi Liguri), pp. 197–202

Cavalieri Manasse, Giuliana, Graziella Massari, and Maria Pia Rossignani. 1982. *Piemonte, Valle d'Aosta, Liguria, Lombardia*, Guida Archeologica Laterza (Bari: Laterza)

Cirelli, Enrico. 2008. *Ravenna. Archeologia di una città* (Florence: All'Insegna del Giglio)

Dadà, Massimo. 2006. 'Archeologia dei monasteri in Lunigiana. Gli enti monastici della diocesi di Luna nel Medioevo', in *Atti del IV Congresso Nazionale di Archeologia Medievale. Scriptorium dell'Abbazia di San Galgano (Chiusdino – Siena) 26–30 Settembre 2006*, ed. by Riccardo Francovich and Marco Valenti (Florence: All'Insegna del Giglio), pp. 340–45

Durante, Anna Maria. 2001. *Città antica di Luna. Lavori in corso* (La Spezia: Luna Editore)

———. 2003. 'La città vescovile di Luna nell'alto Medioevo', in *Roma e la Liguria marittima. Secoli IV–X*, ed. by Mario Marcenaro (Bordighera: Istituto Nazionale di Studi Liguri), pp. 203–14

Durante, Anna Maria, and Lucia Gervasini. 2000. *Luni. Zona archeologica e Museo Nazionale* (Rome: Istituto Poligrafico e Zecca dello Stato)

Fabiani, Roberta. 2018. 'La concia delle pelli e le acque dell'Ilisso', *Hormos*, 10: 371–406

Flohr, Miko. 2013. *The World of the Fullo: Work, Economy, and Society in Roman Italy*, Oxford Studies on the Roman Economy (Oxford: Oxford University Press)

Gelichi, Sauro. 1994. 'L'edilizia residenziale in Romagna tra V e VIII secolo', in *Edilizia residenziale tra V e VIII secolo. IV Seminario sul Tardoantico e l'Altomedioevo in Italia centrosettentrionale (Monte Barro, 1993)*, ed. by Gian Pietro Brogiolo (Mantova: Società Archeologica Padana), pp. 157–67

Genovesi, Stefano, and Rocco Marcheschi. 2020. 'I contenitori da trasporto', in *Il Teatro romano di Luna: 70 anni di ricerche archeologiche*, ed. by Lucia Gervasini and Marcella Mancusi (Genova: Sagep Editori), pp. 202–24

Gervasini, Lucia. 2016. 'Luni e il marmo', in *Notae Lapicidinarum dalle cave di Carrara*, ed. by Emanuela Paribeni and Simonetta Segenni (Pisa: Pisa University Press), pp. 35–41

Gervasini, Lucia, and Marcella Mancusi. 2014. 'Da Splendida Civitas a Civitas Episcopalis', in *Ecce Lignum Crucis. Alle origini della fede*, ed. by Elena Scaravella and Barbara Sisti (La Spezia: Pisa University Press), pp. 61–63

———. 2016. 'Aggiornamenti Lunensi. Studi e ricerche', ed. by Silvia Lusuardi Siena and Giuseppina Legrottaglie, *Quaderni Centro Studi Lunensi*, 10: 69–100

——— (eds). 2020. *Il Teatro romano di Luna: 70 anni di ricerche archeologiche* (Genova: Sagep editori)

Johnson, Paul. 2016. 'Identifying and Understanding Waste Deposits in the Archaeological Record: The Example of Late Antique Rome', in *Paesaggi Urbani Tardo-Antichi. Casi a Confronto*, ed. by Maria Concetta Parello and Maria Serena Rizzo (Bari: Edipuglia), pp. 131–37

Lusuardi Siena, Silvia. 2003. 'Gli scavi della Cattedrale di Luni nel quadro della topografia cittadina tra Tarda Antichità e Medioevo', in *Roma e la Liguria marittima. Secoli IV–X*, ed. by Mario Marcenaro (Bordighera: Istituto Nazionale di Studi Liguri), pp. 195–202

Lusuardi Siena, Silvia, Marco Sannazaro, and Claudia Perassi. 2011. 'Aspetti di Luni bizantina', in *Ai confini dell'Impero. Insediamenti e fortificazioni bizantine nel Mediterraneo occidentale (VI–VIII Sec.)*, ed. by Carlo Varaldo (Bordighera: Istituto Nazionale di Studi Liguri), pp. 261–322

Marsili, Giulia. 2016. 'Il riuso razionale: cantieri di smontaggio e depositi di manufatti marmorei nella documentazione archeologica ed epigrafica di età tardoantica', in *Paesaggi urbani tardo-antichi. Casi a confronto*, ed. by Maria Concetta Parello and Maria Serena Rizzo (Bari: Edipuglia), pp. 149–56

Menchelli, Simonetta. Forthcoming. 'Western Regional Contexts and Their Interconnectivity in the Late Roman Mediterranean: Some Case Studies', in *LRCW6 – Late Roman Coarse Wares 6. Proceedings of the Conference Held in Agrigento, 2017*

Menchelli, Simonetta, Stefano Genovesi, Aurora Maccari, Rocco Marcheschi, Silvia Marini, and others. 2018. 'Luna. Casa e bottega: un nuovo quartiere presso Porta Marina', ed. by Silvia Lusuardi Siena and Giuseppina Legrottaglie, *Quaderni Centro Studi Lunensi*, 11: 37–61

Menchelli, Simonetta, Stefano Genovesi, and Rocco Marcheschi. 2021a. 'Luna tardoantica. Il quartiere presso Porta Marina: continuità e cambiamenti nel sistema insediativo', in *Abitare nel Mediterraneo tardoantico. Atti del III Convegno Internazionale del Centro Interuniversitario di Studi sull'Edilizia abitativa tardoantica nel Mediterraneo (CISEM) (Bologna, 28–31 ottobre 2019)*, ed. by Isabella Baldwin and Carla Sfameni (Bari: Edipuglia), pp. 263–72

Menchelli, Simonetta, Paolo Sangriso, Alberto Cafaro, Stefano Genovesi, Silvia Marini, and others. 2021b. '*Luna*: The Area of Porta Marina between the Republican and the Imperial Periods', in *Archaeological Landscapes of Roman Etruria*, ed. by Alessandro Sebastiani and Carolina Megale, MediTo – Archaeological and Historical Landscapes of Mediterranean Central Italy, 1 (Turnhout: Brepols), pp. 163–74

Menchelli, Simonetta, Paolo Sangriso, Alberto Cafaro, Silvia Marini, and Rocco Marcheschi. 2020. 'Luni. Gli scavi nel quartiere di Porta Marina', *Atti della Pontificia Accademia Romana di Archeologia*, 92: 369–415

Menchelli, Simonetta, Paolo Sangriso, and Stefano Genovesi. 2016. 'Luni: le campagne 2014–2015 nel settore sud-orientale della città', ed. by Silvia Lusuardi Siena and Giuseppina Legrottaglie, *Quaderni Centro Studi Lunensi*, 10: 101–24

Paroli, Lidia, and Laura Vendittelli (eds). 2004. *Roma: Dall'antichità al Medioevo. Contesti tardoantichi ed altomedievali* II (Milan: Electa)

Petrella, Giovanna. 2007. 'La produzione della calce: stato degli studi e proposta di scheda di informatizzazione dei dati di un forno da calce', *Archeologia Postmedievale*, 11: 151–72

Pieri, Dominique. 2005. *Le commerce du vin oriental à l'époque Bizantine (v^e-viie Siècles). Le témoignage des amphores en Gaule* (Beuyrouth: Institut français du Proche-Orient)

Rabotti, Giuseppe, Augusto Vasina, and Currado Curradi (eds). 1985. *Breviarium Ecclesiae Ravennatis Bavarian Codex: VIIth–Xth Centuries* (Rome: Istituto Storico Italiano per il Medioevo)

Reynaert, Julie. 2018. 'A City in Transition, Urban Changes in Late Antiquity and the Contribution of Archaeozoology' (unpublished master's thesis, University of Ghent)

Saguì, Lucia. 2001. 'La circolazione delle merci: il deposito della fine del VII secolo nell'esedra della Cripta Balbi', in *Roma dall'antichità al Medioevo. Archeologia e Storia nel Museo Nazionale Romano Cripta Balbi*, ed. by Maria Stella Arena, Paolo Delogu, Lidia Paroli, Marco Ricci, Lucia Saguì, and others (Milan: Electa), pp. 266–95

Theuws, Frans, and Mirjam Kars (eds). 2017. *The Saint-Servatius Complex in Musstricht. The Vrijthof Excavations (1969–1970). Roman Infrastructure – Merovingian Cemetery – Carolingian Cemetery – Early Town Development* (Bonn: Habelt)

Tjäder, Jan Olof. 1954. *Die Nichtliterarischen Lateinischen Papyri Italiens Aus Der Zeit 445–700*, Skrifter Utgivna Av Svenska Institutet i Rom, 40 (Lund: C. W. K. Gleerup)

Vinchesi, Maria Assunta. 2016. 'Il marmo lunense: le testimonianze letterarie', in *Notae Lapicidinarum dalle cave di Carrara*, ed. by Emanuela Paribeni and Simonetta Segenni (Pisa: Pisa University Press), pp. 23–31

Ward-Perkins, Bryan. 1977. 'Ricerche su Luni medievale. Lo Scavo nella zona nord del Foro (CS). Altri rinvenimenti. Sepolture e pozzi d'acqua', in *Scavi di Luni II. Relazione delle campagne di Scavo 1972–1973–1974*, ed. by Antonio Frova (Rome: L'Erma di Bretschneider), pp. 664–71

——. 1978. 'L'abbandono degli edifici pubblici a Luni', *Quaderni Centro Studi Lunensi*, 3: 33–46

——. 1979. 'Una casa bizantina a Luni. Notizia preliminare', *Quaderni Centro Studi Lunensi*, 4–5: 33–36

——. 1981. 'Two Byzantine Houses at Luni', *Papers of the British School at Rome*, 49: 91–98

Zanini, Enrico. 1998. *Le Italie bizantine. Territorio, insediamenti ed economia nella provincia bizantina d'Italia (VI–VIII Secolo)* (Bari: Edipuglia)

FABIO SAGGIORO

10. When the Countryside Changes

*Landscape between Places of Power and the Environment
in Central and Northern Italy*

Introduction

In this contribution we will try to consider the case studies discussed in this volume within a geographical horizon that affects Central-Northern Italy, emphasizing in particular some aspects of places of power and thinking in relation to the environment and its transformations between Late Antiquity and the early Middle Ages.

Population in the Historiographical Debate: Tuscia, Villages, and Castles

Tackling the issue of the population of the countryside in the Tuscia area means dealing with — at least in a broad point of view — two great historiographic models that have marked the historical-archaeological debate in the second half of the twentieth century and, until now, have remained a point of reference for some of the categories that we use and that we are led to adopt in the scientific debate. We refer to the 'model' of Pierre Toubert (Toubert 1973) and that of Riccardo Francovich (Francovich and Hodges 2003). These are two models that were opposed to each other for a long time, perhaps unjustly (Augenti and Galetti 2019), with both essentially deriving from a different documentary basis: the first developed based on the written sources of the great abbey archives of Farfa; the second based on archaeological data, on extensive excavations, and on territorial studies that marked the development of Italian medieval archaeology (see also Bianchi 2015; Valenti 2018). Both models, as is normal, responded to different cultural solicitations of the time: the first, linked to the debate on the so-called 'feudal' powers, opened up, among many aspects, a look at the complexity of the phenomena of the population of the countryside, while the second experimented not only with new methods but also with a long-term vision of the dynamics of the landscape and the population. Recently, research on these issues has returned to reflect on the solidity of these schemes, updating their contents and perspectives. Francovich, as Giovanna Bianchi (2015) recalls, began to develop the Tuscan model mainly from the results coming from the excavation in the castle of Scarlino and subsequently from those in the castle of Montarrenti (Cantini 2003), further enriching the body of his research with other cases, including Poggibonsi and Miranduolo (Valenti 2018). In the last twenty years, the research carried out in the Tuscan area on these issues has allowed for a wider articulation of the phenomena, contributing to an underlining of, among other aspects (a) the characteristics of the nucleation of the hypothesized Curtense structures (b) the role of the elite, starting from the Carolingian age, in the management of economic processes and transformations in the forms of material culture, and (c) the organization and relationship between forms of power and the resources of the region.

The centralized settlement, built from wood and preferably on a hilltop, would have been characteristic of early medieval Tuscany and then more generally of the peninsula, but this outcome was seen, also and above all, as a possible response to socio-economic needs of the rural world, which had already matured in the early phases of the early Middle Ages. The coincidence of place between *curtes*, villages, and then castles provided a perspective that was not so new on the historiographic level but was 'revolutionary' on the

---

Fabio Saggioro (fabio.saggioro@univr.it) Università di Verona

Archaeological Landscapes of Late Antique and Early Medieval Tuscia: Research and Field Papers, ed. by Riccardo Rao and Alessandro Sebastiani,
MEDITO 3 (Turnhout 2023), pp. 163–171
BREPOLS ❧ PUBLISHERS   DOI 10.1484/M.MEDITO-EB.5.134000

epistemological level (Valenti 2016); in fact, it provided a reading of the archival sources, namely of the terms and 'names' that were contained in them, which were less materially significant than had been previously assumed. The most recent studies, at least in the last decade, have continued to work along these lines, giving strength to an idea of complexity, already intuited by Toubert and then taken up by others, including Aldo Settia (1984), as well as gradually going into detail on the processes, especially the economic ones.

New Perspectives from Vetricella: Settlement, Economy, and Powers in the Early Middle Ages

The ERC nEU-Med project (Bianchi and Hodges 2018, 2020) offered the opportunity to increase the territorial investigation in the area of the Metalliferous Hills, in particular in the coastal areas of the Cornia and Pecora valleys. The multidisciplinary approach (archaeological, geoarchaeological, geochemical, palynological, and micropaleontological) adopted by the project proved to be fundamental for advancing new reconstructive hypotheses of the historical environment of this area; however, within this project, close to the Scarlino site, archaeological evidence has shown how the *curtis*-village-castle connection is not always so rigid (Marasco and Dallai, *infra*).

The investigations carried out within the nEU-Med project show how, between the eighth and eleventh centuries, it was possible to identify activities involving public bodies directly connected to the management of the royal tax authorities. The first traces of occupation of the Vetricella site can be dated to the seventh–eighth centuries when in some sectors, there was evidence of wooden structures. In this first significant and problematic phase of occupation, we can observe evidence of productive activities of a metallurgical nature. Around the middle of the ninth century, an impressive project was then carried out for the construction of a fortified centre of the plain, a sign of a public authority, and equipped with a defensive system consisting of three concentric ditches, which enclose a slightly raised central mound crowned by a tower structure.

In this context, the spaces of (metallurgical) production and forms of power converged in the ninth century (Bianchi and Collavini 2018); however, they did not constitute an aggregation for the population, as was the case in many other Tuscan contexts (Bianchi 2018; Valenti 2018). The distribution of seats of power, seats of population, and seats of the economy over several places contributes to enriching the picture provided by the model of Riccardo Francovich, who observed a more centralized scheme for the innermost areas. The

relationship between early medieval ruling classes and coastal areas, which was highlighted for the early medieval phase, first through Byzantine presence and then in the Lombard period (Bianchi and Collavini 2018; Tomei, *infra*), seems to maintain its centrality. It is a centrality that no longer seems to connect to a Tyrrhenian world *tout-court*, but starting from the ninth century, it would seem to look almost exclusively at the territories of the peninsula, heavily weakening the former connections: Corsica, for example, became more oriented towards the Latium area, with the advantage of a more internal territorial consolidation,. In the light of the archaeological data, this aspect revealed by the written documentation seems to represent not a change in the organization of the population but a change inside the settlements, at least if we refer to the case that has been better studied in recent years — Vetricella. It is in the Carolingian phase that the term *curtis* appears, representing a new form of territorial management linked to the elites in a differentiated form for the different regions, which would have been pushed by initiative and by imperial favour (Tomei, *infra*), especially in the Lucca area.

Empty Landscapes? Data from the Invisible between Man and the Environment

The Emptyscapes project is part of a new approach to the study of landscapes and represents one of the first experiences of this type in the Mediterranean area (also Campana 2017, 2018; Campana and Piro 2019). It deals with the study of non-settled territorial spaces through non-invasive systems (geophysics, remote sensing), then also integrated with stratigraphic excavation, in order to reconstruct not only the settlement network and the population of the countryside but also the environmental balances and the transformations of agricultural spaces and infrastructure. This project is placed in the context of the *ager Rusellanus*, the countryside around the ancient city of *Rusellae* in southern Tuscany (Citter 1996). It is a space that is subject to intense research. In this context, among the different results, it should be noted that during the fifth century, on the part of the area now crossed by the course of the Salica stream and until then occupied by a pond, whether permanent or marsh, some paleo-soils that were used in the early Middle Ages were formed, perhaps for agricultural purposes. Between the fifth and sixth centuries AD, a large part of the wetland was probably reclaimed, and subsequently, around the late ninth or early tenth century, the work was completed by creating a drainage channel and ditches. In this phase, with the definitive drying up of the southern part of the wetland, the northern space saw the birth of a large oval mound settlement, which occupied just under two hectares on a natural hill, was surrounded by two substantial ditches and existed from the tenth to the twelfth century (Campana, *infra*). These data are interesting because these factors could also have had a wider impact on the living conditions of the population. In fact, during the early Middle Ages, a larger coastal lagoon extended inland north-west of Grosseto. This lagoon would have provided vital conditions to support mosquito populations, which thrive in stagnant, brackish water. Although the site of *Rusellae* is located at the top of a hill, the altitude would not have been high enough to escape the mosquitoes, as excavations and analyses on the necropolis of the episcopal church have shown (*infra*). The results that emerged also suggest that this was a biologically heterogeneous site, with individuals who were not only local but also from other parts of the Mediterranean, a subject which merits further study.

We have attempted to develop the theme of 'empty' spaces in areas like northern Italy, such as in an effort aimed at systematizing the traces found by all available air flights, integrated with LiDAR footage and with a study, at least in part, of the historical cartography, to which we must add the systematization of the archaeological data already present for the Veronese plain (Saggioro 2010) (Fig. 10.1) and, though only in part, for that of Brescia (see Saggioro, Breda, and Bosco 2019) (Fig. 10.2). The data acquired in these systematic forms are impressive and show that on the archaeological level there is a very high potential for the information provided by new technologies, with over 15,000 traces of natural origin (palaeo-beds, swamp areas, etc.) and over 3000 of anthropogenic origin. By integrating these data, coming from different types of sources, it was, therefore possible to formulate, albeit with a certain degree of approximation, a location for the wooded and marshy areas mentioned in private documents or monastic bodies, allowing us to compare cartographies and therefore to define the spaces of the past with greater precision, fostering an approach that attempts to analyse the landscape in a more complete way, especially outside the settlement space.

The Villa and the River: A Dynamic and Changing Environment

Taking a step back from a chronological point of view, the case of the Villa dei Vetti offers us a further starting point for reflection on the dynamics between Late Antiquity and the early Middle Ages in these areas. The new acquisitions on the site allow us to consider the hypothesis that the structure could be a river villa with a port and therefore strictly connected to the use of the river (Cantini and Martinez, *infra*); however,

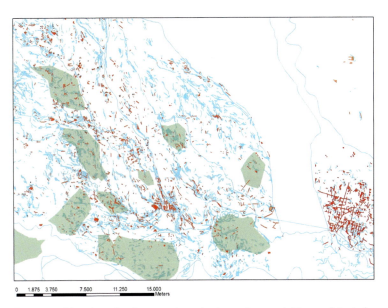

Figure 10.1. Mapping of anthropogenic and paleoenvironmental traces detected by aerial photography and LiDAR in the low Veronese plain (elaboration by the author, reproduced with permission).

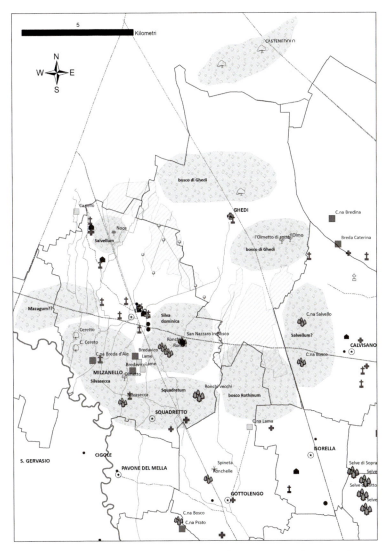

Figure 10.2. Reconstructive hypothesis of the paleoenvironmental topography in the lower Brescia plain (elaboration by the author, reproduced with permission).

during the sixth century we have various testimonies of floods of the Arno, and also in the Villa dei Vetti there are a series of layers of clay and sand dated to this period (Cantini 2017, 12–17) that seem to mark the end of the use of the site. In fact, up to the tenth century, there was only a sporadic use of the nearby hilltop settlement of Montereggi.

Obviously, we cannot reduce this change to climatic explanations alone, but it is certainly possible that, between the sixth and ninth centuries, following a series of environmental transformations, a flood cut a new channel in the sediment of the ancient meander, leading to an extensive redefinition of the area. Changes of this type are noted in the Po valley in the same period and are linked to complex and articulated processes, in which the 'catastrophic' episodes are part of a broader process of the redefinition of rural spaces (Saggioro 2022). For the area of the Great Veronese valleys, it was possible to observe how these changes were the result of progressive changes in the hydrographic basins that had already started in the Roman age. In Late Antiquity and in the early Middle Ages, the complex infrastructural system, which had guaranteed a balance between production spaces, settlements, and the natural environment in some areas of the Po valley, underwent a rapid transformation, probably due to the lack of maintenance. These dynamics, however, are also reflected in mountainous contexts; for example, near Lake Lavarone in Trentino (Filippi and others 2007; on Lake Ledro, see Joannin and others 2014), the level of the lake appears lower in these periods than it was in the past. After having witnessed the arrival of chestnut in the Imperial Roman age, a return of the beech forest can be observed, perhaps as early as Late Antiquity. In the early Middle Ages, deforestation seems to have been common, which according to scholars would have even produced modest landslides (with consequent changes in the environment) and progressive anthropization of the area, a phenomenon that has also been observed in recent studies conducted on Lake Ledro and that would seem to highlight how, after a long phase of substantial stability, the balance between man and the environment was being redefined; for example, in 2011, during the interventions for the recovery and restructuring of the former Manifattura Tabacchi complex (Modena), a buried forest covered by a silt-sandy alluvial layer came to light (Bosi and others 2015; Saggioro 2022). It appeared on the surface to be rich in plant elements such as logs, root systems, and tree roots. Based on the archaeological stratigraphy, the forest seems to have built up over a period of about a century (fifth–sixth centuries AD). Twenty-seven wood samples from the trunks were studied, most of them poplar, alder, oak, and elm. In this case the fifth–sixth centuries also seem to mark an important phase, including on the environmental aspect.

The Turning Point of the Sixth Century: Which Landscapes?

At this point it is interesting to look more carefully at the sixth century and at the data provided here by studies on the coastal landscape (Chirico and Sebastiani *infra*). At the beginning of the sixth century AD, the decline in population would by now have become evident, bringing to completion those first signs of imbalance and disintegration that had manifested themselves in the second half of the fifth century AD. This was a general trend, which by now would have been consolidated. An element of novelty, in this very complex phase, is represented by small fortifications on high ground, which became new military and civil reference points of the region, a phenomenon that seems to have been common. Public powers and rights converged on these Tuscian sites often because they had ports or landings (Castiglione della Pescaia-Serrata Martini) or because they occupied strategic positions along important roads, as in the case of *Rusellae*. These are centres and assets that flowed into Byzantine hands during and after the Gothic War. The countryside continued to be inhabited, but settlement patterns began to gradually change. Numerous small cemeteries have been observed consisting of no more than ten tombs and placed inside Roman ruins, a phenomenon that was widespread in many areas of the peninsula and that has proven very difficult to interpret. If we combine these data with the lines on environmental changes that have already been described, it is more evident that the sixth century represented a phase where the landscape was being redefined (Squatriti 2010).

It is certain, however, that as in the case of the Scoglietto hut, which partly exploits the structures of the abandoned temple, a scattered settlement continued to be observed at this stage, consisting of small production units scattered throughout the region and still in connection with the structure of the previous settlement of the Roman-late antique period. Perhaps it is not a chronological problem, that of scattered (Roman) or centralized (medieval) settlements, but instead a question linked to which system can best reflect an effective balance between man and the environment. It is in this search for balance between economies, powers, and society that religious buildings also begin to assume an important role of reference.

Landscapes of Power between Population and Environment: New Directions between the Ninth and Tenth Centuries

The cases presented in this volume underline the extent to which environmental aspects are becoming central themes for research in the coming years (McCormick and others 2012). If, in fact, the places of resources, those of power, and those of population can be broken down according to different degrees of centralization, an understanding of the environmental aspects, which are necessary in order to state and to contextualize the weight of the transformations, becomes more and more relevant. The environment certainly means resources, but it also means spaces for the individual and the community to work (as in the example of Nogara: Saggioro 2011b, 2020); the degree of detail that our knowledge offers no longer seems to satisfy the level of scientific questions that are produced.

Vetricella, the area of Roselle, and the Villa dei Vetti show in fact how the understanding of the balance of the landscape is a determining factor, but the processes that determine transformations and changes are not yet sufficiently clear. It must also be borne in mind that the changes likewise take on local and sub-regional characteristics, linked to the specificities of the regions. In these examples, in fact, the forms of power referable to the settlements document a close relationship between man and the environment and suggest a management that is not occasional, passive, and of mere exploitation but rather is a planned and structured action for the subsistence of the settlements and for the economy. These are studies, the ones on Tuscia, that find comfort in a broader horizon, even in northern Italy (Saggioro 2022).

Indeed, one of the most complex aspects that research has attempted to address in recent years has certainly been defining the space that the structures of the ancient environment occupied in the past: being able to frame the spaces of the forest and of the swamp but also of the pasture or of cultivated areas, trying to articulate the picture that the vision of the simple settlement can offer. Think of the forest and its transformation over time: its characteristics in its relationship with man have been well analysed in numerous studies, yet the forest has its own physicality in the space that is important and delimited. Those who experience it are able to recognize its boundaries, which are fundamental because they sometimes divide spaces between different economies and systems, between private properties and/or communities. It is a defined place, a regulated space that can be reached, crossed over, and used. The proximity and accessibility to the space of nature are elements of great importance which man recognizes. If in many cases we know that boundary signs had to be placed on natural elements, such as tree trunks (or be themselves represented by natural elements, such as plants or ditches), then in some cases we know that they could have been made instead into particular shapes. During some research it was possible to identify and to observe two elements of boundary stones found a short distance from the village of Nogara (VR) and referring to a nearby forest owned by the abbey of San Zeno di Verona (Saggioro 2010), managed in turn through the monastery of San Pietro in Valle, which was its dependent on the plain. For this oak forest near the village of Nogara (VR), for example, a multiplicity of data has shown a well-structured system of exploitation as early as the ninth century (Saggioro 2011a and 2011b). There are written attestations that reflect a sort of forest breeding/cultivation and management of forest areas that is not occasional and sporadic. The relationship with these environmental resources also helps to determine the identity of the Nogara community, which is a community that manifested itself among the various aspects and also in relation to these resources when, for example, in the first decades of the tenth century, they collectively asked the abbot of Nonantola, who boasted rights over the castle, for their use.

The village-castle of Nogara, like that of Sant'Agata Bolognese, studied by Sauro Gelichi, Mauro Librenti and Marco Marchesini (Gelichi, Librenti, and Marchesini 2014; Marvelli and others 2014) proved a phase of rapid development between the ninth and tenth centuries. Like Nogara (Castiglioni and Rottoli 2011; Marchesini and Marvelli 2011), the early medieval village of Sant'Agata must have been surrounded by oak-hornbeam but above all by large meadows and grazing areas. Analyses have documented that the village was located in an area consisting of mesophilic oak-hornbeam woods (with a prevalence of English, downy, and Turkey oak accompanied by maples, hornbeams, ash, elms, and hazel and, in the suborder, by hygrophilous woods with alders, willows, and poplars) interspersed with large, cultivated areas, meadows, and pastures. Even in cases such as that of the Bagni di Romagna settlement (Saggioro and others 2022a), archaeobotanical investigations have brought to light an area characterized by the presence of extensive grazing areas, with a substantial anthropogenic pressure already in the phases preceding the settlement. In particular, the tree cover in the first phase of population of the area was mainly characterized by the presence of mesophilic plain oak woods with maples, hornbeams, oaks, lime trees, elms, and hazelnuts and, in the lower order, by hygrophilous woods with alders and willows; in the second phase of population (seventh century) there was a reduction in the wooded area. The subsequent phases of settlement saw a shrinking of the forest cover,

Figure 10.3. Image of the early medieval phases of the alpine town of Piuro during the excavation phases 2021 (photo by the author, reproduced with permission).

Figure 10.4. Early medieval building under excavation in Piuro, during the 2019 research campaign (photo by the author, reproduced with permission).

which was increasingly reduced as early as the middle centuries of the Middle Ages.

In recent years, similar data have been highlighted in the case of the monastery of San Benedetto di Leno (BS), where paleoenvironmental analyses have shown a close relationship between site transformations, changes in the economy, and changes in the surrounding environment (Bosco 2019; Saggioro, Breda, and Bosco 2019) (Fig. 10.2). In fact, a work applicable on a microscale has also been replicated in the Brescia plain, where the wooded sectors have been positioned, to better understand the relationship between the monastery's activities and property. Beyond the distinction by species, the palynological analysis has allowed us to appreciate how, up to at least the eleventh century, the presence of the woods around Leno experienced a general growth, a phase of real expansion, perhaps also as a consequence of a series of initiatives planned by the monastery itself. If the first turnaround took place at the end of the century, to the advantage of herbaceous species, it is nevertheless true that the estimated forest cover did not disappear but remained rather high until what could be a true ecological fracture, which occurred not before the fourteenth/fifteenth century, with a decrease in the percentage value of the oak forest group plus woody hygrophytes from an average of 17.5

per cent to 3.84 per cent. Furthermore, starting from the end of the year 1000, the new open areas, more than being cultivated with cereals, the percentages of which were low on average, were covered with grass and used for the breeding of animals, a sector that was in constant expansion. Right from the middle of the eleventh century and then more and more in the following century, the monastery of San Benedetto began to associate its possessions in the lower irrigated plain with others located in the pre-alpine area of Garda and in the upper Franciacorta. Breeding appeared to be an increasingly important phenomenon in the monastery's economy, and in the same regard, archaeobotanical data have indicated that further spaces that were useful for breeding were probably obtained in the surrounding area as well. This leads us to think that forms of economic specialization, more or less marked and which were inevitably supported by a circulation of products at least on a regional scale, had to be present at least since the ninth and tenth centuries, structuring some intuitions and ideas that emerged decades ago in the study of written sources.

Furthermore, for the Alpine area, where at the moment very few sites have been investigated, considering the case of the site of Piuro (Sondrio), data emerges in certain similar aspects (Breda and Saggioro 2018; Saggioro and others 2022b, Saggioro 2022). Piuro was a village that developed during the early Middle Ages and that, with some ups and downs, remained active until September 1618 (Figs 10.3 and 10.4), when a huge landslide overwhelmed it, completely covering it and sealing its fate. It was a village linked to a specialized production, that of soapstone, a material that was widespread in the Po valley in the early Middle Ages. This village provides a settlement model where the spaces of power seem less evident and that seems to show a complex and rational management system, with soapstone quarrying areas along the slopes, small 'mid-slope' settlements with agricultural areas, temporary settlements at high altitude for grazing, a valley floor with major settlements, other small nuclei, and agricultural and open areas. The forest, while present, is therefore not a separate space but a space that is integrated into the life of the communities and probably subject to evolutions and changes. This aspect would therefore reflect, at least in some contexts, the situation of the plains. A known case is that of the buried forest of Concordia sulla Secchia (Marchesini and others 2003; Saggioro and others 2022a), where at least three phases of transformation of the forest cover were observed: in the initial phase there was a lowland wood that can be dated to between the seventh and eighth centuries, with elm dominant and accompanied by oaks, near a stream and a settlement that is more or less close to the area. Following a catastrophic alluvial event, probably attributable to the Po river, during the eleventh century, the meso-hygrophilous forest was submerged and replaced by an open bush of willows with numerous stagnal areas, which gave way to a return of the oak grove, with wide open spaces, in the final years of the Middle Ages.

If the control of resources and spaces was therefore a central element for the early medieval aristocracies of these territories, even a reading of the landscapes of power cannot ignore a more articulated vision of the paleoenvironmental characteristics and their evolutions.

Works Cited

Augenti, Andrea, and Paola Galetti (eds). 2019. *L' incastellamento: storia e archeologia. A 40 anni da Les structures di Pierre Toubert* (Spoleto: CISAM)

Bianchi, Giovanna. 2015. 'Recenti ricerche nelle colline metallifere ed alcune riflessioni sul modello toscano', *Archeologia Medievale*, XLII: 9–26

——. 2018. 'Public Powers, Private Powers, and the Exploitation of Metals for Coinage: The Case of Medieval Tuscany', in *Italy and Early Medieval Europe. Papers for Chris Wickham*, ed. by Ross Balzaretti, Julia Barrow, and Patricia Skinner (Oxford: Oxford University Press), pp. 384–401

Bianchi, Giovanna, and Simone Maria Collavini. 2018. 'Public Estates and Economic Strategies in Early Medieval Tuscany: Toward a New Interpretation', in *Origins of a New Economic Union (7th-12th Centuries): Preliminary Results of the nEU-Med Project, October 2015-March 2017*, ed. by Giovanna Bianchi and Richard Hodges (Florence: All'Insegna del Giglio), pp. 147–62

Bianchi, Giovanna, and Richard Hodges (eds). 2018. *Origins of a New Economic Union (7th-12th Centuries): Preliminary Results of the nEU-Med Project, October 2015-March 2017*, Biblioteca di Archeologia Medievale, 25 (Florence: All'Insegna del Giglio)

—— (eds). 2020. *The nEU-Med project: Vetricella, an Early Medieval Royal Property on Tuscany's Mediterranean*, Biblioteca di Archeologia Medievale, 28 (Florence: All'Insegna del Giglio)

Bosco, Maria. 2019. 'Le analisi archeobotaniche e palinologiche presso il sito di San Benedetto di Leno (BS)', in *Il monastero di San Benedetto di Leno. Archeologia di un paesaggio in età medievale*, ed. by Fabio Saggioro, Andrea Breda, and Maria Bosco, Storie di Paesaggi Medievali, 2 (Florence: All'Insegna del Giglio), pp. 259–300

Bosi, Giovanna, Anna Maria Mercuri, Marta Mazzanti, Assunta Florenzano, Maria Chiara Montecchi, Paola Torri, Donato Labate, and Rossella Rinaldi. 2015. 'The Evolution of Roman Urban Environments through the Archaeobotanical Remains in Modena and Northern Italy', *Journal of Archaeological Science*, 53: 19–31

Breda Andrea, and Fabio Saggioro. 2018. 'Progetto Piuro: primi dati sulle campagne di ricerca 2016–2017. Dalla frana del 1618 alla storia del paesaggio', in *VIII Congresso Nazionale di Archeologia Medievale* (Florence: All'Insegna del Giglio), pp. 26–30

Campana, Stefano. 2017. 'Emptyscapes: Filling an "Empty" Mediterranean Landscape at Rusellae, Italy', *Antiquity*, 91.359: 1223–40

——. 2018. *Mapping the Archaeological Continuum*, Springer Briefs in Archaeology (Cham: Springer International Publishing)

Campana, Stefano, and Salvatore Piro (eds). 2019. *Seeing the Unseen: Geophysics and Landscape Archaeology* (London: Routledge)

Cantini, Federico. 2003, *Il castello di Montarrenti. Lo scavo archeologico 1982–1987. Per la storia della formazione del villaggio medievale in Toscana (secc. VII–XV)* (Florence: All'Insegna del Giglio)

—— (ed.). 2017. 'La villa dei "Vetti" (Capraia e Limite, FI): archeologia di una grande residenza aristocratica nel Valdarno tardoantico', *Archeologia Medievale*, 44: 9–71

Castiglioni, Elisabetta, and Mauro Rottoli. 2011. 'Nogara. L'abitato di Mulino di Sotto. Coltivazione, alimentazione e ambiente nel Medioevo', in *Nogara. Archeologia e storia di un villaggio medievale*, ed. by Fabio Saggioro (Rome: Giorgio Bretschneider), pp. 123–57

Citter, Carlo (ed.). 1996. *Grosseto, Roselle e il Prile* (Mantova: Società Archeologica Padana)

Filippi, Maria Letizia, Oliver Heiri, Enrico Arpenti, Nicola Angeli, Mauro Bortolotti, André Lotter, and Klaas Van der Boorg. 2007, 'Evoluzione paleoambientale dal Tardoglaciale a oggi ricostruita attraverso lo studio dei sedimenti del Lago di Lavarone (Altopiano di Folgaria e Lavarone, Trentino)', *Studi Trentini di Scienze Naturali: Acta Geologica*, 82: 279–98

Francovich, Riccardo, and Richard Hodges. 2003. *Villa to Village: The Transformation of the Roman Countryside* (London: Duckworth)

Gelichi, Sauro, Mauro Librenti, and Marco Marchesini (eds). 2014. *Un villaggio nella pianura. Ricerche archeologiche in un insediamento medievale del territorio di Sant'Agata Bolognese* (Florence: All'Insegna del Giglio)

Joannin, Sebastien, Michel Magny, Odile Peyron, Boris Vannière, and Didier Galop. 2014. 'Climate and Land-use Change during the Late Holocene at Lake Ledro (Southern Alps, Italy)', *Holocene*, 24.5: 591–602

Marchesini, Marco, Silvia Marvelli, Antonella Mancini, and Luisa Forlani. 2003, 'Ricostruzione ambientale del paesaggio vegetale nella bassa pianura modenese-mantovana in età medievale', in *Terre di confine: il territorio di San Giovanni del Dosso e del destra Secchia nel Medioevo*, ed. by Maurizio Perboni (Mantova: Società Archeologica Padana), pp. 137–43

Marchesini, Marco, and Silvia Marvelli. 2011. 'Paesaggio vegetale e antropico circostante l'abitato altomedievale di Nogara (Verona): risultati delle indagini archeopalinologiche', in *Nogara. Archeologia e storia di un villaggio medievale*, ed. by Fabio Saggioro (Rome: Giorgio Bretschneider), pp. 159–92

——. 2012. 'Paesaggio vegetale e ambiente nelle campagne altomedievali della Pianura Padana', in *Paesaggi, Comunità, Villaggi medievali*, ed. by Paola Galetti (Spoleto: CISAM), pp. 463–75

Marvelli, Silvia, Marco Marchesini, Paola Torri, Carla Alberta Accorsi, and Anna Maria Mercuri. 2014. 'Il paesaggio vegetale ricostruito attraverso le analisi polliniche', in *Un villaggio nella pianura. Ricerche archeologiche in un insediamento medievale del territorio di Sant'Agata Bolognese*, ed. by Sauro Gelichi, Mauro Librenti, and Marco Marchesini (Florence: All'Insegna del Giglio), pp. 294–307

McCormick, Michael, Ulf Büntgen, Mark A. Cane, Edward R. Cook, Kyle Harper, Peter Huybers, Thomas Litt, Sturt W. Manning, Paul Andrew Mayewski, Alexander F. M. More, Kurt Nicolussi, and Willy Tegel. 2012. 'Climate Change during the Roman Empire: Reconstructing the Past from Scientific and Historical Evidence', *Journal of Interdisciplinary History*, 42: 251–73

Saggioro, Fabio. 2010. *Paesaggi di pianura. Trasformazioni del popolamento tra Età romana e Medioevo. Insediamento, società ed ambiente tra Mantova e Verona* (Florence: All'Insegna del Giglio)

—— (ed.). 2011a. *Nogara. Archeologia e storia di un villaggio medievale* (Rome: Giorgio Bretschneider)

——. 2011b. 'Nogara. Un villaggio della Pianura Padana tra IX e X secolo', in *Nogara. Archeologia e storia di un villaggio medievale*, ed. by Fabio Saggioro (Rome: Giorgio Bretschneider), pp. 327–42

——. 2020. 'Rural communities and landscapes in Northern Italy (IX–XII A.D.)', in *Social Inequality in Early Medieval Europe. Local Societies and Beyond*, ed. by Quiros Castillo Juan Antonio (Turnhout: Brepols), pp. 227–54

——. 2022. 'Archeologia del paesaggio e relazioni uomo-ambiente: risorse, natura e luoghi in Italia Settentrionale tra V e X secolo d.C.', *Antiquité Tardive*, 29 (2021): 43–56

Saggioro, Fabio, Andrea Breda, and Maria Bosco (eds). 2019. *Il monastero di San Benedetto di Leno. Archeologia di un paesaggio in età medievale*, Storie di Paesaggi Medievali, 2 (Florence: All'Insegna del Giglio)

Saggioro, Fabio, Marco Marchesini, and Silvia Marvelli. 2022a. 'Per un'archeologia del bosco nel medioevo: elementi, dinamiche e processi', in *Il bosco. Biodiversità, diritti e culture dal medioevo al nostro tempo*, ed. by Alessandra Dattero (Rome: Viella), pp. 35–54

Saggioro, Fabio, Nicola Mancassola, Zoni Federico, and Elisa Maccadanza. 2022b. 'Storia di un villaggio alpino: gli scavi presso il sito di Piuro (SO)', in *IX Congresso di Archeologia Medievale*, 2, ed. by Marco Milanese (Florence: All'Insegna del Giglio), pp. 133–38

Settia, Aldo. 1984. *Castelli e villaggi nell'Italia padana. Popolamento, potere e sicurezza fra IX e XII secolo* (Naples: Liguori)

Squatriti, Paolo. 2010. 'The Floods of 589 and Climate Change at the Beginning of the Middle Ages: An Italian Microhistory', *Speculum*, 85: 799–826

Toubert, Pierre. 1973. *Les structures du Latium médiéval: Le Latium méridional de la Sabine du IXe siècle à la fin du XIIe siècle*, 2 vols (Rome: École française de Rome)

Valenti, Marco. 2016. 'Fortified Settlements of the 8th to 10th Centuries. Italy and the Case of Tuscany', in *Fortified Settlements in Early Medieval Europe. Defended communities of the 8th–10th centuries*, ed. by Christie Neil and Herold Hajnalka (Oxford: Oxbow Books), pp. 289–301

——. 2018. 'Changing Rural Settlements in the Early Middle Ages in Central and Northern Italy Towards the Centralization of Rural Property', in *Italy and Early Medieval Europe. Papers for Chris Wickham*, ed. by Ross Balzaretti, Julia Barrow, and Patricia Skinner (Oxford: Oxford University Press), pp. 123–40

Figure 11.1. Cencelle: aerial view of settlement (photo by the author).

Figure 11.2. Cencelle: inscription of Pope Leo IV (photo by the author).

FRANCESCA ROMANA STASOLLA

11. Landscapes between the Sea and the Hills

An Early Medieval City in Roman Tuscia

The development of the Tyrrhenian area in northern Latium between the seashore and the mountainous area called 'Monti della Tolfa' falls within the range of interest of the papal interventions that, during the early Middle Ages, aimed at defining and consolidating the region around Rome through a series of actions, such as the establishment of *domuscultae* and the foundation of *civitates*. Some of those cities, as is well known, had an exclusively symbolic character without a real impact from the point of view of urban planning and not having a subsequent autonomous development. This is not the case, however, of *Leopolis*, the city founded by Pope Leo IV in the hinterland of the Roman port of *Centumcellae*, twelve miles from the seashore, as the *Liber Pontificalis* of the Roman Church states (LP, II, 131–32) (Fig. 11.1).

The source is very detailed, documenting how the citizens of *Centumcellae*, the northernmost point of the port system of Rome, asked the pope for help because of the attacks of the Saracen pirates, which menaced the port and devastated the city. As usual, in the medieval literary *topoi*, the pope had a dream, and upon awakening, he called his *magister militum*, Petrus, and ordered him to look for a suitable place for the foundation of a new urban centre. After much research, a suitable place was identified, with building materials and water available; a city was then built, not too big but equipped with churches and walls. At the end of the construction, on 14 August 854, the solemn consecration of the new centre was celebrated with a triple procession led by the pontiff, who sprinkled the walls with holy water and baptized from his name the new city as *Leopolis*; at the end of the ceremony, the pope performed the *rogationes*.

The story highlights a series of interesting elements, such as the use of the Imperial ceremonial or the reference to the Justinian canons in the necessary requirements for the new urban centre (Gentili, Somma, and Stasolla 2016–2017, 384–92), that find a full confirmation through archaeological documentation. Indeed, in 1994 the Department of Sciences of Antiquity of the University of Rome Sapienza started a research and excavation project in the archaeological site of *Leopolis* that continues without interruptions, supported by the 'Grandi Scavi' programme of the University (Stasolla 2012; Ermini Pani, Somma, and Stasolla 2014). The excavation has clarified how the area on which the city stands — a trachyte hill — was occupied by an Etruscan *oppidum*, which failed at the time of the Roman conquest (Gentili, Somma, and Stasolla 2016–2017, 369–79). Afterward a phase of Roman occupation followed, whose function, probably cultic, is not yet completely clear. In the late Roman period, a church with a funerary area was built in the location. The many funerary inscriptions, also with consular dating (Nastasi 2013), and the fragments of early medieval sculpture of the church's liturgical furniture (Stasolla 2018a, 2018b) testify to this. We do not know to what kind of settlement, certainly rural, this liturgical complex belonged to, but a cistern, reused in the following phases, must be referred to this phase (Stasolla and Doronzo 2018; Doronzo 2019).

Leo IV's project involved a complete reorganization of the spaces: the whole hill on which the city stands was cleared of buildings, and a new foundation was implanted. Therefore, this is a valuable opportunity to try to understand the inspiring criteria of the pontiff who was about to create a real *civitas*. The new urban centre was endowed with a wall with an irregular path, which followed the orography of the hill and enclosed an area of about three hectares. The city wall was built with red lithoid tufa from a nearby quarry reused for the occasion, cut into squared blocks, and placed in

Francesca **Romana Stasolla** (francescaromana.stasolla@uniroma1.it) Università La Sapienza di Roma

Archaeological Landscapes of Late Antique and Early Medieval Tuscia: Research and Field Papers, ed. by Riccardo Rao and Alessandro Sebastiani, MEDITO 3 (Turnhout 2023), pp. 172–183

BREPOLS ❧ PUBLISHERS

DOI 10.1484/M.MEDITO-EB.5.134001

regular rows. This was according to the tradition that distinguishes the papal workers of the eighth–ninth centuries working in Rome and Latium (Ermini Pani and Alvaro 2009; Stasolla, Di Nezza, and Doronzo 2011). It incorporated sections of the city walls of the Etruscan *oppidum*, also made with blocks of red tufa from the same quarry. Even if there is no archaeological certainty, it is presumable that the wall circuit was equipped with towers. The construction had two gates: the main one to the east and a second to the west (De Lellis 2015, 2019).

On the eastern gate the pontiff affixed a large inscription: a *tabula ansata* in white marble, profiled by a three-ply braid. The name of the founding pope recurs in the *ansae*, while the central text contains an invocation for the protection of the city (Ermini Pani and Guerrini 2014) (Fig. 11.2).

This artefact unequivocally links the site to the city mentioned by the *Liber Pontificalis*. The urban plan develops from a central road axis that, starting from the eastern gate, heads to the top of the hill, where there is a church 17 m wide, with three naves perfectly organized in the 2:1 module and presumably concluded by at least one east–west oriented apse. A rich marble apparatus donated by the pontiff survived for a long time; fortunately reused in the later building phases and therefore recovered. It constitutes a significant *corpus* of early medieval sculpture archaeologically documented. It is extremely rare in Italy (Stasolla 2018a). In front of the church, there was a bell tower, while outside, between the left perimeter wall of the church and the city walls, there was a cemetery, already foreseen at the time of the urban planning. Along the left perimeter, and in correspondence with the late antique cistern wall, there is a door, later buffered, which suggests the presence of a baptismal space, according to a scheme recurring in the church, always commissioned by Pope Leo IV, of the SS. Quattro Coronati in Rome (Barelli 2009; Gentili, Somma, and Stasolla 2016–2017, 389–90). This church is identified with one of the two mentioned by the *Liber Pontificalis*, which attributes to Leo IV the commissioning of two sacred buildings, respectively dedicated to St Peter and St Leo. The cathedral of *Centumcellae* was dedicated to St Peter, and the episcopal see was moved to the new centre. This was archaeologically confirmed by the discovery of a small pillar belonging to a seventh-century episcopal chair of Roman production, attributable to the chair that the bishop had to bring with him as a symbol of his office (Stasolla 2018b). A large hall completed the episcopal complex with a wide apse, only partially found and whose function is still uncertain. From the episcopal complex, a secondary road led to the city's western gate. From the main street, the road network was articulated in a radial pattern (Fig. 11.3).

On the opposite side of the episcopal complex, a trapezoidal building made of tufa blocks housed the seat of the civil power. Little is known about residential construction, and the discovery of a wooden building with a rubbish pit — then renovated with a mixed technique in wood and stone in the eleventh century — does not allow us to believe that all buildings were made of wood. The urban model chosen by Leo IV, which placed the episcopal complex as the hierarchical focal point of the topography of the city, has its origins in the Justinian foundations, starting with the sequence of plans for Iustiniana Prima. With the Gothic War, a great part of the Justinian legacy had reached Italy, where it was incorporated, becoming a model for the more conservative episcopal commission, the episcopal one, which would use this scheme for a long time in the recovery of the heights to plant the episcopal complexes in highly visible positions, such as in the case of the pre-Roman and Roman acropolis of southern Latium throughout the early Middle Ages. Thereby cities of secondary importance were defined *civitates* as episcopal sees, gaining at the same time great importance thanks to their location in the landscape as sacred centres, with great cathedrals standing at the top of the acropolis or the hills.

The *civitas* wanted by the pope certainly falls within the framework of the stabilization politics of papal power in the Latium, but it was not just a symbolic gesture. As in many other centres in Latium, the permanence of the name *civitas* depends on the presence of the bishop, who qualifies the site. Furthermore, archaeological data in the coastal city of *Centumcellae* show a drastic decline in the settlement after the eighth century (David, Stasolla, and Zaccagnini 2018). Another significant element comes from toponymy. The name of the city, *Leopolis*, disappeared very soon. Just eighty years after the foundation, the centre is mentioned in the written sources as castrum *Centumcellensis*, thus creating in this way a duplication between the two centres. As a result, some portulans speak explicitly of *civitates Centumcellis* (Nardi Combescure 2013), and only at the end of the eleventh century did the port centre acquire the name of *Civitas Vetula*, leaving the name *Centumcellae* to the Leonine city, later corrupted in the current *Cencelle*. This stabilization with the undoubted transfer of population is connected with the exploitation of a very active territory in Roman times and continued in Late Antiquity and the early Middle Ages. In this way, Cencelle became the cornerstone of an area devoid of urban presences but rich in rural settlements that archaeological research continues to highlight. This confirms the resilience of the *via Aurelia* sector, at least in the Latium (Citter, Nardi Combescure, and Stasolla 2018).

Cencelle's presence arises in the context of the debate on the importance of the city system in south-

11. LANDSCAPES BETWEEN THE SEA AND THE HILLS 175

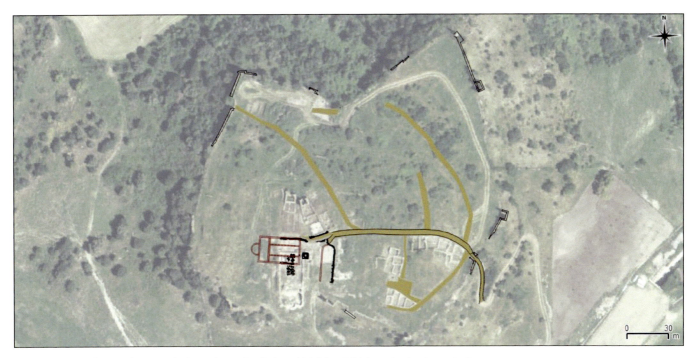

Figure 11.3. Cencelle: aerial view with the early medieval phase highlighted (elaboration by the author).

Figure 11.4. Cencelle: on the right, the Romanesque church; on the left, the political pole of the town (photo by the author).

ern Etruria and how this urban centre could have constituted an objective urban reality rather than only a self-representative model of papal power. Indeed, it was a centre of modest dimensions compared to the large port city. Still, the transfer of the episcopal see constituted a relevant element in the connotation of the urban reality as a legacy of the Roman centre of *Centumcellae*. The ambivalence in the sources, which mention the two *Centumcellae* alternately or simultaneously until the eleventh century, helps to define an equivalence, in the sensibility of contemporaries, between the two demic centres, the coastal one and the one on the hills. The fortune of Cencelle and its continuity of urban life mark its difference with respect to the other papal civitates, different in topographical quality, ideological meaning, and demic consistency. The foundation of Cencelle was not only an expression of the self-representative will of the Roman popes but also a real need for a territory otherwise poor in urban centres, marking its development and fortune. This happened regardless of its modest consistency, which constitutes the characterizing trait of Italian early medieval foundations. The consistency that makes it closer to a *castrum* than to a real *civitas*: in all probability, it is precisely the presence of the episcopal see that characterizes its urban connotation, as was the case in other Latium realities from the late antique period.

Archaeological research has highlighted several activities after the foundation of the city by Pope Leo IV, who died in the following year. Thanks to the inscriptions, we are aware of interventions at the time of his successor, Pope Benedict III, and of an anonymous bishop (Nastasi 2017). Written sources also document the loss of the episcopal dignity of the city following the reorganization of the dioceses of Latium (Stasolla 2019a). Archaeological data show a series of changes in the church of St Peter, the most important of which refers to the closing of the lateral door and the insertion of a small baptismal font at the beginning of the left aisle.

However, starting from the twelfth century, the city was renovated and redefined into a new urban plan, further consolidated during the thirteenth century. In 1108 the bishop of Tuscania, to whose jurisdiction the city belonged, made a donation to the prior of Cencelle for the construction of a church. This is the moment when the early medieval St Peter was demolished, and the construction of a new Romanesque basilica started, a building in tufa cut into quarry ashlars and with semi-columns carved into the blocks themselves. It had three naves with masonry columns, a single access, a raised presbytery, and three apses replicated in the crypt below, accessible by two staircases starting from the side aisles (Pistilli 2016). The floor was paved differently: the central nave and the presbytery were

paved in Cosmatesque *opus*, made by the same workers of the nearby Tarquinia (Stasolla and Brancazi 2019); the side aisles had the floor in grey stone slabs, with the exception of the first part of the right aisle. Here the baptismal font was located, and the space identified by a white marble floor made with reused slabs from the early medieval furniture of the demolished cathedral, often inverted. Therefore, its survival was guaranteed. This building represents an important intervention in the urban plan: the new church was built with a 90° rotation and a north–south orientation, with the facade towards the city centre and the apses towards the city walls (Fig. 11.4). In both cases, these interventions have a strong architectural value. From the twelfth century, written sources document the presence in Cencelle of magistracies that would lead the city to a municipal government endowed with political autonomy. The city was disputed for a long time between Rome and Corneto (the medieval Tarquinia).

The Romanesque church is only the first of a series of urban renewal interventions, including the reuse of the quarries close to the city. The sides of the hill were occupied in order to extract the trachyte, a hard stone to be reduced into small blocks. At the same time, the city was endowed with greater fortifications, making the sides of the hill taller and steeper. The new city walls were built in small blocks of trachyte, taking up the path of the early medieval circuit and incorporating the sections of the still-usable walls of Leo IV. The large epigraph of the founder pope was reassembled on the eastern gate, evidently considered to identify the city. The walls were equipped with seven towers, built at different times and irregular distances. They were arranged in such a way as to guarantee perfect visibility over the surrounding area to the sea (De Lellis 2019). A third gate opened to the south: the rotation of the church enhanced the south-western section of the city, with the same sacred building representing a relevant element of the city wall circuit. Actually, it was built so that its double apses — those of the church and those of the crypt — protrude from the city walls, creating an impressive effect for those who approached the city.

The rebuilding of the city walls also included a military redoubt along the southern side of the city, where a *posterula* probably was opened. It is a large rectangular room with two floors, equipped with three latrines, built in connection with the city walls, and with a stable and a room with a mezzanine floor, probably used for storage. The barn is equipped with a sewage drainage system, which flowed outside the city walls together with the drains of the latrines, where fertilizer was possibly located.

The city's central core included the public government complex in front of the church, which was set up in the area where the early medieval administrative

Figure 11.5. Cencelle, sector III, aerial view of the residential buildings (photo by the author).

buildings were located. Here a first tower with two-tone masonry and an ashlar base was flanked by a refined tufa tower-house, with a staircase leading to the first floor obtained inside the walls, and then the two-store public building, with a *proferulum*. The lower floor of the public building housed a large ceramic workshop divided into three rooms: the first for decanting the clay and turning, the second contained an oven, and the third was for ceramics' decoration and sale. This plant produced common and glazed ceramics, the first archaic majolica being on a scale certainly higher than the city's needs. It remained in use until 1349, when an earthquake that affected the whole of northern Latium destroyed the public building which was rendered unusable. The public building was then rebuilt (Somma and Stasolla 2016).

The archaeological investigations have also involved the residential and artisan districts of the city, as well as the large cemetery near the Romanesque church, allowing us to reconstruct the spectrum of the social life of Cencelle throughout the Middle Ages, at least until the fifteenth century. This was rendered possible by the rather abundant written sources. Particularly significant is a document dated the 29th of September 1220, which sanctions the submission of Cencelle to the municipality of Viterbo in the presence of the entire community, under the leadership of its mayor, *Henricus de Accettante*. The interest of this source lies in the restitution of a very rich social articulation of the small town, at least in comparison with other communities of the Tolfetan area, with the possibility of comparing the archaeological data. This attests the presence of two marquises, a *magister*, and a judge, who would otherwise be unknown to us on the basis of archaeological documentation. Also known from material data are some craftsmen who represented the productive class of the city. There were two blacksmiths, *Matheus*, son of *Alexii*, and *Guarnerius*; a tableware manufacturer, *Benencasa* defined as *scutellarius*; a shoemaker, *Henricus*; some millers, *Martinus, Guidectus, Guido*, and a *Benencasa Guidonis*; some tavern keepers, *Adamus Blasius Iohannis, Ranaldus Iohannis*, and one *Ioannis*, probably father of the other two (Stasolla 2012, 94–122). The archaeological data, in this case, have been surprisingly generous in reconstructing the places where these craftsmen carried out their work.

A residential area was found in the south-eastern part of the city as the result of well-defined urban planning (Fig. 11.5). Starting from tower houses in tufa, groups of terraced houses in trachyte develop, often built with common perimeter walls, all with access to the street front and generally on two floors.

This is a ubiquitous building model in the municipal city in times of demographic increase, and even in

Cencelle, the need to exploit the available space is demonstrated by the sub-excavation of the rock in order to expand the building space. This allowed most of the houses to have part of the ground floor carved in the rocky bank. Like the city walls, houses are all without foundations, but the walls rest directly on the rock, worked to form the starting core to which the first rows of the double curtain are welded. The houses generally have a first storey with a floor in rocky slabs, a fireplace on the ground, and a grain pit dug into the floor, and a second storey with internal and/or external access and a wooden floor. Some of them had stone basins inserted in the masonry upstairs, into which the rainwater from the gutter drains flowed, to guarantee, at least in some periods, a water reserve on the upper floors.

In this district traces of many artisanal activities have been found, which can be identified, by type and by chronology, with those mentioned in the document of the year 1220. In particular, at least two metal working areas have been found, with remains of the production plants and structures for working iron and metal alloys; the archaeological documentation is enriched by the finds of ingots, materials to be remelted, melting slag, and a number of artefacts, certainly the result of the work of blacksmiths. The location at the entrance to the city's main gate certainly favoured the activity of shoeing animals, which did not have to cross the inhabited centre. The discovery of horse and mule shoes constitutes a relevant material indicator. A bakery, a bread sale plant, and a milling plant have been identified, with the latter, however, constructed after the earthquake of 1349, when perhaps the mills outside the city were damaged. In a building, the concentration of litre mugs and game pieces led to the hypothesis of its function as a tavern: the taverns, in fact, did not have specific architectural features that were archaeologically detectable, and a few wooden furnishings were enough in rooms not different from a private house.

In a document dated 1220, a *campanarius* is also mentioned, a man involved in the construction or maintenance of the bells that, as we know from the municipal statutes, played a fundamental role in the social life of medieval cities. In Cencelle we have attestations from the document of the use of the civic bell to call men to the city assemblies. We also have the archaeological evidence of a bell furnace in the right aisle of the Romanesque church, linked to the construction of the basilica (Annoscia, Barone, and Gaudenzi Asinelli 2014).

Archaeological investigations also involved the cemetery near the Romanesque church, located along its left side: here, an intense depositional sequence between the twelfth and fifteenth centuries has led to the discovery of over 500 tombs. These depositions, combined with those of the early medieval cemetery and other ones found inside the church, bring the number of the buried subjects in Cencelle to over 800. It is a significant number of skeletons, all studied by anthropologists of the University of Rome 'Tor Vergata' who have collaborated on a permanent basis with our team and actively participated in the excavation. It is an urban cemetery occupied by inhabitants of a single centre in a rather limited chronological period and is an exceptional sample. The results of the data from the anthropological study, crossed with archaeological and topographical data, allow us to make a series of interesting reflections on different themes.

The first theme is related to the 'archaeology of war', which occupies a significant role in the real and symbolic horizon of the Middle Ages. Archaeological data show a city that is very attentive to defence, taking care to control the territory from afar, making it difficult to access its doors, and which constantly restoring its walls and towers. The wall circuit is equipped with slits for crossbows and throwing machines. In the city we have found swords, daggers, arrowheads, crossbows, knitted armour, etc., and the blacksmith workshops themselves forged a rich set of offensive and defensive weapons (Annoscia 2019; De Lellis 2019; Cocciantelli 2014). The written sources report continuous battles and skirmishes that complicated the life of the city, forcing it to make treaties of alliance, up to the submission to Viterbo, to guarantee protection by a larger municipality. However, the anthropological analysis carried out on many buried subjects has highlighted a very different reality. There are no cuts, with very rare exceptions, nor in any case, pathological scenarios to be traced back to war episodes. Furthermore, the average life-span in the community was medium-high, and the quality of life was particularly good. All the buried, in fact, show good health conditions, all had access to regular and sufficient food resources, all ate wheat and major cereals, and all consumed an adequate quantity of animal proteins. Cases of malnutrition and food stress were not found. The emerging picture excludes war scenarios, and the architectural landscape does not show traces of destruction attributable to a cause of this kind. We can also exclude that the protracted state of belligerence that seems to emerge from written sources affected the territory surrounding the city, from which Cencelle drew its direct supply, given that the population was able to access food resources without interruption (Baldoni and others 2019; Festa and others 2019). The massive presence of weapons can certainly be interpreted as the militarization of the society, a constant of medieval society, to the spread of tournaments and jousting — confirmed by the presence of dedicated weapons and a military garrison to which was entrusted the defence and care of public order. Probably, the war episodes reported by the sources took place outside the city by specialized troops and therefore had relatively little impact on the urban population and its resources. It was a a war delegated to specialists, not territorial, which can only be identified through an integrated reading of not exclusively historical-archaeological sources.

The entire system of water supply is the subject of a specific line of research: the city is served by a small river, the Rio Melledra, which runs at the base of its north-west slopes and flows into the more important Mignone river, which represents the waterway to the sea. Since the early Middle Ages, Cencelle has organized its water supply through cisterns, reused, and increased during the urban reorganization of the municipal age. In this phase, the whole inhabited area appears organized in units of houses gathered around small squares or open spaces with a well in the centre, the mouth of a cistern into which rainwater flows. The flow of wastewater is carefully regulated in the urban plan, as Cencelle is devoid of sewers, like most medieval towns. Firstly, an attempt was made to recover rainwater, considered drinkable, in the cisterns and trays positioned on the roof of the houses. There are also the areas of drainage of the eaves of the roofs between the houses, known as *transende* in the written sources, and the slopes of the streets are calculated so that rainwater and urban discharges are orderly conveyed towards drainage holes made in the city walls. Drainage was positioned in external areas where obvious smells and sewage could create the least possible nuisance (Stasolla and Doronzo 2018).

Another theme of the research are the funeral rituals. Following the disappearance of the funeral equipment after the seventh century, the archaeological traces of the ways in which the dead was accompanied on his afterlife journey gradually diminished. This denotes that the rite becomes less tangible. Archaeological excavations show how medieval cemeteries increasingly hosted indistinct, confused, overlapping burials, especially starting from the twelfth century. Although without concrete evidence, the presence of mass burials has led to the hypothesis that the urban centre was subjected to catastrophic events or epidemics, even before having precise analyses that could confirm these or otherwise. In Cencelle, the uninterrupted and undisturbed sequence of urban cemeteries from the ninth to the fifteenth century allows us to investigate the burial methods and their variations (Stasolla and others 2015), constituting an excellent case study also for evaluating the archaeological challenges posed by an urban cemetery from a methodological and interpretative point of view (Stasolla 2015). The study of the funeral liturgy of the Middle Ages, together with the civil norms, which are contained in the municipal statutes, has showed how the funeral had strict rules, normed both at the religious and civil levels as an expression of the whole community. The set of these rules and rites starting from the early Middle Ages accentuates the immaterial character of the ceremonies that accompany the dead so that their traces are increasingly difficult to read in the archaeological context. All the ceremonies and rituals that regulated the funeral ceremonies took place in the house of the deceased, along the streets of the city (funeral procession), and in the church, with the funeral celebration that concluded the rite. The burial became a mere technical act, more and more often devoid of rituals. Even the rites of memory became less tangible and were performed in the church, with masses and acts of mercy and expiation.

At the archaeological level, some interesting elements should be noted. The first is the symbolism of the sacred buildings, especially those equipped with a baptistery, which often provides a path with a high symbolic value that unites the two fundamental moments of the Christian's life, birth, and death. As in Cencelle, the baptismal font of the other churches is located near a side door, through which the catechumen enters at the moment of receiving the baptism. This access is in front of another door, the one that leads from the left aisle to the cemetery and which was used to lead the bodies to the burial after the funeral. The arrangement of the two entrances, facing each other, is not accidental and occurs in several churches with a high symbolic value, enclosing the whole life of a person who, at the moment of accessing baptism and therefore at the moment of his birth in Christ, sees and prefigures the place and the path of his rebirth to eternal life, the moment of his earthly death (Stasolla 2019b).

The possibility of investigating an entire city allows us to thoroughly analyse the sphere of its social life, an aspect that often escapes archaeological reconstruction and that for the Middle Ages is often delegated more to the reconstruction of written sources than to material ones. Cencelle constitutes a good prototype for a comparative study, and indeed a series of ideas have arisen precisely from the intersection of data gathered from different disciplines. Anthropological studies, for example, are showing a clear differentiation between the skeletal systems of men and women: men have a decidedly more developed musculoskeletal system of the lower limbs, while that of women suggests that their life was unlikely to have taken place outside the city walls (Baldoni 2019).

Such evidence suggests a society in which female labour had to take place in an urban and domestic environment — a wealthy society, which could afford to allow women not to come down from the hill of Cencelle every morning to go to work in the fields and return every evening. This coincides with the general state of nutrition of the women, who present themselves

Figure 11.6. Cencelle, artefacts for women's work (photo by the author).

Figure 11.7. Cencelle, majolica vessels produced locally (photo by the author).

as well-nourished when compared to men. It is not unlikely that women in the city joined men in crafts, as we know from the statutes of the various guilds, but they certainly had to devote themselves to textile and sewing works, whose archaeological documentation is quite abundant (Brancazi 2014) (Fig. 11.6). In this type of social context, studies conducted on children, whose burials are present in a widespread and homogeneous way in the cemeteries of Cencelle, have evidenced the spread of child work, their working age, and the intensity of their work. Not being dictated by stringent needs, it will be interesting to understand how much work is considered in the context of the child's/young adult's educational and start-up processes.

Another aspect is linked to the consumption and use of ceramics for understanding the familiar and social articulation system. In the pottery of daily use, a homogeneous picture emerges for Cencelle in the high Middle Ages, with a prevalence of the 'olla' as kitchen container, index of liquid or semi-liquid preparations, which we find in actual batches, indicating specialized and different use for different food. In kitchen pottery, there is no lack of differentiation in pans, especially in baking pans, which are all in formats suited to heating a single portion, suggesting modest-sized families, even mononuclear units (Stasolla 2018c; Previti 2020). In the decorated ceramics, a massive presence of archaic majolica is highlighted, not only because it is a ubiquitous class of ceramics in northern Latium but because it was directly produced in Cencelle. Its widespread use in the city has allowed for a wide deployment of the decorative heritage, which ranges from the usual motifs of this type of ceramic to elements very limited to northern Latium and even to the local area (Fig. 11.7). The research on decorative motifs, symbolism, choices of the clients, and possible inspiring motifs for the craftsmen is one of the aspects that most stimulates interdisciplinary connections. It is already clear how the observation of artistic realities even nearby — the floors in Cosmatesque work, the early medieval sculptures still visible, the decorative motifs of the goldsmiths, etc. — form part of the decorative heritage from which the ceramic artisans drew their figurative patterns. Furthermore, influences from the preserved pre-medieval substratum, which returned to light or came back into vogue and were reintroduced in stylistic features and minor motifs (Brancazi 2018, 2020), should not be excluded. On the other hand, the discourse involving the higher classes of the population is broader, expressing their status through decorated ceramics, including imported pottery, jewels, personal ornaments, and clothing accessories, such as the first silver or gold buttons (Nastasi 2014).

The network of contacts documented by ceramics and numismatic finds attests to the high circulation especially of Tuscan coins but also of singular artefacts, such as a thirteenth-century French seal, attributable to the period of the Angevin domination of Rome and therefore to the passage of people linked to the Anjou government in northern Latium (Annoscia 2014).

A not-secondary aspect of the research on the social life of the city regards the playful aspects, which in Cencelle appear firmly codified by the mention, in the document of 1220, of a *joculator*, likely an employee in the management of entertainment and public events in the city (Stasolla 2012, 139–40). In such a small town, this presence is not common. It documents the attention to an aspect of social life full of rituals, as it is an opportunity for self-representation, exposure, social rebalancing, and the recomposition of tensions. Even on a more ordinary and everyday level, there is no shortage of simpler artefacts. In fact, an abundant number of bone game dice, ceramic pawns mostly obtained from open forms in archaic majolica, have been found. The most extraordinary pieces, however, are two pawns, one certainly a chess piece, and another a table game element, perhaps another check, also in bone (Stasolla 2019c). There was an element of chess, a king, found in the area of the military garrison, as well as a more singular pawn, representing a moor of elegant and accurate workmanship, found in the area of the public building. These artefacts tell, together with the documentation of the rides and tournaments, of an articulated playful and social life, including upper classes. In fact, the document of 1220 mentions judges, notaries, magisters, and ecclesiastics for whom, as is known, the chess game was the only board game allowed (Fig. 11.8).

In 1349 the city was hit by a strong earthquake that shook northern Latium: structural damage is clearly visible and affected the church of St Peter, the public building with its ceramic workshop, which was closed, and a series of private buildings. Even a northern portion of the city walls collapsed, with the consequent landslide of a modest portion of the hill on which the city stands. The missing part of the walls was compensated with a lower wall, a parapet with holes for the drainage of water. The reconstruction of the public building and the urban renovations document a still-stable municipal power and a still-vital city.

The life of Cencelle, at least as an urban centre, was abruptly interrupted as a consequence of a distant events occurring in the West. The fall of Constantinople in 1453 by the Turks deeply changed the dynamics of trade between East and West, also breaking the commercial monopolies that some Italian cities had firmly established in the eastern areas of the Mediterranean. One of the goods that suddenly disappeared in the West was alum, which was also used to fix colours, not only in paintings and fabrics. Its lack caused great

Figure 11.8. Cencelle, game pieces (photo by the author).

damage to the burgeoning textile industries of Western Europe. A spasmodic search for alunite deposits, the mineral from which alum is obtained, soon started. The deposits present in northern Latium on the Monti della Tolfa, in the area where Cencelle stands, were enhanced by the Apostolic Chamber, the administrative office of the Roman Church. Starting from the first years of the second half of the fifteenth century, a big business of extraction, processing, and trading of alum started, which guaranteed new vitality to the port of Civitavecchia. A new centre, Allumiere, was created a few kilometres from Cencelle, expressly functional to all mining activities and housing the workers involved in the quarries and production processes. The whole area around the quarries was functionally converted into activities, and related economies developed. This marked the end of Cencelle as a city and its transformation into one of the farms serving the *lumiere*, as the alunite quarries were called. The archaeological traces of this transformation are evident above all in the area of the church of St Peter, which was transformed into the management centre of the farm and which survived as such at least until the seventeenth century (Dallai, Bianchi, and Stasolla 2020).

Works Cited

Annoscia, Giorgia Maria. 2014. 'Dalla Francia a Cencelle: storia di un sigillo', in *Forma e vita di una città medievale. Leopoli-Cencelle*, ed. by Letizia Ermini Pani, Maria Carla Somma, and Francesca Romana Stasolla (Spoleto: CISAM), pp. 130–32

——. 2019. 'Scenari bellici nel medioevo. Guerra e territorio tra XI e XVI secolo. Le ragioni di un incontro', in *Scenari bellici nela medioevo: guerra e territorio tra XI e XV secolo (Roma, 17 novembre 1016)*, ed. by Giorgia Maria Annoscia, Past, 3 (Rome: Quasar), pp. 7–27

Annoscia, Giorgia Maria, Nadia Barone, and Mainardo Gaudenzi Asinelli. 2014. 'Nuovi dati sulla fornace da campana di Leopoli-Cencelle', *Scienze dell'Antichità*, 20.1: 303–20

Baldoni, Marica. 2019. 'Beyond the Autopsy Table: The Potentials of a Forensic Anthropology Approach for Biological Profiling of Unknown Skeletal Individuals from Ancient. A Morphological, Metric and Isotopic Analysis of the Medieval Population of Leopoli-Cencelle' (PhD Thesis Scienze Medico Chirurgiche Applicate, University of Rome Tor Vergata)

Baldoni, Marica and others. 2019. 'The Medieval Population of Leopoli-Cencelle (Viterbo, Latium): Dietary Reconstruction through Stable Isotope Analysis from Bone Proteins', *Journal of Archaeological Science: Reports*, 24: 92–101

Barelli, Lia. 2009. 'Il complesso dei SS. Quattro Coronati a Roma: lettura del monumento attraverso l'analisi del palinsesto murario', in *Muri parlanti. Prospettive per l'analisi e la conservazione dell'edilizia storica (Pescara, 26–27 settembre 2008)*, ed. by Claudio Varagnoli (Florence: Alinea editrice), pp. 167–78

Brancazi, Beatrice. 2014. 'Tessuti per abiti', in *Forma vita di una città medievale. Leopoli-Cencelle*, ed. by Letizia Ermini Pani, Maria Carla Somma, and Francesca Romana Stasolla (Spoleto: CISAM), pp. 104–05

——. 2018. 'Dal tratto alla bottega: una produzione ceramica viterbese a Cencelle', *Temporis Signa*, XIII: 15–26

——. 2020. 'I motivi decorative delle ceramiche rivestite bassomedievali a partire dalla Maiolica Arcaica di Cencelle' (PhD Thesis, Archeologia e Antichità post-classiche, Sapienza University of Rome)

Citter Carlo, Sara Nardi Combescure, and Francesca Romana Stasolla (eds). 2018. *Entre la terre et al mer. La via Aurelia et la topographie du littoral du Latium et de la Toscane*, Past, 1 (Rome: Quasar)

Cocciantelli, Letizia. 2014. 'Le armi e l'equipaggiamento militare', in *Forma vita di una città medievale. Leopoli-Cencelle*, ed. by Letizia Ermini Pani, Maria Carla Somma, and Francesca Romana Stasolla (Spoleto: CISAM), p. 73

Dallai, Luisa, Giovanna Bianchi, and Francesca Romana Stasolla (eds). 2020. *I paesaggi dell'allume. Archeologia della produzione ed economia di rete – Alum landscapes. Archaeology of production and network economy*, Biblioteca di Archeologia Medievale, 29 (Florence: All'Insegna del Giglio)

David, Massimiliano, Francesca Romana Stasolla, and Rossella Zaccagnini. 2018. 'Nuove ricerche nel territorio di Civitavecchia. Un progetto per Aquae Tauri', *Scienze dell'Antichità*, 24.1: 149–74

De Lellis, Lorenzo. 2015. 'La cinta muraria di Leopoli-Cencelle. Alcune considerazioni preliminari', *Scienze dell'Antichità*, 21.1: 257–68

——. 2019. '*Urbs haec nulla hominum sed bella nocere valebunt*: le mura e gli apprestamenti difensivi di leopoli-Cencelle', in *Scenari bellici nela medioevo: guerra e territorio tra XI e XV secolo (Roma, 17 novembre 1016)*, ed. by Giorgia Maria Annoscia, Past, 3 (Rome: Quasar), pp. 67–78

Doronzo, Giulia. 2019. 'L'approvvigionamento idrico a Leopoli-Cencelle (Tarquinia, VT). Elaborazioni geomorfologiche e territoriali', *Archeologia e Calcolatori*, XXX: 503–06

Ermini Pani, Letizia, and Corrado Alvaro. 2009. 'L'opera muraria con paramento litico. Un'analisi archeologica', *Temporis Signa*, IV: 1–11

Ermini Pani, Letizia, and Paola Guerrini. 2014. 'L'epigrafe di Leone IV', in *Forma vita di una città medievale. Leopoli-Cencelle*, ed. by Letizia Ermini Pani, Maria Carla Somma, and Francesca Romana Stasolla (Spoleto: CISAM), p. 15

Ermini Pani, Letizia, Maria Carla Somma, and Francesca Romana Stasolla (eds). 2014. *Forma e vita di una città medievale. Leopoli-Cencelle* (Spoleto: CISAM)

Festa, Giulia and others. 2019. 'First Analysis of Ancient Burned Human Skeletal Remains probed by Neutron and Optical Vibrational Spectroscopy', *Sciences Advances*, 30, doi: 10.1126/sciadv.aaw1292

Gentili, Maria Donatella, Maria Carla Somma, and Francesca Romana Stasolla. 2016–2017. '*Ad locum optimum valdeque munitum*: nuovi dati sulla fondazione di Leopoli-Cencelle', *Rendiconti della Pontificia Accademia Romana di Archeologia*, LXXXIX: 367–406

LP *Le Liber Pontificalis*, ed. by Luis Duchesne (Paris: Ernest Thorin Éditeur, 1892)

Nardi Combescure, Sara. 2013. 'Da Centumcellae a Leopoli. Città e campagna nell'entroterra di Civitavecchia dal II al IX secolo d.C.', *Mélanges de l'École française de Rome*, 105.2: 481–533

Nastasi, Arianna. 2013. 'Iscrizioni romane, tardoantiche e altomedievali dallo scavo di Leopoli-Cencelle (VT)', *Scienze dell'Antichità*, 19: 327–45

——. 2014. 'Gioielli e accessori di abbigliamento', in *Forma vita di una città medievale. Leopoli-Cencelle*, ed. by Letizia Ermini Pani, Maria Carla Somma, and Francesca Romana Stasolla (Spoleto: CISAM), p. 109

——. 2017. 'Iscrizioni di committenza a Leopoli-Cencelle (VT) alla luce dei nuovi rinvenimenti epigrafici', *Scienze dell'Antichità*, 23.1: 245–54

Pistilli, Pio Francesco. 2016. 'Una fabbrica ecclesiastica riemersa nella Tuscia romana. La collegiata romanica di San Pietro a Cencelle', in *La fucina di Vulcano. Studi sull'arte per Sergio Rossi*, ed. by Stefano Valeri (Rome: Lithos), pp. 13–24

Previti, Giulia. 2020. 'Il testo da pane a Cencelle: morfologie a confronto per una storia dell'alimentazione', in *VI Ciclo di Studi Medievali (Firenze, 8–9 giugno 2020)* (Lesmo (MB): Edizioni EBS Print), pp. 116–21

Somma, Maria Carla, and Francesca Romana Stasolla. 2016. 'Città fondata e rifondata: Leopoli-Cencelle', in *"Fondare" tra antichità e medioevo (Bologna, 27–29 maggio 2015)*, ed. by Paola Galetti (Spoleto: Fondazione Cisam), pp. 27–43

Stasolla, Francesca Romana. 2012. *Leopoli-Cencelle. Il quartiere sud-orientale* (Spoleto: CISAM)

——. 2015. 'Archeologia dei cimiteri urbani: problemi di scavo, soluzioni interpretative', in *Atti del VII Congresso Nazionale di Archeologia Medievale (Lecce, 9–12 settembre 2015)*, ed. by Paul Arthur and Marco Leo Imperiale (Florence: All'Insegna del Giglio), pp. 201–06

——. 2018a. 'Arredi scultorei altomedievali dalla chiesa di S. Pietro a Leopoli-Cencelle', in *Studi in memoria di Fabiola Ardizzone. 4. Varie*, ed. by Rosa Maria Carra Bonacasa and Emma Vitale, Quaderni digitali di archeologia post classica, 13 (Palermo: Antipodes), pp. 275–88

——. 2018b. 'Prima di Leone IV: scultura altomedievale da Leopoli-Cencelle', in *«Di Bisanzio dirai ciò che è passato, ciò che passa e che sarà». Scritti in onore di Alessandra Guiglia*, ed. by Silvia Pedone and Andrea Paribeni (Rome: Bardi Edizioni), pp. 545–51

——. 2018c. 'Il quotidiano di una città medievale: archeologia dell'alimentazione a Leopoli-Cencelle', in *Le archeologie di Marilli. Miscellanea di studi in ricordo di Maria Maddalena Negro Ponzi Mancini*, ed. by Paolo De Vingo (Alessandria: Edizioni dell'Orso), pp. 511–22

——. 2019a. 'Rileggere le fonti, per la conoscenza archeologica di Cencelle', in *Studi in memoria di Giuseppe Roma*, ed. by Adele Coscarella, Ricerche, XVI (Cosenza: Università della Calabria editore), pp. 232–43

——. 2019b. 'Chiesa e sepolture: simbiosi e alterità in una città di fondazione tra IX e XV secolo', *Hortus Artium Medievalium*, 25: 555–62

——. 2019c. 'Archeologia dei gioco degli scacchi nel Medioevo occidentale: nuovi manufatti in Italia', *Vicino Oriente*, XV: 279–97

Stasolla, Francesca Romana, and Beatrice Brancazi. 2019. 'Pavimenti cosmateschi da Cencelle: la chiesa di S. Pietro', in *Atti del XXIV Colloquio AISCOM (Este, 14–17 marzo 2018)*, ed. by Michele Bueno, Chiara Cecalupo, Marco Emilio Erba, Daniela Massara, and Federica Rinaldi (Rome: Quasar), pp. 255–66

Stasolla Francesca Romana, Sergio Del Ferro, Marica Baldoni, and Cristina Martínez-Labarga. 2015. 'Aree funerarie a Leopoli-Cencelle: riflessioni sui primi dati', *Scienze dell'Antichità*, 21.1: 369–98

Stasolla, Francesca Romana, Maria Di Nezza, and Giulia Doronzo. 2011. 'Materiali, tecniche costruttive e fonti di approvvigionamento a Leopoli-Cencelle', in *Atti del II Convegno di studi in ricordo di Gabriella Maetzke (Viterbo, 26–27 aprile 2010)*, ed. by Elisabetta De Minicis and Carlo Pavolini, Daidalos, 12 (Viterbo: Disbec editore), pp. 299–340

Stasolla, Francesca Romana, and Giulia Doronzo. 2018. 'La gestione e lo smaltimento delle acque nella città di Leopoli-Cencelle tra tradizione romana e nuove pianficazioni nel Lazio dei papi', in *I sistemi di smaltimento delle acque nel mondo antico (Aquileia, 6–8 aprile 2017)*, ed. by Maurizio Buora and Stefano Magnani, *Antichità Altoadriatiche*, LXXXVII: 473–90

12. The Landscapes of Power in Mediterranean Tuscany (c. 750–850)

As a preamble, I will explain the meaning of the title and give general coordinates for orientation. The first words are a reference to concepts elaborated by sociology, political geography, and philosophy.[1] They had a successful application in archaeology with the contribution of Colin Renfrew (1984), *Societies in Space: The Landscape of Power*. Another famous title is the book by Sharon Zukin (1991), *Landscapes of Power: From Detroit to Disney World*.

By 'landscapes of power', we mean the characteristics of the anthropized environment that fulfill political functions in a performative sense; in other words, the ways in which physical space is organized and structured by the minority who give commands, concentrates wealth and prestige to use the definition of elite proposed by Vilfredo Pareto (Bougard, Bührer-Thierry, Le Jan 2013): 'An elite with the resources to extend its ideology through materialization promotes its objectives and legitimacy at the expense of competing groups who lack those resources' (DeMarrais, Castillo, and Earle 1996, 17). Landscape thus becomes an 'agent of social, economic, and political processes' (Groth and Wilson 2003, 74).

From a topological point of view — simplifying Gilles Deleuze's thought — before the advent of modernization, power would gather and develop in political, economic, social, and cultural centres. Furthermore, in Edward Shils's vision it would be possible to identify in the structure of society a central zone to which the symbols, values, and beliefs that govern it can be traced. It also partakes in the nature of the sacred — on this the reference is Mircea Eliade — and is made up of a set of activities, roles, and people within the network of institutions.[2]

Also taking prompts from these reflections, since the 1990s medievalists have gone in search of places and centres of power. A central core irresistibly attracted the elite in the early medieval West: the royal court. It would provide political cohesion and legitimacy, social eminence, and the primary economic resource, the land. The sense of the public is the main inheritance of Rome, preserved by the various fragments into which the Empire had been divided. Proximity, even spatial, was decisive to this central area: the *Königsnähe*. It was coloured by the lexicon of familiarity: to occupy a distinguished place in society, one had to enter the house of the *pater familias*, the King, placed by God at the head of the earthly community, and put oneself at his service. I refer, among others, to the ideal-types of Chris Wickham and the research of Stuart Airlie, Janet Nelson, Mayke de Jong, Jean-Pierre Devroey, and Régine Le Jan, devoted, in particular, to the Frankish world (Wickham 2005; Airlie 2012; Nelson 2007; de Jong 2009; Devroey 2006; Le Jan 1995).

More recently, these studies have been flanked by a return of interest in the material and economic basis of public power, especially in Italian historiography of the last decade. Subjects of investigation are the modes of functioning of states in the post-Roman West, whose rulers acted in economic terms as a *primus inter pares*. Among the elite of landowners, the King was the one who had the greatest supply of land, with a difference of scale depending on the regional context (Carocci and Collavini 2014; Bougard and Loré 2019).

In early medieval Europe, Tuscany stands out for the strength of its public framework, which remained active and vital until almost the end of the eleventh century. It was one of the last regions in which the inheritance of Rome was conserved before the feudal revolution (Wickham 2009). The public authority, whose highest local representative was the Duke, then Count-Marquis of Lucca, here managed to maintain a clear margin in

---

1 On this theoretical reflection see more recently Kühne 2018, 2019.
2 A critical reading, more nuanced and complex, in Remotti 2014.

Paolo Tomei (paolo.tomei1@unipi.it) Università di Pisa

Archaeological Landscapes of Late Antique and Early Medieval Tuscia: Research and Field Papers, ed. by Riccardo Rao and Alessandro Sebastiani, MEDITO 3 (Turnhout 2023), pp. 185–197

land terms with the elite, who continued to gravitate in its orbit (Tomei 2019a).

My reflections on landscapes in Mediterranean Tuscany between Late Antiquity and the early Middle Ages — the topic of this collection of essays — will therefore deal with landscapes of power. The structuring agents of these landscapes are the individuals and groups that occupied the public sphere: officials and aristocrats who were universally recognized as public *actores* and drew sustenance from the resources that moved in this central space by establishing a symbiotic interaction with the ruler. The issues that I am going to present are matured within a research project, called *FISCUS*, under the direction of Simone Collavini. Its aim is to reconstruct the entity, location, and handling forms of the material basis of public power in early and high medieval Tuscany.[3]

For reasons of space and adherence to the theme, I will concentrate on a limited territory, the Tuscan coastal strip and the northern Tyrrhenian islands, which lie opposite the Tuscan mainland, and on a particular conceptual and chronological knot, the century between *c.* 750 and 850, which saw the passage between Lombard and Carolingian domination, or more specifically, on the transformations that were accomplished during the government of Emperor Lothair I in Italy. In this interval, there had been changes in the landscapes of power, as well as in the structures of society and of the documentation.

The dynamics detectable with a narrow scope in Mediterranean Tuscany, as I will show, can be referred to historical processes of more general significance. I will put together different kinds of written sources, the very numerous private charters produced and preserved in the major centre of power in Tuscany, the city of Lucca, and capitularies, legislative provisions issued at court and transmitted separately throughout the Kingdom. By using them it is possible to form conclusions about the social body, on the dialectic between the elite and central government, and on political ideology and power practices. The elements taken from the written sources will be placed in dialogue with palaeography, onomastics, and archaeology.

The main system of power in early medieval Tuscany was represented by an integrated pair of *civitates*, Lucca and Pisa, whose combined influence extended over a large part of the region, with the exception of the southernmost part, in the Lombard age under the aegis of Chiusi.

Pisa was the terminal of one of the main port complexes of the Tyrrhenian coast, generated by the confluence into the sea of two large, navigable rivers, the Arno and the Serchio, which served as a link with the hinterland. Landings in the vicinity of the city were part of a network of cabotage routes that connected Tuscany with Rome, taking advantage of the coastal and lagoon landings at the mouth of the Fine and Cecina, Cornia and Pecora, and Bruna and Ombrone rivers (Pasquinucci 2004).

Lucca, on the other hand, had been in Late Antiquity the seat of the state *fabrica* of swords. It housed a Duke, the main political authority of the region, which was a coherent territorial and identity unit of the Lombard Kingdom, with a discrete margin of autonomy (Pazienza 2016). Tuscany could count on a peripheral geographical position with respect to the Po basin, wholly distinct from it, thanks to the Apennine chain that made the Tuscan territory a sort of entrance vestibule to Rome. There is an interesting parallel between Lucca and Pavia, the main capital of Lombard Italy, also formerly a public manufacture of weapons, specifically bows.[4]

To weld together Lucca and Pisa, there was a vast arch of uncultivated land, coastal lagoons and tombolos, and wooded expanses and rocky reliefs, which from the coast reached the Arno, stretching from the north-west to the south-east, approximately from Massa to Empoli (lakes of Porta and Massaciuccoli, Monti Pisani, lake of Sesto, forest of the Cerbaie, marsh of Fucecchio). By their nature, these were public places (Tomei 2019a, 23–24). The system formed by the two cities, located symmetrically on both sides of the fiscal uncultivated arch and characterized by different functions, enjoyed a continuing socio-economic centrality in Tuscany.

The landscape just outlined is the setting for a historical narrative that starts in the middle of the eighth century. These were the spaces of action of a group of people who have been defined by Collavini (2007a) as 'regional elite' because of their political and social range of action. Within this group the highest political authorities, both civil and ecclesiastical, were chosen: the Duke and the Bishop of Lucca. Some of the holders of these titles also held the honorary title of *vir magnificus*, which signified a close proximity to the royal court in Pavia (Gasparri 1980).

The group was composed of fluid kinships, not yet provided with a cognonymic designation and a definite lineage identity: the kinship of Pertuald and Gumpert, *viri magnifici*, to whom Bishop Peredeus (720–779, son of the former) belonged; the kinship of Bishop Talesperianus (714–730), linked to three brothers, *viri magnifici* and *gasindi* (i.e. personal followers) of the King

---

3   As its first outcomes see Collavini and Tomei 2017; Collavini 2019; Tomei 2019b. The project has since become part of the Research Project of National Interest (PRIN) *Fiscal Estate in Medieval Italy: Continuity and Change (9th – 12th Centuries)*.

4   *Notitia dignitatum* IX. 28–29.

based in Pavia, Ratpert, Teutpert, and Godepert; the kinship of Perprand, *vir magnificus*, son of Duke Walpert (714–736) and brother of Bishop Walprand (728–754); the kinship of the *viri magnifici* Alahis, probably gastald of Lucca, and Alamund, respectively father and son, to whom Duke Allo can be ascribed (761–785).[5]

A dense network of interpersonal ties connected this segment of society. They appeared in the salient moments of life, when the social prestige of an individual was rediscussed and reaffirmed: that is, when a person disposed of his/her immovables, movables, and self-movables — namely slaves — property, establishing the modalities of transmission to the heirs. At that time, acts were produced that filled the set of writings and that were themselves object of the testamentary dispositions as valuable goods, i.e., titles of ownership generating memory and rights.[6]

Hence, the documents concerning this interweaving of kinships serve as an ideal selection in the research. By selecting and analysing them, it is possible to reconstruct an effective and expressive insight into the landscapes of power in Tuscany. One can follow men, places, objects, and ideas that passed through the public sphere. In addition to the examination and study of charters, it is also worthwhile to consider the overviews of this social segment drawn by Chris Wickham (2005, 209–19), Maria Elena Cortese (2017, 35–66), and Stefano Gasparri (2012, 36–73).

The 'regional elite' was the highest level in a poorly differentiated aristocratic social fabric. Compared to the Frankish world, it was less rich in land terms. The value of five major estates can be taken as a ceiling. The land in central-northern Tuscany was much more distributed, scattered in a cluster of small and medium-sized ownerships; therefore, there is a marked discrepancy in power between those owning these areas and those with the authority to hold and manage public land.

Elite status was not derived from ancestry but from office holding. Determining factors for the accumulation of power and prestige were marked by the highest positions and the *Königsnähe*. In each kinship of the group, there is a direct link with the King, which can be traced back even before King Liutprand, who died in 744 and under whose rule there was a veritable documentary revolution with the start of the first substantial series of private charters kept in the ecclesiastical archives. Contacts went back to King Perctarit, who died in 688.

The heritage of this segment was formed, in fact, in the shadow of the King as shown in the *breve de moniminas*, a list of almost one hundred documents

in precious *mobilia* (in gold and silver, coined and non) that concerned the family of the gastald and *vir magnificus* Alahis and the church of San Pietro ai Sette Pini, founded by them in the suburbs of Pisa (Ghignoli 2004). The individuals and kinships closest to the court were able to collect a good number of royal donations. Given their relative smallness in size, it can be assumed that they were broadly widespread and distributed in the social fabric.

The Tuscan elite were generally city oriented. Political structures, institutions, and officials were concentrated in the same places. The Lucca-Pisa system constituted, as said, the regional core. The richest and most influential parental groups were active in this area and were able to accumulate assets in more than one of the surrounding dioceses.

From the first quarter of the eighth century, they promoted religious foundations, which the sources define in a synonymic way as *ecclesiae* and *monasteria*, inside or just outside the city walls: just to give a few examples, in Pisa, the already mentioned San Pietro ai Sette Pini (kinship of the gastald Alahis); in Lucca, San Michele in Cipriano (kinship of Bishop Peredeus), Santa Maria Ursimanni (kinship of Bishop Talesperianus), and San Salvatore Oliole (kinship of Duke Walpert). Churches expressed eminence and devotion, preserved the patrimony, often entrusted to the women of the family who led a religious life there, and attracted pious donations from those who lived nearby or wished to establish a relationship with the group — practices that were regulated by the laws of Liutprand issued after 712, in the first years of his reign (Lazzari 2017).

Like their founders, these institutions enjoyed *Königsnähe*, not least because some of their landholdings were originally fiscally derived; therefore, their subsequent rectors did not stray from the public sphere and sought royal protection to negotiate, defend, and display their economic and social status. A first model of reference for the Tuscan elite was San Frediano, an ancient suburban church that King Cunipert's *maior domus*, Faulo, refounded as a monastery in 685.[7]

Although the tendency of the leading segments of society to converge towards the city, where the seats of power were located, is clear, the exponents of the 'regional elite' were also protagonists in the countryside, where they made considerable investments and ruled important ecclesiastical institutions, above all San Pietro of Camaiore (kinship of the gastald Alahis) and San Pietro of Palazzuolo, not far from the Versilia and Maremma coasts respectively. The latter was founded

---

5 About these kinships see Stoffella 2007; Ghignoli 2004.
6 Themes deepened in Bougard, La Rocca, and Le Jan 2005.

7 *ChLA*, vol. xxx, n. 894; *CDL*, vol. iii, n. 7.

by the Pisan Walfred, with a relative of his, Gunduald from Lucca, and Fortis, Bishop in Corsica.[8]

The powerful ones owned valuable residences in the city (sometimes multi-storey), in suburbs, and in the countryside, yet these are substantially invisible from the archaeological point of view. In the charters they are called *salae* and are remembered as a characteristic element of aristocratic landownership, provided with courtyards including wells, orchards, gardens, and other adjoining buildings. They are also associated with markers of eminence: the presence of granaries and of *balnea*, a feature of continuity with the Roman past. During the eighth century, these complexes could be renovated to house a *monasterium* or a welfare institution (*xenodochium*).

The absence of archaeological evidence can be explained by the limits of the sample, very fragmentary, which is the result of punctual and random surveys, or by the legibility of the archaeological data. It is possible that their value and prestige were visibly expressed through decorative elements, movable and perishable, in the interiors and furnishings of dwellings or by making extensive use of wood construction. In general, material culture returns a context in which capital was spent for immediate ostentation, not invested in the long term. This refers to a hierarchically fluid and little crystallized society structure, where the need to display wealth remained constant and situational.

Indeed, the elite in Lucca are characterized in the written sources by the ownership of precious *mobilia* for personal adornment, in gold, silver, and silk, and to be displayed in war and parade, banquet and assembly. At death, these items, along with slaves, were often given away for the salvation of the soul and the manifestation of status.[9]

Other data from written sources build a profile both individual and collective. These are elements of self-representation and identity. Firstly, there is writing. Armando Petrucci has spoken for the Lombard age of *cancelleresca lucchese*: a type of documentary script produced by a local graphic activity that differs from the normal 'new cursive'. It was used both by writers who professionally drafted charters in Lucca and by the highest representatives of the urban society; for example, Bishop Talesperianus, Bishop Walprand, and Sunderad, nephew of Bishop Peredeus. Lucca maintained ties with the late antique documentary tradition. The 'cancelleresca lucchese' is influenced by the graphic

features of chancellery in the Roman-Byzantine area (Petrucci 1992).

Then comes onomastics (Francovich Onesti 2000; 2012; Haubrichs 2014). Charters primarily enable us to study the onomastic text of *possessores*, who sold, bought, rented, donated, and disputed over the land. The majority of anthroponyms in the eighth century are of Lombard origin. More frequent than elsewhere in the Kingdom are the mixed Latin-Lombard compounds, although they are rare in the highest segment of the *viri magnifici*. There is no shortage of names of Greek derivation such as Ololia, nephew of Duke Walpert, and Bellerifonsus, close to the royal court and to the offspring of the gastald Alahis — I will return to these two figures shortly. The overall image is of strong integration, exchange, and cultural assimilation, with traits of continuity and innovation.

Among the 'regional elite' there are both Latin and Germanic names (kinships of Walfred, Bishop Talesperianus, and Bishop Peredeus). The offspring, according to the ancient Germanic custom, present sequences of alliterative names, the formation of which takes place by variation of one of the two members into which an anthroponym can be broken down (kinships of Duke Walpert, gastald Alahis). There are, however, also new compounds, taken from the common lexicon, such as Talesperianus ('Such we hope'). This is an element that refers to the shapes of kinship: in making an onomastic choice, it was common to draw both from the paternal and maternal onomastic stock.

Now I return to the land, which is the absolute protagonist in charters. I have answered the questions of how much and in which forms, but it remains to say where the 'regional elite' had its land base. In this regard, there are significant matches between charters and land bases, especially in two areas. The 'regional elite' shared possessions in the stretch of coast marked by toponyms that applied to very large territories, on the border between the dioceses of Pisa, Volterra, and Populonia: Rosignano, Vada, Cecina, and *Asilacto* (today Marina di Bibbona).[10] Here they had *salae* with demesnes called *sundria*, lands in direct economy, or *cafagia*, originally game reserves, and salt pans. In the description of the internal structure of the latter, a very particular lexicon is used. It presents a Greek patina that remained in vogue until the fall of the public world in Tuscany at the end of the eleventh century: *alapas* for the basins (a sort of unit of measurement for the salt pans) and *catamarie* and *moralioli* for the tanks and channels of the upstream sea water circuit (Tomei 2020).

Salae, sundria, cafaggia, and salt pans in this area have a prominent place in the charters relating to hereditary

---

8 Schmid 1991. Palazzuolo (a speaking toponym, stands for 'little palace') had a twin institution for the women of the kinship: San Salvatore of Pitiliano, on the banks of the Versilia River.

9 On *mobilia* see Gelichi and La Rocca 2003.

10 On these territories see Ceccarelli Lemut 2006; 2009.

division in the kinships of Duke Walpert and of Bishop Peredeus, as well as in the act of foundation of San Pietro of Palazzuolo by Walfred: *brevia* of division and *pro anima* donations to churches and individuals may also have involved slaves and *mobilia*. They are also attested in similar documents by type but concerning people whose degree of eminence is a little lower. Although they can be counted in the circle of the richest in the Lucchese charters, their parental groups do not include *viri magnifici* (Wickham 2005, 211–12). See the case of the couple Teutprand and Gumpranda, who founded and endowed for themselves and their daughters the church of San Michele within the walls of Lucca (764), and the *vir devotus* Tassilo, son of Autchis (768).[11]

Another sign of continuity is that, in the charters relating to the 'regional elite' and concerning these territories, there is a rich landowner named Praetextatus. His sister Gausperga lived with her husband near Vada (768). His son Wectari was always active on the same stretch of coast (839).[12] For onomastics and space of action, the points of contact with Late Antiquity are remarkable. The reference is to Vettius Agorius Praetextatus, who had huge possessions in Etruria and was close to Publilius Ceionius Caecina Albinus, both among the members of the senatorial aristocracy portrayed by Macrobius in *Saturnalia* (Cantini 2017). In addition, the nephew of the latter, Caecina Decius Aginatius Albinus and his villa near the mouth of the river that from their *gens* had taken the name, namely Cecina, appear in *De reditu* as a stop on Rutilius's sea journey (Donati 2013).

How is it possible to explain this long-term aftermath? In the eighth century there was still a Praetextatus acting in this landscape;[13] however, the differences with respect to the homonym of the fourth century are many, whether or not he was a descendant of him — the fact is in any case irrelevant. Among the senatorial class that had grand estates here and the Lombard elite, the political and social range of action is not comparable. It had definitely contracted. Within the same areas there were new management centres of great landowning, no longer the villas, as archaeological research testifies (Pasquinucci and Menchelli 2006); moreover, the owners of the *salae* now acted in this area because of the *Königsnähe* and the convergence towards the redistribution circuit of public land. The vast senatorial estates must have been largely confiscated (Collavini 2020). Toponymy refers to a widespread possession of the fisc. Among the many possible examples, take Paratino, that is *Palatino*, where one of the most important ecclesiastical institutions of the territory, the baptismal church of San Pietro, stood on the Cecina bank near a crossing point of the river and the sea (Ceccarelli Lemut 2009).

The control of these strategic areas, a system of salt pans and landing points also rich in woodland in the coastal tombolos, guaranteed to the *publicum* the exploitation of non-agrarian resources, in particular salt, and the conservation of a Tyrrhenian projection, through the connection to cabotage routes. The elite participated in this system, accumulating possessions on the coast between Rosignano and *Asilacto* thanks to their adherence to the public sphere, in proportion to their degree of proximity to the court.

This brings me to the second area where the possessions of the 'regional elite' converge: Corsica. Furthermore, only and precisely the kinships of the *viri magnifici* have possessions on the island. This is linked with good probability to the conquest of Corsica. Regarding the chronology of the process, everything remains unknown (Renzi Rizzo 2006). In the middle of the eighth century, after the event, the possessions of Duke Walpert and those offered by Walfred to San Pietro of Palazzuolo are attested on the island.[14] This land pattern must be the cause or consequence of the relationship with the royal court of these parental groups, which must have played a decisive role in the passage of Corsica into Lombard hands, acting on behalf of Pavia. The major imperial abbey of Tuscany, San Salvatore of Sesto, located in the heart of the fiscal uncultivated arch, also had possessions in Corsica. The assets on the island are mentioned in the first diploma preserved for San Salvatore at the beginning of the eleventh century but probably attributable to a much earlier period.[15]

There is a connection between establishment in the system of salt pans and landings on the coast between Rosignano and *Asilacto* and that in Corsica. It was thanks to the *Königsnähe*, starting from the coastal power centres, that the members of the 'regional elite' played a leading role in the Tyrrhenian Sea. Their range of action corresponded to the network of bonds within the group of founders of the Palazzuolo monastery: Lucca and Pisa, the Versilia and Maremma coasts, and Corsica. Such an activity at sea was officially recognized with the task of defence and protection assigned to the Duke of Lucca Allo, of the kinship of

---

11 *ChLA*, vol. XXXIII, n. 981; vol. XXXIV, n. 1000.

12 *ChLA*, vol. XXXIII, n. 969; vol. XXXIV, n. 1003; vol. LXXVII, n. 31; vol. LXXXIV, n. 17.

13 Also, Wectari seems a Germanization of Vettius.

14 *ChLA*, vol. XXXII, n. 939; Molitor 1991. The only identifiable landholding is the one belonging to Palazzuolo, San Pietro of Accia.

15 *DHII.*, n. 425. Sesto owned three *curtes* (*Noce*, *Persicum*, and *Sambucum*) that cannot be located with certainty.

the gastald and *vir magnificus* Alahis, in the first years following the Frankish conquest of the Kingdom.[16] His base was located near *Asilacto*, in a locality still known in the late eleventh century as *sala Allonis ducis*.[17] The role of Allo is nothing new. According to Michael McCormick (2001, 264), Carolingians 'inherited at least a rudimentary maritime infrastructure linking Tuscany to the Lombard territory of Corsica'.

It was the 'regional elite', a social segment anchored to the public sphere, which contributed to the tightness of this tenuous connective tissue. Its demand supported and fed a cabotage route that engulfed the upper Tyrrhenian Sea into a wider maritime network, linking the Aegean to the western Mediterranean (Meo 2018, 220–22). On this point the theory of reference is the 'background noise' of Peregrine Horden and Nicholas Purcell (2000).

The relations with the Byzantine world, and more broadly with the Mediterranean, of the political space centred on Lucca and Pisa are evident on the linguistic front: just think of the lexicon of the salt pans and of the material culture, following for instance the trail of the globular amphorae (Petralia 2015). No less important are the elements provided by written sources. Again, with reference to Duke Allo and his activities on the sea, there are documented contacts of the 'regional elite' with the Byzantine merchants/pirates who sailed along the Tuscan coast, also in search of slaves.[18] I can add three other profiles that positively reflect the Mediterranean aspect of Lombard Tuscany. All of them have an operating presence in the landscapes of power in common.

Mauricius, cellarer (*canavarius*) of King Liutprand, obtained assets in Tuscany from the public redistribution circuit. They were located in the fiscal uncultivated arch, between Lucca and Pisa (730).[19] With him arrived a codex, the Mozarabic Orational, which had been produced in Spain, perhaps Tarragona, and had passed through Sardinia. The manuscript is famous because, in addition to an annotation by Mauricius, it contains the so-called *Aenigma Veronense*, written by another cursive hand at about the same time — one of the oldest extant examples of Italian language in its evolution from Vulgar Latin (Petrucci 2017).

Ololia follows. Her grandfather was Duke Walpert; her uncle was Bishop Walprand. Her father, the *vir magnificus* Perprand, could rely on vast landholdings, including a *sala*, a *sundrium*, and two *cafagia* in the area

of Rosignano and on assets in Corsica.[20] I believe that the specification that distinguished a small monastery within the walls of Lucca, San Salvatore Oliole (later called in Mustolio, from *monasteriolum Oliole*), presumably founded by the woman, refers to her (Belli Barsali 1973, 531). Her name seems to echo that of saint Eulalia/Olalla, sung by Prudentius in *Peristephanon* and much venerated in Visigoth and Mozarabic Spain (Fábrega Grau 1958).

I conclude the portrait gallery with the already mentioned Bellerifonsus, a prominent figure in Lucca, close to Allo and Queen Ansa, who was very active in Rome.[21] It was thanks to the intermediary relationship between the royal and papal courts that he was able to take control of a monastery that was named after him, San Pietro Bellerifonsi (also called in Cortina), already attributed by Kings Aripert II and Liutprand to the Papacy. Situated near the *curtis regia*, the mint and the artisanal and commercial core of Lucca, it housed productions specialized in weaving precious silk manufactures (Tomei 2018). At the request of Charlemagne, Bellerifonsus served as messenger, bringing letters from the Pope to Bishop Egila in Spain.[22]

In the delicate and decisive dialectic between the Papacy and the Frankish and the Lombard courts during the eighth century, the members of the 'regional elite' were key interlocutors and played a leading role thanks to their network of contacts that extended in the Tyrrhenian space. This is recorded in the *Codex Carolinus*, a collection of letters commissioned by Charlemagne in 791 to preserve texts that needed a change of writing support, passing from papyrus to parchment.[23] This is a selected epistolary, functional to present an official version of the Franco-Papal relations since 739 (McKitterick 2004, 146–48).

Some of the letters included therein prove Bellerifonsus's mandate as messenger, Allo's defensive role, and the latter's connivance with the Byzantines. The collection also shows that the 'regional elite' was not a monolithic block but was subjected to pressure in the triangulation between Rome, Pavia, and Charlemagne. Fractures could thus be generated. In particular, there were contrasts between Allo and Gunfred, son of Walfred and rector of San Pietro of Palazzuolo.[24]

After Desiderius's defeat, initially the social hierarchies and the balance of power in the system coordinated

---

16 *Codex Carolinus*, n. 59.

17 *APRI*, vol. II, n. 160. Perhaps identifiable with the current Podere Sala.

18 *Codex Carolinus*, n. 59.

19 *ChLA*, vol. XXVI, n. 802.

---

20 *ChLA*, vol. XXVI, n. 811; vol. XXIII, n. 960; *CAAP*, n. 13. An overview in Collavini 2010, 18–19.

21 *CDL*, vol. II, nn. 236, 257; *ChLA*, vol. XXXVIII, n. 1098; vol. LXXIII, n. 9. A profile in Bianchi and Tomei 2020.

22 *Codex Carolinus*, nn. 95–97.

23 On this change see Internullo 2019.

24 *Codex Carolinus*, nn. 50–51, 59, 95–97. I follow the interpretation given by Collavini 2009, 271–72.

by the Lucca-Pisa couple were not upset, but a soft transition from Lombard to Frankish domination took place; rather, the effects were felt over the course of one/two generations. In the beginning the 'regional elite' profitably sought to bind themselves to the Carolingians.

The group of founders of San Pietro of Palazzuolo still ruled the monastery in the decades at the turn of the ninth century with Andrew (794–810), son of Gunduald, the third abbot after Walfred and Gunfred. At that time San Pietro became an imperial abbey and established a relationship with Reichenau, as recorded by the confraternity book of the abbey in Lake Constance. A hagiographic text was also produced to exalt the figure of the first rector, the *Vita Walfredi*, which circulated north of the Alps along the network of imperial abbeys (Schmid 1991). From this phase all traces of the group's control over the monastery, firmly placed in the public sphere, ceased.

For his part Allo ruled Lucca after the Frankish conquest with the title of Duke, like his predecessors of the Lombard age. He promoted the construction in Lucca of a monastic institution — later known as Santa Giustina — entrusted to San Salvatore of Brescia (Belli Barsali 1973, 531). The abbey in Brescia, founded by the last Lombard King Desiderius and his wife Ansa, maintained a central role with the Carolingians, still functioning as a reserve for fiscal estates and subject to the special protection of the King (Lazzari 2019). After the death of Allo, however, it was no longer possible for the 'regional elite' to hold the ducal office. In the decades between the eighth and ninth centuries, foreign counts settled in Lucca, recruited from the ranks of the *Reichsadel*: first the Frank Wichram (797–810) and then the Bavarian Boniface (812–813), who succeeded in transmitting the office to his son of the same name (Castagnetti 2010, 213–15).

In the meantime the Bishop, still an expression of local society, took an increasingly important place in the political life of Lucca. The brothers John (783–800) and James (801–818) succeeded one after the other on the cathedra. The prominence and valorization of the episcopal office became evident on the urban and rural stage through the political use of relics: the discovery or transfer of holy bodies to the city, an expedient of great fortune in the Frankish world, was functional to the legitimation of the promoting authority. This is testified by the hagiographic production, in particular the second version of the *Passio* of Bishop Fredianus and the *Passio et translatio* of Bishop Regolus (Collavini 2007a, 2007b; Vocino 2008, 2017; Cotza 2019, 572–73). Bishops continued to be chosen among the high clergy of the urban mother church until the advent of Lothair I in the second quarter of the ninth century. Then the *Reichsadel* also took over in this respect.

Therefore, in the fifty years that followed the Carolingian arrival, a new field of forces was established in Lucca. This was a multiform historical process, in which traits of continuity and change intertwined. Social structures were in the end profoundly transformed. The 'regional elite' was scaled down by comparison with the *Reichsadel*, which had a position of greater proximity to the new rulers and a much wider horizon of action — this allowed its members to accumulate *honores* in different areas of the Empire. The social fabric accentuated some of its characteristics, assuming an even less differentiated conformation and an even more urban-centric structure. Thus was formed what has been defined by Collavini (2007a) as 'diocesan elite', a layer in which the kinships of the ancient 'regional elite' and individuals of lower extraction were integrated. It was no longer divided within by the honorary titles widespread in the Lombard age; it was firmly rooted in the city and had, at the most, a diocesan range of action. From this social base, the aristocratic structures still dominant in the eleventh century began to take shape in Lucca, due to the action of imperial power, which under Lothair I controlled both the offices of Count and Bishop (Tomei 2019a).

Focusing on Mediterranean Tuscany, the first element of novelty can be seen very clearly; nevertheless, it has been slightly neglected by historiography. This was the time when a continentalization of the elite took place. For the distinguished segments of society, it was no longer possible to have an autonomous projection and foothold in the Tyrrhenian islands at the time of the March of Tuscany, a political-territorial body headed by the Count-Marquis of Lucca that framed the region in the span between Emperors Lothair I and Henry IV, from the middle of the ninth to the end of the eleventh century. Unlike the Lombard age, the most powerful parental groups in the following period (the sons of Rodilandus, the Cunimundinghi, and the sons of Huscit) had no possessions in Corsica. This is not due to a lack of sources: their land base is well documented (Tomei 2019a).

In order to fully understand and contextualize the continentalization, it is useful to consider the recent study of Stefan Esders (2018) on the capitularies of Lothair I issued in February 825 by the royal *curtis* of Marengo for the recruitment of a military expedition to Corsica (*Capitula de expeditione Corsicana*).[25] Their background is the agreements concluded by the Frankish Empire with Rome, Constantinople, and Baghdad as a response to the incursions into Corsica and Sardinia by the Saracens of Spain and North Africa at the beginning

---

25 *I capitolari italici*, n. 25 (<https://capitularia.uni-koeln.de/capit/ldf/bk-nr-162/>).

of the ninth century.[26] International diplomatic relations, the Saracen raids by sea, the role of protection entrusted to the Count of Lucca, the Bavarian Boniface II, guardian and *praefectus* of Corsica, are themes that are tied in the annalistic and narrative sources of the time produced at court, on all the *Annales Regni Francorum*.[27]

Military recruitment and command powers on the island were reserved in the *Capitula* for the Count, to be understood first and foremost with that of Lucca. Corsica had, in fact, been fiscalized. Another capitulary of Lothair I, moreover, issued by the royal *curtis* of Corteolona a couple of years earlier, had given the Count the power to exile in Corsica the leaders of conspiracies that attacked public order.[28] The Tuscan aristocratic fabric, more rigidly framed by the Carolingian domination, had no freedom of action in the Tyrrhenian space, where it was subjected to the Count of Lucca by imperial mandate. The last trace in the early medieval charters of Corsica refers significantly to the public sphere and to Count Boniface I: a judicial assembly presided over in April 813 also by Petronius, Bishop in Corsica.[29] The echo of the strong control of the Count-Marquis of Lucca on the island can be seen in the rule exercised in Corsica by a branch of the Obertenghi family, the one descended from Adalbert Atto II, at the end of the eleventh century, which probably took over from it (Nobili 2006).

Continentalization is also linked to the changed layout of the Carolingian Tyrrhenian Sea. The synthesis of Antonino Meo (2018, 222–29) on amphoric circulation has finally brought to light the formation of two areas with blurred outlines, whose watershed must be placed at the height of the Roman-Campanian coast. By the first half of the ninth century, a Roman-Carolingian economic system had been established in which Pisa, the main port complex in Tuscany, was located. The glazed pottery of Rome and Latium (*Forum Ware*) can be taken as fossil guide. It was a predominantly closed space, detached from the one still fully integrated with the eastern Mediterranean and one in which the cabotage routes between Rome and Provence intensified. The Tuscan aristocratic demand became embedded in this frame. The fracture of the Tyrrhenian Sea was then only recomposed in the Ottonian age, thanks to the expansion of the Fatimid Palermo, which found a privileged outflow in Pisa.

The disappearance of Corsica from the range of action of the elite is but one of the elements of novelty that can be seen in the aristocratic structures of Carolingian Tuscany compared to the Lombard past. These transformations are related to changes in the ways of exercising and representing power and in the forms of documentation. As in the case of Corsica, they emerge from the systematic study of the charters preserved in Lucca and are reflected in the capitularies, provisions that arise as the outcome of a discussion on specific topical issues, from the meeting between the needs of government and the demands of the parties who came to court and met in assembly (Patzold 2019). Consider, in particular, the intensive series of capitularies issued between 822 and 832 by Lothair I.[30] Here I can only quote some essential features.[31]

The elite adopted a new culture of power that followed a 'curtense' model. Their land base was organized around *curtes*, a bipartite system of managing the great landownership applied primarily by the fisc. Its first isolated traces can already be found in some charters of the eighth century that refer to the 'regional elite' (Wickham 2005, 294–96). The main coordination centre was the directly run land reserve, no longer called *sundrium* but *dominicum*, where there was a church, *salae*, or other buildings of prestige.

From the quantitative point of view, thanks to a process of scalar growth, which experienced phases of acceleration and stasis from the ninth to the eleventh century, the most powerful groups in Lucca in the age of the March reached a value six times greater — thirty *curtes* — than the land base of their predecessors of the Lombard age. Remarkable also is the difference with their contemporary groups whose centre of gravity was located in the neighbouring *civitates* of the March: between ten and twenty *curtes* in Florence and less than ten in Pisa and Pistoia (Cortese 2017, 214–55).

This parable of growth did not rely on the material and symbolic capital accumulated before the ninth century. It was a real social restart made by individuals of the 'diocesan elite' of local origin, who benefited from the imperial favour. The social fabric, shaped by the action of the court, knew a progressive polarization. The Aldobrandeschi family first emerged (Collavini 1998), then in their wake a second circle of kinships (the sons of Rodilandus, the Cunimundinghi, and the sons of Huscit). If the descendants of the ancient 'regional elite' occupied an increasingly marginalized position, far from the centre of the public sphere, the transalpine immigrants were unable to plant deep roots in the territory of Lucca. The ascending parental groups

---

26 Until then the raids were mostly Byzantine initiatives, Del Lungo 2000.

27 *Annales Regni Francorum*, pp. 122–76 (*ad annos* 806–828); Astronomus, *Vita Hludowici* 42.

28 *I capitolari italici*, n. 21 (<https://capitularia.uni-koeln.de/capit/ldf/bk-nr-158/>).

29 *ChLA*, vol. LXXIII, n. 50.

30 *I capitolari italici*, nn. 20–32. On Lothair I see now Schäpers 2018.

31 The general reference is Tomei 2019a.

became the bearer of a new onomastic text that became characteristic of the elite in the March of Tuscany. It does not include anthroponyms of the 'regional elite'.

Exponents of this circle are the protagonists of *livelli* (*chartae ad censum perexolvendum*) and *placitum* reports (*notitiae iudicati*), documentary forms that were typified at the turn of the ninth century and became a feature of the marquisal Tuscany. *Livelli* gave written and legally valid form, ostensible in the assembly, to contractual relationships between *possessores* and were used first of all to reward clients, both their own and others. *Placitum* reports, instead, kept concrete memory of the ritualized liturgy of the public assembly through which the central power surrounded by ranks of counsellors and followers reaffirmed and justified its authority, regulating political competition. Both types make explicit reference in the formulary to *iustitia dominica*, that is, what the individual had to publicly give and do in a society ordered by the *dominus rex* on behalf of the heavenly lord, *dominus dominorum* (Ghignoli 2004, 2009; Tomei 2017). This *iustitia* was debated at length in assembly, as shown by the capitularies issued by the royal *curtes* of Marengo and Corteolona at the time of Lothair I.

The elite also used new graphic forms. For the most powerful exponents close to the centre of power, they moved from 'high and narrow' script in the definition of Petrucci (1992), a gradual local evolution of the 'cancelleresca lucchese', influenced by the protocol of diplomas in the Lombard chancellery, to the Carolingian minuscule. It appears not coincidentally in Lucca at the time of the Bishop of Frankish origin Berengar (837–843) and is used first among the non-foreigners by Heriprand Aldobrandeschi, in the years in which he made a qualitative leap that initiated the process of social differentiation (Collavini 1994).

There is, however, a strong line of continuity, and it concerns the landscapes of power. It is evident by observing two exchanges in which the most powerful figures in Lucca of their time are involved, respectively Allo (782) and the aforementioned Heriprand (840). The former exchanged land with the rector of San Silvestro of Lucca, on which depended the church of Sant'Andrea of *Apuniano*, around Bolgheri. Allo received from him a *casella sundriale*, already a cellar for the conservation of wine in *dolia* (*cella meraria*), and two *case massaricie* in *Asilacto*, with salt pans and appurtenances in the surrounding area. The salt pans located in Cecina were, however, excluded.[32] Heriprand made the exchange with Bishop Berengar. In return for two plots of land in *Asilacto*, one of which bordered on public possessions, he obtained fields located in the neighbouring *Ascla*, adjoining a coastal shrubland (*silva sicha*) and marshland. They bordered on land already belonging to the same Heriprand and with common lands of the men of Vada (*terra de ominibus Vadisiani*).[33]

At the time of Lothair I, the faces but not the places of power had changed. Though renewed in many ways, the elite continued to gravitate around the complex of landings and salt pans between Rosignano and *Asilacto*, where the fisc had had and kept vast properties. The boundaries are eloquent. Those who enjoyed *Königsnähe* ended up accumulating interest in these areas, which remained firmly within the public sphere, drawing on the redistributive circuit moved by the court. This flow remained central to holding power and prestige in Tuscany, namely a substantial land base and authority of command and coercion; however, it does not mean that the circuit remained unchanged — also for this reason it deserves careful study.

Over time it varied in circulation speed and flow density, it benefited different subjects, and as the fiscalization of Corsica and the continentalization of the elite demonstrate, it sometimes encountered limitations which diverted its course. Only the Count-Marquis, because of his public office, from the fiscal *curtes* on the coast could freely have a Mediterranean projection. This was not the case of the other aristocrats, who had to follow in his wake at sea.

---

32 *ChLA*, vol. XXXVII, n. 1084.
33 *ChLA*, vol. LXXVII, n. 41.

Works Cited

Primary Sources

Annales regni Francorum	*Annales regni Francorum inde ab a. 741 usque ad a. 829, qui dicuntur Annales Laurissenses maiores et Einhardi* (*Monumenta Germaniae Historica*, Scriptores rerum Germanicarum, vol. VI), ed. by Friedrich Kurze (Hannover: Hahnsche, 1895)
APRI	*Acta Pontificum Romanorum Inedita*, ed. by Julius von Pflugk-Harttung (Tübingen and Stuttgart: Fues, 1881–1888)
Astronomus, Vita Hludowici	*Thegan. Die Taten Kaiser Ludwigs – Astronomus. Das Leben Kaiser Ludwigs* (*Monumenta Germaniae Historica*, Scriptores rerum Germanicarum, vol. LXIV), ed. by Ernst Tremp (Hannover: Hahnsche, 1995)
CAAP	*Carte dell'Archivio Arcivescovile di Pisa. Fondo arcivescovile*, vol. I, ed. by Antonella Ghignoli, Biblioteca del Bollettino Storico Pisano Fonti, 11 (Pisa: Pacini, 2006).
CDL	*Codice Diplomatico Longobardo*, ed. by Luigi Schiaparelli, Carlrichard Brühl, and Herbert Zielinski, Fonti per la Storia d'Italia, 62–66 (Rome: Istituto Storico Italiano per il Medio Evo, 1929–2003)
ChLA	*Chartae Latinae Antiquiores. Facsimile-edition of the Latin Charters prior to the Ninth Century*, ed. by Albert Bruckner and Robert Marichal (Zürich: Urs Graf, 1954–1998; 2nd Series Ninth Century, ed. by Guglielmo Cavallo and Giovanna Nicolaj (Zürich: Urs Graf, 2004–2017)
Codex Carolinus	*Monumenta Germaniae Historica*, Epistolae Merowingici et Carolini aevi, vol. III, ed. by Wilhelm Gundlach (Berlin: Weidmann, 1892), pp. 476–657
DHII	*Monumenta Germaniae Historica*, Diplomata regum et imperatorum Germaniae, vol. III, Heinrici II. et Arduini Diplomata, ed. by Harry Bresslau (Hannover: Hahnsche, 1900–1903)
I capitolari italici	*I capitolari italici. Storia e diritto della dominazione carolingia in Italia*, ed. by Claudio Azzara and Pierandrea Moro, Altomedioevo, 1 (Rome: Viella, 1998)
Molitor, Stephan. 1991	*Walfreds cartula dotis aus dem Jahre 754*, Karl Schmid (ed.), *Vita Walfredi und Kloster Monteverdi. Toskanisches Mönchtum zwischen langobardischer und fränkischer Herrschaft*, Bibliothek des Deutschen Instituts in Rom, 73 (Tübingen: Niemeyer), pp. 146–73
Notitia dignitatum	*Notitia dignitatum. Accedunt notitia urbis Constantinopolitanae et laterculi provinciarum*, ed. by Otto Seeck (Berlin: Weidmann, 1876; repr. Cambridge: Cambridge University Press, 2019)

Secondary Studies

Airlie, Stuart. 2012. *Power and its Problems in Carolingian Europe*, Variorum Collected Studies Series (Aldershot: Ashgate)

Belli Barsali, Isa. 1973. 'La topografia di Lucca nei secoli VIII-XI', in *Lucca e la Tuscia nell'alto medioevo. Atti del V Congresso internazionale di studi sull'alto medioevo* (Spoleto: CISAM), pp. 461–554

Bianchi, Giovanna, and Paolo Tomei. 2020. 'Risorse e contesti insediativi nelle Colline Metallifere altomedievali: il possibile ruolo dell'allume', in *Alum Landscapes. Archaeology of Production and Network Economy*, ed. by Luisa Dallai, Giovanna Bianchi, and Francesca Romana Stasolla (Florence: All'Insegna del Giglio), pp. 155–66

Bougard, François, Geneviève Bührer-Thierry, and Régine Le Jan. 2013. 'Les élites du haut Moyen Âge. Identités, stratégies, mobilité', *Annales. Histoire, Sciences Sociales*, 68: 1079–112

Bougard, François, Maria Cristina La Rocca, and Régine Le Jan (eds). 2005. *Sauver son âme et se perpétuer. Transmission du patrimoine et mémoire au haut Moyen Âge*, Collection de l'École française de Rome, 351 (Rome: École française de Rome)

Bougard, François, and Vito Loré (eds). 2019. *Biens publics, biens du roi. Les bases économiques des pouvoirs royaux dans le haut Moyen Âge (VIe–début du XIe siècle)*, Seminari internazionali del Centro Interuniversitario per la Storia e l'Archeologia dell'Alto Medioevo, 9 (Turnhout: Brepols)

Cantini, Federico (ed.). 2017. *La villa dei Vetti (Capraia e Limite, FI): archeologia di una grande residenza aristocratica nel Valdarno tardoantico* (Florence: All'Insegna del Giglio)

Carocci, Sandro, and Simone Maria Collavini. 2014. 'The Cost of States: Politics and Exactions in the Christian West (Sixth to Fifteenth Centuries)', in *Diverging Paths? The Shapes of Power and Institutions in Medieval Christendom and Islam*, ed. by John Hudson and Ana Rodríguez, The Medieval Mediterranean, 101 (Leiden: Brill), pp. 123–58

Castagnetti, Andrea. 2010. 'I vassalli imperiali a Lucca in età carolingia', in *Il patrimonio documentario della chiesa di Lucca Prospettive di ricerca*, ed. by Sergio Pagano and Pierantonio Piatti Toscana Sacra, 2 (Florence: Edizioni del Galluzzo), pp. 211–84

Ceccarelli Lemut, Maria Luisa. 2006. 'Inquadramento degli uomini e assetto del territorio: incastellamento, signoria e istituzioni ecclesiastiche', in *Il Medioevo nella provincia di Livorno: i risultati delle recenti indagini*, ed. by Chiara Marcucci and Carolina Megale (Pisa: Pacini), pp. 11–42

——. 2009. 'Un castello e la sua storia. Montescudaio nel Medioevo', in *Storia di Montescudaio*, ed. by Romano Paolo Coppini (Pisa: Felici), pp. 43–70

Collavini, Simone Maria. 1994. 'Aristocrazia d'ufficio e scrittura nella Tuscia dei secoli IX–XI', *Scrittura e civiltà*, 18: 23–51

——. 1998. *Honorabilis domus et spetiosissimus comitatus. Gli Aldobrandeschi da conti a principi territoriali (secoli IX–XIII)*, Studi medioevali, 6 (Pisa: ETS)

——. 2007a. 'Spazi politici e irraggiamento sociale delle élites laiche intermedie (Italia centrale, secoli VIII–X)', in *Les élites et leurs espaces. Mobilité, rayonnement, domination (du VIe au XIe siècle)*, ed. by Philippe Depreux, François Bougard, and Régine Le Jan, Haut Moyen Âge, 5 (Turnhout: Brepols), pp. 319–40

——. 2007b. 'Da società rurale periferica a parte dello spazio politico lucchese: S. Regolo in Gualdo tra VIII e IX secolo', in *Un filo rosso. Studi antichi e nuove ricerche sulle orme di Gabriella Rossetti in occasione dei suoi settanta anni*, ed. by Gabriella Garzella and Enrica Salvatori, Piccola Biblioteca Gisem, 23 (Pisa: ETS), pp. 230–47

——. 2009. 'Des Lombards aux Carolingiens: l'évolution des élites locales', in *Le monde carolingien: bilan, perspectives, champs de recherches*, ed. by Wojciech Falkowski and Yves Sassier, Culture et société médiévales, 18 (Turnhout: Brepols), pp. 263–300

——. 2010. *Rosignano Marittimo. Il medioevo: ambiente, economia, società* (Livorno: Debatte)

——. 2019. 'I beni pubblici: qualche idea per gli studi futuri', in *Biens publics, biens du roi. Les bases économiques des pouvoirs royaux dans le haut Moyen Âge (VIe–début du XIe siècle)*, ed. by François Bougard and Vito Loré, Seminari internazionali del Centro Interuniversitario per la Storia e l'Archeologia dell'Alto Medioevo, 9 (Turnhout: Brepols), pp. 423–31

——. 2020. 'Dall'antichità al medioevo tra archeologia e fonti scritte: considerazioni introduttive', in *La transizione dall'antichità al medioevo nel Mediterraneo centro-orientale*, ed. by Giovanni Salmeri and Paolo Tomei (Pisa: ETS), pp. 9–18

Collavini, Simone Maria, and Paolo Tomei. 2017. 'Beni fiscali e scritturazione. Nuove proposte sui contesti di rilascio e di falsificazione di D. OIII. 269 per il monastero di S. Ponziano di Lucca', in *Originale – Fälschungen – Kopien. Kaiser- und Königsurkunden für Empfänger in Deutschland und Italien (9.–11. Jahrhundert) und ihre Nachwirkung im Hoch- und Spätmittelalter (bis ca. 1500)*, ed. by Nicolangelo D'Acunto, Wolfgang Huschner, and Sebastian Roebert, Italia Regia, 3 (Leipzig: Eudora), pp. 205–16

Cortese, Maria Elena. 2017. *L'aristocrazia toscana. Sette secoli (VI–XII)* (Spoleto: CISAM)

Cotza, Alberto. 2019. 'A proposito della nuova edizione delle passioni di San Miniato', *Archivio Storico Italiano*, 177: 565–75

de Jong, Mayke. 2009. *The Penitential State: Authority and Atonement in the Age of Louis the Pious, 814–840* (Cambridge: Cambridge University Press)

Del Lungo, Stefano. 2000. *Bahr 'as Shâm. La presenza musulmana nel Tirreno centrale e settentrionale nell'Alto Medioevo*, British Archaeological Report International Series, 898 (Oxford: Archaeopress)

DeMarrais, Elizabeth, Castillo, Luis Jaime, and Timothy Earle. 1996. 'Ideology, materialization and power strategies', *Current Anthropology*, 37: 15–31

Devroey, Jean-Pierre. 2006. *Puissants et misérables. Système social et monde paysan dans l'Europe des Francs (VIe–IXe siècles)* (Brussels: Académie Royale de Belgique)

Donati, Fulvia. 2013. *La villa romana dei Cecina a San Vincenzino (Livorno). Materiali sullo scavo e aggiornamenti sulle ricerche* (Pisa: Felici)

Esders, Stefan. 2018. 'Die Capitula de expeditione Corsicana Lothars I. vom Februar 825. Überlieferung, historischer Kontext, Textrekonstruktion und Rechtsinhalt', *Quellen und Forschungen aus italienischen Archiven und Bibliotheken*, 98: 91–144

Fábrega Grau, Ángel. 1958. *Santa Eulalia de Barcelona. Revísión de un problema histórico* (Rome: Iglesia Nacional Española).

Francovich Onesti, Nicoletta. 2000. 'L'antroponimia longobarda della Toscana: caratteri e diffusione', *Rivista italiana di onomastica*, 6: 357–74

——. 2012. 'Discontinuità e integrazione nel sistema onomastico dell'Italia tardoantica: l'incontro coi nomi germanici', in *La trasformazione del mondo romano e le grandi migrazioni. Nuovi popoli dall'Europa settentrionale e centro-orientale alle coste del Mediterraneo*, ed. by Carlo Ebanista and Marcello Rotili, Giornate sulla tarda antichità e il Medioevo, 4 (Cimitile: Tavolario), pp. 33–50

Gasparri, Stefano. 1980. 'Grandi proprietari e sovrani nell'Italia longobarda dell'VIII secolo', *Longobardi e Lombardia: aspetti di civiltà longobarda. Atti del VI Congresso internazionale di studi sull'alto medioevo* (Spoleto: CISAM), pp. 429–42

——. 2012. *Italia longobarda. Il regno, i Franchi, il papato* (Rome: Laterza)

Gelichi, Sauro, and Maria Cristina La Rocca (eds). 2003. *Tesori: forme di accumulazione della ricchezza nell'alto medioevo (secoli V–XI)*, Altomedioevo, 3 (Rome: Viella)

Ghignoli, Antonella. 2004. 'Su due famosi documenti pisani dell'VIII secolo', *Bullettino dell'Istituto Storico Italiano per il Medio Evo*, 106: 1–69

——. 2009. 'Libellario nomine: rileggendo i documenti pisani dei secoli VIII–X', *Bullettino dell'Istituto storico italiano per il Medio Evo*, 111: 1–62

Groth, Paul, and Chris Wilson. 2003. 'Die Polyphonie der Cultural Landscape Studies', in *Landschaftstheorie. Texte der Cultural Landscape Studies*, ed. by Brigitte Franzen and Stefanie Krebs, Kunstwissenschaftliche Bibliothek, 26 (Cologne: König), pp. 58–90

Haubrichs, Wolfgang. 2014. 'Typen der anthroponymischen Indikation von Verwandtschaft bei den "germanischen" gentes: Traditionen – Innovationen – Differenzen', in *Verwandtschaft, Name und soziale Ordnung (300–1000)*, ed. by Steffen Patzold and Karl Ubl, Ergänzungsbände zum Reallexikon der Germanischen Altertumskunde, 90 (Berlin: De Gruyter), pp. 29–71

Horden, Peregrine, and Nicholas Purcell. 2000. *The Corrupting Sea. A Study of Mediterranean History* (Oxford: Blackwell)

Internullo, Dario. 2019. 'Du papyrus au parchemin. Les origines médiévales de la mémoire archivistique en Europe occidentale', *Annales. Histoire, Sciences Sociales*, 74: 521–57

Kühne, Olaf. 2018. *Landscape and Power in Geographical Space as a Social-Aesthetic Construct* (Springer: Wiesbaden)

——. 2019. *Landscape Theories. A Brief Introduction* (Springer: Wiesbaden)

Lazzari, Tiziana. 2017. 'La competizione tra grandi possessores longobardi e il regno: le leggi di Liutprando e il patrimonio delle donne nel secolo VIII', in *Acquérir, prélever, contrôler: les ressources en compétition (400–1100)*, ed. by Geneviève Bührer-Thierry, Régine Le Jan, and Vito Loré, Haut Moyen Âge, 25 (Turnhout: Brepols), pp. 43–60

——. 2019. 'Una santa, una badessa e una principessa: note di lettura sul capitello di santa Giulia nel Museo di Brescia', *Reti Medievali Rivista*, 20: 421–46

Le Jan, Régine. 1995. *Famille et pouvoir dans le monde franc (VIIe–Xe siècle)* (Paris: Publications de la Sorbonne)

McCormick, Michael. 2001. *Origins of the European Economy: Communications and Commerce AD 300–900* (New York: Cambridge University Press)

McKitterick, Rosamond. 2004. *History and Memory in the Carolingian World* (Cambridge: Cambridge University Press)

Meo, Antonino. 2018. 'Anfore, uomini e reti di scambio sul mare pisano (VIII–XII secolo)', *Archeologia Medievale*, 45: 219–38

Nelson, Janet L. 2007. *Courts, Elites, and Gendered Power in the Early Middle Ages: Charlemagne and Others*, Variorum Collected Studies Series (Aldershot: Ashgate)

Nobili, Mario. 2006. 'Sviluppo e caratteri della dominazione obertenga in Corsica fra XI e XII secolo', in *Gli Obertenghi e altri saggi*, ed. by Mario Nobili, Collectanea, 19 (Spoleto: CISAM), pp. 179–214

Pasquinucci, Marinella. 2004. 'Paleografia costiera, porti e approdi in Toscana', in *Evolución paleoambiental de los puertos y fondeadores antiguos en el Mediterráneo occidental*, ed. by Lorenza De Maria and Rita Turchetti (Soveria Manelli: Rubbettino), pp. 61–86

Pasquinucci, Marinella, and Simonetta Menchelli. 2006. 'Goti, Bizantini e Longobardi nella Tuscia nord-occidentale: il tardo-antico a Vada Volaterrana', in *Il Medioevo nella provincia di Livorno: i risultati delle recenti indagini*, ed. by Chiara Marcucci and Carolina Megale (Pisa: Pacini), pp. 43–53

Patzold, Steffen. 2019. 'Capitularies in the Ottonian realm', *Early Medieval Europe*, 27: 112–32

Pazienza, Annamaria. 2016. 'Una regione periferica del Regno? La Tuscia in età longobarda', *I Longobardi oltre Pavia. Conquista, irradiazione e intrecci culturali* (Milan: Cisalpino), pp. 33–52

Petralia, Giuseppe. 2015. 'Tra storia e archeologia: Mediterraneo altomedioevale e spazi regionali italiani (intorno al secolo VIII)', *Studi Storici*, 56: 5–28

Petrucci, Armando. 1992. 'Il codice e i documenti: scrivere a Lucca fra VIII e IX secolo', in *Scriptores in urbibus. Alfabetismo e cultura scritta nell'Italia altomedievale*, ed. by Armando Petrucci and Carlo Romeo (Bologna: Il Mulino), pp. 77–108

——. 2017. 'L'orazionale visigotico di Verona: aggiunte avventizie, indovinello grafico, tagli maffeiani', in *Letteratura italiana: una storia attraverso la scrittura*, ed. by Armando Petrucci (Rome: Carocci editore), pp. 247–64

Remotti, Francesco. 2014. 'Introduzione a un'antropologia dei centri', *Spazio Filosofico*, 11: 257–78

Renfrew, Colin. 1984. 'Societies in Space: the Landscape of Power', in *Approaches to Social Archaeology*, ed. by Colin Renfrew (Edinburgh: Edinburgh University Press), pp. 24–29

Renzi Rizzo, Catia. 2006. 'Corsica longobarda: dalle testimonianze scritte alle risultanze archeologiche, un provvisorio status quaestionis', in *IV Congresso Nazionale di Archeologia Medievale*, ed. by Riccardo Francovich and Marco Valenti (Florence: All'Insegna del Giglio), pp. 530–35

Schäpers, Maria. 2018. *Lothar I. (795–855) und das Frankenreich*, Rheinisches Archiv, 159 (Cologne: Böhlau)

Schmid, Karl (ed.). 1991. *Vita Walfredi und Kloster Monteverdi. Toskanisches Mönchtum zwischen langobardischer und fränkischer Herrschaft*, Bibliothek des Deutschen Historischen Instituts in Rom, 73 (Tübingen: Niemeyer)

Stoffella, Marco. 2007. 'Crisi e trasformazioni delle élites nella Toscana nord-occidentale del secolo VIII: esempi a confronto', *Reti Medievali Rivista*, 8: 1–49

Tomei, Paolo. 2017. 'Censum et iustitia. Le carte di livello come specchio delle trasformazioni della società lucchese (secoli IX–XI)', *Reti Medievali Rivista*, 18: 251–74

——. 2018. 'The Power of the Gift. Early Medieval Lucca and its Court', in *Origins of a New Economic Union (7th–12th Century). Preliminary Results of the nEU-Med Project: October 2015–March 2017*, ed. by Giovanna Bianchi and Richard Hodges (Florence: All'Insegna del Giglio), pp. 123–34

——. 2019a. *Milites elegantes. Le strutture aristocratiche nel territorio lucchese (800–1100 c.)*, Reti Medievali E-Book, 34 (Florence: Florence University Press)

——. 2019b. 'Una nuova categoria documentaria nella Toscana marchionale: la donazione in forma di mandato. Cultura grafica e strutture politiche in una società di corte', *Quellen und Forschungen aus italienischen Archiven und Bibliotheken*, 99: 115–49

——. 2020. 'Il sale e la seta. Sulle risorse pubbliche nel Tirreno settentrionale (secoli V–XI)', in *La transizione dall'antichità al medioevo nel Mediterraneo centro-orientale*, ed. by Giovanni Salmeri and Paolo Tomei (Pisa: ETS), pp. 21–38

Vocino, Giorgia. 2008. 'Le traslazioni di reliquie in età carolingia (fine VIII–IX secolo): uno studio comparativo', *Rivista di storia e letteratura religiosa*, 44: 207 55

——. 2017. 'L'Agiografia dell'Italia centrale (750–950)', *Hagiographies VII*, Corpus Christianorum (Turnhout: Brepols), pp. 95–268

Wickham, Chris. 2005. *Framing the Early Middle Ages: Europe and the Mediterranean, 400–800* (Oxford: Oxford University Press)

——. 2009. *The Inheritance of Rome. A History of Europe from 400 to 1000* (London: Penguin)

Zukin, Sharon. 1991. *Landscapes of Power. From Detroit to Disney World* (Berkeley: University of California Press)

Index

Places

ager Rusellanus: 12, 39, 42–43, 89, 90, 164
Alberese: 12, 70, 89–90, 93, 98
Allumiere: 181
Angkor Wat: 143
Aiali, villa: 41–44, 50–52, 97, 100, 102
Aquae Rusellanae: 90, 94–95, 98, 100, 102
Arena: 22
Asilacto – modern Marina di Bibbona: 188–90, 193

Baghdad: 191
Bagni di Romagna: 167
Bagni di Roselle: 89–90, 94
Benevento: 143
Bolgheri: 193
Brancalete: 41, 51–52
Brescia: 13, 165, 168, 191
Byzantium: 22, 27, 34, 136, 141, 181, 191
see also Constantinople

Campiglia Marittima: 111
Campo Alberguccio: 68, 70
Campi Bagni: 60, 62
Canterbury: 144
Capraia e Limite: 55, 57–58
Carlappiano: 12, 109, 111–15, 122
Carthage: 98, 156
Casal Volpi: 113, 115
Casette di Mota: 42, 70, 97–98, 100–02
Catallo: 27, 30
Cecina: 188, 193
Cencelle: 13–15, 145, 172–81
see also Centumcellae; Leopoli; *Leopolis*
Cerveteri: 44
Chiusi: 71, 186
Civitate Vetere: 30
Civitavecchia: 181
Cosa: 12–14, 68, 70, 72, 88–89, 94, 100, 126–38, 144
Cripta Balbi: 143

Domitiana positio: 97
Donoratico: 145

Empoli: 25, 58, 93–94, 187

Falesia: 109
Fattoria Badiola: 97, 101
Filettole: 22
Florence: 12–13, 27, 32, 55, 63, 144, 192
Follonica: 107–08, 111, 114, 144
Fosso Cortigliano, villa: 97, 100
Franciano, curtis: 114
Frankfurt: 145

Grosseto: 13, 39–44, 49, 50–51, 53–54, 70–71, 78, 82, 89, 100–01, 145, 165

Hasta: 89, 90, 92–94, 98, 100
Heba: 68, 100

Insula Matidia: 97

La Giuncola: 90
Largo Argentina: 143
Le Frasche: 93, 100
see also Montesanto
Le Mortelle, villa: 97
Limite: 22, 58, 60
Lucca: 13, 21–22, 32, 68, 70–71, 143–44, 164, 185–93
Lugnano: 72
Luna (modern Luni): 13–14, 27, 149–52, 154, 158–60

Maastricht: 144, 152
Manifattura Tabacchi: 166
Mainz: 144
Marseilles: 144
Massa Carrara: 186
Massa Marittima: 116, 145
Milan: 13
Miranduolo: 163
Modena: 54, 166
Montarrenti: 163
Montelupo Fiorentino: 57, 62
Montereggi: 60, 62, 166
Monteverdi, monastery: 22
Moscona: 43–46, 49, 50, 52
Mosconcino: 45–46, 49–50, 52, 58, 69
see also La Canonica

Naples: 143
Nogara: 167

Otranto: 143

Paderborn: 145
Paludozzeri: 29
Pavia: 13, 186–87, 189–90
Piazza dei Cavalieri: 22, 29, 31
Piazza Duomo: 24–33
Piazza Venezia: 143
Pisae (modern Pisa): 13–14, 21–35
Piombino: 108, 111
Pistoia: 60, 192
Piuro: 168–69
Podere Casetta: 119–20
Podere Passerini: 94–95, 102
Poggibonsi: 163
Poggio al Marmo: 23
Poggio Franco, villa: 97
Poggio Gramignano: 72
Ponte del Diavolo: 90
Populonia: 12–13, 42, 68, 70–71, 107, 109, 114, 144, 188
Porto alle Conche: 23
Portus Cosanus: 89, 127–28, 137
Portus Fenigliae: 137
Portus Pisanus: 23–24, 128
Portus Scabris: 109, 116, 137, 144
Puntone di Scarlino: 116

Ravenna: 137, 143, 160
Rome: 11, 22, 24, 30, 71, 78–79, 89, 97–98, 136–37, 142–43, 145, 160, 173–74, 176, 181, 185–86, 190–92
Rosignano: 188–89, 190, 193
Rusellae: 13, 13, 39, 40–53, 65–71, 73–79, 81, 88–90, 93–95, 97–98, 100, 102, 107, 144, 164–65, 168

Saint Peter and Marcellinus, basilica: 97
Saint-Servatius, church: 144
Salebro, modern Castiglione della Pescaia: 12, 70, 89, 90, 101–02, 166
Salerno: 143
Samos: 138
San Benedetto di Leno, monastery: 168
San Giorgio, church: 30

San Giovanni, baptistery: 29–30
San Giuliano sul Monte Pisano, church: 22
San Martino *de Plano*: 101
San Michele, church: 22
San Michele in Cipriano, church: 187, 189
San Piero a Grado: 23–24
San Pietro ai Sette Pini, church: 29, 187
San Pietro di Bellerifonsi, monastery: 22
San Pietro 'in Acci', monastery: 22
San Pietro in Cortevecchia, church: 22
San Pietro in Valle, monastery: 167
San Pietro of Camaiore, monastery: 187
San Pietro of Palazzuolo, monastery: 187, 189–91
San Quirico, monastery: 114
San Rossore: 23, 28
San Salvatore of Brescia, monastery: 191
San Salvatore Oliole, monastery: 187, 190
San Sisto in Cortevecchia, church: 29
San Zeno di Verona, abbey: 167
Sant'Agata Bolognese: 167
Sant'Andrea of *Apuniano*, church: 193
Santa Cristina, church: 29
Santa Eufrasia, church: 29
Santa Giustina, monastery: 191
Santa Liberata, villa: 70, 97
Santa Margherita, church: 29
Santa Maria Ursimanni, church: 187
Santa Maria Vergine, church: 29
Santo Stefano ai Lupi: 23
SS. Quattro Coronati, church: 174
Sarzana: 152
Scarlino: 109, 115, 120, 163–64
Scoglietto: 70, 93, 98, 100, 102, 166
  see also Temple of *Diana Umbronensis*
Scoglietto, cave: 100
Serrata Martini – Paduline: 89, 95–97
Siena: 13, 71, 144
Spaccasasso, cave: 100
Spolverino: 90–91, 93, 98, 100
Sterpeto – San Martino, villa: 42, 89–90, 97–98, 100–02

Talamone: 89, 94, 100
Tagliata, villa: 137
Tarquinia: 146, 176
Terme Leopoldine: 94
Torre Mozza: 111, 114, 122
Tours: 144
Trajan's Markets: 143
Tuscania: 176

Umbro flumen: 89–91, 93, 98

Vacchereccia: 93
Vada Volterrana: 32, 188–89, 193
Vecchiano: 22
Veio: 44
Verona: 13
Vetricella: 12, 107, 109, 116–22, 144–45, 165–67
Vetti, villa: 12, 55, 62, 165–67
Vetulonia: 13, 68, 100, 107
Via Aemilia Scauri: 28, 42, 44, 89–90, 94–95
Via Aurelia vetus: 42, 89–90, 93, 95, 100
Via Aurelia nova: 42
Via Cardinale Maffi: 26
Via Galluppi: 25, 28
Vignale: 113, 115
Viterbo: 177, 178
Vulci: 44

Geography

Albano, mount: 57–58
Amiata, mount: 71, 90
Argentario, mount: 70, 97
Arno, river: 12, 23, 27–29, 55, 57–58, 62
Arno, valley: 27
Auser, river: 21, 23, 25, 27–29, 32

Baetica: 90, 94
Botrangolo, stream: 113, 115
Bruna, river: 96, 186

Capraia, island: 70
Cecina, river: 186, 189
Cerbaie, forest: 186
Colline Metallifere: 71, 107, 116, 144–45
Concordia sulla Secchia, forest: 169
Cornia, river: 107, 111, 122, 186
Cornia, valley: 107, 109, 111, 113–15, 122, 164

Corniaccia, river: 113–15
Corsica, island: 15, 22, 35, 164, 188–93
Constance, lake: 191

Elba, island: 70, 107, 116, 122, 144
Etruria: 11, 22, 25, 27, 42, 70, 127, 176, 189

Franciacorta: 169
Fucecchio, marsh: 186

Garda, region: 169
Giannutri, island: 89, 94
Giglio, island: 89, 94

Latium: 14–15, 30, 164, 173–74, 176–77, 180–81, 192
Lavarone, lake: 166
Ledro, lake: 166

Maremma: 43, 71–73, 78, 107, 187, 189
Massaciuccoli, lake: 186
Migliarino, island: 23
Monti della Tolfa: 173, 181
Monti Pisani: 186

Ombrone, river: 42, 89, 90, 186
Ombrone, valley: 40
Orcia, valley: 40

Pannonia: 138
Pecora, river: 107, 116, 122, 186
Pecora, valley: 12, 107, 109, 111, 114–15, 117, 119–20, 122, 164
Porta, lake: 186
Prilis (Prile), lake: 89, 95, 97, 101

Rio Melledra, river: 179
Russia: 138

Salica, river: 41, 44, 47, 50–51, 164
Sardinia, island: 15, 22, 35, 72, 190–91
Scarlino, lake: 116
Serchio, river: 23, 186
Sesto, lake: 186
Sicily: 72, 144
Spain: 190–91

Tarragona: 190
Tavoliere, plain: 44
Tunisia: 22, 90
Tuscia: 11–14, 24, 34, 70, 89–90, 98, 102, 163, 167

Tuscia suburbicaria: 89
Tyrrhenian Sea: 22, 24, 32, 89–90, 95, 116, 144–45, 190, 192

Uganda: 72
Umbria: 24, 72

Valdarno: 25
Valdiserchio: 22
Valnera, river: 113, 115
Veronese, plain: 165–66
Versilia: 187, 189
Versilia, river: 188

People

Adalbert Atto II, count: 192
Aelius Agrippinus: 95
Agilulf, king: 70
Adalgis: 22, 34
Alahis: 187–88, 190
Alamund: 187
Aldobrandeschi, family: 42, 114, 116, 138, 192
Aldobrandeschi, Heriprand: 193
Allo, duke: 189–91, 193
Andrew, abbot: 191
Aripert II, king: 190
Augustine: 141
Augustus, emperor: 141
Aurelia Saturnina: 95
Autchis: 189

Balbinus, bishop: 70–71
Baldwin III, emperor: 136, 138
Benedict III, pope: 176
Boniface I, count: 191
Boniface II, count: 22, 192

Caecina Decius Aginatius Albinus: 189
Caracalla, emperor: 135–36
Cecilianus: 28
Charlemagne, emperor: 190
Cicero: 141
Commodus, emperor: 135
Constantine, emperor: 89, 97–98, 141–42
Constantine II, emperor: 93
Clüver, Phillip, historian: 94
Cunimundinghi, family: 191–92

Dante Alighieri: 78
Desiderius, king: 22, 34, 190–91
Domitian, emperor: 93, 96

Eutichianus, pope: 149

Felice, bishop: 151
Fortis, bishop: 188
Fredianus, bishop: 191

Gaudentius, bishop: 28
Gausperga: 189
Gelasius I, pope: 28
Genseric, king: 98
Gerontius: 151
Giusto of Utens: 63
Godepert: 187
Gordian III, emperor: 135–36
St. Gregory the Great, pope: 21, 22, 70
Gumpranda: 189
Gunduald: 188, 191

Hadrian, emperor: 89, 94–95, 96
Hadrian, pope: 143
Harum al-Rashid, calif: 22
Henry IV, emperor: 191
Hugh, king: 22, 34–35, 119, 122
Huscit: 191–92

Ifrigiye Arabs: 22

James, bishop: 191
Johannes, bishop: 28, 30
John, bishop: 191
Justinian: 102, 136

Lacanius: 24
Leo IV, pope: 14, 143–44, 172–74, 176
Liutprand, king: 187, 190
Lothair I, emperor: 22, 186, 191–93
Louis the Pious, emperor: 97

Macrobius: 189
Malavolti, Orlando: 71
Maxentius, emperor: 90
Maximinus Thrax, emperor: 135–36
Medici, Cosimo I: 60
Medici, Ferdinando I: 63
Medici, family: 58, 71

Obertenghi, family: 192

Paschal I, pope: 143, 146
Peredeus, bishop: 186–89
Perctarit, king: 187
Perprand: 187, 190
Pertualdo: 22

Philip I, emperor: 135–36
Piranesi, Giovanni Battista: 63
Plotina Pompeia: 95
Publius Ceionius Caecina Albinus: 189

Radaldus, bishop: 71
Ratcauso: 22
Ratpert: 187
Regolus, bishop: 191
Rodilandus: 191–92
Rutilius Namatianus, poet: 23–24, 27, 70, 98, 128, 151, 189

Septimius Severus, emperor: 135–36
Severus Alexander, emperor: 135–36
Sidonius Apollinaris, politician: 72
Silvester, pope: 97
Smaragdo, exarch: 21
St. Cerbonius, bishop: 70

Talesperianus, bishop: 186–88
Tassilo: 189
Teutpert: 187, 189
Theodorus, bishop: 71
Trajan, emperor: 89, 94–96

Venanzio, bishop: 151
Vettius Agorius Praetextatus: 189
Vibia Priscilla: 95
Vibius Romulus: 95
Vitalianus, bishop: 68, 70
Vualfredo: 22

Walpert, duke: 187–90
Walprand, bishop: 187–88, 190
Wectari: 189
Wichram, count: 191

Zocchi, Giuseppe: 63

Events

Edict of Theodosius: 70, 150

Gothic War: 27, 96, 102, 136–37, 166, 174

Second World War: 96, 129, 130

MediTo: ARCHAEOLOGICAL AND HISTORICAL
LANDSCAPES OF MEDITERRANEAN CENTRAL ITALY

All volumes in this series are evaluated by an Editorial Board, strictly on academic grounds, based on reports prepared by referees who have been commissioned by virtue of their specialism in the appropriate field. The Board ensures that the screening is done independently and without conflicts of interest. The definitive texts supplied by authors are also subject to review by the Board before being approved for publication. Further, the volumes are copyedited to conform to the publisher's stylebook and to the best international academic standards in the field.

Titles in Series

Archaeological Landscapes of Roman Etruria: Research and Field Papers, ed. by Alessandro Sebastiani and Carolina Megale (2021)

Medieval Landscapes of Southern Etruria: The Excavations at Capalbiaccio Tricosto (1976–2010), ed. by Michelle Hobart (2023)

In Preparation

Archeologia e storia nella rada di Portoferraio: La villa di San Marco, a cura di Franco Cambi, Laura Pagliantini e Edoardo Vanni